# Freedom of Speech
## in the Marketplace of Ideas

# *Freedom of Speech*

## *in the Marketplace of Ideas*

Douglas M. Fraleigh
*California State University,*
*Fresno*

Joseph S. Tuman
*San Francisco State University*

◆◆◆◆◆◆◆◆◆◆◆◆◆◆◆◆◆◆

**Bedford/St. Martin's**
*Boston* ◆ *New York*

*Sponsoring editor:* Suzanne Phelps Weir
*Editorial assistant:* Hanna Shin
*Manager, publishing services:* Emily Berleth
*Publishing services associate:* Meryl Gross
*Project management:* Books By Design, Inc.
*Production supervisor:* Scott Lavelle
*Text design:* Books By Design, Inc.
*Cover design:* Evelyn Horovicz
*Cover photos:* (Front Cover)    Clockwise from top left: Joe Tuman; Joseph D.
Lavenburg, National Geographic Society. Collection of the Supreme Court of the
United States; Dane Penland. Collection of the Supreme Court of the United States;
Richard Strauss, Smithsonian Institution. Collection of the Supreme Court of the
United States; Harris & Ewing. Collection of the Supreme Court of the United States;
*New York Times* (July 9, 1963). Copyright © 1963 *New York Times* Pictures. Reprinted
by permission; Harris & Ewing. Collection of the Supreme Court of the United States.
Center: From *The Rebel Girl: An Autobiography* by Elizabeth Gurley Flynn. International
Publishers (1973), p. 98. Used by permission of International Publishers Company,
New York. (Back Cover)    Photos: Dennis Geaney Photography.

Library of Congress Catalog Card Number: 95-73209

Copyright © 1997 by St. Martin's Press, Inc.

Manufactured in the United States of America.

1
f e d c

For information, write:
Bedford/St. Martin's
75 Arlington Street
Boston, MA 02116
(617-426-7440)

ISBN: 0-312-11715-9

# Contents

# Preface

Few can approach a subject like free expression without any context or experience for it in their own lives. Most of us will understand this best when our free expression has been reduced to something less than free. When we first discussed writing this book, we shared three experiences which informed our understanding of the topic. Two of these experiences were individual to each author; a third was collective from our days in law school. For one of us, it was a reminiscence of childhood, and the memory of a young boy who spent the day in the principal's office being punished for "daring" to speak out at a school assembly, asking why members of a local city council (none of whom rode bicycles) had never bothered to ask students for their input before making new rules prohibiting the riding of bicycles in the downtown area.

A second memory came to one of us not as a child and a student, but as an adult and a teacher, at a faculty workshop on "avoiding legal liability." Here, an administrator encouraged a young professor and his colleagues to take action if a student's speech offended other students. When asked if a student who was sanctioned for his or her speech would not then have a case against the university on First Amendment grounds, the administrator summarily dismissed the concern, stressing only a desire to avoid any lawsuits.

A third and collectively shared recollection came to us from our days studying law at Boalt Hall in Berkeley, when in first-year orientation, all students were encouraged to completely disregard whatever they thought they knew about law and the courts. The orientations professor asserted that we would now read the courts' actual opinions and see for ourselves the text of the statutes and rules in question. We were instructed to let them, and not what our inductive experiences, books, movies, or superficial news treatments might have told us, be our guides.

Both authors were left with the same impression, agreeing that news treatments, movies, books, or our own prejudices were inaccurate guides for understanding law; but how, we wondered, especially in the area of freedom of speech, could we ignore our own experiences?

This book attempts to reconcile these different parts. We feel that we accomplish this reconciliation through the following features.

First, we have divided our approach to freedom of speech into different sections, attempting as comprehensive a look as possible at the range of issues implicated by this freedom. These include a section on the historical origins of free speech, another on limits justified by "protecting society," one for categorical exceptions to free expression, and a final section dealing with content-based regulation of speech. This approach is both comprehensive and contemporary, with emphasis on subjects which should be of special interest, including extensive treatment of campus free-speech issues, as well as special concerns for technology and expression in cyberspace. It is our belief that readers will learn more when the topics they study involve issues they are familiar with in their everyday lives.

Second, in each chapter we offer readers an opportunity to explore judicial opinions which have determined the meaning of freedom of speech and the First Amendment. It is our judgment that readers become active learners by reading the case law for themselves, as well as informed commentary and analysis from others. In this way we hope to demystify free speech law for readers, encouraging them to begin grappling with the complexities offered by each case.

Third, to provide a thorough theoretical grounding in the subject, we also introduce readers to the philosophical justifications for freedom of speech and counter-arguments for speech constraints. Mindful of the need to avoid public misconceptions (for example, the misconception that freedom and free expression are unique inventions of Western culture), we also offer readers a review of the history of free expression in the United States and other countries and cultures.

Fourth, and by choice, we attempt to illuminate the complexity of these issues and encourage readers to think critically about them by using a Marketplace of Ideas metaphor for freedom of speech. We do not advance the claim that free market capitalism is the best economic system (and therefore we need a system of expression that is analogous to a free market); this text is not premised on an economic analysis of the law. We do, however, believe that a Marketplace of Ideas metaphor aids the reader in visualizing a world where the exchange of ideas is unrestrained. While we consider other possible explanations of free speech, we feel this metaphor serves as the best tool for this purpose.

We also want to encourage readers to use their critical thinking skills in developing their vision of an ideal system of expression. Readers will not simply be presented with the current law for free expression and asked to assume this is what the law ought to be. In addition to learning what the law is, readers will be exposed to differing viewpoints as to what the law should be, and challenged to develop their own perspectives.

At the same time, however, we are not eager to encourage readers to dismiss their own memories and experiences with freedom of speech issues.

Such experiences provide valuable context for understanding the nature of free expression. In that spirit, we have carefully worked to select examples which provide readers with a comprehensive review of freedom of speech, while at the same time picking examples which will hopefully be familiar and meaningful to most who read this book.

This book is also designed to be accessible to a wide range of readers, with each chapter offering both a cross-section of case law and analysis designed to provoke inquiry and discussion. In that spirit, we have been careful to provide enough case law to comprehensively satisfy those who want more than an outline of a case, while at the same time providing enough of our own analysis and questions to demystify the law for those who may find its study inhibiting.

We do not pretend to suggest that this effort will resolve all controversies and questions surrounding freedom of speech. In point of fact, most of these issues must be judged case by case—and so this book may at best only result in provoking thoughtful questions and inquiry on the part of the reader. But if we accomplish this much we will be justified, for as James Thurber once wrote: "It is better to ask some of the questions than to know all of the answers."

## *Acknowledgments*

We could not have completed this book, of course, without the very significant assistance of several friends and colleagues. Special thanks are offered to Franklyn S. Haiman for advice and guidance, George Diestel and Nancy McDermid for collegial support and useful suggestions, Suzanne Phelps Weir at St. Martin's for editorial assistance, the library staff at Boalt Hall, School of Law (U.C. Berkeley) and Darrell S. Duncan and Theresa Pollard at San Francisco State University for research assistance, Lisa Kawamura for proofreading, Kazuko Nishita for typing assistance, and Donna Smith for graphic design.

We appreciate the valuable comments and suggestions of the following people who kindly reviewed this manuscript: Nicholas Burnett, California State University, Sacramento; Haig Bosmajian, University of Washington; Tim Gallimore, University of Missouri; Ann Gill, Colorado State University; John Gossett, University of North Texas; Franklyn S. Haiman, Northwestern University; Sean Patrick O'Rourke, Vanderbilt University; Tom Schwartz, Ohio State University; Paul Siegel, Gallaudet University, and Anita Taylor, George Mason University.

We would also like to thank our families for their love and support during this project. In particular, Doug would like to thank his wife, Nancy, for believing in him and never doubting that the book would be completed. He would also like to thank his son, Douglas III, whose karate dojo and hockey rink provided the venue for many after-school work sessions on the book, and his daughter, Whitney Tenaya, who often worked beside him writing her "books" as this manuscript was completed. Finally, he would like to thank the coaches and team members of the Fresno State speech and debate team, who were incredibly supportive of this project even when it meant more work and less coaching for them.

Joe would like to thank his wife, Kirsten, for love, patience, and the critical eye that saw things in the manuscript he sometimes missed. He would also like to thank his children, Helen and Nathaniel, both of whom put up with books, articles, and papers around the kitchen nook for several months, as well as countless lectures and descriptions of the Constitution over a bowl of cereal. For pretending to be interested, their Dad thanks them!

D.M.F.
J.S.T.

*Freedom of Speech*

*in the Marketplace of Ideas*

# CHAPTER 1    *Objectives*

**After reading chapter 1,**
**you should understand**
**the following:**

◆ *The type of* questions *you will seek to answer when you study freedom of speech.*

◆ *The* meaning *of freedom of speech, and the dimensions of this right.*

◆ *The* justifications *for freedom of speech, as well as common arguments in favor of* limiting *free speech rights.*

◆ *The* marketplace of ideas *metaphor for freedom of speech.*

◆ *Two important* implications *of the marketplace metaphor: There is no such thing as a bad idea, and more speech is the appropriate remedy for speech perceived to be harmful.*

◆ *The* procedure *by which the American judicial system determines the meaning of our free speech rights.*

◆ *Major* doctrines *employed by the Supreme Court in deciding freedom of speech cases.*

1 # An Introduction to the Study of Freedom of Speech

## WHAT WILL YOU LEARN ABOUT WHEN YOU STUDY FREEDOM OF SPEECH?

SUPPOSE THAT NINE students are seated in a row at their graduation from a state university. Each wears a robe that has one letter or number attached to the back, so that when the students stand, the message "187 racist" is shown. (The number 187 refers to a ballot proposition that would deny services to undocumented immigrants.) When the students stand to deliver their message, university officials eject them from the ceremony, and the protesters are arrested for disturbing the peace.

Should these students have a right to express themselves freely at their graduation?

Should an opponent of abortion have a right to approach patients entering a clinic and exhort them not to have an abortion? Do gay and lesbian organizations have a right to march on a public street in a parade sponsored by a veterans' organization? Should a novelist be allowed to write a story describing how the protagonist uses a fertilizer bomb to blow up a federal office building? The study of freedom of speech focuses on such issues. As you read further in this book you will learn how to analyze these and other free speech controversies.

You will consider three major lines of inquiry in this text. First, you will study the current state of the law on freedom of speech. What do people in the United States have a right to say? When can the government place limitations on expression? The First Amendment, providing that "Congress shall make no law . . . abridging the freedom of speech, or of the press," does not define our rights with precision. Although the judicial decisions you will read clarify the meaning of the First Amendment, your study of free speech should not end with learning the current state of the law.

A second issue to consider is whether you agree with the current state of the law on freedom of speech in the United States. When you read excerpts from leading Supreme Court cases, you will study why the Court ruled as it did. You will examine the viewpoints of justices who were in the minority (called **dissenting opinions**) as well as the opinions of scholars who have disagreed with the Court. Your professor is likely to present additional viewpoints in class.

You should consider these diverse perspectives on freedom of speech, along with your thoughts on the issues, and reach your conclusions about what our right to freedom of speech *should* consist of. One of the most important skills you can develop during your college education is the ability to apply critical thinking to the theories and principles you are learning. As a citizen in a free country, you have a right to voice your support or opposition to the rules that govern society. Thus, to be an effective advocate for your viewpoint on freedom of speech, it is important to understand the justifications for, and criticisms of, free speech law.

A third topic of study is the history of free speech protection. Freedom of speech is not an American invention. Ancient cultures had traditions that facilitated—and inhibited—free expression. Americans' experiences with freedom of speech, first as British subjects and later as citizens of an independent nation, evidence the slow and difficult process by which this right was obtained and developed. Twentieth-century experiences, such as persecution of alleged Communists during the 1950s, show how fragile freedom of speech can be if it is not vigilantly protected.

Before you begin to study the history of freedom of speech as well as its current status in the United States, it is helpful to understand the concept of free speech. This chapter will elaborate on the meaning of freedom of speech, discuss some fundamental justifications for that freedom, and introduce a metaphor that helps to explain how freedom of speech functions in the United States. Finally, this chapter will illustrate how freedom of speech controversies are resolved in our society and provide tips for effective study.

## THE MEANING OF FREEDOM OF SPEECH

### The Definitions of Freedom and Speech

To define freedom of speech, it is necessary to consider what constitutes speech and what we mean when we say that speech is free. This section discusses the meanings of speech and freedom in the context of the study of freedom of speech. We also present four significant dimensions of freedom of speech.

*The Meaning of Freedom.*    Finding a suitable definition for freedom in a free speech context is a challenge, because the literal definition of *freedom* would protect speech that even the staunchest of civil libertarians would not defend. Freedom of speech cannot mean the freedom to say anything we want at the time and place of our choosing. It is common sense that freedom of speech does not include the right to tell a cashier, "I have a gun, give me all your money"; nor to interrupt a doctor who is performing brain surgery with a screaming tirade about medical malpractice; nor to falsely tell a child that his or her parents have just died.

Freedom of speech can more accurately be defined as the right to be free from unreasonable constraints on expression. Of course, defining an "unreasonable constraint" presents the most daunting challenge here. As you read the free speech cases in this text, you will learn about how the Supreme Court has set the boundaries between reasonable and unreasonable constraints in a variety of communication contexts. These boundaries define what freedom of speech is in the United States.

*The Meaning of Speech.* In its contemporary usage, *freedom of speech* often refers to the freedom of communication by diverse means, including but not limited to use of the spoken word.[1] For example, if you have a First Amendment right to call a person a "sexist pig" in a speech, you are likely to have the same right if you use those words again in a newspaper article or an electronic mail transmission.

The right to communicate still varies at times, depending on the medium of communication.[2] Nevertheless, when scholars or jurists write about freedom of speech, they are ordinarily referring to the freedom to *communicate* a message, instead of the narrower right to express that message orally. Therefore, the terms *freedom of speech, freedom of expression,* and *First Amendment freedoms* will be used interchangeably to refer to the same basic right to communicate.

As you read this text, you will examine four major dimensions of freedom of speech. The Supreme Court has not held that all of these aspects of free expression are uniformly protected by the First Amendment. Nevertheless, each dimension has an effect on our communication, and each should be considered when deciding how free our speech is in the United States or any other society.

### Four Criteria for Evaluating the Extent of Freedom of Speech

*Freedom to Communicate without Fear of Government Sanction or Censorship.* If freedom of expression is to exist, the government must provide a compelling justification before it can impose a **prior restraint.** Prior restraint is the censorship of information before it is communicated, as is the case when government officials have the power to remove objectionable articles from a newspaper before publication. Another essential condition for free expression

---

1. See, e.g., 16B *Corpus Juris Secundum,* "Constitutional Law," Section 539, pp. 4–5. "[T]he constitutional right to free speech is not limited to public addresses, pamphlets, or words of an individual, but it also embraces every form and manner of dissemination of ideas that appeal best fitted to bring such ideas and views to the attention of the general populace."
2. See, e.g., chapters 10 and 13 for examples of rules that place restrictions on messages only when they are transmitted through a certain type of channel.

is limitation of the government's ability to penalize people after they communicate their ideas. The government's power to punish communicators or impose prior restraints is ordinarily checked by an independent institution, such
as the U.S. Supreme Court.

The majority of free speech cases that you will study in this text involve
the government's attempt to punish or control communicators, based on the
content of the message they express. Government constraints on communicators are typically involved in freedom of speech cases, because the Constitution
forbids Congress[3] from abridging freedom of speech.

The government does not provide the only constraint on uninhibited
expression in our society. For example, throughout history, women's ability
to express themselves has been determined by the extent to which they were
controlled by their fathers and husbands (often with the law's blessing). Our
own history documents the coercion exerted by private citizens upon abolitionists to discourage them from promoting antislavery. In modern times, it
has been argued that social pressures have encouraged people to avoid politically incorrect speech, particularly on campus.[4] And if your employer tells
you to stop speaking out in favor of environmental protection (because the
firm's clients may not like your message), the risk of losing your job may motivate you to curtail your speech. When the pressure to refrain from expressing your viewpoints comes from nongovernmental sources, your right to
self-expression is *not* guaranteed by the First Amendment—which only forbids *governmental* abridgment of speech.

*Freedom from Compulsory Speech.*  If the government can force you to
express a particular message, you lack the freedom to remain silent or to sub-
stitute a message that more accurately states your viewpoint. This comes into
play when public schools require students to salute the flag[5] or recite a prayer.
This type of government control on speech is also implicated when public employees are required to sign a document certifying that they are not Communists, and when physicians in government-funded health clinics are told what
to say when discussing abortion.[6]

*Freedom of Access to Effective Channels of Communication.*  Another
important condition for freedom of speech is the speaker's ability to communicate with his or her target audience. That freedom would be circumscribed if
people could express themselves only in private conversations or private
places such as their homes. The Supreme Court has recognized that public
places such as streets and parks may be used by the public for communicating
their thoughts, subject to reasonable regulations.[7] In chapter 10, you will

3. The Constitution was also interpreted to proscribe the states from abridging the rights of free
expression in *Gitlow v. New York,* discussed here in chapter 4.
4. See, e.g., Jerry Adler et al., *Taking Offense,* Newsweek 48 (December 24, 1990).
5. The compulsory flag salute issue is discussed in chapter 11.
6. These issues are addressed in chapter 12.
7. *Hague v. C.I.O.,* 307 U.S. 496 (1939).

study the tests for what constitutes a public place and what constitutes a reasonable regulation.

Access to effective communication technology is related to the question of access to public places. Does freedom of speech exist when some of us have the resources to convey opinions to mass audiences while others must rely on smaller-scale methods of communication? The television station owner and the person who can afford a significant financial contribution to an elected representative has a greater opportunity to be heard than does the low-income individual who holds up a handmade sign on a street corner.

Inequalities in the means of exercising free speech rights have concerned commentators in our society. For example, Michael Lind, a senior editor of *Harper's* magazine, has written about an American "overclass," the richest twenty percent of the population, contending that this group is monopolizing wealth at the expense of the poor and middle class. Lind views their greater ability to use their First Amendment rights as an important cause of their success. He writes that this "overclass manages to protect itself from popular insurgencies, not only through its ownership of the news media but also by its financial control of elections."[8] University of California journalism professor Ben Bagdikian has also critiqued the decrease in the number and diversity of persons with control over the means of mass communication:

> Almost without exception they [the chief executives of the twenty-three corporations that control most of what Americans can see and read] are economic conservatives. They can, if they wish, use control of their newspapers, broadcast stations, magazines, books, and movies to promote their own corporate values to the exclusion of others.[9]

Despite the arguments against existing inequalities, access to effective means of communication has not usually been recognized as a part of our First Amendment rights. The Supreme Court has held that when available radio or television frequencies are scarce, it is consistent with the First Amendment that the federal government require station owners to broadcast a diversity of viewpoints.[10] When there has not been scarcity of channels in a communication medium, the right of access has not been viewed as a First Amendment freedom,[11] and the First Amendment rights of the owner of the communication technology have been held to be paramount.

***Freedom from Government Domination of the Free Speech Environment.*** Government can influence public discourse, even if it does not censor any particular viewpoints. It may publish posters and create television advertisements to encourage citizens to join the armed forces. It may attempt to provide funding for artists who write patriotic music, while denying funds to

8. Michael Lind, *To Have and Have Not: Notes on the Progress of the American Class War*, 290 Harper's 35, 41 (June 1995).
9. Ben H. Bagdikian, *The Media Monopoly*, p. 6 (Beacon Press, 3rd ed 1990).
10. See *Red Lion Broadcasting Co. v. F.C.C.*, 395 U.S. 367, discussed in chapter 13.
11. See, e.g., *Miami Herald Publishing Co. v. Tornillo*, 418 U.S. 241 (1974).

those whose work contains homoerotic themes. The government may also withhold information that could help the public resolve controversial issues, such as a confidential memorandum by government economists criticizing a President's budget plan.

Although the government has not overtly prevented expression in any of these examples, pacifists, artists who wish to express gay or lesbian themes, or critics of the President's budget are all likely to feel that the government is attempting to stack the deck in favor of its position on these issues.

Freedom of speech may be compromised when the government promotes one viewpoint and refuses to provide equal resources for the expression of opposing views. First Amendment freedoms may also be harmed when members of the public lack access to information that would help them make a stronger case for their side of an argument. Chapter 12, on government-subsidized speech, will analyze these questions. The issue of access to government information that is withheld in the name of national security will be considered in chapter 5.

Now that you have read about several of the primary dimensions of freedom of speech, we must analyze another fundamental question: Why should this bundle of rights we call freedom of speech be highly valued?

## JUSTIFICATION AND CRITIQUE OF FREEDOM OF SPEECH

This section will help you develop your own perspective on the importance of free speech. First, we introduce four of the primary rationales that are offered to support free speech. In support of each rationale, we present the thoughts of some of the most eloquent past and present defenders of freedom of speech. However, freedom of expression has had its share of scholarly critics. The second part of this section will discuss some of the ideological challenges to freedom of speech in the United States.

### Reasons for Freedom of Speech

Why is freedom of speech justified? The four most important reasons are: (1) it is vital to our system of self-government; (2) it facilitates the discovery of the truth; (3) it promotes individual dignity and self-worth; and (4) any regime for speech control would be unworkable and deleterious. It is important to note that the Supreme Court has not consistently vindicated all of these interests in free speech. Throughout this text, you will read judicial decisions that have emphasized certain justifications (particularly, those facilitating democracy and discovering the truth) and limited the importance of others (especially, those promoting individual autonomy).

***Freedom of Speech Is Vital to Self-Government.***   In a democratic society, the people hold the ultimate power to control their government. To make rational decisions about the fate of society, citizens must have access to all ideas about government policy. Professor Alexander Meiklejohn, a leading proponent of this justification for the First Amendment, argued:

> These conflicting views [that a military draft is moral or immoral, and that American political institutions are superior or inferior to Russia's] may be expressed, must be expressed, not because they are valid, but because they are relevant. If they are responsibly entertained by anyone, we, the voters need to hear them. . . . To be afraid of ideas, any idea, is to be unfit for self-government.[12]

Free speech also promotes democratic values by helping to expose government wrongdoing. Professor Vincent Blasi has noted that exposure of government abuses such as Watergate enables the public to remedy the wrong. The fear of public exposure also deters official malfeasance.[13]

***Freedom of Speech Promotes Discovery of the Truth.*** The viewpoint that truth will emerge from an open competition of ideas has ancient origins. Aristotle wrote that "the true and the just are by nature stronger than their opposites," and that true and better facts "are by nature always more productive of good syllogisms and, in a word, more persuasive."[14] If true ideas are inherently more powerful than false ones, and all ideas are freely expressed, the public will ultimately come to accept the truth.

In 1644, the English poet John Milton expressed a similar optimism about truth in *Areopagitica*, a landmark tract in defense of free expression. Milton argued in opposition to Parliament's Licensing Order of 1643, which gave that body the power to control what was printed in England. In defending the ability of truth to emerge from free expression, Milton wrote:

> And though all the windes of doctrin were let loose to play upon the earth, so Truth be in the field, we do injuriously by licencing and prohibiting to misdoubt her strength. Let her and Falsehood grapple; who ever knew Truth put to the wors, in a free and open encounter.[15]

Historically, censorship has been employed to deny the emergence of ideas now universally accepted as true. In seventeenth-century Europe, religious authorities insisted that an immobile earth stood at the center of the universe. An expression of doubt about this doctrine could be punished by death,[16] and under threat of torture and execution,[17] the astronomer Galileo was forced to sign a statement renouncing the view that the sun was at the

---

12. Alexander Meiklejohn, *Free Speech and Its Relation to Self-Government*, p. 27 (Harper, 1948).
13. Vincent Blasi, *The Checking Value in First Amendment Theory*, 1977 American Bar Foundation Research Journal 521.
14. George A. Kennedy, *Aristotle on Rhetoric: A Theory of Civic Discourse*, pp. 34–35 (Oxford Univ. Press, 1991).
15. J. Max Patrick, *The Prose of John Milton*, p. 327 (New York Univ. Press, 1968).
16. Albert Einstein, introduction to *Dialogue Concerning the Two Chief World Systems, Ptolemaic and Copernican*, p. xvii (Univ. of California Press, 1953).
17. Stillman Drake, id., p. xxiv. Galileo was then imprisoned for the rest of his life, although his surroundings were comfortable and he was allowed to pursue research with his favorite pupils.

center of the universe. In nineteenth-century America, southern states severely restricted arguments against slavery. The aim of the powers-that-be is obvious: suppress new and often better reasons and ideas when they threaten the status quo.

The preceding theories find value in free speech as a means to desirable ends. The third justification emphasizes the importance of liberty, even if it benefits the individual rather than society.

*Freedom of Speech Promotes Individual Autonomy.*   When human beings are constrained from expressing their feelings, an element of their humanity is suppressed. First Amendment scholar Thomas Emerson called this a suppression of human dignity and a negation of one's essential nature.[18] Therefore, according to former California Chief Justice Rose Bird, the benefits that are achieved by the communicator provide an independent justification for freedom of speech:

> Free speech is also guaranteed because of our fundamental respect for individual development and self realization. The right to self expression is inherent in any political system which respects individual dignity.[19]

According to Milton, a good book is the product of reason, based on the very faculties that separate us from animals and make us more godlike or angelic. When good books are suppressed, it is a denial of the writer's essential humanity, a destruction of what is best in a person. Because ideas can outlive their inventor, this suppression "slays an immortality."[20]

John Stuart Mill argued that the power to control the expression of even one person was illegitimate:

> If all mankind minus one were of one opinion, and only one person were of the contrary opinion, mankind would be no more justified in silencing that one person, than he, if he had the power, would be justified in silencing mankind.[21]

In addition to arguing that free speech is justified because of the good it produces for society or for its individual members, freedom of speech can also be justified on the grounds that even if certain speech is detrimental to society, any attempt to regulate it will produce more harm than good.

*Regulations Directed at "Harmful" Speech Will Inevitably Be Abused to Constrain Worthwhile Speech.*   Another argument against curtailing speech is that even if some speech is harmful, any effort to limit this expression will also constrain speech that should be protected. Furthermore, no agent of control can be relied upon to regulate speech in a manner that serves the public interest.

---

18. Thomas I. Emerson, *The System of Freedom of Expression,* p. 6 (Random House, 1970).
19. *Guglielmi v. Spelling-Goldberg Productions,* 25 Cal.3d 860, 866 (1979) (Bird, C. J., concurring).
20. Patrick, pp. 256, 272.
21. John Stuart Mill, *On Liberty: Annotated Text Sources and Background Criticism,* ed. David Spitz, p. 18 (W.W. Norton, 1975).

Who should have the power to limit speech? Many people would not object to censorship if they were given the power to censor. As you read the cases in this text, you may encounter speakers whose ideas you consider dangerous, disgusting, discourteous, or just plain foolish. It is tempting to say, "I do not believe that type of expression is necessary; I do not talk that way; therefore, it does not need First Amendment protection." But does any one of us have a moral right to suppress the ideas of another? John Locke considered the problem more than three centuries ago:

> We should do well to commiserate our mutual ignorance . . . and not instantly treat others ill . . . because they will not renounce their own and receive our opinions. . . . For where is the man that has uncontestable evidence of the truth of all that he holds, or of the falsehood of all he condemns?[22]

If each of us lacks proof of the moral superiority of our own claims, why not rely on majority rule to determine what speech is permissible? One difficulty is that the conventional wisdom of society often turns out to be wrong. Wrote Mill, "Ages are no more infallible than individuals; every age having held many opinions which subsequent ages have deemed not only false but absurd."[23]

For example, the music of Elvis Presley and the Beatles was once labeled as dangerous and revolutionary, but their lyrics now seem mild when compared to those contemporary "merchants of doom," such as grunge rockers and rap musicians.[24] In turn, the music of the next generation is likely to face similar condemnation from young adults who enjoy today's controversial music. If history is a reliable predictor of the future, no majority of society will permanently corner the market on truth (or taste).

If the will of the majority could silence speech, it is likely that at some point each of us would be subject to having his or her ideas suppressed. The issue of equal rights provides one example of this phenomenon. American Civil Liberties Union president Nadine Strossen noted that if the First Amendment protected only popular ideas, majorities could have silenced the civil rights movement of the 1960s and advocacy of the Equal Rights Amendment in the 1970s.[25] Conversely, if one believes that victims of discrimination have been given too many privileges, a politically correct majority could silence 1990s arguments against affirmative action or welfare if they believed that it would be dangerous for society to roll back these programs.

If the limits on speech cannot be set by any one of us and should not be established through majority vote, could we allow a government agency to set

---

22. John Locke, *An Essay Concerning Human Understanding*, p. 560 (Routledge, 6th ed 1910).
23. Mill, p. 19.
24. The issue of rap music and the First Amendment is considered in chapters 4 and 9.
25. Nadine Strossen, *Defending Pornography: Free Speech, Sex, and the Fight for Women's Rights*, p. 61 (Scribner's, 1991).

the limits on speech? Entrusting the government with greater control over expression is a risky proposition. Because public officials are likely to want to preserve their own power, "a government deciding what historical, political, and moral ideas to suppress is bound to be affected by aims other than the disinterested pursuit of truth."[26]

It is ironic for people to distrust government on the one hand and on the other advocate greater government control of speech. Political conservatives are distrustful of big government, yet argue for government control of speech that they consider obscene or detrimental to "family values." Persons on the left vilify a government that institutionalizes racism and patriarchy, yet support that government's placing constraints on hate speech and sexist advertising. The paradox of distrusting government while supporting such limits on speech illustrates the risk inherent in giving government more power to control speech.

Every time constraints on speech are proposed, we must consider who is to implement the restriction and how it will be done. If certain types of expression are deemed harmful or worthless, the government must write and enforce a law against such speech. Will government officials, with their own interests and agendas, only use the law to punish "valueless speech"? How do officials *know* when speech is harmful? Can lawmakers write a rule that clearly defines what speech is prohibited without encroaching on speech that should be protected? These concerns cause civil libertarians to oppose government controls unless expression will cause imminent serious harm that cannot be prevented by any other means.[27]

Fear caused by the inability of any persons or institutions to make good judgments about the control of speech can be minimized through rules which protect freedom of speech. This freedom can also promote democratic government, truth seeking, and individual autonomy. These benefits can be contrasted with the views of commentators who believe free speech rights can be overemphasized.

### Arguments in Support of Restricting Freedom of Speech

Justifications for limiting speech have been offered throughout history. Two ubiquitous examples are the suppression of speech to foster a favorable opinion of a ruler and to prevent denial of prevailing religious doctrine. When restrictions on speech are advocated in modern times, these arguments are not ordinarily cited in their defense, although they remain motives for speech control. A new set of arguments is offered instead.

***Individual Rights Should Not Supersede Communitarian Needs.*** Communitarians argue that the United States has overemphasized the rights of the individual and neglected the individual's duties to his or her community. Pro-

---

26. Kent Greenawalt, *Speech, Crime, and the Uses of Language*, p. 22 (Oxford Univ. Press, 1989).
27. Strossen, pp. 41–42.

fessor Mary Ann Glendon of Harvard has decried the "exaggerated absoluteness of our American rights rhetoric" and "a near silence concerning responsibility."[28] Another leading spokesperson for this point of view, Professor Amitai Etzioni from George Washington University, argues;

> [B]oth the individual and the community have the *same basic primary moral standing.* . . . One cannot use the needs of society—or individual rights—to shut out the other considerations, as for instance, do First Amendment absolutists.[29]

Communitarians argue that there is an interdependence between our community needs and our individual rights. The communities we belong to (neighborhoods, workplaces, political entities, etc.) must be healthy, or a society capable of preserving our individual rights cannot be sustained.[30]

What duties might we owe society with respect to our expression? Temple University Professor Molefi Kete Asante argues that civility ought to be a guiding principle. He suggests that "no area of our social compact agitates us so much as how we speak to each other in conversation and in the public forum."[31] Professor Asante notes three important aspects of civility: courtesy, safety, and common sense.

Courtesy involves expressing your feelings in a manner that recognizes the humanity of other people, even when you disagree with them.[32] Vilification of one social group is a denial of that norm. Equality of all persons, despite social differences, is a fundamental principle of our political community. When expression denies the personhood of some community members, equality is denied.[33]

The principle of safety states that speech should not be used to create conditions of physical harm to oneself or to others.[34] Thus, speech should not be used to provoke a fight or incite violence toward others. Speech that genuinely jeopardizes our national security would also fit in this category.

Common sense refers to the viewpoint that some expression is inappropriate in a decent society. An "anything goes" philosophy, fueled by music videos and movies, has replaced the standards once exemplified by orators and writers. Professor Asante argues that as a society, we have lost a common understanding of what constitutes good taste in expression, and he challenges communication scholars to help society find a common ground.[35]

28. Mary Ann Glendon, *Rights Talk*, p. 45 (Free Press, 1991).
29. Amitai Etzioni, *A Responsive Society*, p. 138 (Jossey-Bass, 1991).
30. Daniel Bell, *Communitarianism and Its Critics*, p. i (Clarendon, 1993).
31. Molefi Kete Asante, *Unraveling the Edges of Free Speech*, 75 National Forum 12 (Spring 1995).
32. Id, pp. 12–13.
33. *A Communitarian Defense of Group Libel Laws*, 101 Harvard Law Review, 682, 690–91 (Jan. 1988).
34. Asante, p. 13.
35. Id., p. 14.

A communitarian philosophy does not necessarily advocate censorship as a means of enforcing speech duties. For example, communitarians have advocated freedom with respect to the use of hate speech but urged individuals not to exercise their right to insult any human being with racist, sexist, or homophobic slurs.[36] The individual can voluntarily be the agent of change and agree to use his or her First Amendment rights in a way that promotes a healthy community.

*Speech Rights Should Not Supersede Other Individual Rights.*   Another justification for restricting speech does not advocate a new balance between individual rights and community rights. Instead, it argues that freedom of speech should not automatically "trump" other individual rights. The United States is different from many other countries because of the primacy it places on speech rights. Many Western European countries, for example, put the right to government protection of health and welfare on a par with freedom of speech.[37]

Some scholars have called for more balance between the First and Fourteenth Amendments. The Fourteenth Amendment mandates that no state shall "deny to any person within its jurisdiction the equal protection of the laws." Stanford professor Charles Lawrence III has argued that claims of free speech rights to make racist statements should be balanced against the Fourteenth Amendment right of equal protection for people of color.[38] Michigan Law professor Catharine MacKinnon decries the First Amendment protection of Nazis, Klansmen, and pornographers, and calls for the state to provide "relief from injury to equality through speech."[39] The Supreme Court of Canada provided an example of this reasoning when it upheld an obscenity conviction. The Canadian Court noted, "[If] true equality between male and female persons is to be achieved, we cannot ignore the threat to equality resulting from exposure to audiences of certain types of violent and degrading material."[40]

*Speech Rights Do Not Guarantee Effective Freedom.*   Some commentators also argue that a greater emphasis should be placed on the guarantee of effective freedom than on formal freedom.[41] In a free speech context, formal freedom refers to our rules about free speech, such as the Constitution's command against *government* abridgment of speech. If the Constitution guarantees all persons this right, then there is the formal right to freedom of speech.

---

36. Samuel Walker, *Hate Speech: The History of an American Controversy*, p. 142 (Univ. of Nebraska Press, 1994). Professor Asante also makes it clear that he is not advocating legislation to require decency in speech.
37. Glendon, p. 99.
38. Charles Lawrence III, *Words That Wound*, p. 64 (Westview, 1993).
39. Catharine A. MacKinnon, *Only Words*, p. 109 (Harvard Univ. Press, 1993).
40. Id. at 101. Quoting *Butler v. Regina*, 2 W.W.R. 577 (Can. 1992).
41. See, e.g. Philip Selznick, *The Moral Commonwealth: Social Theory and Promise of Community*, p. 374 (Univ. of California Press, 1992).

An analysis of effective freedom would view freedom of speech in a broader context. If some segments of society have the economic resources to communicate their viewpoints to mass audiences, and others do not, there would not be effective freedom.[42] Effective freedom would also be denied if a racist judicial system, or the financial inability to hire a capable attorney, prevented some social groups from vindicating their free speech rights in court. If pornography creates a climate where women are inhibited from freely expressing themselves, or if racist speech in the classroom deters ethnic minorities from participating in class, effective freedom is reduced. When freedom of speech is criticized on the grounds of effective freedom, the argument often takes the form that the speech of one person is denying the ability of another person to speak out.[43]

The previous sections provide us with major arguments that are advanced in support of freedom of speech and in defense of restrictions on speech. They do not, however, provide a framework for resolving conflicts between freedom of speech and other societal values. One framework is to consider freedom of speech in the United States as a marketplace of ideas. The marketplace metaphor will be presented in the next section of this chapter. We are not suggesting that there is an absolutely free marketplace of ideas in the United States, nor insisting that a marketplace approach will always produce the best outcomes for society. However, this model explains many of the judicial decisions you will read in this text and provides an analytical tool for studying our system of freedom of speech.

## A METAPHOR FOR FREE SPEECH IN THE UNITED STATES

### The Marketplace Concept

The marketplace of ideas is a metaphor for an environment in which the government's regulation of communication is limited. In an economic free marketplace, such as a bazaar or swap meet, sellers are free to offer their products for sale at any price they choose. Buyers are free to accept the goods on the seller's terms, offer a lower price, or reject the seller's wares. In a marketplace of ideas, the source of the message is the seller. She or he is allowed to express ideas to anyone who is willing to listen. The receiver of the message is like the buyer, and may freely decide to agree or disagree with the message.

The marketplace metaphor was developed in a series of judicial opinions by justices Oliver Wendell Holmes and Louis Brandeis. As you will read in chapter 4, the concepts developed by Holmes and Brandeis remain an integral part of contemporary legal reasoning on the First Amendment.

---

42. See e.g. David Kairys, *With Liberty and Justice for Some: A Critique of the Conservative Supreme Court*, p. 62 (New Press, 1993). Kairys argues that the Supreme Court has "narrowed and restricted the free speech rights available to people of ordinary means, enlarged the free speech rights of wealthy people and corporations, and erected a free-speech barrier to public access to the media."
43. See, e.g., Lawrence, p. 79.

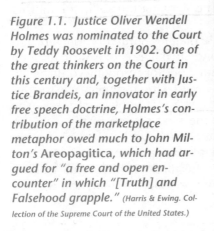

*Figure 1.1. Justice Oliver Wendell Holmes was nominated to the Court by Teddy Roosevelt in 1902. One of the great thinkers on the Court in this century and, together with Justice Brandeis, an innovator in early free speech doctrine, Holmes's contribution of the marketplace metaphor owed much to John Milton's Areopagitica, which had argued for "a free and open encounter" in which "[Truth] and Falsehood grapple."* (Harris & Ewing. Collection of the Supreme Court of the United States.)

Justice Holmes first used the marketplace metaphor in 1920 (see Fig. 1.1). He argued that the First Amendment should protect exhortations to resist United States participation in World War I. He reasoned that even if a majority of Americans were convinced that the U.S. role in the war was correct, opposing viewpoints should not be suppressed. Instead, Justice Holmes argued for a truth-seeking perspective on the First Amendment. He argued that "the ultimate good desired is better reached by free trade in ideas, and that the best test of truth is the power of the thought to get itself accepted in the competition of the market."[44]

The marketplace of ideas provides a context for analyzing freedom of speech in subsequent chapters of this text. When the government allows for a marketplace of ideas, freedom of speech is enhanced. When the government places restrictions on the marketplace, freedom of speech is curtailed. If we ac-

---

44. *Abrams v. United States,* 250 U.S. 616, 630 (1919) (Holmes, J., dissenting). The *Abrams* case is discussed in detail in chapter 4.

cept the marketplace of ideas as a desirable end for freedom of speech law, we must accept other corollaries of this model.

## Implications of the Marketplace of Ideas Metaphor

*Freedom of Speech Protects Speech We May Despise.* If there is to be a free marketplace of ideas, the government must tolerate expression that many of its citizens may find repugnant. Nazis must be allowed to shout messages of hate, rap musicians must be allowed to argue that all white persons are racists, and extremists of all political persuasions must have the right to characterize government officials as "jackbooted thugs."

Justice Holmes argued that all Americans must take this principle to heart if there is to be free speech in the United States. He wrote:

> If there is any principle of the Constitution that more imperatively calls for attachment than any other it is the principle of free thought—not free thought for those who agree with us but freedom for the thought we hate.[45]

In this text, you will read about free speech issues involving communicators from all segments of society. In some cases, you will agree with their messages; in others you may find their expressions reprehensible. If there is to be a free marketplace of ideas, the rights of all these defendants must be supported.

*The Remedy for Bad Ideas Is More Speech.* When there is a free marketplace of ideas, suppression of speech is not an appropriate remedy for speech that is considered offensive or dangerous. Instead, the preferred response is to speak out against the disfavored idea. This doctrine was first expressed by Justice Louis Brandeis when he argued that the First Amendment protected the right to be a member of the Communist Party, even if that organization supported the overthrow of the U.S. government. According to Justice Brandeis, suppression of Communist ideas was not the proper response. Instead, he argued, "the fitting remedy for evil counsels is good ones."[46] Whenever there was time to avert an alleged evil through discussion, "the remedy to be applied is more speech, not enforced silence."[47]

Under a marketplace of ideas system, people are free to speak out against speech they find threatening or offensive. If you fear that references to federal law enforcement authorities as "jackbooted thugs" will undermine law and order in society, you should attempt to persuade people to speak more

---

45. *United States v. Schwimmer*, 279 U.S. 644, 645–55 (1927) (Holmes, J., dissenting).
46. *Whitney v. California*, 274 U.S. 357, 375 (1927) (Brandeis, J., concurring). The *Whitney* decision is discussed in detail in chapter 4.
47. Id. at 377.

respectfully of these agencies, and point to these agencies' accomplishments. If you believe that calls for the repeal of affirmative action are racist, you are free to denounce this advocacy as racism, and argue that affirmative action has benefited society. Instead of advocating repression of speech, you should use your First Amendment rights to counter the speech you abhor.

Now that you have studied the theory of a marketplace of ideas, it is time to proceed to the question of how our constitutional system of government decides what speech will be allowed into the marketplace.

## THE COURT SYSTEM IN THE UNITED STATES AND ITS ROLE IN INTERPRETING THE FIRST AMENDMENT

### The Role of the Judiciary

As we noted earlier in this chapter, the text of the First Amendment does not precisely define our free speech rights. Figure 1.2 provides a model of how the court system operates to define the meaning of freedom of speech in the United States.

Under our system of government, the Supreme Court has the last word on interpreting the text of the U.S. Constitution.[48] However, the Court does not establish regulations and guidelines that define our First Amendment rights as thoroughly as possible *before* free speech disputes arise. Instead, the function of the judicial system is to resolve cases and controversies[49] *after* the alleged denial of rights has occurred. We will use the hypothetical case of the student protest at graduation to demonstrate how our First Amendment rights are ordinarily interpreted.

### The Process for Resolving Free Speech Questions

*The Communicator Delivers a Message.*    A freedom of speech case begins with the act of communication. In the hypothetical case on page 1, the students used the written word to convey their views on Proposition 187—the aforementioned immigration reform initiative. In the cases you will study, a variety of means of communication will be used, including speeches, pamphlets, music, electronic mail, and symbolic acts, such as the burning of a flag.

*The Communicator's Right Is Challenged.*    The Constitution protects us from abridgment of our free speech rights. An abridgment may take a variety of forms. The student protesters were ejected from their graduation ceremony. They were also subjected to **criminal** prosecution for the offense of disturbing the peace. A communicator may be subjected to a **civil** lawsuit, in which he or she is sued by a private citizen who claims to have been harmed by the speaker's words. In other cases, the challenge to speech rights is made by a

---

48. *Marbury v. Madison*, 1 Cranch 137 (1803).
49. *U.S. Const.*, Article III.

## *Figure 1.2*  FREEDOM OF SPEECH ISSUES ARE RESOLVED BY THE STATE AND FEDERAL COURT SYSTEM

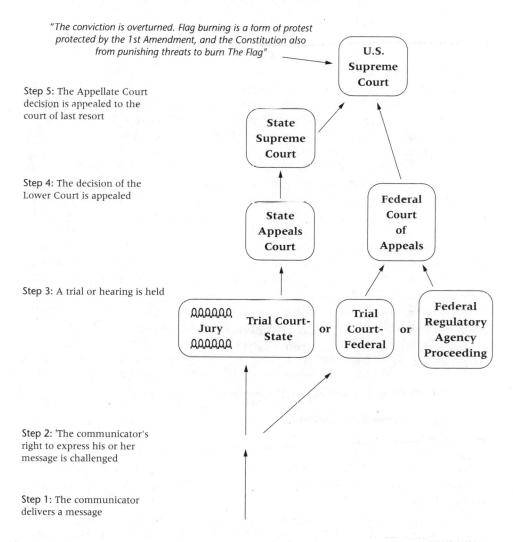

"*The conviction is overturned. Flag burning is a form of protest protected by the 1st Amendment, and the Constitution also from punishing threats to burn The Flag*"

U.S. Supreme Court

Step 5: The Appellate Court decision is appealed to the court of last resort

State Supreme Court

Step 4: The decision of the Lower Court is appealed

State Appeals Court

Federal Court of Appeals

Step 3: A trial or hearing is held

Jury

Trial Court-State

or

Trial Court-Federal

or

Federal Regulatory Agency Proceeding

Step 2: 'The communicator's right to express his or her message is challenged

Step 1: The communicator delivers a message

governmental regulatory agency, such as when a radio station is denied a re-
newal of its license because it had broadcast obscene stories.

   *A Trial or Hearing Is Held.*   The person whose speech rights are challenged is entitled to his or her day in court. The student protesters may sue
the university for denying them the right to participate in their graduation.
Before the protesters can be fined or imprisoned for violating any law (such as
one against breach of the peace) they are entitled to a trial, at which the prosecution must prove that their expression violated the law. In civil cases, the
**plaintiff** (the person who initiated the lawsuit) must prove that he or she has
been wronged by the communicator's words in a way that entitles the plaintiff
to money damages or other remedies.

   The defendant in a trial or hearing has the option of arguing that his or
her expression may not be punished because it is protected by the Constitution. This challenge may be made even if the defendant is guilty of breaking
the law in question. The challenge is allowed because the Constitution is the
highest law of the land, and no other law can be used to deny our constitutional rights. Thus, our graduation protesters could argue that even if the state
law against disturbing the peace clearly forbids people from standing up and
protesting during a public ceremony, that law must give way to a higher
law—the First Amendment.

   After a constitutional challenge is made, the judge may rule that charges
against the defendant must be dropped, or that a verdict against the defendant
may not be enforced, because the defendant's conduct is protected by the First
Amendment. The judge should decide the case based on **precedents,** which
are previous decisions by higher courts that provide guidance on how the
Constitution should be interpreted.

   Deciding on the correct precedent to follow may not be an easy task for
the judge. The facts of cases that have been decided by the Supreme Court
and other higher courts will not be identical to those in the particular case the
judge must resolve, so she or he has a judgment call to make. In our hypothetical graduation, assume that there is no prior case involving a silent
protest at a college ceremony. The judge would need to look to a related case
for guidance—in this case, perhaps a Supreme Court ruling that a high school
student may be barred from delivering a graduation speech, because he previously had delivered a speech to the student body that was replete with sexual
innuendoes.[50] Based on that ruling, assume that the judge concludes that
there is no constitutional right to disrupt a college graduation ceremony.

   *The Trial Court's Ruling Is Appealed.*   The decision of the trial court
can be appealed on the grounds that the judge did not apply the Constitution

---

50. *Bethel School District v. Fraser,* 478 U.S. 675 (1986).

correctly. Thus, the defendants may turn to an **appellate court** and argue that the trial court's decision should be overturned.

Appeals courts exist for both the state and federal court system. If the trial were held in federal court, any appeal would be heard by a federal court of appeals. Each state also has its own appeals courts, as well as a court of last resort, usually called the state supreme court. These courts would be the initial forum for an appeal of the state trial court's decision.

In our hypothetical example, the students would take their case to a state appeals court and claim that the trial judge should have found their protest to be protected by the U.S. Constitution. However, suppose the appeals court and state supreme court both agreed that the trial judge had correctly applied the First Amendment by finding no constitutional right to protest at a college graduation. The students would have one remaining opportunity to have their right to protest vindicated.

**The Case Is Appealed to the Supreme Court.** The U.S. Supreme Court has the final authority to resolve questions of constitutional law. If one side disagrees with the ruling of the state supreme court, and the case raises a substantial federal question (such as a possible denial of rights guaranteed by the U.S. Constitution), that party may petition the Supreme Court for a **writ of certiorari.** A party whose claim has been denied by a U.S. court of appeals may do the same. The Supreme Court grants certiorari only "when there are special and important reasons therefore."[51] If the writ is granted, the justices will read the written briefs by both sides, do their own research on the legal issues involved (and/or consult with their clerks about their research), conduct an oral argument between the parties' attorneys, engage in formal and informal deliberations, and write opinions that explain their decisions.

The Supreme Court will consider a limited number of freedom of speech cases in such detail in any given year. The Court decides most cases on its docket without writing an opinion. Typically, the Court writes less than two hundred full opinions per year on all subjects, from accomplice liability to zoning, in addition to freedom of speech. If the Court does not vote to hear a case, the decision of the appellate court will stand.

Suppose that the Supreme Court granted certiorari. The decision of the Court will establish a precedent for protests of this nature, in the context of a university graduation ceremony. The Court could conclude that since a high school may restrict freedom of speech in order to preserve decorum at its graduation, a college has the right to do the same. More likely, the Supreme Court would reason differently, perhaps focusing on a case that held that a *silent* protest in a library is protected by the First Amendment.[52] Because the

---

51. Henry J. Abraham, *The Judicial Process*, p. 185 (Oxford Univ. Press, 4th ed 1980).
52. *Brown v. Louisiana*, 383 U.S. 131 (1966).

student demonstrators made no noise, and did not cause a disturbance, assume that the Supreme Court found that the students' protest was protected by the First Amendment.

Our demonstrators would be delighted, as their freedom of speech has been vindicated. However, it is important to understand that the Court would have resolved only a narrow freedom of speech issue. What if students engaged in a noisier protest the next year, or used an obscene gesture to convey their message? Because those facts are different from the facts in our earlier hypothetical case, the noisy or obscene protesters could not count on being protected by the precedent set in the initial graduation protest case.

When the Supreme Court formulates its opinion in a free speech controversy, the justices do not simply follow their intuition and vote for one side or the other. There are decision rules that they rely on in an effort to decide whether the government has offered a sufficient reason to impose limitations on speech. A set of such doctrines has emerged from Supreme Court opinions in the twentieth century. Some doctrines have been supported by a majority of the Court over a period of fifty years or more. Others have only been adhered to by a minority, or have had a short life span as the prevailing view. The following section will introduce you to the most significant doctrines. When you read twentieth-century Supreme Court decisions (beginning in chapter 4), you will see most of these doctrines in operation.

### THE MODERN ERA: EMERGING DOCTRINES

### The Absolutist Position

**Absolutism** refers to the viewpoint that all speech is protected by the First Amendment. The First Amendment guarantees that Congress shall pass *no law* abridging freedom of speech; it does not allow for any exceptions.

This position was often put forward by justices William O. Douglas and Hugo Black. In their opinion, when the founders debated the wording of the Bill of Rights, they considered the costs and benefits of protecting all speech and made a purposeful choice not to create any exceptions.

Under an absolutist approach to free speech cases, the duty of the Court is to interpret the meaning of "abridge" and "freedom of speech," and then decide whether the government restriction in question does abridge that freedom. If the answer is yes, the restriction should be held unconstitutional, regardless of the government's justification.

The difficulty with the absolutist position is that an overwhelming majority of jurists (and citizens) see the need for some limitations on speech. The most famous example of this philosophy is the oft-quoted statement that one cannot falsely shout "Fire!" in a crowded theater, thereby causing a panic. Few would defend the right of a witness in a judicial proceeding to perjure himself or herself, or of a person to offer a "hired gun" $100,000 to kill an enemy. Because the absolutist position on freedom of speech is so difficult to defend, the other doctrines we will consider all assume that speech can be regulated to some extent, but differ in the criteria they use to determine when regulation is appropriate.

### A Hierarchy of Classes of Speech

Historically, different categories of speech have been afforded divergent levels of protection by the Supreme Court. The Court has been more willing to protect speech deemed valuable to society and increasingly less willing to protect expression as its perceived benefit to society decreases.

*High Value Speech.*    Political speech, discussing issues deemed vital to self-government, has usually been considered worthy of the highest level of First Amendment protection. Many Supreme Court justices would not accept Professor Meiklejohn's call for absolute protection of speech concerning government policy,[53] but the Court usually has required a strong showing of need before a regulation on political speech will be sustained. Academic freedom (in *higher* education) also has been called a special concern of the First Amendment.[54] When freedom of speech is protected in the university environment, the truth-seeking function of the First Amendment is served because faculty and students can put forward any opinion without fear of retribution.

The fact that political speech (and perhaps academic freedom) often has been placed at the top of the hierarchy does not ensure that such speech will be protected. In chapter 4, you will read about the effect of the Communist scare of the 1950s on freedom of speech. Although the desirability of communism as an alternative to capitalism is a textbook example of a political issue, advocacy of communism was not allowed an equal footing in the marketplace of ideas, and the university campus was a major venue of repression.

*Intermediate Value Speech.*    A second tier of speech categories has been held to merit fewer protections than political speech. The government cannot restrict speech that fits the intermediate value category at will. However, the burden the government must overcome to defend a regulation on this expression is less stringent than in the case of high value speech.

One example of such speech is advertising, which is not protected when it is false but is entitled to First Amendment protection when true.[55] Regulations on "indecent" expression, such as nude dancing, require a greater

---

53. See chapter 1, p. 7.
54. See chapter 7.
55. See *Virginia State Board of Pharmacy v. Virginia Citizens Consumer Council,* 425 U.S. 748, 770–73 (1976).

justification[56] than restrictions on expression found to be obscene.[57] The right to freedom of expression on inherently scarce channels of communication, such as radio and television airwaves,[58] receives less protection than the right to give a speech or print a book.

*Low Value Speech.*   Other categories of speech have been held to be subject to regulation, with minimal judicial scrutiny of the justification for the restriction. These classes of speech, often called "categorical exceptions" to the First Amendment, are considered to be

> [N]o essential part of any exposition of ideas, and . . . of such slight social value as a step to the truth that the benefit that may be derived from them is clearly outweighed by the social interest in order and morality.[59]

Three categories of speech that have been consistently identified as worthless are **defamation, obscenity,** and **fighting words.** In the 1990s, some social critics have argued that racist and sexist **hate speech** should be added to the worthless speech list. (Each of these categories will be discussed in a later chapter.)

The premise behind the categorical exceptions doctrine is that certain categories of speech need not be protected because they do not help society to discover the truth on the issues confronting it. For example, a speaker need not use the "f-word" to criticize the president because there are more polite expressions that would effectively convey opposition to the president's policies.

The categorical exceptions doctrine assumes that the only purpose of the First Amendment is to facilitate the discovery of the truth. This doctrine places no value on the individual autonomy that can be gained when communicators may choose which words best convey their feelings.

### Tests That Evaluate Government Justifications for Speech Restriction

Undeniably, freedom of expression may entail costs to society. Speech may inspire violence, offend other persons, or ruin an innocent person's career. The Supreme Court has used several tests to decide when the government has established a sufficient need to restrict speech. Different tests have been favored (and disfavored) during this century, depending on the judicial philosophies of the members of the Court. The test used by the Court also has

---

56. *Barnes v. Glen Theatre* 115 L. Ed. 2d 504 (1991).
57. See *Miller v. California* 413 U.S. 15 (1973) discussed in chapter 9, for the current Supreme Court definition of obscenity.
58. See *Red Lion Broadcasting Co. v. FCC,* 395 U.S. 367 (1969).
59. *Chaplinsky v. New Hampshire,* 315 U.S. 568, 572 (1942).

varied, depending on where the speech at issue fits in the hierarchy of expression we previously described. You will see examples of these tests in operation beginning in chapter 4, when we move on to free speech jurisprudence in the twentieth century.

*Incitement to Illegal Conduct Tests.* One accepted basis for regulating speech is proof that the speech in question may cause illegal action. When the risk of illegal conduct is the justification for restricting speech, the Supreme Court has not compared the harm to society that the speech could cause with the benefits of allowing such expression. Instead, the Court has asked whether the *probability* is high enough that some kind of illegal conduct will result.

How high must the probability of illegal conduct be to justify a limitation on speech? Originally, the Court followed the bad tendency test.[60] Under this rule, if the speech was intended to bring about an illegal result (such as avoiding the military draft), it could be punished if that were the result. As you will read in chapter 4, over time the Court has required the government to make a much higher showing that illegal conduct will result before speech can be penalized.

*Balancing Tests.* The Court has decided many free speech issues by balancing freedom of speech against the government's justification for constraining speech. The weight given to freedom of speech in this cost-benefit analysis varies from test to test.

Often, restrictions on speech need to be **narrowly tailored** to further a significant or compelling **government interest.** This test requires that the state provide a good reason for limitations on speech. Furthermore, the restrictions must be no broader than necessary to further the government's interest. For example, suppose the government justified a ban on all abortion protests because sometimes noisy protesters disrupted the work at health care facilities. The Court would likely find that the government restriction was not narrowly tailored because not all abortion protests take place near clinics, and some protests (e.g., silent vigils) make no noise.

The **preferred position** theory was introduced by Justice (later Chief Justice) Harlan Stone in 1938. Although the Court of that era rubber-stamped many of the economic regulations of the New Deal, Stone argued for a different calculus when individual rights were at stake. He wrote, "[T]here may be a narrower scope for operation of the *presumption* of constitutionality when legislation appears on its face to be within a specific presumption of the Constitution, such as those of the first ten Amendments" (emphasis added).[61] This

---

60. See chapter 4.
61. *United States v. Carolene Products,* 304 U.S. 144 (1938).

doctrine shifted the presumption toward constitutional rights and effectively placed the burden of proof on the government to justify its restrictions.

The government has a particularly high burden of proof when it attempts to control speech through a prior restraint. As we pointed out earlier in this chapter, prior restraints limit communication *before* the expression can ever reach the marketplace of ideas. This form of censorship is argued to be the most severe restriction on communication. In chapters 2 and 3, you will learn how British monarchs used prior restraint to control expression. This practice has been unpopular in the United States since the American Revolution. This sentiment is reflected in the Supreme Court's oft-cited decision that "any system of prior restraints of expression comes to this Court bearing a heavy presumption against its constitutional validity."[62]

An **ad hoc balancing** approach simply compares the costs and benefits of restrictions on speech on a case-by-case basis, without a presumption in favor of freedom of speech. Justice Felix Frankfurter was a strong proponent of such a balancing test,[63] and in *American Communications Associations v. Douds*,[64] Justice Fred Vinson maintained that the probable effects of a statute on freedom of speech needed to be balanced against the evil that Congress sought to regulate. *Douds* involved a federal law requiring that labor union officers swear that they were not Communists. Justice Vinson balanced the right to hold or express Communist beliefs against the perceived threat to interstate commerce (assuming a Communist union official might call for a political work strike) and held the regulation valid.[65]

The Supreme Court may also choose to give **deference** to a legislative judgment that a regulation on expression is necessary. This test is likely to be employed when low value speech, such as obscenity or fighting words, is at stake. Rather than carefully considering the government's restriction on speech, the Court will merely ask if there is a rational basis for the restriction. For example, if an obscenity statute were being challenged on First Amendment grounds, the Court could assume that obscenity restrictions are needed to protect the public morals without requiring proof that the regulations would have this effect.

### Other Doctrinal Tools—Vagueness and Overbreadth

The doctrines of **vagueness** and **overbreadth** have often been used by the Supreme Court to protect freedom of expression during the past three decades. These doctrines do not focus on the legitimacy of the government's

---

62. See, e.g., *New York Times Co. v. United States*, 403 U.S. 713 (1971).
63. *Kovacs v. Cooper*, 336 U.S. 77 (1949) (Frankfurter, J., concurring).
64. 339 U.S. 382 (1949).
65. Id. at 399.

*reason* for restricting speech. Instead, they evaluate the *text* of the government's restriction to ensure that the law does not constrain expression protected by the First Amendment.

A law may be void for vagueness if it contains imprecise wording, such that people of reasonable intelligence may differ at its construction and meaning.[66] For example, a law forbidding "obscene art depicting immoral sex" without defining those terms probably would be found unconstitutionally vague, even though obscenity is a category of low value speech that can be regulated. What is art? Is it limited to works such as painting and sculpture, or does it include photographs or films? Is sex "depicted" if it is implied that the actors are doing the act behind closed doors? If they are covered by a sheet? When is sex immoral? These are questions of value that will differ from person to person. Reasonable people would need to guess at the meaning of this hypothetical law.

The **chilling effect** is a by-product of vague restrictions on speech that is mitigated by the void for vagueness doctrine. A chilling effect means that because an individual finds a law vague, he or she may forgo any expression that might break the law, rather than risk a faulty interpretation of the rule. When this occurs, the speaker's expression has been chilled[67] and his or her rights under the First Amendment have been violated.

A restriction is overbroad if, in addition to regulating conduct or expression not protected by the First Amendment, it regulates a substantial amount of constitutionally protected expression.[68] This type of rule can be analogized to a large fishing net that, when cast into the sea, captures not only its legal quota of salmon, but also an illegal catch of endangered dolphins.

An example of an overbroad law would be one that held that "any discussion of killing the president of the United States is illegal." Certain speech that would fit that definition could be constitutionally regulated. For example, a conspiracy to assassinate the president could be outlawed, as well as a direct threat made by a person standing five feet away holding a machine gun. However, the law would also forbid characters in a book or a movie from discussing an assassination. As the law is written, a conversation about who really killed John F. Kennedy also would be prohibited. Because the law prohibits speech that is almost certainly protected by the First Amendment, as well as that which is not, it may well be overbroad.

### SUMMARY

In this chapter we have developed a definition of freedom of speech as the ability to communicate a message by many diverse means, freed from

---

66. See, e.g., *Cromp v. Board of Public Instruction*, 386 U.S. 278 (1961).
67. See, e.g., *Broadrick v. Oklahoma*, 413 U.S. 601 (1973).
68. See, e.g., *Village of Hoffman Estates v. Flipside, Hoffman Estates, Inc.*, 455 U.S. 489 (1982).

unreasonable constraints. At the same time, although some would like this to be an absolute freedom, it has never been so allowed. Much of the debate over free speech, therefore, has turned on the "reasonableness" of the constraint.

In evaluating the extent of free expression (or conversely, the nature of any constraint upon free expression), we also reviewed four different criteria that could in summary be posed as questions. First, is there freedom to communicate without fear of government sanction or censorship? Second, are we free from compulsory speech? Third, do we have access to *effective* channels of communication? Fourth, are we free from government domination of the free speech environment? Free expression is best understood and contextualized in your exploration of these criteria.

To this end, we also discussed the major rationales used to support freedom of expression: (1) it is vital to our system of self-government; (2) it facilitates the discovery of truth; (3) it promotes individual autonomy; and (4) any controls over "harmful" speech would inevitably constrain worthwhile speech. These we contrasted with the primary justifications for constraining speech, including the notions that communitarian needs may take precedence over individual rights, that individual speech rights should not be used to constrain other constitutional rights, and that formal speech rights are no guarantee of effective freedom to speak.

To help us determine how we might resolve the conflict among these rationales, we also introduced a dominant metaphor in the debate over free expression: the marketplace of ideas. The appeal of this metaphor rests in its ability to conceptualize our communications as if in a free marketplace or bazaar, where messages are traded and sold freely, where buyers and sellers are free to move about with no constraints other than those that the marketplace itself may impose for the effective functioning of its commerce. By necessity, this suggests that freedom of speech in such a marketplace may protect speech we despise. It also suggests that that the remedy for "bad" speech is more speech.

In the final section of chapter 1, we reviewed our judicial system, looking to see how it might resolve issues in freedom of expression and how our metaphor might be applied. We observed the process by which objectionable speech might be regulated and the regulation in turn challenged as unconstitutional. We followed this process through to the Supreme Court, and also observed the doctrinal approaches and tools of the Court for this issue since the early part of this century. As noted before, some have tried to see this from an absolutist perspective; others have chosen to view speech protection as variable, depending on where a type of speech fits in a hierarchy of classes of speech. There are also a diversity of approaches for factoring in the government's justification for suppressing speech, some of which give great weight to the government's reasons and others that presume speech should be protected from government incursion.

As you move into the next two chapters, you will find it useful to contrast the aforementioned criteria—the rationales (both for and against free speech) and the metaphor of the marketplace of ideas—with earlier development of free speech concepts, both in this country and other parts of the world across history. As you read chapter 1 and move into chapters 2 and 3, think about which rationales (for or against) you support, and decide whether you agree that speech should take place in a free marketplace of ideas.

# CHAPTER 2      Objectives

**After reading chapter 2,**
**you should understand**
**the following:**

◆ *The ways in which many of the world's cultures have experienced traditions that both* **support** *and* **inhibit** *freedom of speech.*

◆ *The reasons why freedom of speech has been* **slow** *to develop throughout the history of the world.*

◆ *The* **content** *of speech that typically has been repressed.*

◆ *The* **practices** *that have been used to control speech.*

◆ *The fact that freedom of speech rights typically* **wax** *and* **wane** *over time in any given culture.*

◆ *The reality that free speech practices often* **exclude** *significant segments of the population, particularly women.*

◆ *The* **constraints** *on freedom of expression in England, many of which would be replicated in the American colonies.*

# 2  Freedom of Speech: A Historical Perspective

ALTHOUGH POPULAR SENTIMENT maintains that freedom of speech is a product of Western culture,[1] many different societies have contributed to the history of freedom of speech. It is mistaken to assume that free expression was born in Greece, refined in England, and perfected in the United States. For example, there is evidence to support the argument that the Chinese experience rivaled that of the Greeks, and that the Dutch enjoyed far more freedom in the seventeenth century than did the British. Beginning in chapter 4, you will read about many instances in which freedom of speech has been limited in twentieth-century America.

In this chapter, we survey the freedom of speech experiences of a variety of cultures, during the many centuries that predate the founding of the United States. In so doing, we will demonstrate that the popular sentiment referenced above is in fact a misconception of free speech history.

Freedom of speech is a relatively recent concept. Current research indicates that our species has been capable of communication for at least two million years, and has used symbols to communicate for approximately one hundred thousand years.[2] However, the issue of *freedom* to speak did not become salient to humanity until most of those hundred thousand years had passed.

Certain conditions must be met before freedom of speech is realized. Human beings first need to conceive of themselves as individuals, whose needs or ideas may differ from group norms or from the will of their leaders. Humans also need to believe that it is appropriate to communicate their disagreements with respect to the traditions of society or the decisions of their leaders. Finally, and paradoxically,

---

1. See, e.g., R. W. Livingstone, *The Legacy of Greece*, pp. 251–52 (Clarendon, 1921). "The Greeks were the most remarkable people who have yet existed. . . . They were the beginners of nearly everything, Christianity excepted, of which the modern world makes its boast . . . "; and Mary Ann Glendon, *Rights Talk*, p. 16 (Free Press, 1991). "Many of us [Americans] harbor, too, a patriotic conviction that, where freedom is concerned, the U.S. was there first with the best and the most."
2. Marcel Danesi, *Vico, Metaphor, and the Origin of Language*, pp. 26–28 (Indiana Univ. Press, 1993).

individuals must agree as a societal group to establish laws and institutions that preserve their freedom, even in the face of opposition from the ruling hierarchy, who ordinarily would prefer to limit this freedom.

This chapter provides an overview of the history of free speech in many different cultures, and shows that conditions favorable to free expression have been very slow to develop. In the world's earliest societies, people were not likely to challenge their leaders. Later centuries produced more examples of cultures with some free speech practices. However, even in these societies, people did not devise any means to maintain a free speech environment under a succession of leadership changes.

As we begin this study, it is important to note that the historical record is not a list of undeniable facts. Interpretation of historical evidence is subjective and becomes increasingly so when we analyze the tiny percentage of ancient artifacts that have survived. When written evidence from antiquity is found, we cannot be certain of the writer's objectivity or expertise in assessing the facts. Preliterate societies left no written records, and we must draw inferences about freedom of speech from whatever artifacts have been recovered.

In this chapter, we put forward our analysis of the historical record on freedom of speech, recognizing that differing interpretations of the evidence are possible and that future discoveries will add to our understanding of history. This chapter is extensively footnoted so that you can explore the basis for our conclusions in more detail.

## FREEDOM OF SPEECH IN THE WORLD'S FIRST SOCIETIES

### Freedom of Speech before Written History

Imagine that you and your family are part of a nomadic band of hunters fifteen thousand years ago. The leader of your hunting pack indicates that you will move to the plains, where your group always hunts in the spring. You notice a narrow passage through the mountains to the east, where a mammoth would have difficulty running from hunters. Would you challenge the orders of your leader, or would you accept the commands as part of the natural state of affairs? If you tried to speak out, and the leader told you not to talk, would you imagine that you had a right to speak? If you lived in the days before written history, the answer to these questions could be no.

In the time before written history, it is doubtful that humans imagined themselves as individuals, with their own unique personalities. As language grew more sophisticated, one of its first uses was to transmit cultural expectations for behavior, which were beginning to replace animal-like instincts as causes of behavior.[3] A member of the family or tribe had to exercise leadership, first to ensure the coordinated effort necessary to hunt the animals necessary for subsistence and later to organize humanity's first villages. People in

---

3. Grahame Clark, *Aspects of Prehistory*, p. 111 (Univ. of California Press, 1970).

these cultures ordinarily accepted the directions they were given; this can be evidenced by the fact that jails and police forces are not found in primitive societies.[4] According to one historian, "individual independence of action must still have been a virtually unknown concept"[5] to early villagers.

Ironically, although the citizens of the world's first societies may not have been cognizant of any need for freedom of speech, the structure of their communities might have facilitated conditions favorable to freedom of speech. Early preliterate societies seem to have been more egalitarian than their successors, without the hierarchy of power that would characterize later states, such as the pharaohs' Egypt. This earlier environment would be conducive to freedom of expression.[6] We observe similar circumstances in the primitive villages of modern times, where leaders do not ordinarily rule by brute, totalitarian force.[7] Therefore, abuses of power, such as those that compelled Nelson Mandela and Bishop Desmond Tutu to speak out against South African apartheid, might have been less likely to necessitate any demand for freedom in early societies.

About five thousand years ago, the world's earliest civilizations began to emerge in Egypt and Mesopotamia. The historical record of these societies reveals belief systems that ensured slow progress for free speech.

### Freedom of Speech in Ancient Egypt

The concept of the sacred monarchy inhibited the growth of freedom in ancient civilizations. Many societies believed that their rulers were descendants of their god(s).[8] This theory was taken to its furthest extreme in Egypt, wherein the pharaoh *was* a god—not a representative of the gods, but "Horus the Hawk God, the personification of heaven, who had descended to Earth from on high."[9] The pharaoh could bring on rain, make the sun shine, and control the harvest.[10]

As long as the pharaoh was a god, freedom of speech was not a salient concept for Egyptians. It is easy to speak critically of leaders in modern society, where politicians are sometimes assigned a subhuman status;[11] understandably such dissention is less palatable when the ruler is a deity who makes all earthly laws and divines the forces of nature. The Egyptians were in such awe of the pharaoh that they dared not look at him when he appeared in public.[12] Dissent would be further inhibited by a feeling that laws were inevitable when given by gods rather than written by mere mortals.

---

4. Herbert J. Muller, *Freedom in the Ancient World*, p. 18 (Harper, 1961).
5. Chester G. Starr, *A History of the Ancient World*, p. 19 (Oxford Univ. Press, 4th ed 1991).
6. Murray Bookchin, *The Ecology of Freedom*, p. 5 (Cheshire, 1982).
7. Id.
8. William J. Perry, *The Children of the Sun*, p. 140 (Methuen, republished 1968).
9. Mario Attilo Levi, *Political Power in the Ancient World*, p. 1 (Weidenfeld & Nicholson, 1965).
10. Perry, p. 131.
11. Jane Blankenship, "Naming and Name Calling as Acts of Definition," in *Perspectives on Argumentation*, pp. 168–70 (Waveland, 1990).
12. Perry, p. 131.

Because of this perspective, and the absolute power of the pharaoh, it is not surprising that there are only a few examples of free speech in Egypt. One instance of dissent came when the prophet Ipuwer addressed the king (about 2000 B.C.E.). Part of a written record of this oration has survived,[13] and it shows that Ipuwer lamented some of the same conditions that plague modern society—defiance of the law, inadequate revenue in the treasury, and a lack of public safety. The prophet went on to describe the ideal king, and asked, "Where is he today? Doth he sleep perchance? Behold his might is not seen."[14] Equal speech rights for all Egyptians were endorsed in another document, the *Maxims of Ptahhotep*. Ptahhotep was the grand vizier (chief administrative assistant) for King Userkaf, and the maxims were advice for the vizier's son, who would be succeeding him soon. Ptahhotep advised: "Take counsel with the unlearned as with the learned. . . . Worthy speech is more hidden than greenstone, being found even among the slave women at the millstone."[15] In the *Tale of the Eloquent Peasant*, anonymously written about four thousand years ago, a minor government official seizes a peasant's donkeys. The peasant appeals to the grand steward, who is so impressed with the peasant's oratorical skills that he continues to postpone his decision on the appeal, so that he can hear the peasant give more speeches. The king finally orders the grand steward to decide the peasant's case after the steward hears nine addresses.[16] This popular story, which continued to be quoted in Egypt centuries later, provides evidence that advocacy of social justice was sometimes permitted.[17]

Without an earthly check on the pharaoh, freedom would be only intermittent in Egypt. The major constraint on totalitarianism was the Egyptian concept of *ma'at*, or justice. According to Egyptian theology, upon their death, the god-rulers had to account for their actions, and would face the flames of the underworld if they had not acted honestly and justly.[18] Unfortunately, *ma'at* was not always a sufficient guarantor of freedom. When Amhose I expelled the Hyksos from Egypt in the middle of the sixteenth century B.C.E., he built Egypt into a powerful military machine, with the best horses and chariots, as well as fearsome archers. The impact of such a powerful leader on freedom was described by archaeologist James Henry Breasted:

> With such a force at his back, he ruled in absolute power; there was none
> to offer a breath of opposition; there was not a whisper of that modern
> monitor of kings, public opinion.[19]

13. The oration was recorded some four thousand years ago, on paper made from papyrus, a reed that grows near the Nile.
14. James Henry Breasted, *The Dawn of Conscience*, p. 199 (Scribner's, 1933).
15. Id., p. 130.
16. We do not know the grand steward's decision because the ending of the tale has yet to be found.
17. Breasted, p. 193.
18. Levi, pp. 2–3.
19. Breasted, *A History of Egypt from the Earliest Times to the Persian Conquest*, p. 235 (Scribner's, 1929).

## Freedom of Speech in Sumeria

Sumeria, located between the Tigris and Euphrates rivers in what is now Iraq, was another of the earliest recorded civilizations. In 2500 B.C.E., Sumeria, like Egypt, had a sacred monarchy. The Sumerians believed that the air-god Enlil was king of all the lands, and that Enlil crowned the earthly king.[20] Therefore, there would be no debate about public affairs. The royal annals of one ruler stated that "the king's word is right; his utterance, like that of a god, cannot be changed."[21]

Although the prospects for individual rights might seem bleak in such circumstances, the Sumerians did make one major contribution to freedom's history. The earliest recorded use of the word *freedom* was found on a clay cone excavated at the site of the Sumerian city-state of Lagash. The inscription on the cone was written in the twenty-fourth century B.C.E., to commemorate the dedication of a new canal. The symbols on the cone pictured in Figure 2.1

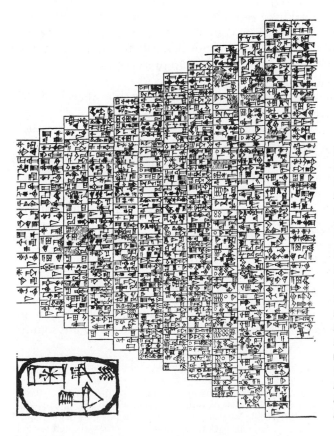

*Figure 2.1 The earliest known recorded use of the word freedom was inscribed on a clay cone in ancient Sumeria during the twenty-fourth century B.C.E. The text on the cone has been translated to read that King Uru'inimgina established the freedom of the citizens of Lagash.* (Copy of text inscribed on clay cone excavated by French at Tello, site of ancient Lagash. From History Begins at Sumer: Thirty-Nine Firsts in Man's Recorded History, The Third Revised Edition by Samuel Noah Kramer; (c) 1981 by the University of Pennsylvania Press. All rights reserved. Reprinted by permission.)

20. Samuel N. Kramer, *The Sumerians,* pp. 119–21 (Univ. of Chicago Press, 1963).
21. Muller, p. 50.

described the achievements of King Uru'inimgina, who was the ruler of Lagash at that time. According to this ancient record, Uru'inimgina "established
the freedom" of the citizens.[22]

The freedom established was not free speech but primarily freedom from
economic abuses. The text asserts that under some previous regimes there
were excessive charges for services (he who brought the dead man to the
cemetery for burial received 420 loaves of bread and seven pitchers of beer),
starving artisans, and an ever-present tax collector. It is then revealed that *the
gods* first gave the kingship to Uru'inimgina, and then set up divine "decrees of
former days," suggesting that certain freedoms probably existed during earlier
regimes. These decrees included a reduction in fees charged to the citizens, a
ban on injustices against orphans and widows, and a development that would
please any modern tax protester—"from the borders of Ningirsu [a god of La-
gash] to the sea, there was no tax collector."[23]

The information on the ancient cone provides a lesson about freedom
that is consistent in early civilizations. Uru'inimgina believed that the freedoms he established were willed by the great god Enlil. However, not all rulers
received the same message from Enlil, as the cone's chronicle of abuses by the
preceding dynasty reveals. Consequently, without an independent institution
(such as a judiciary) that had the power and duty to preserve the rights of the
people, freedom depended on the good will of a ruler.

Furthermore, the document provides no evidence that speech rights
were part of the freedoms established. Uru'inimgina's code did not grant the
freedom to disagree with his reforms or to speak one's mind on any other
topic.[24] Who would dare voice an objection to Uru'inimgina's interpretation of
the will of Enlil? The Sumerians gained no right to debate the issues of the
day and make collective decisions about the appropriate policies for their city-
state. Subsequent literature from this region indicates that there was little
protest. Babylonian writings revealed little controversy, and intellectual life
was "directed towards expression of orthodox opinions."[25] Not until nearly
2000 years after King Uru'inimgina's reign would the concept of freedom expand to include freedom of speech.

## FIRST SIGNS OF FREE SPEECH PROTECTION

During the first millennium B.C.E., several different peoples began to
make progress toward freedom of speech. In these societies, there are signifi-

22. Kramer, *History Begins at Sumer*, p. 45 (Univ. of Pennsylvania Press, 1981).
23. Kramer, *The Sumerians*, p. 318.
24. Political freedoms are not emphasized in later Mesopotamian law codes either. Many of Hammurabi's rules governed economic disputes or set criminal punishments; Starr, pp. 47–48.
Kramer, *The Sumerians*, pp. 336–39. Thirty-eight laws are included in the portions of the Lipit-
Ishtar code that have been found. Most of these also relate to economic topics, although several
do pertain to the rights of slaves, slave owners, and family members.
25. Arnaldo Momigliano, "Freedom of Speech in Antiquity," in *Dictionary of the History of Ideas*,
p. 253 (Philip Weiner, ed., Scribner's, 1973).

cant examples of people who were willing to speak out against their leaders or challenge traditional beliefs. These states did not provide ideal guarantees of freedom of speech, and at times, criticism of the wrong person could cost speakers their lives. Nevertheless, the freedom of speech evidenced in Israel, Athens, Rome, and China was exceptional at that time, and it is not matched by all modern nations.

### The Hebrews: No Sacred Monarchy in Control

The Hebrews made an important contribution to the history of free speech, because their theology did not allow for a sacred monarchy. Yahweh (God) entered into a covenant with all of the Hebrew people, rather than anointing a ruler. Initially, there were no kings or legislators—the law was believed to have come from God, transmitted through Moses.[26]

Even when the people of Israel came to be ruled by kings, the prophets (believed to be messengers of Yahweh) often reminded officials that Yahweh was the true ruler, and they criticized the leaders for straying from God's will.[27] Prophets such as Amos, Hosea, and Micah made fervent demands for social justice.[28] The kings did not often punish the prophets, even if their preaching was threatening to the government.[29] The texts of more historical books of the Bible, as well as recovered letters from the seventh and sixth centuries B.C.E., provide evidence that the Hebrew people were also informal and outspoken when dealing with their leaders.[30]

Although the absence of a sacred monarchy facilitated open criticism of Hebrew rulers, the Hebrews' theology did not foster a comprehensive system of free expression. Even under the most liberal of kings, freedom was limited by the insistence that Judaism was the only true religion. Yahweh was a jealous god, who would not permit worship of other gods. There was no concept of freedom of conscience in ancient Israel.[31] More authoritarian rulers chilled expression on a wider variety of topics. For example, during the despotic reign of Ahab, an overwhelming majority of prophets had followed a safe route by predicting Ahab's success in battle. Only one, Micaiah, was courageous enough to predict that Ahab would lose. His dissenting opinion turned out to be correct, as the king died at the hands of the Syrians.[32]

Another king, Jehoiakim, provided an ancient example of book burning. The prophet Jeremiah had predicted that the kingdom of Judah would be destroyed, so Jehoiakim demanded the scroll on which the prophecy had been

26. Leo Pfeffer, *Church, State, and Freedom*, p. 6 (Beacon Press, 1967).
27. Donald W. Treadgold, *Freedom, a History*, p. 30 (New York Univ. Press, 1990). The word *Yahweh* is mentioned 241 times in the Old Testament, and 221 of these references are made by prophets. See also Momigliano, p. 225.
28. Treadgold, p. 33.
29. Pfeffer, p. 8.
30. Momigliano, p. 255.
31. Muller, pp. 131–32.
32. Treadgold, pp. 29–30.

written. As this forecast was read to the king, he cut off one section of the scroll at a time, and threw each into the fire. Jeremiah had to go into hiding to escape the king's wrath.[33]

### Ancient Athens: Golden Age for Freedom of Speech?

There are two sides to the historical development of free speech in the Greek city-state of Athens. Although freedom of speech was explicitly recognized, and Athenian *citizens* had unprecedented opportunities to speak freely against their government, this right was not extended to women, slaves, or men who were not citizens. There were also laws and customs that constrained citizens' speech.

***Athenian Contributions to Freedom of Speech.*** The barriers that had inhibited free speech throughout society in earlier civilizations were less significant in the city-state of Athens, particularly during Pericles' rule in the fifth century B.C.E. Greek citizens did not believe the gods to be the source of their laws; instead, they prided themselves on living under laws of their own making. They believed that there was a fundamental difference between themselves and "barbarians," whom they thought were willing to obey authority without reason.[34]

Athenians' free speech ideology was reflected in their system of government. Their assembly was open to every citizen, each of whom had a vote on proposals.[35] The Greek word *isegoria* was used to refer to the right of citizens to speak out in the assembly, and debates were begun by the herald's words, "What man has good advice to give the polis and wishes to make it known?"[36]

Freedom of speech for Athenian citizens extended beyond debates in the assembly. Greek comedy was performed before large audiences[37] at state-sponsored festivals. The climate of attitudes there "permitted, and even encouraged, the liberty of comedy to indulge in forms of personal ridicule."[38] The topics of Greek plays had been taboo in earlier societies, and some of the plays focused on subjects that are still controversial in the twentieth century. Greek gods were among the characters brought on stage, and sometimes they were portrayed as stupid or cowardly.[39] In Aristophanes' *The Wasps*, the Athenian legal system was taken to task for creating excessive litigation. *Lysistrata* told of a woman who formed a creative plan to end the Peloponnesian

33. David Daube, *Civil Disobedience in Antiquity*, pp. 69–70 (Edinburgh Univ. Press, 1972).
34. Muller, p. 145.
35. M. I. Finley, *Politics in the Ancient World*, p. 71 (Cambridge Univ. Press, 1983). Up to 6,000 citizens (out of a citizen population of 35,000 to 40,000) attended assemblies in the fifth century B.C.E. Id., pp. 59, 73.
36. Id., p. 139.
37. Id., p. 125. More than ten thousand were present when Sophocles' play *Antigone* was performed about 442 B.C.E.
38. Stephen Halliwell, *Comic Satire and Freedom of Speech in Classical Athens*, 111 Journal of Hellenic Studies 48, 69 (1991).
39. Douglas M. MacDowell, *The Law in Classical Athens*, p. 200 (Cornell Univ. Press, 1978).

War—the women of Greece would cease all sexual relations with the men until the fighting stopped. Euripides' *The Trojan Women* criticized the death and suffering inflicted when Athens attacked Melos, a neutral island.

The Athenians were both aware of the free speech concept and proud to uphold it. They regularly used the word *parrhesia* to refer to the freedom of citizens to speak openly in public and private affairs.[40] When a young Sophist named Polus demanded a right to burst into a conversation, Socrates is reported to have said, "Strange it were, my good fellow, if having come to Athens, where there is the greatest liberty of speech in all Greece, you alone should be denied here."[41]

***Athenian Constraints on Freedom of Speech.*** Although the liberty of speech in ancient Athens was significant for a society of the fifth century B.C.E., serious restraints on speech remained. One needed to be a citizen to submit a proposal to the Boule (the council that decided whether to bring proposals before the assembly), and Athenian residents who were not citizens were denied the right to vote in the assembly.[42] As you will see later in this chapter, the rights of women were actually more limited than they were in earlier sacred monarchies. Finally, slavery was practiced in Athens, and slaves did not have the rights of citizens.

The threat of ostracism, a procedure under which the people of Athens could vote to banish a citizen for ten years,[43] was another constraint on free expression. When Protagoras wrote that "concerning the gods, I am unable to know either that they exist or they do not exist,"[44] he was condemned to exile. Furthermore, copies of his book were gathered and burned.[45] Although ostracism was not frequently invoked, the threat of such proceedings had a deterrent effect on free speech. Citizens were well aware that this powerful weapon could be used on them if they were deemed public enemies by the people.[46] The ultimate ostracism for the expression of ideas was inflicted on Socrates, who had been accused of not recognizing state-sanctioned gods, introducing new divinities, and corrupting the young.[47] In a close vote, the jury found him guilty, and he was sentenced to death (see Figure 2.2).[48]

---

40. Finley, *Censorship in Classical Antiquity,* Times Literary Supplement 923 (July 29, 1977).
41. Max Radin, *Freedom of Speech in Ancient Athens,* 48 American Journal of Philology 215, 215–16 (1927).
42. MacDowell, pp. 44–45.
43. Victor Ehrenberg, *Man, State, and Deity,* p. 30 (London: Methuen, 1974).
44. MacDowell, p. 201.
45. Id.
46. Matthew R. Christ, *Ostracism, Sycophancy, and Deception of the Demos,* 42 Classical Quarterly 336, 338–39 (No. 2, 1992).
47. MacDowell, p. 201.
48. Daube, p. 73. Socrates was found guilty by a margin of only six out of 501 jurors. After the verdict, but before the penalty was fixed, Socrates made a sarcastic speech, contending that the "punishment" should be a state pension. His death sentence was then approved by a margin of 86.

*Figure 2.2  In this rendition of the* **Death of Socrates**
*by Jacques Louis David, Socrates is being given deadly
poison. The free speech traditions of Athens were not
sufficient to protect the renowned philosopher from a
sentence of death for expressing his ideas.* (Oil on Canvas by

Jacques Louis David (1748–1825). Metropolitan Museum of Art, Wolfe Fund, 1931.

Catherine Lorillard Wolfe Collection. Photographic Services, The Metropolitan Mu-

seum of Art, New York, N.Y. 10028. Reprinted by permission.)

Freedom of speech also suffered because the Athenian city-state had no
bill of rights. Consequently, restrictions on the content of speech could be established through the democratic process. One type of forbidden speech was verbal
abuse of the dead. Verbal abuse of the living was restricted *only* when it was inflicted at temples, courts, official buildings, and games;[49] thus, Athens had one
of history's earliest time, place, and manner restrictions (see chapter 10). The
reputation of the city-state could be protected from criticism when foreign officials were present at festivals.[50] Certain words were unsayable, and could not be
used to attack the character of another person unless the charge were true. The
law prevented one from saying that a man had flung away his shield in battle (a

49. Halliwell, p. 49.
50. During the Peloponnesian war, ambassadors of Athens' allies were present at the festival of
Dionysus. A comic poet had been accused of slandering the city, perhaps suggesting that its leaders were corrupt demagogues. J. E. Atkinson, *Curbing the Comedians: Cleon Versus Aristophanes and
Syracosius' Decree,* 42 Classical Quarterly, 56, 58 (1992). The politician Cleon had been instrumental in bringing the case against the poet; Halliwell, p. 65. One year later, a character in Aristophanes' play *Acharnians* said the line, "What I am going to say will be blunt, but fair comment. At
least this time Cleon will not be attacking me for speaking ill of the city in the presence of foreigners. For it is just ourselves . . . there are no foreigners here yet." Atkinson, p. 58.

Greek analogy to modern-day allegations that a politician's military service has been unacceptable), committed murder, or beaten his father or mother.[51]

The Greek colony of Thourioi implemented an alarming policy for chilling free speech. In Thourioi, any person who wanted to propose an amendment to the laws was required to speak with his head in a noose. If the speaker's proposal was unconvincing, the noose was immediately tightened, and the person was strangled.[52] Imagine how willing a United States senator might be to filibuster if such a practice were followed today.

### The Roman Republic: Free Speech Customs and Limits

Freedom of speech was not a hallmark of Roman society, as it was in ancient Athens. The Romans did not have a counterpart for *parrhesia,* the Athenian concept of free speech, and the prevailing attitude was that only persons in authority were guaranteed that right.[53] But despite the lack of legal guarantees for speech, caustic criticism of public officials was not uncommon. Some scholars have even contended that the Romans did have a tradition of free speech.[54] Such divergent views exist because the historical record of Rome is mixed, with evidence of robust verbal and written attacks that were not punished, as well as examples of speech that was repressed.

One of the sharpest differences between free expression in Greece and Rome existed in the theater. Gnaeus Naevius was a third-century B.C.E. playwright who offended the powerful Metelli family when he wrote, "by fate [i.e., not by ability], the Metelli become consuls at Rome."[55] Naevius reportedly was imprisoned and later exiled because of this insult, and possibly because he had offended other aristocratic families as well.[56] Writers and actors did not have the same social status in Rome as they did in Greece,[57] and they rarely would risk an attack on important public figures or discuss major political questions.[58] The fact that dramatic productions were paid for by the government and selected by state magistrates also served to mute criticism of the Roman leadership.[59]

Roman leaders used various tools to repress speech with which they disagreed. The laws of the Twelve Tables (c. 450 B.C.E.), a codification of Roman law, were displayed on twelve bronze or wood tablets in the Forum.[60] One

---

51. MacDowell, p. 128.
52. Kathleen Freeman, *Greek City-States,* p. 38 (W.W. Norton, republished 1963).
53. Momigliano, p. 261.
54. Tenney Frank, *Naevius and Free Speech,* 48 American Journal of Philology 105, 109 (1927); Laura Robinson, *Freedom of Speech in the Roman Republic,* p. 84 (Published PhD Dissertation, Johns Hopkins Univ., 1940).
55. Richard C. Beacham, *The Roman Theatre and Its Audience,* p. 25 (Harvard Univ. Press, 1992).
56. Id.
57. H. D. Jocelyn, *The Tragedies of Ennius,* p. 22 (Cambridge Univ. Press, 1967). During the time that Naevius wrote, script-writing and acting were considered to be lowly activities, and magistrates would sometimes use slaves to act in productions they sponsored.
58. Finley, *Politics,* p. 127. As it happened in Athens when political leaders attempted to punish dramatic expressions, Roman dramatists resorted to innuendo about public issues and officials; Robinson, pp. 28, 43.
59. Robinson, p. 5.
60. Treadgold, p. 55.

law prohibited defamation (verbal attacks on reputation) and the offense apparently was punishable by death.[61] The Twelve Tables also included a prohibition against magical incantations, and this may have been stretched to punish defamatory statements such as the ones made by the playwright Naevius.[62] Another effective tactic to silence objectionable speakers was expulsion. This penalty was used to silence teachers whose viewpoints were considered dangerous, particularly foreign philosophers and rhetoricians.[63] The Roman attitude was summed up in a speech by Cato, who said: "Let them return to their schools and practice their dialectics with Greek boys; Roman youths shall listen to the laws and the magistrates as heretofore."[64] Another alternative was book burning. In 213 B.C.E., the government burned many popular books containing oracles' predictions.[65]

The politicians of Rome enjoyed greater freedom of speech. The Roman Senate had complete freedom of speech during its deliberations.[66] Senators would attack each other, as well as state officials, "by every device of invective language, sometimes with little basis of fact."[67] Cicero, one of history's most renowned orators, often delivered virulent attacks in the Senate. He accused his opponents of murder, adultery, incest, and unnatural relations with young millionaires. In rebuttal to one criticism, Cicero referred to an opponent as a "plague, beast, funeral pyre of the state, mud, dog of Clodius, trunk of a tree, donkey, hog, piece of flesh."[68] Speech was more limited in the Roman popular assembly, the body that had the power to approve legislation. Members came to the assembly to vote, not to speak. Some discussions took place in more informal meetings before the assemblies. But even there, speech was constrained because the magistrate in charge of the meetings had the power either to conduct an open discussion or to allow only the individuals of his choice to speak.[69]

Despite a lack of free speech *guarantees,* the Roman Republic often tolerated acrimonious speech against political leaders. In the second century B.C.E., a satirist named Lucilius regularly lampooned the radicalism of Tiberius and Gaius Gracchus,[70] Roman leaders who wanted to distribute state lands to

61. See Momigliano, p. 261; and Finley, *Censorship,* p. 924. Eighteenth-century jurist Blackstone described the provision as follows: "[A]nd so a law was passed, and punishment imposed, to forbid that anyone should be described by malicious verses:—they changed their note, compelled through dread of death by cudgelling" (William Blackstone, *Commentaries on the Laws of England,* ed. William Carey Jones, Book IV, p. 151 [Bancroft-Whitney, 1916]).
62. Frank, pp. 108–109. Professor Frank disagreed with the claims of other scholars that the Twelve Tables allowed defamation to be punished by death. Id., p. 109.
63. Momigliano, p. 261.
64. Finley, *Censorship,* p. 924.
65. Daube, p. 72.
66. The Roman Senate was not democratically elected, and only elite members of society served in it. The Senate was an advisory body, rather than a lawmaking one; nevertheless, it exerted great influence on Roman policies.
67. Robinson, p. 38.
68. Id., pp. 39–40.
69. Momigliano, p. 261.
70. Robinson, p. 16.

peasants. When Julius Caesar was accused of womanizing, plundering the allies of Rome, and stealing from the capital, he attempted to use tact to win over his critics, rather than censoring them.[71] In the last decades of the Roman Republic, political invective was often passed on in verses and songs, as well as on placards known as *libelli*. The typical response to the most vicious of political claims was simply a counterpamphlet.[72]

Freedom of speech took a turn for the worse in Rome after emperors began to assume dictatorial powers near the end of the first century B.C.E. The Roman treason law, once interpreted to ban only treasonous *acts*, was extended to cover *words* spoken in disrespect of the emperor. A prosecution for treason often resulted in financial ruin or death, depending on the whim of the emperor:[73] Caligula ordered a writer to be burned alive in the amphitheater; Nero exiled several critics who had taunted and satirized him, and condemned one critic to death. When Stoic philosophers criticized the military regime and yearned for a republic, Vespasian condemned the philosopher Helvidius Priscus to death.

The emperor Domitian was particularly arbitrary. At the gladiatorial games, one man supported the Thracians, whom the emperor despised. This man was thrown to the dogs, with a sign reading "A Thracian supporter who spoke impiously" attached to his back.[74] When the historian Hermogenes Tarsus made slighting references to Domitian's regime, the emperor executed Tarsus and ordered that his secretaries be crucified as well.[75] Arbitrary repression had come to replace the relative freedom of speech that the citizens had enjoyed when Rome was a republic.

## Ancient China: Expression of Diverse Philosophies

The excesses of Chairman Mao Zedong's Cultural Revolution and the more recent shootings at Tienanmen Square often reinforce the mistaken belief that China has always repressed antigovernment expression. In reality, the world's oldest written history reveals significant examples of freedom in China, as well as incidents of censorship.

There were no explicit guarantees of free speech in the states that were to become unified as China; in fact, the Chinese language did not contain a word for "rights."[76] Nevertheless, from the time of Confucius, (K'ung-Fu-tze, 551–479 B.C.E.) to the end of the third century B.C.E. (a time span much longer than that of the golden age of Athens), rulers showed considerable tolerance for the expression of ideas. The Chinese concept of the relationship between the ruler and spiritual beings differed from that found in previous

71. Id., pp. 50–51.
72. Finley, *Censorship*, p. 923.
73. Vasily Rudich, *Political Dissidence Under Nero*, p. xxv (Routledge, 1993).
74. Brian W. Jones, *The Emperor Domitian*, p. 124 (Routledge, 1992).
75. Robinson, pp. 82–83.
76. Muller, p. 112.

sacred monarchies. Under the Mandate of Heaven, the king's right to rule could be given or taken away by Heaven, depending on the ruler's performance. Ancient Chinese classics repeatedly reminded leaders that they should follow the people's wishes.[77]

A wide variety of viewpoints on government and philosophy were expounded in China. K'ung-Fu-tze contended that if leaders exhibited *te* (virtue), their subjects would also be virtuous.[78] Legalist philosophers countered with the claim that a strong government was necessary, because most persons are selfish and can be motivated only by a fear of stern punishments.[79] Many other philosophical schools also existed, and thousands of scholars taught disciples or traveled among the states in China, offering their advice.[80] They advocated diverse systems of government, and nearly every political and economic philosophy that was known in the Western world at that time was tried somewhere in China.[81] The intellectual climate in this era easily rivaled that of ancient Greece.[82]

Unfortunately, ancient China lacked any system of checks and balances that would continually ensure a wise interpretation of the Mandate of Heaven. Freedom of speech was stamped out after the Ch'in state achieved a series of military victories over the other Chinese states and unified China in 221 B.C.E. The Ch'in king who unified China took on the title of Shih-huang-ti, the First Emperor.[83] After abolishing feudalism, the emperor found himself being criticized by Confucian philosophers, who advocated a return to the feudal system. According to the *Shih Chi*,[84] the grand councillor Li Ssu advised the emperor:

> At present Your Majesty possesses a unified empire, has laid down the distinctions of right and wrong. . . . Yet there are those who . . . teach to others what is not according to the laws. When they hear orders promulgated, they criticize them upon the streets. To cast disrepute on their ruler they regard as a thing worthy of fame; to accept different views they regard as high (conduct); they lead the people to create slander.
>
> Your servant suggests . . . that all persons in the empire, save those who hold a function under the control of the bureau of the scholars of wide

77. Charles Holcombe, *Liberty in Early Medieval China*, 54 The Historian 609, 611 (Summer 1992); For example, K'ung-Fu-tze's disciple Meng-tzu ("Mencius") wrote that "the people are the most important, the state is next, and the ruler is least important," and that the people could "change the mandate" if the ruler abused it. Muller, p. 112.
78. Derk Bodde, *China's First Unifier*, p. 184 (Hong Kong Univ. Press, 1967).
79. Derk Bodde and Clarence Morris, *Law in Imperial China*, p. 23 (Harvard Univ. Press, 1967).
80. Bodde, p. 2.
81. Ernst Diez, *The Ancient Worlds of Asia*, pp. 215–17 (Macdonald, 1961).
82. Bodde, p. 181.
83. Yang Chen Ching, introduction to Arthur Cotterell, *The First Emperor of China*, p. 9 (Holt, 1981).
84. The *Shih Chi* (Records of the Historian) was compiled by Ssu-ma Ch'ien, who was the grand historian at Emperor Wu's court. His 130-chapter work covers Chinese history from the earliest times to the time of the author (c. 145–90 B.C.E.). Burton Watson, *Records of the Grand Historian of China*, p. 3 (Columbia Univ. Press, 1961).

learning, daring to store the *Shih*, the *Shu*,[85] and the discussions of the various philosophers, should go to the administrative and military governors so that these books may be indiscriminately burned. Those who dare to discuss the *Shih* and the *Shu* among themselves should be (executed and their bodies) exposed on the marketplace. Those who use the past to criticize the present, should be put to death together with their relatives.[86]

Shih-huang-ti was eager to put an end to the "hundred schools of thought,"[87] so he granted approval to this recommendation. Many men brought their books to the capital city of Hsienyang, where fires burned for days. Others hid their texts, but if they were discovered, the owner was either killed or branded and sent to work on the Great Wall, which the emperor had ordered to be completed.[88] According to the *Shih Chi*, Shih-huang-ti also was outraged that scholars he had assembled were criticizing his virtue and spreading rumors to confuse the people. To chill further criticism, 460 scholars were buried alive in Hsienyang.[89] Even the emperor's favorite son, Crown Prince Fu-su, was punished for disagreeing with his father. When Fu-su objected to the burying of the scholars, he was sent to supervise the work on the Great Wall. This was the equivalent of banishment,[90] the sanction invoked against unpopular speakers in Greece and Rome.

Shih-huang-ti died in 210 B.C.E., and a rebellion ended the Ch'in dynasty three years later. Under the successor Han dynasty, which ruled for more than four hundred years, a measure of freedom returned to China. Persons were allowed to speak out on issues such as forced labor, high taxes, and the seizure of land by the wealthy. An assembly was held in 81 B.C.E., and sixty scholars from all parts of China came to submit grievances of the people.[91] Books that had been hidden during Ch'in rule slowly reemerged, but unfortunately their literary accuracy may have been distorted. A new script had been developed, and the meaning of many passages changed during translation.[92] Han scholars also edited, and even falsified, banned texts that had been recovered.[93]

---

85. The *Shih Ching*, or Book of Odes, and the *Shu Ching*, or Book of History, were regularly referred to by Confucians as reminders of the past, where kings were said to rule with virtue rather than by force. Bodde, p. 164.
86. Id., pp. 82–83.
87. Daube, p. 72.
88. Leonard Cottrell, *The Tiger of Ch'in*, p. 150 (Holt, Rinehart, & Winston, 1962).
89. Arthur Cotterell, p. 154; p. 150. Shih-huang-ti was so hated that we cannot be positive that all accounts of his excesses are true; Leonard Cottrell, Bodde notes that histories written under the Han Dynasty, which replaced the Ch'in, could exaggerate Ch'in excesses. Nevertheless, he also notes that even allowing for exaggeration, "there is little doubt that the laws of Ch'in were particularly strict and harsh." (Bodde, p. 167); Arthur Cotterell, p. 12. Yang Chen Ching, curator of the Museum of Warriors and Horse Figures from the tomb of Shih-huang-ti in the People's Republic of China, corroborates that the emperor burned books and buried scholars alive. *The First Emperor of China*, p. 12.
90. Elizabeth Seeger, *The Pageant of Chinese History*, p. 119 (McKay, 4th ed 1962).
91. Bodde, pp. 174–75.
92. Diez, p. 219.
93. Bodde, p. 165.

Our study of ancient China, Israel, Greece, and Rome reveals that free speech traditions were beginning to assert themselves in the first millennium B.C.E. Although freedom of speech was not a constant in these cultures, each had periods of time during which people were relatively free to criticize their rulers or advocate societal change without fear of sanction. Were these free speech experiences aberrations, or was the world moving in the direction of freedom of speech? We answer that question as we move on to the study of other cultures.

### PROGRESS AND SETBACKS

The gains in freedom achieved in different cultures during the first millennium B.C.E. did not serve as a catalyst for the growth of freedom of speech during humanity's most recent two thousand years. Despite progress in some societies, most of the world's people have not been free to speak. The absolute power of governments and the influential voice of religious authorities were two major reasons this freedom has been denied. Pervasive sexism also ensured that women had less freedom of speech than men. These generalizations are borne out by the experiences of disparate peoples.

### Diverse Traditions on the African Continent

Historically, there has never been a single African philosophy of freedom of speech. Rather, the many nations and tribes of Africa fashioned different political systems, ranging from stateless societies to sacred monarchies. None of these entities had explicit guarantees of free speech, but the nature of each influenced the extent to which people could speak without fear of reprisal.

It was not uncommon for Africans to live in societies without any ruler, even when they lived near organized states. In such societies, the family was essentially the government,[94] and adult males had more speech rights than did many of their contemporaries in African states or Europe. For example, the Lugbara people of the Uganda region held councils to deal with the affairs of their villages and made decisions after open discussions.[95] Decisions for Afikpo Ibo villages in Nigeria were made by men of age sixty-five to eighty-three, but all adult males could join the elders in discussions, and all had a right to speak.[96]

In the states of the West African forests, religious and philosophical questions were debated by priests and intellectuals. Traveling storytellers recited parables and humorous stories, some of which (such as Brer Rabbit) were brought to the United States by slaves and became a part of American folk literature.[97]

---

94. Robert July, *A History of the African People*, p. 127 (Scribner's, 1980).
95. Norman R. Bennett, *Africa and Europe from Roman Times to National Independence*, p. 12 (Africana, 2nd ed 1984).
96. Id., p. 13.
97. E. Jefferson Murphy, *History of African Civilization*, p. 154 (Crowell, 1972).

Muslim historian Ibn Battuta told of a custom he observed in Mali, which gave traveling speakers a unique kind of free speech. On certain feast days, a bard (disguised in a feathered dress and a bird's head mask) was allowed to deliver an address to the king, admonishing the ruler and encouraging him to live up to the high standards of his predecessors.[98]

In the western Sudan, fifteenth-century Islamic scholars went on lecture tours and spoke before large crowds.[99] An environment similar to that at medieval universities existed in the mosques of sixteenth-century African cities such as Gao, Jenne, and Timbuktu. The scholarship achieved at Timbuktu was particularly renowned in the Islamic world.[100]

In other African societies, there was little freedom to speak. In many kingdoms, the king was believed to be sacred and imbued with supernatural powers.[101] One example was the king of the Monomatapa (near modern Zimbabwe), whom people approached by crawling on their stomachs. Audiences were not allowed to look at him, and when he spoke to his subjects he remained behind a screen.[102] Where kings were regarded as divine, there was a corresponding decrease in popular input into decision making.[103] This was exemplified in the total power of King Mutesa, who ruled Buganoa from 1857–1881. Although a council of ministers existed, the word of Mutesa was absolute, and he alone made the laws.[104]

Other African rulers were not necessarily viewed as sacred, but they still wielded absolute power. The rulers of Dahomey had a unique way of compelling their subjects to communicate their allegiance. Leading men of the kingdom were required to symbolically surrender their horses to the king. After this ritual of support was concluded, the horses would be reunited with their rightful owners.[105] But defiance was answered with terror: entire villages would be destroyed if they were judged disloyal.

### The Conflict between Free Speech and Fundamentalist Islamic Beliefs

In the days before Islam, Arab peoples enjoyed a degree of freedom of speech. An elder *(shaikh)* was elected to be the leader of a tribe or clan, and he

---

98. Galbraith Welch, *From Freedom to Freedom,* ed. M. Bain and E. Lewis, p. 39 (Random House, 1977).
99. A. Adu Boahen, *From Freedom to Freedom,* p. 69.
100. Margaret Shinnie, *Ancient African Kingdoms,* p. 59 (London: Arnold, 1965); The intellectual climate in Timbuktu was greatly impaired after Morocco invaded the city in 1591. Religious scholars were instrumental in the resistance to the Moroccans. Consequently, their private libraries were confiscated, and some scholars were killed or exiled. Pascal James Imperato, *Mali: A Search for Direction,* pp. 28–29 (Westview, 1989).
101. Philip Curtin, et. al., *African History,* p. 30 (Little, Brown, 1978).
102. Shinnie, p. 119.
103. Basil Davidson, *Africa in History,* p. 103 (Macmillan, 1991).
104. Shinnie, p. 98.
105. Gailey, pp. 100–2.

was often simply first among equals in the council of elders *(majlis)*. The *shaikh*'s dealings with the tribe were often informal and democratic.[106]

This system of governance changed early in the seventh century C.E. According to Islamic beliefs, the Prophet Muhammad began to receive revelations from Allah (God). These revelations became the basis of the *shari'a*, a divinely ordained system of laws.[107] The major purpose of government became protecting the faith, and over time, the *imam* or caliph (ruler) came to be viewed as the "shadow of God on earth."[108] Because Allah appointed this ruler to enforce the *shari'a*, it was the duty of the Muslim to obey him without question, whether the ruler appeared to be moral or immoral, fair or unfair.[109]

Consequently, individuals had no freedom to disagree with the ruler in Islamic fundamentalist states. The belief was that they should simply obey the caliph without question, and any injustice would be settled on the day of judgment.[110] There could be no debate about the religious purpose of the state, and criticism of the state was considered **heresy**.[111] For instance, the caliph Mutawakkil (847–61) cruelly persecuted not only Christians and Jews but also Muslims who dared to express unorthodox beliefs. The Mu'tazilites, Muslims who believed in a deity of justice and reason, were particularly victimized.[112]

The Islamic belief that the ruler was the shadow of God on earth resembled the concept of the sacred monarchy, an idea that had operated to limit freedom of speech throughout history. Islam was not the only religion that had this kind of influence on free expression, as we shall see in our study of Europe.

### Freedom of Speech for European Peoples

After the demise of the Roman Republic, the issue of freedom of speech was dormant in Europe for about one thousand years. The Europeans who migrated to Iceland then established a system of government without a king, at the same time that the authority of kings was expanding on their native continent.[113] The Icelandic Althing, founded about 930, was a general assembly that made laws for the entire nation. Only chieftains could vote, but the proceedings were held in public, with the participants sitting on benches in the open air.[114] Each summer, hundreds of people from throughout the island

106. Kemal A. Faruki, *The Evolution of Islamic Constitutional Theory and Practice*, p. 9 (Karachi: National Publishing House, 1971).
107. Id., p. 12.
108. Ann K. S. Lambton, *State and Government in Medieval Islam*, pp. 13, 309 (Oxford Univ. Press, 1981).
109. Faruki, pp. 234–35.
110. Id., p. 52.
111. Lambton, p. 307. Heretical speech is that which contradicts the teachings of God.
112. Treadgold, p. 97.
113. Magnus Magnusson, *Iceland Saga*, p. 107 (Bodley Head, 1987).
114. Jesse L. Byock, *Medieval Iceland*, p. 61 (Univ. of California Press, 1988).

traveled to the Althing. Observers sat on the slopes surrounding the wooden benches, and likely participated in the discussions of legal issues.[115]

On the continent of Europe, most political and religious leaders were moving in an opposite direction. The participation of citizens in their own government was not even considered.[116]

Expression of religious opinions was particularly risky in Europe. Rulers cooperated with the Church by imposing the death penalty for heresy. Beginning in the tenth century, many heretics were burned at the stake or strangled. Then in the thirteenth century, Pope Innocent III laid the groundwork for the Inquisition. The goal of the Inquisition was to exterminate heretical speech. The Dominican order was assigned the task of traveling from town to town, asking the inhabitants to identify heretics. Once accusations were gathered, alleged heretics were subjected to secret proceedings in which they were presumed guilty. Torture was common if the accused would not confess, and no person was ever found innocent. The Spanish Inquisition was particularly brutal, and wholesale massacres frightened many Jews and Muslims into accepting baptism as Christians. As late as 1781, heretics were still being burned at the stake in Spain.[117]

Sixteenth-century universities also repressed unorthodox religious and political expression. The faculties of institutions such as Oxford, the Sorbonne, and the Berlin Academy of Sciences had the power of censorship. European universities often had their Colleges of Censors affiliated with Commissioners on Heresy.[118]

The Dutch provided a notable exception to the anti–free speech tendencies in Europe. One French writer noted that in Holland, "nobody is troubled on account of his religion. One is free to say what he chooses, even of the magistrates and to denounce them."[119] The Dutch press was the first free press, and its newspapers were sought throughout Europe because they were known to be free from the government control that plagued other European nations. A French king once asked to have a Dutch publisher suppressed, and to his surprise, he was told that this was impossible.[120]

### The British Experience: Legacy for Freedom of Speech in the United States?

British documents and British writers contributed ideas that have become part of the American free speech tradition. Unfortunately, the traditions of England also provided justifications for restricting speech in the United

---

115. Id., pp. 61–64.
116. Treadgold, p. 136.
117. Leo Pfeffer, *Church, State, and Freedom,* pp. 21–22 (Beacon, 1967).
118. Morris L. Ernst and Alan U. Schwartz, *Censorship, The Search for the Obscene,* pp. 8–9 (Macmillan, 1964).
119. H. Taine, *Lectures on Art,* p. 324 (Henry Holt, 1901).
120. Will Durant and Ariel Durant, *The Age of Reason Begins,* p. 480 (Simon & Schuster, 1961).

States. Many of the limitations found in Britain would be transplanted to the American colonies. Furthermore, as you will read in chapter 3, English justifications for curtailing speech rights would also be used as the basis for limiting speech in the United States long after the Revolutionary War had ended.

***Early Limitations on Speech.*** One of the most famous documents in English history is the Magna Carta, or Great Charter. This proclamation, obtained from King John in 1215, granted free men important rights, including the right to a trial by one's peers.[121] Although no free speech rights were granted by the Magna Carta, the charter was significant because it was premised on a concept vital to liberty of expression: Law can create rights that even the king cannot take away. Despite the potential of this document as a catalyst for liberty, for centuries English monarchs, parliaments, and judges were able to limit the Magna Carta's spirit from fostering freedom of expression.

One of the first constraints on speech came in 1275, when Parliament outlawed "false news or tales whereby discord or slander may grow between the king and his people."[122] One hundred years later the statute was reenacted, and punishment came to be administered by the king's council, sitting in the **Star Chamber.**[123] These Star Chamber proceedings were secret, and the King's prerogatives in his council included the use of torture to obtain confessions.[124] The Treason Act of 1351 defined that offense to include merely imagining "the death of our lord the King or of our lady his Queen, or of their eldest son and heir."[125]

The English monarch's power was said to come from God, and kings and queens could define religious orthodoxy. In 1539, Henry VIII had the "Bloody Statute" passed by Parliament. This act made the denial of the doctrine of transubstantiation punishable by burning at the stake.[126] Under Queen Elizabeth I, Jesuits and priests who sought converts faced the death penalty on the grounds that their efforts were treasonous.[127]

Advocacy of free speech rights also had little success in England. Elizabeth I arrested Peter Wentworth for speaking out in favor of free speech.[128] When the English Bill of Rights was finally passed in 1689, free speech was granted only to members of Parliament.[129]

---

121. Treadgold, p. 108.
122. Leonard W. Levy, *Freedom of Speech and Press in Early American History: Legacy of Suppression*, p. 16 (Harper & Row, 1963).
123. Id., p. 8. The Star Chamber was so named because the council met in a room decorated with stars on the ceiling.
124. Frederick Siebert, *Freedom of the Press in England, 1476–1776*, p. 29 (Univ. of Illinois Press, 1952); The Star Chamber operated until 1641, and physical punishments, such as removal of the offender's ears, were meted out along with fines and imprisonment. Id., p. 121.
125. Alan Wharam, *The Treason Trials, 1794*, p. 277 (Leicester Univ. Press, 1992).
126. Pfeffer, p. 27. The Bloody Statute elevated this doctrine to the official faith of the Church of England.
127. Id.
128. Treadgold, p. 153.
129. Levy, p. 16.

***British Restrictions on the Press.***　　Freedom of the press was severely constrained in England. With the advent of printing in England in 1450, the potential for communicating ideas that were not approved by the Crown or the Church was greatly expanded. New laws were enacted to deal with this threat, including Henry VIII's 1529 list of prohibited books. The list included books by Martin Luther and other "heretics," as well as any book that reproached, rebuked, or slandered the King or his honorable council. Under the Proclamation of 1538, all books printed in English were subjected to a licensing system.[130] The power to license books was a royal prerogative, a right that belonged only to the King.[131] All manuscripts had to be submitted to the King's officials, who had the power to censor passages as well as to approve or deny a license.

The licensing system evolved and grew, much to the detriment of publishers. Printers who violated the licensing regulations were fined, imprisoned, and required to post £100 bonds. These bonds were to be forfeited if the printer violated King Henry's Proclamation. One bookseller was committed to the English fleet for violating these provisions, and three persons were executed for rendering erroneous religious opinions.[132]

The incorporation of the Stationers' Company added another source of oppression. The Craft of Writers of the Text Letter was a venerable organization that had the power to make rules governing writers and elect wardens to enforce these rules. Their organization was incorporated as the Stationers' Company (so named because many members operated out of stations, or stalls, near St. Paul's in London), and given a monopoly on printing in England. In return for this favor, the Stationers' Company was to search for heretical and seditious books. Company wardens had the power to destroy the books, imprison the offenders, and levy fines that were shared with the King.[133]

The English maintained a licensing system until 1694.[134] Even after the licensing rules expired, the press was freed only from *prior restraint.* The risk of subsequent punishment (being penalized for disseminating objectionable ideas after they have been printed) remained. In an oft-quoted commentary, British jurist William Blackstone explained how freedom of the press was a narrow concept in England:

> The liberty of the press is indeed essential to the nature of a free state; but this consists in laying no previous restraints upon publications, and not in freedom from censure for criminal matter when published. Every freeman has an undoubted right to lay what sentiments he pleases before

130. Siebert, p. 49.
131. Lord Birkett, "The Changing Law," in *To Deprave and Corrupt . . . Original Studies in the Nature and Definition of Obscenity,* p. 76 (Association Press, 1962).
132. Siebert, p. 50.
133. Birkett, pp. 77–78.
134. Levy, p. 9.

the public: to forbid this is to destroy the freedom of the press, but if he publishes what is improper, mischievous or illegal, he must take the consequences of his own temerity.[135]

The Crown would use subsequent punishment to suppress a wide variety of disagreeable expression.

*The Four Libels in Britain.*   English courts established four major categories of speech that could be punished as criminal libel. As you will read in later chapters, each of these content areas has been invoked as a basis for limiting freedom of speech in the United States as well. The types of libel are sedition, obscenity, blasphemy, and private libel.

Communicators were often punished for **seditious libel,** or unfavorable speech about the government.[136] The English rulers believed that they could not survive in power if they were subject to criticism. In Tutchin's Case (1704), Chief Justice John Holt explained this basis for punishing seditious libel:

> If people should not be called to account for possessing the people with an ill opinion of the government, no government can subsist. For it is very necessary for all governments that the people should have a good opinion of it.[137]

Seditious libel was so broadly defined that any words "which were designed to bring the government into disrepute"[138] could be punished. Communicators could be punished, even if their criticism of the government was justified. Under the English common law, truth only made the libel worse, since true allegations exacerbated any scandal against the government.[139] Furthermore, the role of the jury was circumscribed in seditious libel cases. The jury determined only whether the defendant had spoken the words in question; the judge decided whether the words were seditious.[140]

The penalties for seditious libel could be quite severe. William Twyn printed a book endorsing the right to revolution, and in 1663 he was sentenced to be hanged, emasculated, disemboweled, quartered, and beheaded.[141] Twenty years later Algernon Sidney was executed, even though his writings on government had never been published.[142] In 1793 attorney John Frost was disbarred, pilloried, and jailed for remarking that he supported "equality, no king, and a better constitution."[143]

---

135. Blackstone, p. 152.
136. Siebert, p. 269. Sixteen trials for seditious libel were held from April 30, 1684 to November 28, 1684 alone.
137. *Rex v. Tutchin,* 14 Howell's State Trials 1095, 1118 (1704).
138. Wharam, p. 132.
139. Levy, p. 13.
140. Birkett, p. 79. In 1792, Fox's Libel Act gave the jury the power to decide if the words were libelous.
141. *Rex v. Twyn* 6 Howell's State Trials 513, 536 (1663).
142. *Rex v. Sidney,* 9 Howell's State Trials 818 (1683).
143. *Rex v. Frost,* 22 Howell's State Trials 471 (1793).

Obscene libel was not initially punished by the British government; consequently "bawdy book[s] could be published in England with impunity."[144] In 1727, however, Chief Justice Robert Raymond ruled that obscenity could be punished as a criminal offense, accepting the attorney general's argument that "it tends to corrupt the morals of the King's subjects, and is thus against the peace of the King."[145]

The British produced a definition of obscenity that would be the law in England and the United States for nearly one hundred years. The Hicklin case (1868) was a prosecution under the Obscene Publications Act of 1857.[146] The defendant possessed 250 copies of a pamphlet entitled "The Confessional Unmasked; shewing the depravity of the Roman priesthood, the iniquity of the Confessional, and the questions put to females in confession."[147] The pamphlet was part of the Protestant Electoral Union's efforts to malign Catholicism and elect more Protestants to Parliament. Chief Justice Alexander Cockburn upheld the ruling that the pamphlet was obscene, and provided a very broad definition of the term *obscenity:*

> I think the test of obscenity is this, whether the tendency of the matter charged as obscenity is to deprave and corrupt those whose minds are open to such immoral influences, and into whose hands a publication of this sort might fall.[148]

The chief justice believed that the pamphlet in this case "would suggest to the minds of the young of either sex, or even to persons of more advanced years, thoughts of a most impure and libidinous character."[149]

The third category of libel was blasphemy. For 250 years, Christian doctrine was protected by the common law of England. Examples of forbidden speech included denying God's existence, reproaching Jesus Christ, or bringing any doctrine of the Christian religion into disbelief or ridicule.[150] Tom Paine's publisher was convicted of blasphemous libel because the book *The Age of Reason* contended that accounts of savage conduct in the Old Testament had brutalized and corrupted mankind. When Justice William Ashurst sentenced the publisher, he noted that "all offenses of this kind are not only offenses to God but crimes against the law of the land . . . inasmuch as they tend to destroy those obligations whereby a civil society is bound together."[151]

---

144. Haig Bosmajian, *Obscenity and Freedom of Expression,* p. ii (Burt Franklin, 1976).
145. Birkett, p. 80. As a result, the author of *Venus in the Cloister, or the Nun in Her Smock* was forced to stand in the pillory.
146. This act gave judges the power to issue warrants authorizing searches for obscene publications, and allowing seizure of any obscene works which were discovered.
147. Bosmajian, p. ii.
148. William B. Lockhart and Robert C. McClure, "Why Obscene?" in *To Deprave and Corrupt,* p. 54.
149. Id.
150. Birkett, p. 82.
151. Id.

The law of blasphemy gradually became less severe in England. In 1842, Justice John Taylor Coleridge ruled that it was legal to reverently doubt or deny Christian doctrines. Finally, in 1917, the British House of Lords formally rejected the contention that blasphemous speech was dangerous, noting that "in the present day, reasonable men do not apprehend the dissolution or downfall of society because religion is publicly assailed by methods not scandalous."[152]

A fourth category of punishable expression was private libel, or speech that attacked the reputation of another person. One thousand years ago, Anglo-Saxon law provided that a speaker who insulted another person could sometimes be punished by excision of the tongue.[153] More fortunate defendants were simply required to hold their noses and call themselves liars.[154] Blackstone notes that malicious defamations of any person, made public in order to expose him to public hatred, contempt, and ridicule, constituted libel. The English punished such speech because the words were believed to have a direct tendency to cause a breach of the peace by inciting the recipient of the insult to seek revenge.[155]

The theories under which speech was restricted in England differed from those of strict Islamic regimes or repressive African nations. But the end result on much of three continents was the same. As late as the eighteenth century, freedom of speech had not made lasting progress in any region of the world. And for one half of the world's population, progress was particularly slow.

## Repression of Women's Speech Rights

The history of free speech rights for women does not parallel that of men. When men obtained free speech for themselves, they often left customs and institutions in place that limited women's ability to speak freely. Although history includes examples of valiant women who were willing to voice their opinions, the record also reveals severe repression.

*Evidence from Prehistory.* Some of the most ancient cultures may have had a more favorable climate for the free expression of women than did later societies. Archaeological evidence (dating between 7000 and 3500 B.C.E.) shows that the social organization of peoples living in modern-day Eastern Europe was different from the later societies we have studied in this chapter. An example of evidence used to support this theory is provided by author Riane Eisler, who contends that there is no proof of any elaborate burial plots for chieftains, and that no pictures depicting war (or artifacts of deities carrying spears or swords) have been found.[156] This suggests a peaceful society,

152. Id., p. 83.
153. Theodore F. T. Plucknett, *A Concise History of the Common Law*, p. 483 (Little, Brown, 1956).
154. Id.
155. Blackstone, p. 150.
156. Riane Eisler, *The Chalice and the Blade: Our History, Our Future*, p. 18 (Harper & Row, 1987).

without a rigid hierarchy of leaders and subjects. The most famous scholar associated with this viewpoint is Marija Gimbutas,[157] who was a professor of European archaeology at UCLA. She argued that this European civilization had the mother-goddess as its deity (rather than following a religion based on male dominance) and was based on peaceful egalitarian coexistence, with "no apparent social superiority of men over women."[158] In a society of this nature, freedom of speech could easily have been perceived as a given, and there would not have been a hierarchy of male leaders suppressing the speech of women.

The nature of these prehistoric civilizations has been the subject of scholarly debate, however. For example, University of Toronto anthropology professor Gillian Gillison argues that goddess worship is not a sign of equal status for women.[159] Ruth Tringham of the University of California at Berkeley contends that Professor Gimbutas's construction of European history is based on a very subjective interpretation of the data and is "deeply unsettling."[160] Lynn Meskell of Cambridge University argues that there is considerable evidence of social hierarchy in prehistoric European communities, as well as human sacrifice and weaponry. Meskell argues that "the romanticized view of antiquity . . . has more to do with creating an idealized past to contrast with our own secular, impersonal, and industrialized present than with archaeological facts."[161]

***Egypt and Sumeria.*** In ancient Egypt, women had the same right as men to request justice from the king. Females could institute legal proceedings and testify on their own behalf in court. Women took their place on the picket line, supporting the first recorded labor strike in history."[162] A second-century C.E. papyrus extols Isis (the most popular Egyptian goddess) with the words "you have made a power for the women equal to that of the men."[163] Perhaps Egyptian women benefited from the fact that laws came from the sacred monarch, rather than the men of Egypt. The literature written by male Egyptian mortals includes striking examples of sexism.[164] In Sumeria, where the king also was believed to be selected by God, royal texts cautioned that the

157. See, e.g., Marija Gimbutas, *The Civilization of the Goddess* (Harper Collins, 1991); and *The Language of the Goddess* (Harper & Row, 1989).
158. Anne Baring and Jules Cashford, *The Myth of the Goddess: Evolution of an Image*, p. 56 (Penguin, 1991).
159. Nancy J. White, *Belief in Peaceful Goddess Societies Religion to Some Feminists, Myth to Others*, The Vancouver Sun (July 12, 1995),. p. C6.
160. Ruth Tringham, book review, *The Civilization of the Goddess*, 95 American Anthropologist 196, 97 (March 1993).
161. Lynn Meskell, *Goddesses, Gimbutas and "New Age" Archaeology*, 69 Antiquity 74, 79 (March 1995).
162. Barbara S. Lesko, *The Remarkable Women of Ancient Egypt*, p. 31 (Scribe, 1978).
163. Barbara Watterson, *Women in Ancient Egypt*, p. 27 (St. Martin's, 1991).
164. Watterson, p. 12. The *Wisdom Texts and Instructions* contain stereotypical maxims such as "Never confide in your wife—what you say to her goes straight into the street"; In Egyptian tales, women are often portrayed as stubborn and unreasonable, and they are rarely in heroic roles. Id., p. 14.

king should not show partiality. Thus the legal rights given to men usually applied to women as well.[165] The earliest poems attributed to an author were
written by Enheduanna, a Sumerian priestess in the city of Ur (c. 2300
B.C.E.).[166] Furthermore, women were able to testify on their own behalf in
court,[167] and during the rule of Hammurabi there were female judges.[168]

*Athens and Rome.*    Ancient Athens was famed for its freedom of speech
among free male citizens, yet Athenian women had less of this liberty than
did their counterparts in Egypt and Sumeria. Each Athenian woman was subject to a *kyrios* ("lord" or "master"), usually her husband (or her father if she
was not married). She was expected to obey this man, and the kyrios spoke
for his "dependent" when a woman was involved in court proceedings.[169]
Women's participation in government was not imaginable to men, and
women had no right to vote in the assembly.[170] Aristophanes' *The Female Parliament* poked fun at the idea of women in government. In this comedy,
women dressed as men arrive at the Assembly before the men have awakened. They vote for the government to be run by women, and the newly
elected female legislators enact a provision whereby a man must bed with an
older or less attractive woman before he can have a liaison with the woman of
his dreams. Women rarely attended Greek comedies, and Aristophanes must
have believed that male audiences would find the very idea of women making
speeches and voting quite amusing.[171]

The Roman Republic also discouraged public speaking by women. Ordinarily, a woman would find a male to plead her case in court. One exception
to this rule was Gaia Afrania, who litigated many cases by herself. Her uncom-
promising style was not appreciated by the males she dealt with,[172] and Romans began applying the name Gaia Afrania to any woman who was believed
to have low morals.[173] To prevent an expansion of female advocates, an edict
was issued declaring that no woman could appear in court on behalf of another person.[174]

When a woman's public speaking was tolerated in Rome, the orator was
likely to be a member of the elite or one who was speaking on her husband's
behalf. After a special tax was instituted on wealthy women in 42 B.C.E., the
aggrieved female taxpayers marched into the Forum. Hortensia, herself the

165. Muller, p. 59.
166. Tikva Frymer-Kensky, *In the Wake of the Goddesses*, pp. 42, 79 (Free Press, 1992).
167. Kramer, *The Sumerians*, p. 78.
168. Muller, p. 59.
169. Finley, *Politics*, p. 84.
170. Mary R. Lefkowitz, *Images of Women in Antiquity*, ed. Averil Cameron and Amelie Kuhrt, p. 56
(Wayne State Univ. Press, 1983).
171. Id., p. 54.
172. Daube, p. 25.
173. Lefkowitz, p. 60.
174. Daube, p. 26.

daughter of a famous orator, spoke on behalf of the women who were subjected to the tax. She argued that if women could not hold positions of authority, they should not be taxed. Her argument was successful—the taxes on women were decreased, and taxes on land-owning males were increased to make up the deficiency.[175] Sometimes women could communicate their support of their husbands' political causes. For example, graffiti that survived on the walls of Pompeii noted that "Amadio, along with his wife, asks you to vote for Gnaeus Sabinus.[176]

*Hypatia of Alexandria.* About five hundred years after the demise of the Roman Republic, Hypatia of Alexandria, a remarkable African scholar, held the chair in philosophy at the University of Alexandria. A noteworthy mathematician, she lectured and wrote commentaries on the works of Ptolemy and Euclid. Hypatia was also an acknowledged leader in the field of non-Christian thought, and a mob of Christian fanatics murdered her and dismembered her body.[177]

*European Repression.* In Europe, women were severely persecuted for expressing their religious viewpoints. During the thirteenth century, sects holding beliefs inconsistent with those of the Catholic Church began to proliferate. In these sects, women often had a greater role than was allowed by the Church. The *Passau Anonymous,* a German document written about 1260, decried an interpretation of the Bible suggesting that all men and women should be allowed to preach.[178] The author cited a biblical passage advising that "women should keep their silence in Church, for it is not permitted for them to speak."[179] Women were also subjected to the Inquisition. A detailed record exists of inquisitor Jacques Fournier's interrogation in 1320 of Beatrice de Planissoles, a Cathar[180] woman. The proceedings lasted for several days, and Beatrice finally stated that she regretted her belief in Cathar heresies and was ready to accept her penance. Beatrice was luckier than many Cathars—she was very ill, and her death sentence was commuted. She was required merely to wear a double cross to signify that she was a heretic.[181]

During the time of the Inquisition, local clerics had the power to silence women by condemning them as witches without even the semblance of a fair trial. Any outspoken woman that the priests disliked could simply be branded a

175. Daube, p. 30.
176. Lefkowitz, p. 59.
177. Beatrice Lumpkin, "Hypatia and Women's Rights in Ancient Egypt," in *Black Women in Antiquity,* p. 155 (Transaction Books, 1988).
178. "The Passau Anonymous," in *Women's Lives in Medieval Europe,* p. 306 (Routledge, 1993).
179. I Corinthians 14:34.
180. Abt, p. 306. The Cathars, or Albigensians, rejected many orthodox Christian doctrines, including the incarnation of Jesus Christ. A large number died at the hands of the Inquisition.
181. "Inquisition Records of Jacques Fournier: Life of a Cathar Woman," in *Women's Lives in Medieval Europe,* pp. 312–13.

witch or a heretic.[182] Between the years 1300 and 1700, hundreds of thousands of women were classified as witches and burned or hanged.[183] In England, a woman could also be punished for being "a common scold." A 1375 record from the London court documented the case of Alice Shether, who was accused of this offense. Apparently, "all the neighbors . . . by her malicious words and abuse were . . . greatly molested and annoyed."[184] She was sentenced to stand in the pillory.

In eighteenth-century France, women had played a significant role in the French Revolution and were not shy about voicing their opinions. Female citizens (perhaps more than 4,500) petitioned the National Convention, demanding that more nobles be arrested and that those already imprisoned have their date with the guillotine expedited.[185] Olympe de Gouges wrote *The Declaration of the Rights of Woman*, advocating legal equality between the sexes, admission of women to all occupations, and education for girls.[186] When bread was scarce in Paris during the winter of 1794, hundreds of women came to the Convention to protest. Women entered the tribunes and prevented the politicians from being heard—a tactic they had used in the past. Laws were then passed to ensure that women's protest would be silenced. Women were barred from entering the tribunes, prohibited from participating in any political assembly, and could face arrest if they gathered in the street in groups of five or more. Non-Parisian war widows who had congregated in the capital, where they could attract sympathy, were forced to move to provincial towns.[187]

Although women may have enjoyed some freedoms of speech along with men in ancient Egypt and Sumer, the more common pattern throughout history has been repression. Greek men, despite their own love of free speech, could not imagine how women deserved the same right. In medieval Europe, women paid for their unpopular views by being executed as heretics or witches. And even in a relatively egalitarian society determined to increase the liberty of men, oppressive measures were undertaken in France to ensure that women could not voice their opinions.

Would the American revolutionaries break this mold and guarantee free speech for all? Would the protections be extended regardless of race and gender, and remain strongly enforced in the face of popular opposition? As you will read in chapter 3, our new republic was in no hurry to extend freedom of speech to both sexes.

182. Nancy van Vuuren, *The Subversion of Women*, p. 42 (Westminster, 1973).
183. Id., p. 71.
184. "London Records: Crimes and Punishments," in *Women's Lives in Medieval Europe*, p. 74.
185. Olwen H. Hufton, *Women and the Limitis of Citizenship in the French Revolution*, p. 34 (Univ. of Toronto Press, 1992).
186. Joan B. Landes, *Women and the Public Sphere in the Age of the French Revolution*, pp. 124–25 (Cornell Univ. Press, 1988). Gouges also was a royalist, and offered to defend King Louis XVI in his trial before the National Convention.
187. Hufton, p. 49.

## SUMMARY

In this chapter, we have examined some of the origins of the free speech concept, expanding our review beyond an exclusively Western bias. Freedom of speech is not just a Greek, British, or American idea. As we have seen, many cultures confronted this issue and contributed to our present understanding of this valuable liberty.

Whether we discuss freedom of speech from the perspective of ancient Egyptians, Romans of Caesar's time, or seventeenth-century Britons, certain themes recur. The availability of free speech rights waxed and waned in many cultures. With no institutions in place to guarantee the protection of free speech, this right was largely dependent on the good will of a ruler. When rulers opposed freedom of speech, they could be ruthless in suppressing dissent.

At various points throughout our history, dissenting voices were heard, and greater participation in governance resulted. However, to say that many cultures exercised freedom of speech during such times would be to assume a very limited definition of that right. In most societies, many groups did not enjoy that liberty.

Ultimately, some of the forces that operated to limit speech rights would be challenged by one of the world's younger nations, the United States. As you study the history of freedom of speech in America, evaluate the extent to which the United States has overcome the barriers that still limit speech in many societies.

## CHAPTER 3     *Objectives*

**After reading chapter 3,
you should understand
the following:**

◆ *The nature of freedom of speech in the American colonies, including constraints on expression as well as practices and events that promoted free speech.*

◆ *The history of the adoption of the Bill of Rights.*

◆ *The evidence for and against the hypothesis that the American colonists valued freedom of speech.*

◆ *The* **limitations** *on the exercise of freedom of expression during the years leading up to the Civil War, particularly restrictions on* **women, slaves,** *and* **abolitionists.**

◆ *The changes in freedom of speech rights that took place during the* **Civil War,** *which exemplify how rights are curtailed in time of war.*

◆ *The limited development of First Amendment rights during the years between the Civil War and World War I, and the* **legal doctrines** *that inhibited such development.*

# 3   *Freedom of Speech in America: 1600–1917*

POPULAR MEDIA IMAGES of attempts at democratic elections in Haiti, the Philippines, and the nations of the former Soviet Union can fuel the imagination. What would we do if given the opportunity to build a new country? What type of rules would we agree to govern (and to be governed) by? Would we recognize free expression as a right that the new government could not take away? If so, how would we guarantee that right? As recent history has demonstrated, instituting democratic reforms where democracy did not previously exist is a challenging task. To confirm this proposition, we need look no farther than our own comparatively young republic.

Freedom of speech did not instantly take root in North America as Europeans began to colonize the continent. It is more myth than historical fact that immigrants came to America and later fought the Revolutionary War to live in a land where speech was free. The evidence is more consistent with John Roche's contention that "Colonial America was an open society dotted with closed enclaves, and one could generally settle with his co-believers in safety and comfort and exercise the right of oppression."[1]

This chapter discusses the evolution of free speech rights and traditions in Colonial times and during the first 125 years of United States history. You will see how some of the first colonizers, such as the Puritans and William Penn, regulated speech; and how popularly elected assemblies as well as British officials later asserted their rights to control speech.

Progress would come when the infant American nation ratified the Bill of Rights in 1791. Nevertheless, the new Constitution would be interpreted to provide only limited speech rights, and you will read of many persons who were punished for expression that would be

---

1. John P. Roche, "American Liberty: An Examination of the 'Tradition' of Freedom," in *Aspects of Liberty*, p. 137 (Cornell Univ. Press, 1958).

protected in modern times. This chapter discusses the powerful urge to censor divergent opinions in America, which prevailed for 300 years. You will see that the First Amendment provided only limited assistance to speakers with unpopular ideas throughout the nineteenth century.

## FREEDOM OF SPEECH IN SEVENTEENTH-CENTURY AMERICA

### Native American Traditions

The European immigrants who came to North America did not arrive in a land populated by violent savages who lacked the ability to provide for human rights. To the west of the Massachusetts colonists resided the five nations of the Iroquois Confederacy: The Seneca, Onondaga, Oneida, Mohawk, and Cayuga. These nations had achieved peace with one another, based on the *Kaianerekowa,* or Great Law of Peace.

The business of the confederacy was conducted by a council of the league, which included chiefs from all the nations. The Great Law required that chiefs tolerate the criticism of their people:

> The chiefs of the league of Five Nations shall be mentors of the people for all time. The thickness of their skins shall be seven spans, which is to say that they shall be proof against anger, offensive action and criticism.[2]

The men and/or women of the league had a right to bring complaints about the chiefs to the council, and after three warnings, the chief could be removed.[3]

### Limitations on Speech by the First English Settlers

***Governor Dale's Virginia Code.***    The early English settlers established less tolerant traditions of their own. In Virginia, Governor Dale's Code created restrictions on speech. The code, established in 1610, imposed the death penalty for speaking against the "Articles of the Christian faith" and called for severe punishment if one took the name of God in vain.[4] Minor punishments were meted out for blasphemy, but those who spoke out against the governor were punished more harshly: One man had both arms broken and an awl driven through his tongue.[5]

***Puritan Attitudes toward Free Speech.***    In the Massachusetts Bay Colony of the 1630s, the Puritans sought to recreate the City of God. They endeavored to achieve this utopia through religion, hard work, and poverty.[6]

---

2. Bruce E. Johansen, *Forgotten Founders,* p. 27 (Gambit, 1982).
3. *Id.,* p. 26.
4. Leonard W. Levy, *Blasphemy,* p. 238 (Knopf, 1993).
5. *Id.,* p. 239.
6. James Holstun, *A Rational Millennium,* p. 106 (Oxford Univ. Press, 1987).

The Puritan *Body of Liberties,* adopted in 1641, was not a significant advancement in human rights. This document was really a collection of Puritan statutes, and it included the "right" to be executed for adultery.[7]

In the colony, the brethren (male colonists) were allowed to choose their magistrates,[8] but once they did so, the elected government had powers not unlike those of the ancient sacred monarchs. The people were expected to obey the magistrate, as if his voice were the word of God.[9] John Winthrop, the founder of the Massachusetts Bay Colony, suggested in his *Journal* that a petition to have an order repealed "savors of resisting an order of God."[10]

Winthrop's *Journal* reveals how speech was suppressed. Philip Ratcliff was sentenced to be whipped, lose his ears, and be banished for uttering "most foul, scandalous invectives against [Puritan] churches and government."[11] Henry Linne was whipped and banished for writing letters to England that slandered the colony's administration.[12] And Abigail Gifford was sent back to England for being "a very bothersome woman."[13] Rather than fleeing to a new world of free speech and religious tolerance, the Puritans had definite ideas about what should be said and believed. They feared that dissent against the bedrock principles of their religion would divide the community and destroy their experiment.[14]

The fate of Anne Hutchinson reveals how the Puritans feared diversity of opinion. Hutchinson, upset that females were excluded from private meetings of the church brethren, set up meetings for the women of the church; she attracted some male supporters as well.[15] Her theology included the belief that God's spirit could directly enter the soul. The Puritan authorities found this viewpoint threatening, as people who believed in personal revelations from God might feel no need for church officials or biblical commandments.[16]

Governor Winthrop feared that Hutchinson would convert many church members, and the ministers of Boston contended that she was dangerous to the state.[17] She was called upon to retract twenty-nine "errors of

---

7. John Adair, *Founding Fathers: The Puritans in England and America,* p. 177 (London: J.M. Dent, 1982). There were more progressive elements of the code, such as a ban on husbands' physical punishment of their wives.

8. Pfeffer, pp. 74–75. A limited number of persons actually participated in the governing of the colony, because only those who professed the precise religious doctrines of the Puritans could vote.

9. Joshua Miller, *The Rise and Fall of Democracy in Early America, 1630–1789,* p. 27 (Pennsylvania State Univ. Press, 1991).

10. James Hosmer, ed., *Winthrop's Journal,* Vol. I, p. 303 (Scribner's, 1908).

11. *Id.,* p. 64.

12. *Id.,* p. 67.

13. *Id.,* p. 144.

14. Miller, p. 29.

15. Peleg W. Chandler, *American Criminal Trials,* Vol. I, pp. 4–5 (Boston: Little and Brown, 1841).

16. Levy, p. 246. The term *antimonian* (against the law) was applied to those whose beliefs were similar to Ms. Hutchinson's.

17. *Id.,* p. 247.

doctrine." When she would not, she was excommunicated from the church and banished.

Mary Dyer was another woman whose ideas threatened the Puritans. She was a traveling Quaker minister in England, who came to Boston in 1657. The Massachusetts leaders banished her to Rhode Island, and one year later they passed a law banishing all Quakers, to be enforced by execution. In 1659, Mary Dyer went to Boston with a group of Quakers, "determined to 'look their bloody laws in the face.'"[17a] She was actually led to the gallows before her execution was stayed. When she returned to Boston in 1660, she was sentenced to death and hung.[17b]

Throughout New England, blasphemous speech was severely punished. A Connecticut woman was whipped for giving blasphemous speeches about the Bible and was warned of greater punishment for repeat offenses. In Boston, John Crossman was beaten and had the letter *B* burned into his forehead.[18] The first president of Harvard, Henry Dunster, was convicted for breaching the peace because he gave a sermon on infant baptism.[19]

***Signs of Tolerance in the Colonies.***   Other parts of seventeenth-century America enjoyed greater acceptance of religious expression. Some colonies issued significant documents that expanded individual freedoms. However, free speech was not assured in these jurisdictions.

The greatest tolerance was probably found in Rhode Island. The colony's founder, Roger Williams, had been sanctioned by the Puritans. Their leaders had accused Williams of uttering "divers dangerous opinions"[20] and in 1636 decided to send him back to England. Instead, Williams moved to Providence and set up a community for Baptists, Quakers, and others who did not hold orthodox views. The Rhode Island charter, obtained from the British crown in 1663, allowed the settlers to conduct their "livelie experiment." It provided that persons in the colony could not be punished for differences of opinion in religious matters unless they disturbed the civil peace.[21]

The Maryland Act of Toleration, passed in 1649, gave rights to Christians by ensuring that anyone who professed a belief in Jesus Christ should not be troubled because of his or her religion or "the free exercise thereof."[22] By contrast, Maryland law allowed execution by burning for those who spoke wickedly of God or denied that Jesus Christ was the son of God. In practice,

17a. Margaret Hope Bacon, *Mothers of Feminism: The Story of Quaker Women in America*, p. 26, (Harper & Row, 1986).
17b. *Id.*
18. Levy., p. 253.
19. Leonard W. Levy, *Freedom of Speech and Press in Early American History: Legacy of Suppression*, p. 31 (Harper & Row, 1963). The question of infant baptism was highly controversial in Massachusetts. The Baptists, who opposed the practice, were despised by the Congregationalists, who held the power in the colony.
20. *Winthrop's Journal*, p. 154.
21. Pfeffer, p. 85.
22. *American State Papers on Freedom in Religion*, p. 47 (Religious Liberty Association, 1949).

capital punishment for blasphemy was rare in Maryland (and other colonies), but whippings were not uncommon.[23]

Pennsylvania also professed acceptance of diverse religious viewpoints. The Quakers had been persecuted both in England and in the New World. (The Quakers used some creative forms of **symbolic speech** to respond to these Puritan abuses.)[24] William Penn, who had been imprisoned in England for joining the Quaker sect, acquired the land that would become Pennsylvania and sought to attract settlers with a promise of religious freedom. Pennsylvania's Great Law of 1682 assured that no one who acknowledged one God was to be disturbed because of his religious faith. However, those who did not believe in God received less acceptance.[25] Another limitation on free speech in Pennsylvania was a ban on the use of profanity.[26]

Although religious speech was not truly free in the colonies, one positive seventeenth-century trend was greater tolerance for criticism of government officials. Widener University Professor Larry Eldridge studied the records of 1,244 seditious speech prosecutions in colonial courts. He concluded that "colonists experienced a dramatic expansion of their freedom to criticize government and its officials across the seventeenth century."[27] Eldridge attributed the progress of free speech to both an increase in the stability of colonial governments (making them less threatened by criticism) and a decrease in respect for authority of all types (governmental, religious, and family).[28]

The colonists' increasing insistence on the freedom to criticize their leaders would make conflict inevitable as the British sought to exercise greater control and as tension grew between the people and their elected representatives.

### THE EIGHTEENTH CENTURY

For most of the seventeenth century, the British government was preoccupied by events at home and could not devote much attention to the colonies. Near the end of that century, the Crown took a more active role in asserting control over its American subjects.[29] While the king's representatives in the New World endeavored to control the colonists' expression, the

23. Levy, *Blasphemy*, p. 253.
24. The earliest Quakers to arrive in Boston, Anne Austin and Mary Fisher, had their books burnt by the hangman, and they were imprisoned for five weeks; Chandler, p. 35. Penalties for Quakers in Massachusetts included beating, loss of an ear, and imprisonment without bedding or heat during the winter. Symbolic speech protests by Quakers included appearing naked in public streets and in Puritan churches to symbolize the spiritual nakedness of the Congregationalist church. Levy, *Blasphemy*, p. 257.
25. Pfeffer, p. 89. Sunday was required as a day of rest in Pennsylvania to provide time for reading the scriptures and to forestall the growth of atheism.
26. *Id.*
27. Larry D. Eldridge, *A Distant Heritage: The Growth of Free Speech in Early America*, p. 3 (New York Univ. Press, 1994).
28. *Id.*, pp. 138–139.
29. Leonard Woods Labaree, *Royal Government in America*, p. 173 (Yale Univ. Press, 1930).

people's own representatives often posed the greatest threat to freedom of speech.

### Royal Authorities' Attempts to Control Speech

As you read in chapter 2, freedom of speech was limited in eighteenth-century Britain, and it is no surprise that the king's officials placed constraints on speech in the colonies. In New York, Peter Chocke was prosecuted for calling the governor the worst in the history of the province.[30] In Virginia, four individuals were punished for stirring up sedition, having spread an "evill opinion" of the government.[31] In 1723, a Pennsylvania man was arrested for making derogatory comments about the king. At the man's sedition trial, the judge informed the jury that subjects should "quietly submit themselves to those whom Providence has placed over them," and the defendant was sentenced to forty-one lashes.[32]

The Massachusetts governor and his council were equally unkind to the printed word. The first newspaper in the colonies, Benjamin Harris's *Publick Occurrences Both Foreign and Domestic,* was shut down after its first issue. The governor was upset because an article criticized Indians, allied with the British, for failure to show up for a key attack on the French. Puritan clergy were upset about a story claiming the French king slept with his daughter-in-law; in their opinion, such "lustful" information should not have been provided to the public.[33]

The trial of John Peter Zenger marked a watershed in the efforts of the colonists to assert their freedom of expression. Zenger, publisher of the *New York Weekly Journal,* was jailed for printing several seditious libels that allegedly inflamed the minds of the people with contempt for the king's government (particularly that of unpopular Governor William Cosby).[34] The so-called libels included two ballads celebrating the results of an election of city magistrates, in which most of the candidates opposed to Governor Cosby won. One song insinuated that Cosby and his political allies were "pettyfogging knaves" and promised to "make the scoundrel raskals fly."[35] While awaiting trial, Zenger's wife and friends continued to publish the paper, with Mr. Zenger communicating "thro' the Hole of the Door of the Prison."[36]

At his trial, Zenger was defended by eighty-year-old Philadelphian Andrew Hamilton, one of the most respected lawyers in colonial America. Hamilton argued that Zenger's complaint against the governor was one that every freeborn subject had a right to make, and he told the jury that Zenger could

---

30. Levy, *Freedom of Speech,* p. 23.
31. *Id.,* p. 22.
32. *Id.,* pp. 50–51.
33. Nat Hentoff, *The First Freedom,* pp. 61–62 (Delacorte, 1980).
34. Livingston Rutherfurd, *John Peter Zenger: His Press, His Trial,* pp. 45–46 (Dodd, Mead, reprinted 1941).
35. *Id.,* pp. 38–39.
36. *Id.,* p. 47.

be convicted only if his words were false. Chief Justice De Lancey admonished Hamilton, asserting the British rule that truth was not a defense to the charge of seditious libel.[37] Hamilton disregarded the judge, saying the British rule was reminiscent of the days of the Star Chamber. Hamilton turned to face the jury and asked them to use their best judgment on the issue, noting that Zenger's safety rested with them.[38]

The jury found Zenger not guilty, the citizens in the crowded courtroom responded with "three huzzas," and Hamilton received a dinner at the Black Horse Tavern.[39] Mr. Hamilton was even made an honorary citizen of New York.[40]

The Zenger case created no legal precedent; the law of seditious libel remained unchanged. The jury had simply chosen to ignore the law. The verdict did serve as evidence that public opinion in the colonies would not tolerate the prosecution of those who criticized royal officials. The case drew much interest throughout the colonies, and the Boston and Philadelphia newspapers published detailed descriptions of the proceedings.[41]

The Zenger case was the last seditious libel case tried before royal judges.[42] However, the people's own representatives in colonial assemblies felt no need to extend free speech guarantees to criticism of their actions.

### Colonial Legislatures' Attempts to Control Speech

Colonial assemblies claimed parliamentary privilege to control speech. The privilege was an English concept based on rights possessed by the British parliament, including freedom of speech (for themselves rather than their constituents) and freedom from molestation.[43] Over time, molestation came to mean not just physical assault but also unfavorable words directed against the assembly.[44]

Boston printer James Franklin was one victim of the privilege. In 1722, his *New-England Courant* contained a statement that the government of Massachusetts would pursue a band of pirates "sometime this Month, if the Wind and Weather permit." Both houses of the legislature were offended by Franklin's innuendo that their pirate defense policy was inadequate. They summoned him to appear, and he was imprisoned for breach of privilege until the end of the legislative session.[45] While James was incarcerated, his sixteen-year-old brother, Benjamin Franklin, published the paper. Ben Franklin

37. Rutherfurd, p. 124. The Chief Justice cited *Tutchin's Case,* covered on p. 50 of this text.
38. Michael R. Belknap, *American Political Trials,* pp. 34–35 (Greenwood, 1981).
39. Rutherfurd, p. 126.
40. Belknap, p. 35.
41. Rutherfurd, p. 126.
42. Levy, *Freedom of Speech,* p. 20.
43. Mary Patterson Clarke, *Parliamentary Privilege in the American Colonies,* p. 2 (Yale Univ. Press, 1943).
44. *Id.,* p. 130.
45. Jeffrey A. Smith, *Printers and Press Freedom,* p. 101 (Oxford Univ. Press, 1988).

avoided direct criticism of the legislature's action against his brother, but he did publish the following words penned by anonymous London essayists:

> [I]n those wretched countries where a man cannot call his tongue his own, he can scarce call anything else his own. Whoever would overthrow the liberty of a nation must begin by subduing the freeness of speech.[46]

The New York Assembly was reminiscent of the Star Chamber in the case of Alexander McDougall. A handbill had been circulated criticizing an assembly vote to help supply the King's troops in New York City in return for the governor's authorization of credit. An informant claimed that the anonymous author, a "Son of Liberty," was in fact a merchant named Alexander McDougall. The alleged author was arrested and brought before the House. When McDougall refused to respond to the assembly's questioning, Representative de Noyelles contended that the house could extort his answer through torture.[47] When McDougall provided a written statement of the reasons he would not enter a plea,[48] the Speaker of the House deemed that statement insulting to the honor and dignity of the house. McDougall was then jailed for nearly three months.[49]

Punishment for criticizing the "people's representatives" was not an isolated phenomenon. According to History Professor Mary Patterson Clarke, "scores of people, probably hundreds," were tracked down and brought to colonial assemblies to account for their words.[50]

Once the colonists won the Revolutionary War, the infant nation would be able to establish its own tradition of freedom of speech, with no interference from the British. Would the American people demand, and their representatives approve, strong free speech guarantees? Or would it be more accurate to say that British law on free expression remained in the United States long after the king's troops went home?

## THE NEW NATION ADOPTS THE BILL OF RIGHTS

Scholars differ in their interpretations of the historical evidence regarding the sentiment for free expression in the new American nation. Harvard Law Professor Zechariah Chafee, Sr., perhaps the leading free speech scholar of his era, contended that

> The First Amendment was written by men . . . who intended to wipe out the common law of sedition, and make further prosecutions for criticism of

---

46. Hentoff, pp. 62–63.
47. *Id.,* p. 83. The torture threatened was *peine forte et dure,* in which the victim is spread-eagled and weights are placed on his body. For each day the prisoner is silent, more weights are added.
48. Because the Assembly had already voted that the pamphlet was seditious libel, McDougall did not believe he would obtain a fair trial.
49. Levy, *Freedom of Speech,* p. 85.
50. Clarke, p. 117.

the government, without any incitement to law-breaking, forever impossible in the United States of America.[51]

This viewpoint, endorsed by twentieth-century Supreme Court justices in major freedom of speech opinions,[52] has been criticized by revisionist historians. Professor Leonard Levy from Brandeis University argued that "the persistent image of colonial America as a society in which freedom of expression was cherished is an hallucination of sentiment that ignores history."[53]

Did American citizens and their representatives in the new government voice a strong desire for free speech? The history of the Constitution and the Bill of Rights provides evidence both for and against this proposition.

### Drafters of the Constitution Omit Free Speech

After winning the Revolutionary War, the American people needed a blueprint for self-government. Delegates to the constitutional convention spent the long, hot summer of 1787 working in Philadelphia, and were hoping to submit their work to Congress and return home. The constitution they intended to propose had no bill of rights whatsoever. According to Pennsylvania delegate James Wilson, many of his colleagues had never even thought about such guarantees.[54]

One delegate was troubled by this omission. On September 12, 1787, Virginia's George Mason said he wished the Constitution had included a bill of rights. Mason believed it would "give great quiet" to the people, and said that he could write one in a few hours. Despite Mason's enthusiasm, a motion to have a committee prepare the bill lost 10–0. Another motion to declare that "the liberty of the press should be inviolably observed" was also defeated.[55] No delegate went on record against protecting individual rights;[56] they simply did not believe that a bill of rights was necessary to ensure such protection.

On September 17, 1787, the Constitution was drafted and the Convention adjourned. Each state would then need to vote on approving the document. The ratification issue produced a heated debate in the states. The Federalists, who included Alexander Hamilton, James Madison, and John Jay among their ranks, supported the new Constitution. They believed that the central government needed the power to collect taxes and provide an

---

51. Zechariah Chafee, Jr., *Free Speech in the United States*, p. 21 (Harvard Univ. Press, 1948).
52. See, e.g., *Abrams v. United States* 250 U.S. 616, 630 (1919) (Holmes, J., dissenting), and *N.Y. Times v Sullivan*, 376 U.S. 254, 270 (1964).
53. Levy, *Freedom of Speech*, p. 18.
54. Bernard Schwartz, *The Bill of Rights: A Documentary History*, Vol. II, p. 627 (Chelsea House, 1971).
55. Levy, *Original Intent and the Framers' Constitution*, p. 148 (Macmillan, 1988).
56. George Washington wrote the Marquis de Lafayette, "[T]here was not a member of the Convention, I believe, who had the least objection to what is contended for by the advocates of a Bill of Rights." *The Writings of George Washington*, Vol. 11, pp. 254–59, cited in Schwartz, p. 987–88.

adequate defense for the new nation.[57] The Anti-Federalists[58] were opposed to the Constitution because they believed it gave the national government too much power at the expense of the states.

### Political Pressure for a Bill of Rights

The Anti-Federalists found that their arguments against the Constitution were strengthened by the absence of a bill of rights. Opponents of the Constitution were able to use this issue as a focal point, because, in modern terms, the missing bill was a political "hot-button" issue. The popularity of a bill of rights was manifested in several ways. In states such as Pennsylvania, where the Federalists held a clear majority at the ratifying convention, the minority argued that the Constitution lacked an explicit guarantee of rights.[59] Massachusetts voted to ratify the Constitution, but only after Governor John Hancock submitted nine proposed amendments. Massachusetts' Congressional representatives were directed to use their influence to attempt to have the amendments added to the Constitution.[60] Virginia and New York delegates approved ratification in conjunction with a recommendation that a bill of rights be added. In addition, state documents, such as the Virginia Declaration of Rights and the Pennsylvania Constitution of 1776, included protection of free expression.[61]

The Federalists could see the political benefits of supporting a bill of rights. New York's Governor Clinton sent a letter to other governors in the hope that one of the new Congress's first acts would be to call a convention to consider Constitutional amendments.[62] James Madison, involved in a close election against James Monroe (an Anti-Federalist who supported a bill of rights) changed his position on the issue.[63] Thus, the Constitution was ratified, with a promise that a bill of rights would soon be added.[64]

---

57. Craig R. Smith, *To Form a More Perfect Union: The Ratification of the Constitution and the Bill of Rights 1787–1791*, p. 19 (University Press of America, 1993).
58. The Anti-Federalists preferred to call themselves Democratic Republicans, but Federalist usage of the more derogatory term "Anti-Federalist" led to the common public adoption of the latter term.
59. Craig R. Smith, p. 41.
60. *Id.*, p. 67. These amendments did not include freedom of speech or the press.
61. Virginia's declaration provided that "freedom of the Press is one of the greatest bulwarks of liberty, and can never be restrained but by despotick Governments." Pennsylvania's constitution proclaimed that "the people have a right to freedom of speech, and of writing, and publishing their sentiments."
62. Craig R. Smith, pp. 25–26. The letter was drafted by leading New York Federalists, including Alexander Hamilton.
63. Madison wrote to George Eve, a campaign worker, that the first Congress should prepare amendments making "the most satisfactory provisions for all essential rights, particularly the rights of Conscience in the fullest latitude, [and] the freedom of the press." *The Writings of James Madison*, cited in Schwartz, p. 997.
64. Levy, *Original Intent*, p. 163.

## Debate in the House

James Madison took the lead and introduced a bill of rights to the House on June 8, 1789. Madison's proposal included seventeen amendments, most of which were consistent with those the states had put forward. Freedom of expression was not the most common amendment,[65] but five of the eight states that proposed amendments did include free press guarantees, and three states also added freedom of speech.[66]

Madison's draft included a guarantee of free expression, using language similar to the Virginia and Pennsylvania recommendations.[67] Relatively few statements about this guarantee were made when the House debated the amendments. Madison asked the rhetorical question of whether the amendments (including freedom of speech and press) were not the very ones most strenuously required by the Constitution's opponents.[68] When a clause prohibiting *the states* from infringing on rights such as free expression was being debated, Madison contended that this provision was the most valuable amendment.[69]

The final House version included seventeen amendments. The fourth amendment approved by the House provided that

> The freedom of speech, and of the press, and the right of the people to assemble, and consult for the common good, and to apply to the government for redress of grievances, shall not be infringed.

## Debate in the Senate

The Senate made a significant change to the free speech guarantees proposed by the House. Many opponents of the Constitution believed that the document already placed too many limitations on the states. The Senate therefore changed the House's language to provide that "*Congress* shall make no law abridging The Freedom of Speech, or of the press" (emphasis added).

As a result of the Senate's change, for well over one hundred years the U.S. Constitution would not stand in the way of state efforts to abridge freedom of speech. As you will read later in this chapter, the loss of Madison's "most valuable amendment" would have grave consequences for speakers with unpopular viewpoints.

We have a record of one other argument made in the Senate about freedom of expression. A proposal to specify that freedom of the press was to be

---

65. All eight states wanted powers not delegated to the federal government to be reserved to the states; seven advocated trial by jury; and six supported religious freedom.
66. Schwartz, p. 983.
67. *Id.*, p. 1026. "The people shall not be deprived or abridged of their right to speak, to write, or to publish their sentiments; and the freedom of the press, as one of the great bulwarks of liberty, shall be inviolable."
68. *Id.*, p. 1104.
69. *Id.*, p. 1113.

protected in "as ample a manner as had been secured by common law" was defeated.[70] This was the only effort, during either the House or the Senate proceedings, to add precision to the definition of freedom of speech or press. Because no clear answer can be found in the text of the Constitution, debates about the extent to which it protects free expression have continued for the past two hundred years.[71]

After the Senate made significant changes in the text of the House's draft of the Bill of Rights, the two bodies agreed on the Senate's wording of the amendments, and twelve amendments were sent to the states for approval in October 1789.

### The States Approve the Bill of Rights

Several states, such as New Jersey, Maryland, and North Carolina rapidly approved the amendments to the Constitution. Maryland's vote to approve followed a Senate debate that focused on freedom of the press.[72] Some states, such as Delaware, approved all but the original first or second amendments. These amendments—dealing with the number of representatives and compensation for Congress—were not approved by a sufficient number of states. Consequently, the guarantees of free speech, press, religion, and assembly moved from their original position to become the First Amendment. By November 1791, ten of the eleven states needed had ratified the Bill of Rights,[73] but final passage would not come easily due to Anti-Federalist opposition in other states.

In Massachusetts, the ratification process stalled while Anti-Federalists proposed further amendments to strengthen state power at the expense of Congress.[74] The Anti-Federalists in Virginia's Senate voted to reject several of the amendments, including freedom of speech and press. Another resolution, to put the issue back in the public's hands and hold a referendum on the controversial amendments, narrowly missed adoption by that state's House and Senate. In the end, some key Virginia Anti-Federalists came out in support of the amendments, believing that Congress would do no better and that the Bill of Rights would "inculcate upon the minds of the people, just ideas of their rights."[75] On December 15, 1791, the Virginia Senate concurred with the vote of their colleagues in the House, and the ten amendments that are now the Bill of Rights became part of our Constitution.

70. Craig R. Smith, p. 132.
71. Freedom of speech and press could be construed very narrowly if one adopted English jurist William Blackstone's contention that freedom of the press only means freedom from prior restraints (see Chapter 1, *infra*). At the other end of the spectrum, First Amendment absolutists would argue that there can be no restraints whatsoever on speech. See Justice Black's opinion in *Dennis v United States*, 341 U.S. 494, 580 (1951) (Black, J., dissenting).
72. Craig R. Smith, p. 160.
73. Three-fourths of the states needed to ratify an amendment before it could pass. With the addition of Vermont to the Union, there were fourteen states, necessitating the approval of eleven.
74. Craig R. Smith, p. 163.
75. *Id.*, p. 160.

The Bill of Rights did not prevent states from infringing on speech, and it failed to provide a definition of the freedom of speech that Congress could not abridge. As you will read later in this chapter, the Bill of Rights was not applied to protect the rights of many unpopular speakers, including women, slaves, abolitionists, and social reformers. Nevertheless, the bill is a very significant document in the history of freedom. For the first time, the people of a nation had a written guarantee that certain speech rights were beyond the reach of the national government. This guarantee was adopted through representative democracy, rather than being a product of a generous sacred monarch or a king's royal prerogative. Furthermore, as Thomas Jefferson noted, the existence of an independent judiciary would reduce the risk that a political majority could punish the expression of minority viewpoints.[76] Perhaps most important was the fact that the Bill of Rights created a framework, from which courts of the twentieth century would significantly expand our freedom of speech.

In chapter 2, we noted a pattern in which free speech rights would expand and contract at different times in any given nation's history. The United States proved to be no exception. The passage of the Bill of Rights was a sign of progress for free expression in the infant nation. Within a decade, however, this right was seriously challenged. A law known as the Sedition Act was passed, and it severely tested the American citizens' commitment to freedom of speech.

### THE SEDITION ACT OF 1798

France declared war on England in 1793, and America's loyalties were divided. The Federalists supported Great Britain, and their political opponents, the Republicans, showed more sympathy to the French. The French, believing that the United States favored Britain, initiated attacks on American shipping and broke off diplomatic relations. Tensions were so high that Congress authorized a military buildup; at the same time, President Adams's emissaries were trying to negotiate a settlement with the French. The French negotiators made an insulting secret offer, and once it became public knowledge, opposition to the French was running high throughout the United States.[77]

The Federalists believed that war with France was inevitable. To curb antigovernment speech, they introduced the Sedition Act in Congress. The text of the Sedition Act is found on page 73. The Federalist leaders were tired of being attacked by the Republican press, and it was their belief that the peo-

---

76. Levy, *Original Intent*, p. 164.
77. The French negotiators' demands included a loan from the U.S. government, a bribe for the French Directory, and a public apology for President Adams's speech recommending that Congress prepare for war. Because the Americans had promised not to divulge the names of the French negotiators, President Adams merely referred to them as agents W, X, Y, and Z. The incident became known as the XYZ affair.

ple could be "manipulated" into opposing the Federalist government.[78] In the wake of public dissatisfaction with France's arrogant negotiating stance, they believed that the political climate was ripe for them to push through an anti-sedition law.[79] Federalists in Congress passed the Sedition Law, which President Adams signed on July 14, 1798.

On its face, the Sedition Act should have been barred by the First Amendment. Congress had passed a law that authorized imprisonment for communicators who criticized the government, clearly an abridgment of expression at the core of freedom of speech.[80] Republicans in Congress made this argument,[81] but Federalists countered that the First Amendment merely codified Blackstone's definition,[82] which protected communicators from prior restraint but allowed them to be punished after speaking or publishing.[83]

Federalists also argued that under the Constitution, the federal government possessed an inherent power to protect itself. For example, representatives Otis and Harper maintained that the government could not function "if sedition for opposing its laws, and libels against its officers, itself, and its proceedings, are to pass unpunished."[84]

The Supreme Court never ruled on the Sedition Act's constitutionality. Lower courts did uphold the act, and three Supreme Court justices, while sitting on federal circuit courts, did the same.[85] John Marshall, later to become Chief Justice, was one of few Federalists to oppose the law. But he based his opposition on the belief that the law was useless and counterproductive. Marshall defended the Sedition Act's constitutionality in writing.[86]

The Federalists arrested at least twenty-five people for violations of the Sedition Act, and ten cases resulted in conviction.[87] Prosecutions were initiated against four of the five leading Anti-Federalist newspapers in the country. These included the *Aurora*, whose editor, Benjamin Franklin Bache (Ben

78. Dale A. Herbeck, New York Times v. Sullivan: *Justice Brennan's Beautiful Lie*, 28 Free Speech Yearbook 37, 41 (1990). The Federalists were convinced that since they knew the "truth" about the best policies for the nation, there was no purpose in public discussion of their policies.

79. James Morton Smith, *Freedom's Fetters: The Alien and Sedition Laws and American Civil Liberties*, p. 142 (Cornell Univ. Press, 1956).

80. See, e.g., Alexander Meiklejohn, *Political Freedom: The Constitutional Powers of the People*, p. 27 (Harper, 1948).

81. For example, Representative Albert Gallatin maintained that it was an evasion of the Constitution to say, "You may write and publish what you please, but if you publish anything against us, we will punish you for it. So long as we do not prevent, but only punish your writings, it is no abridgment of your liberty." (*Annals of Congress* [5th Congress, July 10, 1798], pp. 2160).

82. See page 49 of this text.

83. James Morton Smith, p. 136.

84. *Id.*, p. 132. This was the same argument that a British judge made nearly one hundred years earlier, when he upheld the British government's right to punish seditious libels. See page 50 of this text.

85. Thomas I. Emerson, David Haber, and Norman Dorsen, *Political and Civil Rights in the United States*, Vol. I, p. 38 (Little, Brown, 1967).

86. James Morton Smith, p. 151.

87. Emerson et al., p. 37.

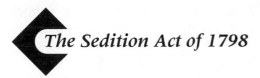

# The Sedition Act of 1798

Section 2. [I]f any person shall write, print, utter or publish . . . any false, scandalous and malicious writing or writings against the government of the United States, or either house of the Congress of the United States, or the President of the United States, with intent to defame . . . or to bring them . . . into contempt or disrepute; or to excite against them . . . the hatred of the good people of the United States, or to stir up sedition within the United States . . . then such person . . . shall be punished by a fine not exceeding two thousand dollars, and by imprisonment not exceeding two years."[1]

[1]*Source: United States Statutes at Large*, Vol. I (1798), pp. 596–97.

Franklin's grandson), had portrayed the Federalists as warmongers.[88] And Luther Baldwin, a common citizen, was convicted because he opined that for all he cared, someone could fire a cannon through President Adams's ass.

A noteworthy victim of the Sedition Act was Republican Congressman Matthew Lyon, the first person put on trial for breaking that law. During his reelection campaign in Vermont, Lyon had often quoted a letter that was critical of President Adams's policies toward France, and concluded by asking why Congress had not sent Adams to the madhouse. Lyon also wrote a letter to the editor of *Spooner's Vermont Journal* contending that the President had "an unbounded thirst for ridiculous pomp, [and] foolish adulation."[89]

Congressman Lyon was convicted for violating the Sedition Act and sentenced to four months in jail. He served that sentence in an unheated cell, sharing his quarters with horse thieves and other vagrant prisoners. According to Lyon, the cell reeked with "a stench about equal to the Philadelphia docks in the month of August."[90]

Thomas Jefferson and James Madison authored resolutions against the Sedition Act, which were adopted by the legislatures of Kentucky and Virginia. Jefferson and Madison feared that this opposition could cause them to be indicted under the act, so they kept their participation secret.[91]

The Sedition Act had an effect on freedom of speech and the press in America, but it was not the one the Federalists had hoped for. After answering

88. Jeffrey A. Smith, p. 160. The Federalists were so upset with Bache's writings that they prosecuted him for common law seditious libel before the Sedition Act had been passed.
89. Aleine Austin, *Matthew Lyon: "New Man" of the Democratic Revolution*, p. 109 (Pennsylvania State Univ. Press, 1981).
90. *Id.*, p. 119.
91. Herbeck, p. 43.

the seditious libel charge in court, Bache noted in the *Aurora* that neither prosecution nor persecution would cause him to abandon the cause of truth. He continued to write that the Sedition Act was unconstitutional.[92] The number of Republican newspapers in the United States rose from fewer than twenty to more than fifty in two years, and their circulation blossomed.[93] Matthew Lyon was reelected to Congress while in jail. The Sedition Act was a major issue in the election of 1800, but it failed to deter frequent attacks on the character of John Adams.[94] When an electoral college tie between presidential candidates Thomas Jefferson and Aaron Burr forced the House of Representatives to select the President, it was Representative Matthew Lyon who cast the deciding vote for Jefferson. The Sedition Act expired March 3, 1801; Jefferson pardoned all defendants who had been convicted under the act, and Congress repaid most of the fines.[95]

Thomas Jefferson had considered the Sedition Act to be an "experiment on the American mind, to see how far it will bear an avowed violation of the Constitution."[96] The American people made it clear that federal punishment of those who criticize government officials would not be tolerated. But the battle for freedom of speech was far from over. The Sedition Act crisis would be replaced by other free speech controversies.

### THE NINETEENTH CENTURY: 1800–1860

### Judicial Decisions Provide Limited Protection for Speech

Although our modern judiciary has often interpreted the Constitution to protect the rights of communicators, the courts of the nineteenth century developed doctrines that were less protective of speech.

One of the most significant limitations on judicial protection of speech was a by-product of an 1833 case, *Barron v. The Mayor and City Council of Baltimore.*[97] In *Barron,* the Supreme Court ruled that the Bill of Rights limited only the authority of Congress, and that these amendments did not protect individuals from state encroachments on their rights.[98] This decision should not be surprising, since concerns about states' rights had caused the Senate to write the First Amendment so that it would limit only Congress's power. The political climate of the 1830s was still strongly supportive of states' rights,[99] and appointees to the Supreme Court shared the public's enthusiasm for state autonomy.

92. Jeffrey A. Smith, p. 160.
93. John C. Miller, *Crisis in Freedom: The Alien and Sedition Acts,* p. 222 (Little, Brown, 1951).
94. As one author described the character attacks, had an innocent bystander heard the arguments, he may have concluded that Adams was on trial for murder and robbery rather than running for president. *Id.,* p. 223.
95. Emerson et al., p. 38.
96. John C. Miller, p. 166.
97. 7 Peters 243 (1833).
98. *Id.,* p. 250.
99. Donald G. Morgan, "The Marshall Court and Civil Liberties," in *Aspects of Liberty,* p. 174.

The Court was reluctant to make decisions that might seem radical to the public. The idea that an independent Supreme Court could nullify the acts of elected representatives was unprecedented.[100] If the American people were to come to accept the legitimacy of the Supreme Court's rulings, even when the decisions were counter to the will of the majority, the Court could not be perceived to be too far out of step with the American people.

The second judicial doctrine that limited the utility of the First Amendment was an acceptance of the Blackstone definition of freedom of the press. Supreme Court Justice Joseph Story's influential treatise on Constitutional Law noted that

> It is plain then, that the language of [the First Amendment] imports no more than that every man shall have a right to speak, write, and print his opinions upon any subject whatsoever, without prior restraint."[101]

Justice Story's treatise went on to note that Blackstone's doctrine had not been repudiated by any state court. In fact, Story's definition of freedom of the press was cited by the courts more often than any other definition in the first half of the nineteenth century.[102]

This limited judicial construction of First Amendment rights was consistent with the attitudes of the American people in that era. Although there was generally strong support for the public's right to criticize their elected officials,[103] speech on controversial issues and speech by oppressed members of society was often constrained.

### No Freedom of Speech for African American Slaves

The male citizens of Greece saw no inconsistency in providing for their own freedom of speech while denying this human right to their slaves. Here, the southern states were guilty of the same flawed reasoning. Many whites in those states feared the possibility of a slave revolt. These states adopted slave codes, which included substantial limits on freedom of expression. The death penalty was imposed for anybody caught planning a slave revolt. Slaves could not hold dances or other social events, nor could black preachers conduct services unless a white person was present. Slaves were not allowed to own horns or drums. Perhaps most significant, in many southern states it was forbidden to teach black slaves how to read and write.[104] Gabriel, Denmark

---

100. It was not self-evident that the Constitution gave the Supreme Court, rather than Congress, the power to decide the meaning of the Constitution. In *Marbury v. Madison*, 1 Cranch 137 (1803), Justice Marshall's opinion asserted that an act of Congress that is repugnant to the Constitution cannot become law. If the American people did not assent to the legitimacy of this ruling, the Court would have found it very difficult to compel acceptance of its decision.

101. Joseph Story, *Commentaries on the Constitution of the United States* (Little and Brown, 1833), quoted in Timothy W. Gleason, *19th Century Legal Practice and Freedom of the Press: An Introduction to an Unfamiliar Terrain*, 14 Journalism History 26, 29 (Spring 1987).

102. *Id.*, p. 30.

103. *Id.*, p. 31.

104. Clement Eaton, *Freedom of Thought in the Old South*, p. 114 (Peter Smith, 1951).

Vesey, and Nat Turner were three major figures who planned or led slave in-
surrections, and all three had been educated.[105] White Southerners also feared
that literate slaves would read about the slave revolt in Haiti and about the
French revolution, and also be incited to revolt by the dreaded abolitionist literature from the north.[106]

The response of slaves to these oppressive codes provides impressive evidence of the human desire to communicate, even under the most difficult of
circumstances. Slaves held clandestine meetings in the night, and news concerning family members who had been sold could be conveyed. The meetings
also served as an opportunity to continue a beloved African tradition, story
telling (see chapter 2). These stories connected slaves to their African past,
and provided a means for them to hand down their perspective of the slavery
experience, rather than being dependent on their masters' versions of
history.[107]

Music also was a means of circumventing the slave codes. By singing
spirituals such as "Go Down, Moses," and "Nobody Knows the Trouble I've
Seen," slaves could protest against bondage.[108] Plantation owners may have
interpreted such singing as evidence of contentment, but in reality the music
served other purposes. Slaves used it as a code, to communicate information
to other plantations and to signal warnings to runaway slaves. They also cir-
cumvented bans on musical instruments. As one slave named Silas Jackson
explained, "we . . . used to take the horn of [a] dead cow or bull, cut the end
off of it, we could blow it, some having different notes. We could tell who was
blowing, and from what plantation."[109]

### Freedom of Speech and the Antislavery Cause

The institution of slavery provoked other free speech battles. Abolitionists were determined to convince the nation of the evils of slavery. William
Lloyd Garrison's fast-growing American Anti-Slavery Society raised the funds
to send one million publications to the southern states. Their literature
showed the horrors of slavery with pictures as well as descriptive language.[110]

Southern states feared the spread of antislavery persuasion. With the
memory of Nat Turner's revolt fresh in the minds of Southerners, they feared
that antislavery publications would incite more slave rebellions.[111] All southern states, except Kentucky, passed legislation that restricted discussion of

105. Gladys-Marie Fry, *Night Riders in Black Folk History*, p. 41 (Univ. of Tennessee Press, 1975).
106. *Id.*, p. 43.
107. *Id.*, pp. 212–13.
108. Leslie Howard Owens, *This Species of Property: Slave Life and Culture in the Old South*, p. 171–72. (Oxford Univ. Press, 1976).
109. *Id.*, pp. 174–75.
110. Donna Lee Dickerson, *The Course of Tolerance: Freedom of the Press in Nineteenth-Century America*, p. 86 (Greenwood, 1990).
111. *Id.*, p. 90. Ex-slave David Walker's "Appeal in Four Articles Together with a Preamble to the Colored Citizens of the World" directly advocated a slave revolt. Harold L. Nelson, *Freedom of the Press From Hamilton to the Warren Court*, p. 167 (Bobbs-Merrill, 1967).

abolitionist issues. A Virginia law punished any person who "by speaking or writing maintains that owners have no right of property in slaves," and Louisiana outlawed conversations "having a tendency to promote discontent among free colored people, or insubordination among slaves."[112]

In addition, southern universities denied faculty and students freedom of discussion about slavery. These forums of higher learning could have provided "progressive thought" on the problem of slavery, but the South had moved beyond the point where even self-criticism was acceptable.[113] Faculty members who renounced the institution of slavery were likely to lose their jobs.[114]

Southern states also attempted to halt the spread of abolitionist literature through the postal system. Virginia passed a law requiring postmasters to notify a judge should they come across mail that encouraged rebellion or denied that slaves were their owners' property. The judge would then have the writings burned in his presence.[115] Acting on their own volition, many postmasters in the South refused to deliver abolitionist literature. Legislation was introduced in Congress to require postmasters to remove antislavery publications from the mail if these were forbidden by state law. Northern senators believed this bill would repeat the mistakes of the Sedition Act, and it was rejected.[116]

However, the North was not blameless when it came to repressing abolitionist speech. Many Northerners were racists, and they assumed that freedom for the slaves would result in black men wandering the streets, taking white jobs, and exercising the right to vote.[117] In 1835, William Lloyd Garrison was dragged through the streets in Boston by an angry mob, who tore off most of his clothes. He was forced to spend the night in jail for his own safety.

The Rev. Elijah Lovejoy, publisher of an antislavery journal, *The Observer*, had his press destroyed three times by the hostile citizens of Alton, Illinois. They passed a resolution insisting that the First Amendment did not apply to abolitionists, who were attempting to incite insurrection and anarchy. When Lovejoy brought in a fourth press, he was attacked and shot to death.[118]

The Lovejoy incident created a martyr, and in the northern states, public attitudes became more supportive of freedom of the press.[119] The abolition controversy increased free expression in another way, when it opened doors for an increasing participation of women in the public debate.

112. Joseph Nye, *Fettered Freedom: Civil Liberties and the Slavery Controversy 1830–60*, p. 175 (Michigan State Univ. Press, 1963).
113. *Id.*, pp. 100–1.
114. Hentoff, p. 90.
115. Nelson, p. 178.
116. Dickerson, p. 103.
117. *Id.*, p. 88. The earliest black newspaper, *Freedom's Journal*, noted in a March 16, 1827, editorial that "our friends . . . seem to have fallen into the current of popular feeling and are . . . actually living in the practice of prejudice, while they adjure it in theory." Herbert Aptheker, *Abolitionism: A Revolutionary Movement*, p. 65 (Boston: Twayne, 1989).
118. Merton L. Dillon, *Elijah P. Lovejoy, Abolitionist Editor*, pp. 66, 169 (Univ. of Illinois Press, 1961).
119. Nye, pp. 127–28.

### Free Speech Rights for Women

In chapter 2, you read how the free speech rights of women usually lag behind those of men in any given culture. The United States is no exception. The Constitution did not deny First Amendment rights to women, but sexist attitudes and traditions placed severe limitations on their exercise of free speech. In the 1820s, the prevailing belief was that women who wanted to speak in public were unwomanly and irreligious.[120] One of the first women to defy these conventions was Frances Wright. She advocated equal rights for women, challenged established religion, and supported workers' rights. She lectured to workers in many cities, and her opponents' typical response was to label her an atheist and a supporter of free love. Men would show their disdain for future women's rights advocates by calling them "Fanny Wrightists."[121]

The educational system limited women's opportunities to obtain the training needed to participate in public affairs. Conventional wisdom held that women did not need a formal education, for their lives would be spent in the home. Even when higher education became available to women, the colleges' objective was to prepare "daughters of the land to be good mothers."[122]

Oberlin College, in Ohio, was the first college to admit students of any race or gender, but even that liberal institution did not provide an equal education for women. Initially, women took an easier course of study, because it was believed that they would have more difficulty learning than men. Antoinette Brown and Lucy Stone, frustrated by the lack of any oratorical opportunities in the women's courses, organized a debating society. Meetings took place in an African American woman's home on the edge of town, and occasionally in the woods, where a guard was posted to warn of intruders.[123] Later, advanced coeducational courses were offered; but women, who had been socialized not to speak in the presence of men, requested separate classes in rhetoric.[124]

The abolitionist movement created new opportunities for women. Women gathered most of the signatures on the petitions against slavery that were sent to Congress.[125] In 1839, abolitionist women began dissolving their auxiliary organizations, took offices in the American Anti-Slavery Society, and gave increasing numbers of public lectures.[126] Angelina Grimke was one of the

---

120. Angela Howard Zophy, ed., *Handbook of American Women's History*, p. 499 (Garland, 1990).
121. Eleanor Flexner, *Century of Struggle: The Woman's Rights Movement in the United States*, pp. 27–28 (Belknap, 1975).
122. Daphne Spain, *Gendered Spaces*, p. 145 (Univ. of North Carolina Press, 1992).
123. Ellen Carol DuBois, *Feminism and Suffrage: The Emergence of an Independent Women's Movement in America*, p. 29 (Cornell Univ. Press, 1978).
124. *Id.*, p. 126.
125. Malvina Halberstam and Elizabeth F. Defeis, *Women's Legal Rights: International Covenants an Alternative to ERA?*, p. 10 (Transnational, 1987).
126. DuBois, *The Elizabeth Cady Stanton–Susan B. Anthony Reader*, p. 8 (Northeastern Univ. Press, 1992).

most effective speakers for the Society. An eloquent orator, she pulled audiences into her presentations with descriptions of abuse she had witnessed while growing up in South Carolina.[127] Other women who would later become leaders in the women's rights movement, such as Elizabeth Cady Stanton, Susan B. Anthony, and Lucy Stone, were also active in the Society.[128]

This effort by women to take a more active role in public speaking was not welcomed in all segments of society. A pastoral letter written by the Massachusetts Council of Congregationalist Ministers chastised Angelina Grimke and her sister Sarah, noting that "when [a woman] assumes the place and tone of man as a public reformer . . . her character becomes unnatural."[129] Elizabeth Cady Stanton wrote to Susan B. Anthony of the pain she felt when her father, whom she adored, was critical of her efforts:

> I cannot tell you how deep the iron entered my soul. I never felt more keenly the degradation of my sex. To think that all in me of which my father would have felt a proper pride had I been a man, is deeply mortifying to him because I am a woman. . . . They [her father and husband] are not willing that I should write even on the woman question. But I will both write and speak.[130]

Even the 1840 World Anti-Slavery Convention, in London, refused to admit the American female delegates.

Societal attitudes against women addressing a *promiscuous* audience (one in which men and women are present) provided another barrier to free expression, particularly in the 1830s. The use of that pejorative label had a chilling effect, as women engaged in "promiscuous" communication would hardly be viewed as moral. When women addressed men, society would assume that they were relying on their powers of seduction, rather than rational argument, to persuade.[131]

The societal barriers that worked against women's exercise of their constitutional rights convinced female orators that their plight was similar to that of the slaves. Sarah Grimke's *Letters on the Equality of the Sexes* discussed the ways in which slaves and women were denied basic human liberties.[132] Under the leadership of Elizabeth Cady Stanton, the first women's rights convention was held in 1848, at Seneca Falls, New York. One of the most noteworthy resolutions passed at the convention was the Declaration of Sentiments, modeled on the Declaration of Independence. This document argued that women were

---

127. Zophy, p. 242. Grimke's pamphlet, *An Appeal to Christian Women in the South*, asked women to appeal to their husbands and sons to end slavery. The pamphlet was burned and a warrant for her arrest was issued in South Carolina. *Id.*
128. DuBois, *The Elizabeth Cady Stanton–Susan B. Anthony Reader*, p. 8.
129. Elizabeth Ann Bartlett, *Letters on the Equality of the Sexes and Other Essays*, p. 2 (Yale Univ. Press, 1988).
130. DuBois, *The Elizabeth Cady Stanton–Susan B. Anthony Reader*, pp. 58–59.
131. Susan Zaeske, *The "Promiscuous Audience" Controversy and the Emergence of the Early Woman's Rights Movement*, 81 Quarterly Journal of Speech 191, 197–98 (May 1995).
132. Bartlett, p. 18.

equal to men, and contended that women should have all the rights and privileges of U.S. citizens.[133]

In the aftermath of the Seneca Falls convention, more women began to speak in public. Susan B. Anthony, Amelia Bloomer, and Rev. Antoinette Brown were the first women to lecture publicly in Manhattan; three thousand people attended. Historian Phoebe Hanaford estimated that by 1876, more than thirty women had achieved national recognition for their public speaking.[134]

## THE CIVIL WAR

In times of war, civil liberties are often given a low priority by governments fearing that any dissention will compromise the war effort. The Civil War was no exception.

### Curtailment of Speech Rights in the North

President Lincoln took direct actions to establish censorship during the war. After seizing control of the telegraph lines, he claimed the right to censor all transmissions. In addition, he suspended *habeas corpus*, the process under which a person can challenge the legality of his or her arrest. Lincoln took this action despite a judicial ruling that this power belonged only to Congress and not the President.[135] After *habeas corpus* was suspended, people were arrested for communicative acts, including expressing satisfaction with a Confederate victory, displaying Confederate emblems, and singing Confederate songs.[136]

Military and government officials were particularly intolerant of the "Copperhead press." Copperheads, named after the poisonous snake, were northern Democrats who opposed abolitionism and the war. According to a reference book of that era, authorities suppressed more than two dozen newspapers during the Civil War.[137] General Ambrose Burnside issued an order terminating publication of the *Chicago Times*, because it repeatedly expressed disloyal and incendiary sentiments.[138] Although President Lincoln countermanded Burnside's order in Chicago, Lincoln subsequently suspended the *New York World* and *New York Journal of Commerce*, and ordered the arrest of their proprietors.[139] The two newspapers had reported that the President wrote a letter announcing that 400,000 additional men were to be drafted. When the letter was revealed to be a forgery perpetrated by two Wall Street

133. Halberstam and Defeis, p. 9.
134. Zophy, p. 499.
135. Chief Justice Taney, while sitting on a Maryland appeals court, heard a case challenging Lincoln's suspension of *habeas corpus* and ruled that the Constitution does not give this power to the President. Linfield, p. 26.
136. *Id.*, p. 27.
137. *The American Annual Cyclopaedia and Register of Important Events, 1862–1865* (Appelton, 1862–75), cited in Dickerson, p. 165.
138. Nelson, pp. 230–31.
139. *Id.*, pp. 232–33.

speculators who hoped to profit from rising gold and silver prices, Lincoln rescinded the order to arrest the newspapers' editors.[140]

## Freedom of Speech in the Confederacy

Professor Stephen Smith's study of free expression in the Confederate states concluded that practices in the South did not significantly differ from those in the North.[141] For white Southerners, the Confederate constitution mirrored the First Amendment's guarantees of freedom of speech and press.[142] However, the slave codes insured that African Americans did not share in this freedom.

Wartime restrictions imposed by the Confederates were similar to those of their northern counterparts. Telegraph lines were censored, and the Confederate Congress authorized the President to suspend *habeas corpus*. The Confederate military sometimes took censorship into their own hands. For example, General Earl Van Dorn declared that in his jurisdiction, it would be illegal to speak or write anything that would impair Confederate currency or decrease confidence in Confederate officers.[143] A Georgia regiment, enraged by pro-Union editorials in the Raleigh *Standard*, raided the newspaper's office and scattered type in the street.[144]

Southern newspapers often criticized Confederate President Jefferson Davis. Although the press faced verbal attacks in Congress,[145] newspapers were not suppressed. When Davis was asked about suppressing a hostile Richmond newspaper, he responded that "there would be nothing gained to win independence by losing liberties."[146] William Brownlow, a pro-Union editor of the *Knoxville Whig*, was arrested for writing editorials against the Confederacy; Davis ordered Brownlow released and allowed him to go north.[147]

### AFTER THE WAR: TO 1917

In the fifty years following the Civil War, the American public was exposed to a plethora of new ideas. These included birth control, workers' rights, and radical new forms of government for the United States. Before the war,

---

140. Dickerson, p. 178. The speculators had noticed the rise of gold and silver prices in response to previous announcements that more men were to be drafted; they were arrested for forgery.
141. Stephen A. Smith, "Freedom of Expression in the Confederate States of America," in *Perspectives on Freedom of Speech*, p. 45 (Southern Illinois Univ. Press, 1987).
142. Article I, Section 9.12 provided that "Congress shall make no law . . . abridging the freedom of speech, or of the press." Marshall DeRosa, *The Confederate Constitution of 1861*, p. 142 (Univ. of Missouri Press, 1991).
143. Stephen A. Smith, p. 35.
144. Dickerson, p. 199.
145. House Speaker Bocok suggested that the Richmond *Examiner* should be destroyed and its editors hanged. Merton Coulter, *The Confederate States of America*, p. 503 (Louisiana State Univ. Press, 1950).
146. *Id.*
147. Stephen A. Smith, p. 39.

there had been a basic consensus of values among the American people. Afterwards, urbanization, industrialization, and immigration led to a breakdown of America's homogeneity.[148] These new ideas threatened the established order, and reactionaries "banded together to impose their views of a properly ordered society on the entire nation."[149]

### Anthony Comstock and the Obscenity Controversy

No crusader was more determined to impose his moral standards on the American people than Anthony Comstock. While working in a New York City dry goods store, Comstock reacted to the sexually explicit reading material of his co-workers with great offense. He became determined to save the American people from a great sin, and in 1872 joined with the Young Men's Christian Association (YMCA) to create the Committee for the Suppression of Vice.[150]

Comstock and his committee were highly successful. In 1873 they pressured Congress to pass the Comstock Act. This law prohibited the mailing of obscene books, pamphlets, newspapers, and periodicals.[151] The Committee was active in the enforcement of this new law: Comstock would ferret out offenders by ordering suspected works in the mail under an assumed name. In New York State, the criminal code was amended to allow vice society agents to be deputized and to arrest persons caught violating any state or federal obscenity law. Many other states passed their own versions of "little Comstock laws" to combat obscenity.[152]

Under the Comstock Act, Aristophanes' *Lysistrata* (see p. 36) was banned from the mails, and French masterpieces were taken from a New York art gallery. Comstock was particularly offended by the works of George Bernard Shaw. After Comstock attacked Shaw's play *Mrs. Warren's Profession,* which dealt with prostitution, the playwright created the term "Comstockery" to refer to excessive prudery.[153]

Comstock traveled 200,000 miles in his mission to save the country from sin. Thanks to his efforts, about 700 persons were arrested, resulting in 300 prison sentences and $60,000 in fines.[154]

The federal courts of this era did not confront the question of whether anti-obscenity laws violated the First Amendment. Employing the British definition of obscenity announced in *Reg. v. Hicklin*, a federal circuit court upheld D. M. Bennet's conviction for mailing *Cupid's Yokes.*[155] The Hicklin definition

148. Alexis J. Anderson, *The Formative Period of First Amendment Theory, 1870–1915,* 24 American Journal of Legal History 56, 58 (January 1980).
149. Margaret A. Blanchard, *Revolutionary Sparks: Freedom of Expression in Modern America,* p. 3 (Oxford Univ. Press, 1992).
150. *Id.,* p. 15.
151. Bosmajian, *Obscenity,* pp. iii–iv.
152. Blanchard, pp. 17–18.
153. *Id.,* p. 21.
154. Joan Dash, *A Life of One's Own: Three Gifted Women and the Men They Married,* p. 27 (Harper & Row, 1973).
155. Bosmajian, *Obscenity,* p. iv. Bennet was caught when he mailed a book to one G. Brackett, a pseudonym used by Anthony Comstock. The *Hicklin* case is discussed in chapter 2 of this text.

provided a very low threshold for finding a work obscene. In the 1883 case of *United States v. Bretton,* the Court held that

It is not a question of whether it would corrupt the morals of every person. . . . It is within the law if it would suggest impure and libidinous thoughts in the minds of the young and inexperienced."[156] ◆◆◆

## Margaret Sanger and the Birth Control Movement

Margaret Sanger also challenged the morals of established society. In 1914, she began publishing *The Woman Rebel,* a monthly newspaper devoted to the interests of working women. Sanger believed that a woman's right to control her own body included freedom from involuntary pregnancy; the term *birth control* was first used in her newspaper.[157] When Sanger wrote that she was going to publish information about birth control in *The Woman Rebel,* post office officials told her that her newspaper violated obscenity laws and would be banned from the mail.

Sanger defied the post office and published eight issues of *The Woman Rebel.* She had decided to print the birth control information in a different pamphlet, but the government indicted her anyway. The charge was that she had printed an article, "In Defense of Assassination," in *The Woman Rebel.* To some, the agenda behind the indictment was a desire to persecute Sanger for her birth control advocacy. While her trial was pending, she received significant support. British dignitaries such as H. G. Wells and Dr. Marie Stopes wrote President Wilson and defended freedom of speech on birth control. Segments of the media came to Sanger's defense, and even some socially prominent women supported her.[158] The government decided to dismiss the charges. Margaret Sanger toured the country to promote the cause of birth control,[159] and she was instrumental in making her cause a national movement.

## The Free Speech Campaigns of the IWW

The Industrial Workers of the World, or "Wobblies," posed a different threat to the established order. Their goal was to abolish capitalism and replace it with egalitarian socialism. Unlike more established unions, they accepted workers from all walks of life—including itinerants, immigrants, and people of color (see Figure 3.1).[160]

156. *Id.*
157. Zophy, p. 667.
158. Dash, pp. 48–49. These women included Sanger's childhood friend, Mrs. Thomas Hepburn, the mother of Katharine Hepburn. *Id.,* p. 49.
159. While in Portland, Oregon, Sanger was arrested for distributing *Family Limitation,* which was not supposed to be illegal in that state. Hundreds of women followed her to jail, and the police had to lock the doors to keep them out. The publicity generated by this arrest led to a barrage of requests for *Family Limitation.* Dash, p. 51.
160. Hentoff, pp. 102–3.

*Figure 3.1. Elizabeth Gurley Flynn, activist in the Industrial Workers of the World's "free speech" campaigns. In this 1909 picture, she is with IWW leader William D. ("Big Bill") Haywood (right) and Socialist speaker Hubert Harrison.* (From The Rebel Girl: An Autobiography *by Elizabeth Gurly Flynn. International Publishers (1973), p. 98. Used by permission of International Publishers Company, New York.)*

Freedom of speech was an integral part of the IWW's recruiting efforts. IWW speakers would go to the skid rows of western towns and stand on soapboxes while making their appeal for members.[161]

Many communities responded by passing ordinances that outlawed speaking on the streets where workers tended to congregate.[162] The IWW responded with free speech campaigns. Their strategy was to have one speaker address the crowd, get arrested,[163] and then be replaced by another IWW member. Large numbers of Wobblies would participate in these protests, and it was not uncommon for jails to be filled beyond capacity as each replacement speaker was arrested.[164]

---

161. Terry W. Cole, "The Right to Speak: The Free Speech Fights of the Industrial Workers of the World," in *Perspectives on Freedom of Speech,* p. 47.
162. Blanchard, p. 46.
163. Id. The police would arrest the Wobblies regardless of the content of their speech. One member was arrested for reading the Declaration of Independence.
164. Donald E. Winters, Jr., *The Soul of the Wobblies,* pp. 52–53 (Greenwood, 1985).

The IWW organized more than twenty free speech protests in different cities, and police brutality was the typical response. In San Diego, Wobblies were forced to run a gauntlet of men with whips, after which they had to kiss the flag and sing the national anthem. In Fresno, they were "showered" by high-pressure fire hoses. In Spokane, during the middle of winter, they were first placed in sweatboxes and then moved into unheated cells.[165] When two boatloads of Wobblies attempted to sail into Everett, Washington, for a free speech campaign, they were fired on by police and vigilantes, leading to seven deaths.[166]

Why was the First Amendment often unavailable to protect the rights of political protesters and social reformers? One major reason was the Supreme Court's narrow interpretation of the First Amendment during the period from the Civil War to World War I.

### Judicial Decisions on Free Expression, 1866–1917

It would appear that the First Amendment was largely ignored by the courts prior to World War I.[167] Many of the free speech issues you have read about in this chapter involve communicators whose speech rights were not protected. Nevertheless, this does not mean that the courts were avoiding free speech cases. More accurately, judicial doctrines were failing to extend protection to speech.

*Free Speech and Press Guarantees Applied Only to Congressional Acts.* In 1907, *Patterson v. Colorado*[168] gave the Supreme Court an opportunity to revisit the doctrine that the First Amendment only prevents *Congress* from restricting speech and the press. In *Patterson*, the defendant was held in contempt of court for publishing articles and a cartoon that impugned the motives of the state supreme court. The Court did not discuss the legitimacy of state limitations on free expression. Instead, it held that even if free speech and press were protected from state abridgment, the purpose of the speech and press clause was to prevent "all such previous restraints upon publications, as had been practiced by other governments.[169] In other words, the doctrine of Blackstone was alive and well.

Infringement on First Amendment rights by private citizens was tolerated in *United States v. Cruikshank*.[170] This case involved African American citizens in Louisiana, who wanted to meet for political purposes. The defendants—whites opposed to these gatherings—were charged with banding together to threaten

165. Cole, p. 50.
166. Winters, p. 103.
167. David M. Rabban, *The First Amendment in Its Forgotten Years*, 90 Yale Law Journal 514, 515–16 (January 1981). Even the Supreme Court wrote that "no important case involving free speech was decided by this Court prior to *Schenck v United States*" (*Dennis v United States*, 341 U.S. 494, 503) (1951).
168. 205 U.S. 454 (1907).
169. *Id.* at 462.
170. 92 U.S. 542 (1876).

and intimidate citizens of African descent and prevent them from exercising their constitutional rights. The Supreme Court rejected this cause of action against the defendants, ruling that the First Amendment protected citizens only from congressional abridgments of speech.[171]

*Freedom of Expression Did Not Apply to Films.*   The nation was suspicious of the new medium of motion pictures. Community leaders feared *The Great Train Robbery* because it involved crime and violence. Congress barred films of prizefights from interstate commerce, because one film showed African American heavyweight champion Jack Johnson defeating Jim Jefferies, a white former champion.[172] Many states and localities responded to public fears of motion pictures by establishing censorship boards.

*Mutual Film Corporation v. Industrial Commission of Ohio*[173] involved a challenge to an Ohio law creating a censorship board for films. The board of censors was to approve only films that were "of a moral, educational, or amusing and harmless character."[174] The Supreme Court rejected Mutual's First Amendment challenge to the law, ruling that although motion pictures may be mediums of thought—like the circus and other shows and spectacles—it would be wrong to extend the guarantee of free speech to "the multitudinous shows which are advertised on the billboards of our cities and towns."[175]

*The Government Could Control Speech When It Owned the Place or Means of Communication.*   William Davis had been preaching on public property, the Boston Common, without a permit from the mayor. A Boston ordinance made it illegal to make a public address, on any public grounds, except in accordance with a permit from the mayor. The defendant argued that the Common belonged to the people of the city, and has been used by the public in many ways, including the preaching of the gospel. In *Davis v. Massachusetts,*[176] the Supreme Court rejected this argument, and upheld the ordinance. The Court held that "for the legislature absolutely or conditionally to forbid public speaking in a highway or public park is no more an infringement of the rights of a member of the public than for the owner of a private house to forbid it in his house."[177]

Congress justified control of the mails using similar analysis. When considering a case called *In the Matter of Orlando Jackson,*[178] the Court upheld a ban on sending lottery information in the mails. Justice Stephen Field's majority opinion noted that because Congress has the power to regulate the entire postal system, it could decide what should and should not be carried. The

171. *Id.* at 552.
172. Blanchard, pp. 51–53.
173. 236 U.S. 230 (1915).
174. *Id.* at 240.
175. *Id.* at 243.
176. 167 U.S. 43 (1897).
177. *Id.* at 47.

Court did not find a First Amendment violation, because Congress was merely refusing to allow *its facilities* to be used to distribute matter deemed injurious to public morals.

### SUMMARY

This chapter began by indicating that freedom of speech did not easily take hold in the colonies. Ironically, the people who fled religious intolerance in Europe were intolerant of others' expression here. As the British exercised greater control of their colonies in the 1700s, clashes between colonists and the agents of the Crown intensified.

Following the American Revolution, the new Constitution made no provision for freedom of speech. This right was included in the Bill of Rights, but its inclusion was as much a product of *realpolitik* as of principled decision making. The First Amendment did not prevent the federal government from enforcing the Sedition Act in 1798, and it did not apply to state abridgments of speech for more than one hundred years after that.

In the 1800s, our legal system did recognize a constitutionally protected right of expression. Unfortunately, that right was seldom enforced to protect persons with divergent views—abolitionists, women's rights advocates, labor agitators, or the critics of government during time of war.

Significant developments in our free speech rights would not begin until well into the twentieth century. The remaining chapters of this text will show how, in a variety of contexts, the Supreme Court has taken a stronger role in protecting our freedom of expression.

178. 96 U.S. 727 (1878).

# CHAPTER 4    *Objectives*

**After reading chapter 4,
you should understand
the following:**

◆ *The conflict between protecting free
expression and protecting society by limiting speech that may persuade audience
members to break the law.*

◆ *The context of typical incitement to illegal conduct cases, which involve prosecution of communicators who critique social conditions and advocate reform of
government policy—two subjects that are
central to the purposes of the First
Amendment.*

◆ *The evolution of First Amendment
protection, from the weak "bad tendency"
test of Schenck v. United States to the significantly more protective test announced
in Brandenburg v. Ohio.*

◆ *The landmark minority opinions of
justices Holmes and Brandeis in Abrams,
Gitlow, and Whitney, which developed
the marketplace of ideas theory and provided the reasoning by which future Court
majorities would expand freedom of
speech.*

◆ *The significance of Gitlow v. New
York, which applied freedom of speech
guarantees to the actions of the stage governments.*

◆ *The diverse theories of jurists and
scholars, which give students the background to develop their own viewpoints
on when speech that may lead to illegal
conduct should be regulated.*

*Incitement to Illegal Conduct*

THERE IS AN INEVITABLE tension between protecting freedom of speech and reducing the risk that speech will inspire others to break the law. We maximize our freedom of speech when all expression is protected, including inflammatory political rhetoric, songs that glorify violence and drug abuse, and even the inane expressions of television characters who cackle moronically at the sight of burning objects.[1] Throughout American history, however, the forces of law and order have feared the power of persuasive communication as an instigator of unlawful actions. Can the marketplace of ideas tolerate incitement of illegal conduct? Should a line be drawn? How high should the probability be that any instance of speech will cause illegal conduct before our society is willing to place limits on freedom of speech?

To understand the complexity of this issue, consider the following hypothetical situation: Jake, a college student, is studying the rhetoric of animal liberation in his rhetorical criticism course. His professor, Sally Goodheart, is an activist on this issue. As part of her course, students study the effectiveness of various rhetorical strategies employed by the animal liberation movement. This includes the rhetorical implications of acts of "liberation," whereby activists break into testing laboratories and free research animals. Dr. Goodheart has a fine rapport with her students and invites several of them to dinner. During the vegetarian meal, she expresses her outrage at the ongoing chemical testing on rabbits at a local cosmetics facility. All the students nod in agreement, at which point Prof. Goodheart produces a pamphlet that she intends to distribute. The pamphlet calls for a boycott of the perfume in question and includes a "call upon the conscience of all

---

1. After watching MTV's notorious *Beavis and Butthead* show, one young fan set his family's home on fire, resulting in the death of his two-year-old sister. See Laura W. Brill, *The First Amendment and the Power of Suggestion: Protecting "Negligent" Speakers in Cases of Imitative Harm*, 94 Columbia Law Review 984, 985 (April 1994).

good people to do whatever is necessary to end the suffering of these animals, and free them once and for all."

Animal liberation activists have caused no trouble at the perfume factory to date. Would law enforcement officials be justified in seizing the pamphlets and arresting Dr. Goodheart for trying to encourage breaking and entering, vandalism, or theft at the facility? Would your answer change if you knew that the day after the dinner, Jake was arrested for breaking into the factory and trying to free some of the animals? What if the police found Dr. Goodheart's pamphlet in Jake's pocket?

This chapter chronicles the Supreme Court's efforts to address the issue of where to draw the line on incitement to illegal conduct. Think about how you might resolve the issue of Dr. Goodheart's pamphlet as you read the Court's analysis on the incitement issue. Under the test followed by the Court in each case, would Professor Goodheart be punished? Do you agree, or would you resolve the case differently?

### THE CLEAR AND PRESENT DANGER TEST

World War I provided the context for the development of an incitement to illegal conduct doctrine. Once the federal government made the decision to enter the war, it was determined to ensure that no dissidents would cause any risk to U.S. military capabilities. That determination was manifested, in part, by the Espionage Act of 1917 (see p. 91), which punished certain types of speech that could impair the war effort.

The Espionage Act was aggressively enforced during World War I. Although scholars have concluded that no spies or saboteurs were punished for violating the act, more than two thousand people were prosecuted because they expressed antiwar ideas. More than half of the defendants were convicted.[2] It was criminal to say that war was contrary to the teachings of Christ, or to criticize the Red Cross or the Y.M.C.A. States passed their own repressive espionage acts. In Minnesota, it was a crime for a person to tell women who were knitting socks for servicemen that "no soldier ever sees these socks," because this obstructed the war effort.[3]

Critics of the war who were convicted for violating the Espionage Act did not submit meekly. Several defendants appealed their convictions on the grounds that their expression was protected by the First Amendment. Some of these appeals reached the Supreme Court, which needed to formulate a doctrine to govern cases where communicators were alleged to be inciting illegal conduct.

2. Margaret A. Blanchard, *Revolutionary Sparks: Freedom of Expression in Modern America*, p. 76 (Oxford University Press, 1992).
3. Zechariah Chafee Jr., *Free Speech in the United States*, p. 51 (Harvard Univ. Press, 1948).

# The Espionage Act of 1917, as Amended, 1918

Section 3 of the Espionage Act prohibited a wide variety of antigovernment speech. The prohibitions extended to

—Anyone who shall willfully make false reports or false statements with intent to interfere with the operation or success of the military . . . of the United States, . . .

—or shall willfully make or convey false reports or false statements or say or do anything except by way of bona fide and not disloyal advice to an investor or investors, with intent to obstruct the sale by the United States of bonds or other securities of the United States. . . .

—and whoever, when the United States is at war, shall willfully cause or attempt to cause, or incite or attempt to incite, insubordination, disloyalty, mutiny, or refusal of duty, in the military or naval forces of the United States, or shall willfully obstruct or attempt to obstruct the recruiting or enlistment service of the United States, and

—whoever, when the United States is at war, shall willfully utter, print, write, or publish any disloyal, profane, scurrilous, or abusive language about the form of government of the United States, or the Constitution of the United States, or the military or naval forces of the United States, or the flag of the United States, or the uniform of the Army or Navy of the United States in contempt, scorn, contumely, or disrepute, or

—shall willfully utter, print, write, or publish any language intended to incite, provoke, or encourage resistance to the United States, or to promote the cause of its enemies,

—or shall willfully display the flag of any foreign enemy,

—or shall willfully by utterance, writing, printing, publication, or language spoken, urge, incite or advocate any curtailment of production in this country of any thing or things, product or products, necessary or essential to the prosecution of the war in which the United States may be engaged, with intent by such curtailment to cripple or hinder the United States in the prosecution of the war. . . .

shall be punished by a fine of not more than \$10,000 or imprisonment for not more than twenty years, or both.[1]

[1] Source: 40 U.S. Statutes at Large (1918), pp. 553–54.

◆◆◆

### The Origin of the Clear and Present Danger Test

The Court's first important ruling in the Espionage Act cases came in *Schenck v. United States.* Because this is the first Supreme Court opinion to be considered in detail in this text, we will provide some guidelines on reading judicial opinions.

*Studying Judicial Decisions: A Note to the Reader.* At this point in your text, you will begin to study major twentieth-century Supreme Court decisions on freedom of speech. This text's presentation of the *Schenck* case will be similar to the way that we will present other major cases. You will read a significant portion of the Supreme Court's opinion in these cases. In some instances, you will also read concurring and/or dissenting opinions, which do not make law but often contain a point of view on free speech issues that you should be aware of. In some cases, the author of a dissenting opinion has offered important insights on freedom of speech, which were eventually accepted by a majority of the Court.

As you read text excerpted from the Court's opinions, try to answer these three important questions:

1. What communication by the defendant led to his or her conviction?

2. What test did the Court use to decide if the defendant's conviction was constitutional? What reasons, if any, did the Court give for employing this test?

3. How did the Court apply the test to the defendant's communication to decide if his or her free speech rights were violated?

Consider these questions as you read *Schenck v United States.* Example answers are included in your text following the *Schenck* opinion (see p. 94).

### The Schenck Decision.

### Schenck v. United States, 249 U.S. 47 (1919)

Mr. Justice Holmes delivered the opinion of the court:

The first [count of the indictment] charges a conspiracy to violate the Espionage Act of June 15, 1917, by causing and attempting to cause insubordination, etc., in the military and naval forces of the United States, and to obstruct the recruiting and enlistment service of the United States. [It is alleged that] the defendant willfully conspired to have printed and circulated to men who had been called and accepted for military service, . . . a document set forth and alleged to be calculated to cause such insubordination and obstruction. . . .

The defendants were found guilty on all counts. They set up the 1st Amendment to the Constitution, forbidding Congress to make any law abridging the freedom of speech or of the press [as a defense]. . . .

According to the testimony, Schenck said he was general secretary of the Socialist Party and had charge of the Socialist headquarters from which the documents were sent. . . . [According to the minutes of the executive committee of the party,] there was a resolve that Comrade Schenck be allowed $125 for sending leaflets through the mail. He said that he had about fifteen or sixteen thousand printed. . . .

The document in question, upon its first printed side, recited the 1st section of the 13th Amendment,[4] said that the idea embodied in it was violated by the Conscription Act, and that a conscript is little better than a convict. In impassioned language it intimated that conscription was despotism in its worst form and a monstrous wrong against humanity, in the interest of Wall Street's chosen few. It said, "Do not submit to intimidation"; [but in form at least confined itself to peaceful measures, such as a petition for the repeal of the act.] . . . It denied the power to send our citizens away to foreign shores to shoot up the people of other lands. . . .

Of course the document would not have been sent unless it had been intended to have some effect, and we do not see what effect it could be expected to have upon persons subject to the draft except to influence them to obstruct the carrying of it out. The defendants do not deny that the jury might find against them on this point.

*But it is said, suppose that was the tendency of this circular, it is protected by the 1st Amendment to the Constitution* (emphasis added). We admit that in many places and in ordinary times the defendants, in saying all that was said in the circular, would have been within their constitutional rights. But the character of every act depends upon the circumstances in which it is done. *The most stringent protection of free speech would not protect a man in falsely shouting fire in a theater, and causing a panic. . . . The question in every case is whether the words used are used in such circumstances and are of such a nature as to create a clear and present danger that they will bring about the substantive evils that Congress has a right to prevent* (emphasis added).

It is a question of proximity and degree. When a nation is at war many things that might be said in time of peace are such a hindrance to its effort that their utterance will not be endured so long as men fight, and that no court could regard them as protected by any constitutional right.

It seems to be admitted that if an actual obstruction of the recruiting service were proved, liability for words that produced that effect might be enforced. . . . If the act (speaking, or circulating a paper), its tendency and the intent with which it is done, are the same, we perceive no ground for saying that success alone warrants making the act a crime. ◆◆◆

***More Defeats for Free Speech.*** The Court decided two more Espionage Act cases one week after *Schenck*. These cases did not analyze whether the defendants' speech created a clear or present danger to the government's military recruiting efforts. To uphold the defendants' convictions, using *Schenck* as

---

4. The Thirteenth Amendment stipulates in part that "Neither slavery nor involuntary servitude, except as a punishment for crime whereof the party shall have been duly convicted, shall exist within the United States, or any place subject to their jurisdiction." (*U.S. Const.*, Art. XIII, Sec. 1).

# ◆ *Analyzing a Judicial Opinion*

When you read the text of a judicial decision, we recommend that you look for the answers to three major questions. For *Schenck v. United States*, you might answer the questions as follows:

**1.  What communication by the defendant led to his or her conviction?**

Schenck had prepared a leaflet for distribution to men who had been drafted. The leaflet argued that the draft was unconstitutional and encouraged draftees "not to submit to intimidation." Schenck was convicted for violating the Espionage Act.

**2.  What test did the Court use to decide if the defendant's conviction was constitutional? What reasons did the Court give for employing this test?**

The Court announced the "clear and present danger" test in *Schenck*. This test allows speech to be punished "when the words are used in such circumstances and are of such a nature as to create a clear and present danger that they will bring about the substantive evils that Congress has a right to prevent." The Court reasoned that free speech rights are not absolute because, after all, freedom of speech would not protect a man who falsely shouted "Fire!" in a theatre and caused a panic.

**3.  How did the Court apply the test to the defendant's communication to decide if the defendant's free speech rights were violated?**

The Court held that Schenck's speech could be punished because Schenck intended to obstruct the recruiting service and because his leaflets "tended" to cause such an obstruction. The Court did not require the government to prove that Schenck actually caused a disruption, reasoning that success (in impeding recruiting for the military) is not required before Schenck's speech can be punished as a crime.   ◆◆◆

a precedent, the Court required only that the communicators' words tended to cause harm. Thus, the clear and present danger test used by the Court could more accurately be called a "bad tendency" rule.[5]

In *Frohwerk v. United States*,[6] the defendant was convicted for violating the Espionage Act and sentenced to ten years in prison. The defendant had as-

---

5. Professor Zechariah Chafee used the term *bad tendency test* to describe an eighteenth-century British doctrine, which maintained that speech could be penalized if it was liable to cause harm in the future and therefore should be "nipped in the bud." See Zechariah Chafee, *Free Speech in the United States*, p. 322 (Harvard Univ. Press, 1948).
6. 249 U.S. 204 (1919).

sisted in the production of twelve articles in the *Missouri Staats Zeitung*, which were said to impair recruiting for the armed forces. The articles maintained that United States participation in World War I was wrong, that the American Army sent to France was raised illegally, and that the war was being fought only to protect the investments of the wealthy. One article asked the question, "Who . . . will pronounce a verdict of guilty upon him [any man who has been drafted] if he stops reasoning and follows the first impulse of nature— self preservation?"[7]

The Supreme Court rejected Frohwerk's First Amendment challenge to his conviction. The Court's opinion noted that there was not much difference between the expressions found in the *Missouri Staats Zeitung* and those that were sufficient to justify punishment of Schenck's speech. Although the Court noted that Frohwerk made no special effort to reach men who were subject to the draft, and that the paper had a small circulation, the Court still found a bad tendency in the articles. Justice Holmes's opinion noted that the jury "might have found that the circulation of the paper was in quarters where a little breath would be enough to kindle a flame, and that the fact was known and relied upon by those who sent the paper out."[8]

The Court reached a similar conclusion in *Debs v. United States*.[9] The defendant, Eugene V. Debs (see Figure 4.1),[10] had been convicted for violating the Espionage Act by obstructing military recruiting and enlistment. The basis of the conviction was a speech Debs gave in Canton, Ohio, in 1918. Debs argued that "the working class, who furnish the corpses, have never yet had a voice in declaring war," and he told his audience that "you need to know that you are fit for something better than slavery and cannon fodder."[11] Debs praised Rose Pastor Stokes, who had been convicted for attempting to cause insubordination and refusal of duty in the military forces; and noted that if she was guilty, so was he.

The Court rejected Debs's claim that his speech was protected by the First Amendment, again based on the rationale that Debs's speech had a bad tendency. The Court's opinion maintained that the jury was warranted in finding that "the opposition [to World War I] was so expressed that its natural and intended effect would be to obstruct recruiting," and that obstruction would be the "natural tendency and reasonably probable effect" of Debs's words.[12]

*Schenck, Frohwerk,* and *Debs* were all unanimous decisions, and the results of those cases could have made opposition to any future war very hazardous. Based on the reasoning of these cases, the First Amendment would not pro-

7. *Id.* at 208.
8. *Id.* at 208–9.
9. 249 U.S. 211 (1919).
10. Debs was the Socialist Party's five-time candidate for President. He received more than 900,000 votes in 1920, while serving his prison sentence for violating the Espionage Act.
11. *Id.*, p. 214.
12. *Id.*, p. 215–16.

*Figure 4.1.  Eugene Debs, giving his famous speech in
Canton.*

tect a defendant's speech if there was a risk that the speech could impair military recruitment.

We can use the hypothetical case of Dr. Goodheart's animal liberation
pamphlet to analyze how the bad tendency rule works to punish speech. Jake
and his classmates are a potentially willing audience for an approachable professor who has gone to the trouble to invite them to dinner. Is her pamphlet,
calling for all good people to do "whatever is necessary" to end the laboratory
animals' suffering and free them, a call for illegal action?

Under the reasoning of *Schenck,* her words would probably be found to
have a tendency to cause trespassing and theft at the perfume facility. Like defendants Schenck, Frohwerk, and Debs, she has conveyed words that might
inspire others to break the law. The words *whatever is necessary* are capable of
multiple interpretations, and do not necessarily invite illegal acts. For example, if Dr. Goodheart told her students to do "whatever is necessary" to do
well in the course, she presumably would not want them to plagiarize reports
or cheat on exams. Nevertheless, under the bad tendency rule, her words
would be taken literally, rather than as rhetorical hyperbole, and she would
be likely to be unprotected by the First Amendment. It would not matter if
Jake and his classmates had never gone near the laboratory, for *Schenck* made
it clear that successful persuasion is not required before incitement of illegal
conduct can be punished.

### A Call to Require a More "Clear and Present" Danger

In major freedom of speech cases of the 1920s, justices Holmes and
Brandeis began to disagree with the Court's majority and insist that the First

Amendment should give way only if the danger posed by speech is truly clear and present. As you read their opinions, look for two important lines of argument. First, find the reasons why Holmes and Brandeis did not believe the defendants' communication created a clear and present danger. Second, understand their perspectives on the role of freedom of speech in the United States. The positions they developed form the core of the marketplace of ideas concept, and they were probably the most persuasive impetus for the demise of bad tendency analysis.[13]

***Abrams v. United States.***[14]    Jacob Abrams and his co-defendants were Russian natives living in the United States. They were convicted for Espionage Act violations, based on two leaflets, one in English and the other in Yiddish, which the defendants had circulated.[15] The leaflets contained messages to the workers of America. One informed workers in ammunition factories that they are producing munitions not only to murder Germans, but also "your dearest, best, who are in Russia and are fighting for freedom."[16] The leaflet also made the following claim about American involvement in World War I: "Workers, our reply to the barbaric intervention has to be a general strike! An open challenge only will let the government know that not only the Russian Worker fights for freedom, but also here in America lives the spirit of Revolution."[17]

The majority opinion in *Abrams* rejected the claim that the leaflets were protected by the First Amendment, noting that this issue had been sufficiently discussed and definitely negatived in *Schenck* and *Frohwerk.*[18]

Justice Holmes did not believe that Abrams's leaflets presented a clear and present danger. His dissenting opinion, joined by Justice Brandeis,[19] made the case for greater protection of First Amendment rights in incitement to illegal conduct cases.

---

13. Professor Donald Fishman has pointed out that the critical period for the creation of First Amendment doctrine came immediately after World War I. He credits Brandeis and Holmes for bringing about Supreme Court debate on the appropriate boundaries for constitutional protection for freedom of expression. See Donald Fishman, "Emerging Conceptions of Freedom of Speech in the Aftermath of World War I: Abrams to Whitney," Paper Presented at the Western States Communication Association Convention, Portland, Oregon, February 13, 1995. In *Dennis v. United States,* 341 U.S. 491 (1951), Chief Justice Vinson's opinion noted that the majority opinions in *Whitney* and *Gitlow* had not been overruled, but that there was "little doubt that subsequent opinions have inclined toward the Holmes-Brandeis rationale" *id.,* at 507.

14. 250 U.S. 616 (1919).

15. Some copies of the leaflets had been circulated covertly, but others had been thrown from the window of a building where one of the defendants worked.

16. 250 U.S. at 621.

17. *Id.*

18. *Id.,* at 619. The majority found a bad tendency in the appeal to the munitions workers, because "the obvious effect of this appeal, if it should become effective—as [the defendants] hoped it might—would be to persuade persons . . . not to work in ammunition factories." *Id.* at 621. Regarding the call for a general strike, the majority reasoned that "the plain purpose of [the defendants'] propaganda was to excite, at the supreme crisis of the war, disaffection, sedition, riots, and, as they hoped, revolution in this country." *Id.,* at 623.

19. When justices agree about the result of a case and the reasons for the decision, one justice will write an opinion to express the position of all the justices who agree with him or her.

### *Abrams v. United States,* 250 U.S. 616, 624 (1919)

Mr. Justice Holmes, dissenting:

But, as against dangers peculiar to war, as against others, the principle of the right to free speech is always the same. *It is only the present danger of immediate evil or an intent to bring it about that warrants Congress in setting a limit to the expression of opinion where private rights are not concerned* (emphasis added). Congress certainly cannot forbid all effort to change the mind of the country. Now nobody can suppose that the surreptitious publishing of a silly leaflet by an unknown man, without more, would present any immediate danger that its opinions would hinder the success of the government arms or have any appreciable tendency to do so. . . .

In this case sentences of twenty years imprisonment have been imposed for the publishing of two leaflets that I believe the defendants had as much right to publish as the government has the right to publish the Constitution of the United States now vainly invoked by them. Even if I am technically wrong, and enough can be squeezed from these poor and puny anonymities to turn the color of legal litmus paper . . . the most nominal punishment seems to me all that possibly could be inflicted, unless the defendants are to be made to suffer not for what the indictment alleges, but for the creed that they avow,—a creed that I believe to be the creed of ignorance and immaturity when honestly held. . . .

Persecution for the expression of opinions seems to me perfectly logical. If you have no doubt of your premises or your power and want a certain result with all your heart you naturally express your wishes in law and sweep away all opposition. . . . But when men have realized that time has upset many fighting faiths, they may come to believe, even more than they believe the very foundations of their own conduct, *that the ultimate good desired is better reached by free trade in ideas,—that the best test of truth is the power of the thought to get itself accepted in the competition of the market* (emphasis added). . . . That, at any rate, is the theory of our Constitution. . . .

[W]e should be eternally vigilant against attempts to check the expression of opinions that we loathe and believe to be fraught with death, unless they so imminently threaten immediate interference with the lawful and pressing purposes of the law that an immediate check is required to save the country. . . . *Only the emergency that makes it immediately dangerous to leave the correction of evil counsels to time warrants making any exception to the sweeping command, "Congress shall make no law abridging the freedom of speech"* (emphasis added).   ◆◆◆

*Gitlow v. New York.*[20]   The majority opinion in *Gitlow* made a vital contribution to the protection of freedom of speech in the United States, which will be discussed in the next section of this chapter. Justice Holmes's dissenting opinion in *Gitlow* is significant as well, because it further develops his ar-

---

20. 268 U.S. 652 (1925).

gument about the necessity for speech to create an *imminent* danger before it can be punished.

The defendant, Benjamin Gitlow, was a member of the national council of the left wing of the Socialist Party. He had arranged for the printing of sixteen thousand copies of the *Left Wing Manifesto*. The manifesto rejected the achievement of socialism through democratic channels, and instead advocated a "mass strike" by the proletariat.[21] The manifesto noted that the final objective of this action would be "the conquest of the power of the state, the annihilation of the bourgeois parliamentary state, and the introduction of the transition proletarian state, functioning as a revolutionary dictatorship of the proletariat."[22]

Although Gitlow was represented by one of the nation's premier defense lawyers, Clarence Darrow, his conviction was ruled constitutional. The majority opinion in *Gitlow* upheld the state of New York's right to punish this expression, accepting the state legislature's judgment that this type of language constituted a clear and present danger.[23] The majority reached this conclusion, although their opinion acknowledged that "there was no evidence of any effect resulting from the publication and circulation of the Manifesto."[24] Justice Holmes's dissenting opinion, joined by Justice Brandeis, argued that no clear and present danger existed.

### *Gitlow v. New York*, 268 U.S. 652, 672 (1925)

Mr. Justice Holmes, dissenting:

If what I think the correct test is applied, it is manifest that there was no present danger of an attempt to overthrow the government by force on the part of the admittedly small minority who shared the defendant's views.

It is said that this Manifesto was more than a theory, that it was an incitement. Every idea is an incitement. It offers itself for belief, and if believed, it is acted on unless some other belief outweighs it, or some failure of energy stifles the movement at its birth. . . .

But whatever may be thought of the redundant discourse before us, it had no chance of starting a present conflagration. If, in the long run, the beliefs expressed in proletarian dictatorship are destined to be accepted by the dominant forces of the community, the only meaning of free speech is that they should be given their chance and have their way.

---

21. Marxist theory maintains that the proletariat (labor class) must overthrow the capital owning class (the bourgeoisie) through revolution. See Edward Hyams, *A Dictionary of Modern Revolution*, p. 36 (Taplinger, 1973).

22. 268 U.S. at 656, n. 2.

23. *Id.* at 671. The defendants had been convicted for violating New York's criminal anarchy law. The law defined criminal anarchy as "the doctrine that organized government should be overthrown by force or violence, or by the assassination of the executive head or of any of the executive officials of government, or by any unlawful means." It made the advocacy of this doctrine, by word of mouth or writing, a felony. *Id.* at 654.

24. *Id.*, at 656.

If the publication of this document had been laid as an attempt to induce an uprising against government at once, and not at some indefinite time in the future, it would have presented a different question. The object would have been one with which the law might deal, subject to the doubt whether there was any danger that the publication could produce any result; or, in other words, whether it was not futile and too remote from possible consequences. But the indictment alleges the publication [of the Manifesto] and nothing more.   ◆◆◆


*Whitney v. California.*[25]    Charlotte Anita Whitney, a member of the social elite and the niece of former Supreme Court Justice Stephen J. Field, had been convicted for violating California's Criminal Syndicalism Act.[26] Whitney's impeccable social credentials may have been the very reason she was vigorously prosecuted, as the authorities wanted to make an example out of this "parlor pink."[27]

The record in Ms. Whitney's case acknowledged that she was an active member of the California branch of the Communist Labor Party and that she served on the group's resolutions committee at the Party's organizing convention. Although her committee had advocated the value of working within the democratic process to achieve revolutionary change, the final constitution approved by the membership rejected this resolution.

The majority in *Whitney* upheld her conviction on the grounds that freedom of speech could be overridden. This gave great presumption to the California legislature's decision that membership in the Communist Party "involves such a danger to the public peace and the security of the state" that it could be punished.[28]

The most noteworthy aspect of the *Whitney* decision was Justice Brandeis's concurring opinion, joined by Justice Holmes. Brandeis (see Figure 4.2) agreed that Whitney's conviction should be upheld on the technical ground that she never asserted the lack of a clear and present danger as a defense.[29] Although Brandeis's opinion did little to help Anita Whitney, it developed important ideas about freedom of speech, which would be used by future courts and advocates in defense of that freedom.

---

25. 274 U.S. 357 (1927).
26. California's Criminal Syndicalism Act was similar to the New York law under which Benjamin Gitlow had been punished. The act provided that any person who "organizes or assists in organizing, *or is knowingly a member* (emphasis added) of any organization. . .assembled to advocate, teach or aid and abet criminal syndicalism. . .is guilty of a felony and punishable by imprisonment." Criminal Syndicalism was defined as any doctrine advocating the commission of crime, sabotage, or unlawful acts of force and violence as a means of accomplishing a change in industrial ownership or control, or effecting any political change (*id.* at 359–60). A number of states had passed such laws in the aftermath of the assassination of President McKinley by an immigrant who was alleged to be an Anarchist. See Hentoff, p. 101. After World War I, when the American public became afraid of the rise of communism, these criminal syndicalism laws provided a tool for arresting Communists and left-wing Socialists.
27. Blanchard, p. 124.
28. 274 U.S. at 371.
29. *Id.* at 379 (Brandeis, J., concurring).

*Figure 4.2. Justice Louis D. Brandeis, first Jewish Justice on the Court and one of the great innovators in developing First Amendment doctrine. Justice Brandeis was nominated by President Wilson in 1916 to replace Joseph Lamar. His concurring opinion in* **Whitney v. California** *follows.* (Harris & Ewing. Collection of the Supreme Court of the United States)

## Whitney v. California, 274 U.S. 357, 372 (1927)

Mr. Justice Brandeis, concurring:

This court has not yet fixed the standard by which to determine when a danger shall be deemed clear; how remote the danger may be and yet be deemed present; and what degree of evil shall be deemed sufficiently substantial to justify resort to abridgment of free speech and assembly as the means of protection. To reach sound conclusions on these matters, we must bear in mind why a state is, ordinarily, denied the power to prohibit dissemination of social, economic and political doctrine which a vast majority of its citizens believes to be false and fraught with evil consequences.

Those who won our independence . . . valued liberty both as an end and as a means. They believed liberty to be the secret of happiness and courage to be the secret of liberty. They believed that freedom to think as you will and to speak as you think are means indispensable to the discovery and spread of political truth; *that without free speech and assembly, discussion would be futile; that with them, discussion affords ordinarily adequate protection against the dissemination of noxious doctrine* (emphasis added); that the greatest menace to freedom is an inert people; that public discussion is a political duty; and that this should be a fundamental principle of the American government. . . .

[T]hey knew that . . . the path of safety lies in the opportunity to discuss freely supposed grievances and proposed remedies; and that the fitting remedy for evil counsels is good ones. Believing in the power of reason as applied through public discussion, they eschewed silence coerced by law—the argument of force in its worst form. Recognizing the occasional tyrannies of governing majorities, they amended the Constitution so that free speech and assembly should be guaranteed.

Fear of serious injury cannot alone justify suppression of speech and assembly. Men feared witches and burned women. It is the function of speech to free men from the bondage of irrational fears. To justify suppression of free speech, there must be reasonable ground to fear that serious evil will result if free speech is practiced. There must be reasonable ground to believe that the danger apprehended is imminent. There must be reasonable ground to believe that the evil to be prevented is a serious one.

Every denunciation of existing law tends in some measure to increase the probability that there will be a violation of it. . . . [E]ven advocacy of violation, however reprehensible morally, is not a justification for denying free speech where the advocacy falls short of incitement and there is nothing to indicate that the advocacy would be immediately acted on.

Those who won our independence by revolution were not cowards. They did not fear political change. They did not exalt order at the cost of liberty. To courageous, self-reliant men, with confidence in the power of free and fearless reasoning applied through the process of popular government, no danger flowing from speech can be deemed clear and present unless the incidence of the evil apprehended is so imminent that it may befall before there is opportunity for full discussion. *If there be time to expose through discussion the falsehood and fallacies, to avert the evil by the processes of education, the remedy to be applied is more speech, not enforced silence* (emphasis added). Only such an emergency can justify repression. Such must be the rule if authority is to be reconciled with freedom. Such, in my opinion, is the command of the Constitution. It is, therefore, always open to Americans to challenge a law abridging free speech and assembly by showing that there was no emergency justifying it. ◆◆◆

After reading the opinions of justices Holmes and Brandeis in *Whitney, Gitlow,* and *Abrams,* do you think they would have ruled that Prof. Goodheart's pamphlet was protected by the First Amendment? Justice Holmes called Abrams's pamphlet a silly leaflet by an unknown man. Could those words also describe the pamphlet Dr. Goodheart distributed? Was there the danger of an immediate evil after she distributed her literature? Would this be a case where more speech, such as discussion among the students involved, or the feedback of friends and family, would dissuade the students from undertaking an animal rescue?

### Critical Thinking: When Should Speakers Be Held Accountable?

In their *Abrams, Gitlow,* and *Whitney* opinions, justices Holmes and Brandeis answered the key question posed by this chapter—Under what circumstances can speech be punished on the grounds that it risks inciting lawbreaking? Other commentators have attempted to answer this same question. This section summarizes a sampling of their analyses. There is no single right answer to be memorized after studying these different perspectives. It is more important that you understand these perspectives and use your own critical thinking skills to decide when, if ever, you believe the government can punish speakers for encouraging illegal acts. You can also analyze the impact each of these four scholars' viewpoints would have on free expression by considering whether they would agree that Dr. Goodheart's animal rights pamphlet should be protected.

***Dean Wigmore's Critique of Clear and Present Danger.*** One of the earliest critics of the clear and present danger test suggested that the rule gave too many rights to communicators. John Wigmore, a respected law school dean, viewed the test as "an unnecessary bleeding-heart concern" for the First Amendment.[30] To Dean Wigmore, "the moral right of the majority to enter upon the war imparts the moral right to secure success by suppressing public agitation against the completion of the struggle."[31]

***Professor Meiklejohn's Absolute Freedom for Political Speech.*** Professor Alexander Meiklejohn argued that the *Schenck* holding "annuls the most significant purpose of the First Amendment," and "destroys the intellectual basis of our plan of self government." If the First Amendment were rewritten in light of the clear and present danger test, Meiklejohn maintains that it would read, "Congress shall pass no law abridging freedom of speech 'except when it finds it advisable to do so.'"[32] Meiklejohn advocated absolute protection for freedom of speech on public issues, with no exceptions tolerated.[33]

***Professor Haiman's Free Choice Standard.*** Northwestern Professor Emeritus Franklyn Haiman has argued that the key issue in incitement cases should be whether the communicator takes away the free choice of the audience. For example, if the orator deliberately deceives the audience, he or she should take responsibility for the consequences. The same would be true if the speaker coerced the listeners into taking illegal action. However, if the audience retains the capacity to reject the solicitation, the speaker should not be punished. Professor Haiman argues that human beings are not "piles of kindling waiting for a spark to ignite them," and "should not be relieved of responsibility for their own behavior by the buck being passed to someone else who may have planted an idea in their minds."[34]

30. Franklyn S. Haiman, *Speech and Law in a Free Society*, p. 279 (Univ. of Chicago Press, 1981).
31. John H. Wigmore, Abrams v. U.S.: *Freedom of Speech and Freedom of Thuggery in War-Time and Peace-Time*, 14 Illinois Law Review 554 (1920), as quoted in Haiman.
32. Alexander Meiklejohn, *Political Freedom: The Constitutional Powers of the People*, p. 30 (Harper & Brothers, 1948).
33. *Id.*, p. 27. To Professor Meiklejohn, no citizen could be barred from speaking because his or her ideas were believed to be false or dangerous. In a system of self-government, the people should be exposed to every perspective on an issue, and decide for themselves which viewpoint to accept. No higher authority should have the power to decide if certain ideas are too dangerous to be presented to the public.
34. Haiman, p. 277–78.

*William Bailey's Application of Communication Theory to Incitement Issues.* William Bailey of the University of Arizona has argued that the Supreme Court's assumptions in incitement cases are based on a faulty model of communication.[35] According to Bailey, the Court assumes that speech has a unidirectional influence; that is, that the speaker is the cause of whatever effects ensue after the audience has heard a speech.[36] For example, if a speaker says "resist the draft," and a member of the audience later flees to Canada to avoid conscription, the speech is assumed to have caused the flight.

Modern communication theory provides reasons for rejecting the causal link between advocacy and audience action. In the first place, it is an outdated assumption that the speaker-audience relationship constitutes a one-way process, whereby ideas are poured into the minds of a passive audience. Instead, communication is viewed as an interaction between the two parties, with both the audience and speaker capable of influencing each other.[37] Furthermore, as J. A. C. Brown, former Deputy Director of the Institute of Social Psychiatry, London, pointed out, people are very resistant "to messages that fail to fit into their own picture of the world," and "seek out only those views which agree with their own."[38]

Bailey provides additional evidence against the existence of a causal link between incitement and violence. He cites Paul Harris's research of Black Power advocacy and forcible action. Harris concluded that

> In each of the cases where speech and violence are closely related in time and space there are significant independent factors intervening between the advocacy and the action. The only proof of a causal relationship between black power advocacy and the forcible action is the time and space relationship itself.[39]

Bailey argues that if the Court adopted an empirical view of speech efficacy, there could be no more incitement prosecutions. This is because it cannot be proven that advocacy caused violence, unless the audience was predisposed towards committing violence. And when the audience is so predisposed, it is not possible to separate the speaker's contribution from the audience's.[40] Bailey finds it ironic that the law assumes that humans have free will and holds them responsible for their individual acts,[41] yet is willing to

---

35. William A. Bailey, "The Supreme Court and Communication Theory: Contrasting Models of Speech Efficacy," in *Perspectives on Freedom of Speech*, p. 91 (Southern Illinois Univ. Press, 1987).
36. *Id.*, p. 98.
37. *Id.*, p. 101.
38. J. A. C. Brown, *Techniques of Persuasion* (London, 1963), as quoted in Bailey, *id.*, p. 102.
39. Paul Harris, *Black Power Advocacy: Criminal Anarchy or Free Speech*, 56 California Law Review 702, 732 (May 1968).
40. Bailey, p. 105.
41. For example, a person who was convicted for shooting the President could not avoid criminal responsibility by proving that he or she committed the act because of persuasive Communist propaganda.

punish a speaker for what the audience did, as if the speaker were a "warlock or wizard who could deprive the individual of his reason and autonomy."[42]

These four theorists have offered interesting perspectives on how the incitement to illegal conduct question could be resolved. Over time, the Supreme Court itself would alter its conception of the clear and present danger test and provide greater protection for communicators. Before those changes took place, however, the Court extended freedom of speech rights in a different, and equally important, manner.

## THE *GITLOW* DECISION PROTECTS FREEDOM OF SPEECH FROM STATE ABRIDGMENT

Nearly one hundred years before *Gitlow*, Justice Marshall's opinion in *Barron v. Baltimore* (discussed in chapter 3) had ruled that the Bill of Rights limited the authority only of Congress. Consequently, if a state wanted to jail a member of the Industrial Workers of the World for standing on a soapbox and reading the First Amendment; deny abolitionists the right to protest slavery; or even prosecute someone for saying that knitted socks would never reach the American troops in Europe, the First Amendment would not stand in the way.

In the 1907 case of *Patterson v. Colorado* (see chapter 3), the Supreme Court majority declined to reconsider the question of extending free speech and press guarantees to the states. Justice Harlan wrote a dissenting opinion in *Patterson* and made the case for applying the First Amendment to the states. His reasoning began with the Fourteenth Amendment, which forbids *states* from making laws that abridge the privileges of U.S. citizens and also disallows states from depriving any person of liberty without due process of law.[43] Harlan then argued that the privileges of free speech and press belong to every citizen, and that they are "essential parts of every man's liberty." He argued that it was "impossible to conceive of liberty, as secured by the Constitution against hostile action, whether by the nation or by the states, which does not embrace the right to enjoy free speech and the right to have a free press."[44]

No other member on the 1907 Court was willing to agree with Justice Harlan and hold that free expression was a fundamental liberty that should be protected from state encroachment. However, by 1925, the Court member-

---

42. Bailey, p. 106.
43. The text of the Fourteenth Amendment includes the following: "No state shall make or enforce any law which shall abridge the privileges or immunities of citizens of the United States; nor shall any state deprive any person of life, liberty, or property, without due process of law" (*U.S. Constitution,* Amendment 14, Sec. 1). The Fourteenth Amendment was a key element in Congress's efforts to give rights to African Americans in southern states after the Civil War. Congress required that new state governments in the South ratify the Fourteenth Amendment before they could be readmitted to the Union.
44. *Patterson v. Colorado,* 205 U.S. at 465 (Harlan, J., dissenting).

ship had changed, and in *Gitlow* the guarantees of the First Amendment were expanded with little fanfare.

### *Gitlow v. New York,* 268 U.S. 652, 666 (1925)

Mr. Justice Sanford delivered the opinion of the Court:

For present purposes we may and do assume that freedom of speech and of the press—which are protected by the First Amendment from abridgment by Congress—are among the fundamental personal rights and "liberties" protected by the due process clause of the 14th Amendment from impairment by the states.

◆◆◆

In one paragraph, the Supreme Court lifted a substantial constraint on freedom of speech. In subsequent chapters, you will read many cases in which free speech rights were protected from state abridgment. Although the *Gitlow* decision did not prevent the conviction of the defendant (the Court ruled that Gitlow's speech presented a clear and present danger, thereby justifying state restraints), it did pave the way for many other communicators to exercise their right to freedom of speech.

### FREEDOM OF SPEECH FOR COMMUNISTS—
### CLEAR AND PRESENT DANGER?

Speech in defense of Communism provided the context for cases involving the clear and present danger doctrine in the 1930s, 1940s, and 1950s. Arguments in favor of friendship with Communist governments abroad or in defense of a Communist government for the United States relate to a classic function of the First Amendment. These viewpoints convey dissatisfaction with our current form of government and call for a change in government policies.

The American public did not view pro-Communist speech as a viewpoint that could be entrusted to the marketplace of ideas. The anxiety began when the Bolsheviks[45] seized power in Russia in November 1917, and then established an organization dedicated to exporting the Soviet revolution.[46] Soon, the Party began to establish a foothold in the United States.[47]

Communist theory justified revolution followed by the establishment of a dictatorship of the proletariat. Was this merely an "abstract doctrine," which posited that someday the workers would get angry and revolt; or an immediate goal for which the Communists were actively preparing? These questions would be critical when Communist speech cases reached the Supreme Court.

---

45. A minority party of Socialists, led by Vladimir Lenin.
46. Blanchard, p. 111.
47. In 1928, the Communist Party appeared on the ballot in thirty-four states, and its presidential ticket of William Foster and Benjamin Gitlow received 48,228 votes. See Irving Howe and Lewis Coser, *The American Communist Party: A Critical History,* p.176 (Da Capo, 1974).

Intense efforts were undertaken to deprive Communists of their free speech rights. William O'Brien, a candidate for governor in Arizona, was arrested and beaten while in jail. Presidential candidate William Z. Foster was arrested in Wilmington, Delaware. The charge against Foster was distribution of an inflammatory slogan—he had distributed a leaflet that declared, "Abolish Lynching!"[48]

Despite the American public's fear of Communism, freedom of speech scored one major victory in the 1930s. Dirk De Jonge, a Communist speaker, was convicted for violating Oregon's criminal syndicalism law. De Jonge was a direct beneficiary of the holding in *Gitlow*, which prevented states from abridging free speech guarantees.

### Speech at a Communist Meeting Is Not Inherently a Clear and Present Danger

Dirk De Jonge had given a speech at a Portland, Oregon, meeting organized by the Communist Party. He had protested against conditions in the county jail and criticized police actions against striking maritime workers. There was testimony that De Jonge had asked the audience to work harder in recruiting members for the Party, but no evidence that he had advocated the violent overthrow of the U.S. government or called for any other unlawful conduct. The Oregon Supreme Court upheld De Jonge's conviction because he had assisted in conducting a meeting of the Communist Party, and Communist literature advocated criminal syndicalism and sabotage.[49] In a unanimous decision, the Supreme Court argued that these facts were not sufficient to justify an abridgment of free speech rights.

### De Jonge v. State of Oregon, 299 U.S. 353 (1937)

Mr. Chief Justice Hughes delivered the opinion of the Court:
While the States are entitled to protect themselves from the abuse of the privileges of our institutions through an attempted substitution of force and violence in the place of peaceful political action in order to effect revolutionary changes in government, none of our decisions go to the length in sustaining such a curtailment of the right of free speech and assembly as the Oregon statute demands in its present application. . . .

Freedom of speech and of the press are fundamental rights which are safeguarded by the due process clause of the Fourteenth Amendment of the Federal Constitution. . . .

---

48. *Id.*
49. *De Jonge v. State of Oregon,* 299 U.S. 353, 359–62 (1937). None of the literature distributed at the meeting advocated criminal syndicalism or other illegal acts. The prosecution had argued that literature found elsewhere proved that the Communist Party supported criminal syndicalism. *Id.* at 360.

These rights may be abused by using speech or press or assembly in order to incite to violence and crime. The people through their Legislatures may protect themselves against that abuse. . . .

[But] the greater the importance of safeguarding the community from incitements to the overthrow of our institutions by force and violence, the more imperative is the need to preserve inviolate the constitutional rights of free speech, free press, and free assembly in order to maintain the opportunity for free political discussion, to the end that government may be responsive to the will of the people and that changes, if desired, may be obtained by peaceful means. Therein lies the security of the Republic, the very foundation of constitutional government.

It follows from these considerations that, consistently with the Federal Constitution, peaceable assembly for lawful discussion cannot be made a crime. . . . Notwithstanding [the objectives of the Communist Party], the defendant still enjoyed his personal right of free speech and to take part in a peaceable assembly having a lawful purpose, although called by that party. The defendant was none the less entitled to discuss the public issues of the day, and this in a lawful manner, without incitement to violence or crime, to seek redress of alleged grievances.

◆◆◆

### Persecution of Communists Intensifies in *Dennis v. United States*

· In the 1940s and 1950s, the public's fear of Communism intensified. Joseph Stalin ruled in the Soviet Union, and his brand of Communism was uniquely repressive. After World War II, the Soviet military occupied much of Eastern Europe, and Winston Churchill gave his classic warning: "From Stettin in the Baltic to Trieste in the Adriatic, an iron curtain has descended across the continent. . . . What they [the Soviets] desire is the fruits of war and the indefinite expansion of their power and doctrines."

The tools that would be used to suppress American Communists were originally created to deal with Fascists. The 1930s saw a growing concern about the possibility of a Hitler or Mussolini coming to power in the United States. In 1940, the Alien Registration Act, also known as the Smith Act,[50] was enacted (see p. 110). The act required aliens to register and be fingerprinted, so that the government could keep track of them. In addition, the Smith Act contained provisions against seditious speech on the part of U.S. citizens, as well as aliens.[51]

The Smith Act was rarely enforced during World War II. The war was popular in the United States, and there was little dissent. However, after the war, the act was employed against the Communists with a vengeance. Under

---

50. Named for the act's author, Congressman Howard Smith.
51. Section 2 of the Smith Act made it unlawful to "knowingly or willfully advocate, abet, advise, or teach the duty, necessity, desirability, or propriety of overthrowing or destroying any government in the U.S. by force or violence," and "to organize or help to organize any society, group, or assembly of persons who teach, advocate, or encourage the overthrow or destruction of any government in the United States by force or violence; or to be or become a member of, or affiliate with, any such society, group, or assembly of persons, knowing the purposes thereof."

political pressure to take the initiative against Communists, U.S. Attorney General Tom Clark brought charges against twelve leading members of the U.S. Communist Party, including party chair William Foster and general secretary Eugene Dennis. The claim was that they had violated the Smith Act by conspiring to teach and advocate the doctrine of Communism. Eleven defendants were convicted (the charges against Foster were dropped because he was ill), and ten received five-year prison terms.[52]

The case was appealed to the Supreme Court. The two most important issues to consider when reading the *Dennis* opinion are (1) what did the defendants do to create a risk that illegal conduct (a Communist revolution) would come about?[53] and (2) was the risk created by the defendants sufficient to justify an abridgment of their First Amendment rights? You will read the **plurality opinion** as well as passages from Justice Douglas's dissent. After reading these opinions, you can decide for yourself whether you agree that the defendants in *Dennis* had created a clear and present danger.

### *Dennis v. United States,* 341 U.S. 494 (1951)

Mr. Chief Justice Vinson announced the judgment of the Court and an opinion in which Mr. Justice Reed, Mr. Justice Burton, and Mr. Justice Minton joined:

Petitioners [Eugene Dennis and his co-defendants] dispute the meaning to be drawn from the evidence, contending that the Marxist-Leninist doctrine they advocated taught that force and violence to achieve a Communist form of government in an existing democratic state would be necessary only because the ruling classes of that state would never permit the transformation to be accomplished peacefully, but would use force and violence to defeat any peaceful political and economic gain the Communists could achieve.

[T]he Court of Appeals held that the record supports the following broad conclusions: By virtue of their control over the political apparatus of the Communist Political Association, petitioners were able to transform that organization into the Communist Party; that the policies of the Association were changed from peaceful cooperation with the U.S. and its economic and political structure to a policy . . . which worked for the overthrow of the Government by force and violence; that the Communist Party is a highly disciplined organization, adept at infiltration into strategic positions . . . that the literature of the Party and the statements and activities of its leaders, petitioners here, advocate, and the general goal of the Party was, during the period in question, to achieve a successful overthrow of the existing order by force and violence. . . .

---

52. Blanchard, pp. 244–45.
53. Determining the facts of the *Dennis* case is highly complicated. The trial lasted for nine months, and the record in the case was 16,000 pages long. The jury made its decision after all of this evidence had been presented. Juries only find the defendant guilty or not guilty; they do not state which portions of the evidence they found to be true. Therefore it is not known which facts the jury found true or false as it sifted through thousands of pages of testimony.

# The Alien Registration Act of 1940 (The Smith Act)

Section 2.

(a) It shall be unlawful for any person—

(1) to knowingly or willfully advocate, abet, advise, or teach the duty, necessity, desirability, or propriety of overthrowing or destroying any government in the United States by force or violence, or by the assassination of any officer of any such government; . . .

(3) to organize or help to organize any society, group, or assembly of persons who teach, advocate, or encourage the overthrow or destruction of any government in the United States by force or violence; or to be or become a member of, or affiliate with, any such society, group, or assembly of persons, knowing the purposes thereof. . . .

Section 5.

(a) Any person who violates any of the provisions of this title shall, upon conviction thereof, be fined not more than $10,000 or imprisoned for not more than ten years, or both.[1]

[1] *Source:* 54 *U.S. Statutes at Large* 670–671 (1940). This law, with some modifications, remains on the books, and can now be found at 18 *U.S. Code Annotated*, Section 2385 (West 1970).

◆◆◆

In this case we are squarely presented with the application of the "clear and present danger test," and must decide what that phrase imports. We first note that many of the cases in which this Court has reversed convictions by use of this or similar tests have been based on the fact that the interest which the State was attempting to protect was itself too insubstantial to warrant restriction of speech. . . .

Overthrow of the Government by force and violence is certainly a substantial enough interest for the Government to limit speech. Indeed, this is the ultimate value of any society, for if a society cannot protect its very structure from armed internal attack, it must follow that no subordinate value can be protected. If, then, this interest may be protected, the literal problem which is presented is what has been meant by the use of the phrase "clear and present danger" of the utterances bringing about the evil within the power of Congress to punish.

Obviously the words cannot mean that before the Government may act, it must wait until the *putsch* is about to be executed, the plans have been laid and the signal is awaited. If Government is aware that a group aiming at its overthrow is attempting to indoctrinate its members and to commit them to a course whereby they will strike when the leaders feel the circumstances permit, action by the Government is required. . . .

The situation with which [j]ustices Holmes and Brandeis were concerned in *Gitlow* was a comparatively isolated event, bearing little relation in their minds to any substantial threat to the safety of the community. . . . They were not confronted with any situation comparable to the instant one—the development of an apparatus designed and dedicated to the overthrow of the Government, in the context of world crisis after crisis.

Likewise, we are in accord with the court below, which affirmed the trial court's finding that the requisite danger existed. The mere fact that from the period 1945 to 1948 petitioners' activities did not result in an attempt to overthrow the Government by force and violence is of course no answer to the fact that there was a group that was ready to make the attempt. The formation by petitioners of such a highly organized conspiracy, with rigidly disciplined members subject to call when the leaders, these petitioners, felt that the time had come for action, coupled with the inflammable nature of world conditions, similar uprisings in other countries, and the touch-and-go nature of our relations with countries with whom petitioners were in the very least ideologically attuned, convince us that their convictions were justified on this score.

Mr. Justice Douglas, dissenting.

If this were a case where those who claimed protection under the First Amendment were teaching the techniques of sabotage, . . . the planting of bombs, the art of street warfare, and the like, I would have no doubts. The freedom to speak is not absolute; the teaching of methods of terror and other seditious conduct should be beyond the pale along with obscenity and immorality. . . .

So far as the present record is concerned, what petitioners did was to organize people to teach and themselves teach the Marxist-Leninist doctrine contained chiefly in four books: *Foundations of Leninism* by Stalin (1924); *The Communist Manifesto* by Marx and Engels (1848); *State and Revolution* by Lenin (1917); *History of the Communist Party of the Soviet Union* (B.) (1939). . . .

There was a time in England when the concept of constructive treason flourished. Men were punished not for raising a hand against the king but for thinking murderous thoughts about him. The Framers of the Constitution were alive to that abuse and took steps to see that the practice would not flourish here. . . .

[F]ree speech is the rule, not the exception. The restraint, to be constitutional, must be based on more than fear, on more than passionate opposition against speech. . . . There must be some immediate injury to society that is likely if speech is allowed. . . .

This record, however, contains no evidence whatsoever showing that the acts charged vis. the teaching of the Soviet theory of revolution with the hope that it will be realized, have created any clear and present danger to the Nation. . . . Communists in this country have never made a respectable or serious showing in any election. . . . Communism has been so thoroughly exposed in this country that it has been crippled as a political force. Free speech has destroyed it as an effective political party. . . . How it can be said that there is a clear and present danger that this advocacy will succeed is, therefore, a mystery. Some nations less resilient than the U.S., where illiteracy is high and where democratic traditions are only budding might have to take drastic steps and jail these men for merely speaking their creed. . . .

Vishinsky wrote in 1938 in *The Law of the Soviet State*, "In our state, naturally, there is and can be no place for freedom of speech, press, and so on for the foes of socialism."

Our concern should be that we accept no such standard for the United States. Our faith should be that our people will never give support to these advocates of revolution, so long as we remain loyal to the purposes for which our Nation was founded.   ◆◆◆

In the years following *Dennis*, people who wanted to advocate Communism had more to fear than prosecutions under the Smith Act. Wisconsin Senator Joseph McCarthy made it his personal mission to lead a national crusade, ferreting alleged Communists out of government and other institutions. Often, McCarthy would merely allege that people were Communists, and many journalists would report his opinions as fact without requiring any proof.[54] The Senate Internal Security Subcommittee believed that world Communist leaders were encouraging the infiltration of schools and colleges, and many teachers were called before investigating committees to answer to charges that they were Communists. To remain employed in academia, it was necessary to be inconspicuous and noncontroversial.[55] In the entertainment field, a blacklist of actors, producers, directors, and writers with suspect political beliefs was compiled. Many careers were destroyed.[56]

### Repression of Communist Speech Decreases

Although many Americans were caught up in the anti-Communist hysteria, some were willing to speak out. Republican Senator Margaret Chase Smith of Maine pointed out that those who were talking the most about "Americanism" were ignoring fundamental American principles, such as the right to hold unpopular beliefs and the right to protest. In her opinion, the fear of being labeled a Communist was creating a chilling effect on free speech. She wrote the "Declaration of Conscience," a document condemning rampant anti-Communism, which was signed by seven Republican senators. By 1954, many members of the Senate were fed up with McCarthy's behavior, and a resolution of censure was passed—only the fourth in the history of the Senate.

The Supreme Court also took the momentum out of Smith Act prosecutions in the case of *Yates v. United States.*[57] In that case, Oleta Yates and thirteen co-defendants were convicted for violating the act by teaching the duty and

54. Blanchard, p. 246.
55. *Id.,* p. 255.
56. *Id.,* pp. 257–58.
57. 354 U.S. 298 (1957).

necessity of overthrowing the government of the United States by force and violence. The *Yates* defense, in their appeal, argued that advocacy of forcible overthrow of the government, as mere abstract doctrine, was protected by the First Amendment.

The Supreme Court agreed with the defense and held that the trial judge should have instructed the jury that advocacy of abstract doctrine could not be punished. The Court construed the holding in *Dennis* to mean that "language of incitement is not constitutionally protected when the group [being indoctrinated] is of sufficient size and cohesiveness, is sufficiently oriented towards action, and other circumstances are such as reasonably to justify apprehension that action will occur."[58]

The Court distinguished the facts in *Yates* from those in *Dennis*. Justice Harlan wrote that advocacy of abstract doctrine, even when accompanied by the hope that it will eventually lead to violent revolution, is too remote from concrete action. The statement of an idea, which may prompt listeners to take unlawful action, is protected by the First Amendment, whereas advocacy that such action be taken is not.[59]

Once the Supreme Court required the government to prove that the *Yates* defendants had directly advocated illegal action, the government dropped the prosecution. No charges were filed for other Smith Act violations after the *Yates* decision. Speech that could be interpreted as pro-Communist was not received warmly in America after *Yates*, but by the late 1950s, the mass hysteria had subsided.

### *BRANDENBURG V. OHIO:* STRENGTHENING THE PROTECTION OF SPEECH

#### The Court's Opinion Strengthens Protection for Speakers

The cause of Clarence Brandenburg was not noble (see Figure 4.3).

He was a leader of the Ku Klux Klan in Ohio. Nevertheless, a speech he gave resulted in a landmark 1969 Supreme Court decision, which gave significant added protection to communicators of all persuasions.

#### *Brandenburg v. Ohio,* 395 U.S. 444 (1969)

Per Curiam.[60]

The appellant, a leader of a Ku Klux Klan group, was convicted under the Ohio Criminal Syndicalism statute for "advocat[ing] . . . the duty, necessity, or propriety of crime, sabotage, violence, or unlawful methods of terrorism as a means of

---

58. *Id.* at 321.
59. *Id.* at 322.
60. The Latin *per curiam,* which translates to "by the Court," means that the Court is issuing a decision without acknowledging a specific author of the opinion.

*Figure 4.3. Clarence Brandenburg was the KKK leader whose threat of "Revengance" was protected under the current incitement test.*
(New York Times (June 9, 1969). (c) 1969 New York Times *Pictures. Reprinted by permission.*)

accomplishing industrial or political reform" and for "voluntarily assembl[ing] with any society, group, or assemblage of persons formed to teach or advocate the doctrines of criminal syndicalism." . . . He was fined $1,000 and sentenced to one to 10 years' imprisonment. The appellant challenged the constitutionality of the criminal syndicalism statute under the First and Fourteenth Amendments to the U.S. Constitution. . . .

✳   The record shows that . . . the appellant telephoned an announcer-reporter [at] a Cincinnati television station and invited him to come to a Ku Klux Klan "rally" to be held at a farm in Hamilton County. With the cooperation of the organizers, the reporter and a cameraman attended the meeting and filmed the events. . . .

One film showed 12 hooded figures, some of whom carried firearms. They were gathered around a large wooden cross, which they burned. No one was present other than the participants and the newsmen who made the film. . . .

[A] scene on the film showed the appellant, in Klan regalia, making a speech. The speech, in full, was as follows:

> "This is an organizers' meeting. We have had quite a few members here today which are—we have hundreds, hundreds of members throughout the State of Ohio. I can quote from a newspaper clipping from the Columbus, Ohio [*Dispatch,*] five weeks ago Sunday morning. The Klan has more members in the State of Ohio than does any other organization. We're not a revengent organization, but if our President, our Congress, our Supreme Court, continues to suppress the white, Caucasian race, it's possible that there might have to be some revengance taken.
>
> We are marching on Congress July the Fourth, four hundred thousand strong. From there we are dividing into two groups, one to march on to St. Augustine, Florida, and the other group to march into Mississippi. Thank you."

✳ In 1927, this Court sustained the constitutionality of California's Criminal Syndicalism Act . . . the text of which is quite similar to that of the laws of Ohio, [in] *Whitney v. California.* . . . But *Whitney* has been thoroughly discredited by later decisions. See *Dennis v. United States* (citation omitted). These later decisions have fashioned the principle that *the constitutional guarantees of free speech and free press do not permit a State to forbid or proscribe advocacy of the use of force or of law violation except where such advocacy is directed to inciting or producing iminent lawless action and is likely to incite or produce such action* (emphasis added). . . .

As we said in *Noto v. United States,*[61] "the mere abstract teaching . . . of the moral propriety or even moral necessity for a resort to force and violence, is not the same as preparing a group for violent action and steeling it to such action." . . . A statute which fails to draw this distinction impermissibly intrudes upon the freedoms guaranteed by the First and Fourteenth Amendments. It sweeps within its condemnation speech which our constitution has immunized from government control. . . .

Measured by this test, Ohio's Criminal Syndicalism Act cannot be sustained. . . . Neither the indictment nor the trial judge's instructions to the jury in any way refined the statute's bald definition of the crime in terms of mere advocacy not distinguished from incitement to imminent lawless action. ◆◆◆

✂ The *Brandenburg* opinion purported[62] to describe changes in the Court's position on incitement to illegal conduct, in the years following the 1927 *Whitney* decision. Regardless of whether the Court was simply following past precedent or breaking new Constitutional ground, the words it used in *Brandenburg* operationalized clear and present danger in a way that provided significant protection to communicators.

As a result of *Brandenburg,* the government cannot punish speech because it has a tendency, or even a reasonable possibility, of inciting illegal conduct. Before the government can punish speech on the grounds that it is incitement, a three-part criterion must be met. First, the speech must be *directed* to inciting lawless action. Second, the advocacy must be calling for *imminent* lawbreaking, rather than illegal conduct at some future time. Finally, the advocacy must be *likely* to produce such conduct.

By revisiting the hypothetical case of Dr. Goodheart, we can see the added protection provided by the *Brandenburg* test. If you will recall, under the bad tendency test a court could easily have held that Dr. Goodheart could be punished because her pamphlet tended to encourage her students to trespass and rescue the research animals. Under *Brandenburg,* the government would need to prove three facts before Goodheart's First Amendment rights

---

61. 367 U.S. 290, 297–98 (1961).
62. The cases cited to show that *Whitney* has been discredited were *Dennis* and *Yates.* See 395 U.S. at 447. After studying the holdings in *Dennis* and *Yates,* the reader may fairly question whether the test announced in *Brandenburg* was the same one followed in those two cases.

could be denied. First, was her action directed to inciting an animal rescue? The facts do not demonstrate that she had that intent. Second, did she advocate imminent illegal conduct? Once again, not on these facts. Like the defendants in *Yates*, she was at most calling for a rescue in the indefinite future. Third, was her advocacy likely to produce illegal conduct? You can use your own experience to predict the answer to that question. Even if you oppose the testing of cosmetics on animals, could any of your professors persuade you to plan and execute a raid on a research facility to rescue the animals?

### Black and Douglas Concurrences—Farewell to Clear and Present Danger?

Justices Black and Douglas agreed with the Court's decision not to punish Brandenburg's speech. In addition, they wrote concurring opinions that they hoped would herald an end to the clear and present danger test. Justice Black's short opinion indicated his agreement with Douglas. Black said that he understood the **per curiam** opinion to simply be citing *Dennis* but not indicating "any agreement on the Court's part with the 'clear and present danger' doctrine on which *Dennis* purported to rely."[63]

Justice Douglas wrote a longer opinion critiquing the clear and present danger rule. As you read the opinion, look for the reasons Douglas believed the test had been harmful for free speech, and see what test he would use instead.

### *Brandenburg v. Ohio*, 395 U.S. 444, 450 (1969)

Mr. Justice Douglas, concurring.

While I join in the opinion of the Court, I desire to enter a *caveat*. The "clear and present danger" test was adumbrated by Mr. Justice Holmes in a case arising during World War I. . . .

Though I doubt if the "clear and present danger" test is congenial to the First Amendment in time of a declared war, I am certain it is not reconcilable with the First Amendment in days of peace. . . .

[I]n *Dennis* . . . we opened wide the door, distorting the "clear and present danger" test beyond recognition. . . .

I see no place in the regime of the First Amendment for any "clear and present danger" test, whether strict and tight as some would make it, or free-wheeling as the Court in *Dennis* rephrased it.

When one reads the opinions closely and sees when and how the "clear and present danger" test has been applied, great misgivings are aroused. First, the threats were often loud but always puny and made serious only by judges so wedded to the *status quo* that critical analysis made them nervous. Second, the test was so twisted and perverted in *Dennis* as to make the trial of those teachers of

63. 395 U.S. at 449–50 (Black, J., concurring).

Marxism an all-out political trial which was part and parcel of the cold war that has eroded substantial parts of the First Amendment. . . .

I think that all matters of belief are beyond the reach of subpoenas or the probings of investigators. . . . That is the deep-seated fault in the infamous loyalty-security hearings which, since 1947 when President Truman launched them, have processed 20,000,000 men and women. Those hearings were the most blatant violations of the First Amendment we have ever known.

*The line between what is permissible and not subject to control and what may be made impermissible and subject to regulation is the line between ideas and overt acts* (emphasis added).   ◆◆◆

The federal cases that have come after *Brandenburg* suggest that the majority opinion has not been applied in a manner that would allow punishment of speech by looking for, and easily discovering, a clear and present danger created by such speech. Federal courts have remained loyal to the three tests set forth in *Brandenburg,* and have not used the clear and present danger standard.

### Federal Cases Apply the *Brandenburg* Test

Subsequent federal cases have dealt with elements of the *Brandenburg* test.[64] The requirement that the illegality advocated must be *imminent* was upheld in *Hess v. Indiana.*[65] In *Hess,* the police had cleared antiwar demonstrators from a public street near the University of Indiana. The defendant said, "We'll take the fucking street later," addressing his remarks to no particular person. He was convicted for disorderly conduct, and the Indiana Supreme Court upheld his conviction on the grounds that his statement "was intended to incite further lawless action on the part of the crowd in the vicinity . . . and was likely to produce such action."[66]

The Supreme Court reversed Hess's conviction, based on a lack of imminence. The Court held that "at best, the statement could be taken as counsel for present moderation; at worst, it amounted to nothing more than advocacy of illegal action at some indefinite future time." However, *Brandenburg* does not allow a state to punish advocacy of illegal conduct when it is not directed to producing "*imminent* lawless action."[67]

The Tenth Circuit Court of Appeals also relied on *Brandenburg*'s imminence requirement to invalidate a conviction in *National Gay Task Force v. Board of Education.*[68] At issue in this case was an Oklahoma law that allowed public school teachers to be terminated if they made statements that advo-

---

64. For an excellent analysis of post-*Brandenburg* incitement cases through 1985, see Paul Siegel, "Protecting Political Speech: *Brandenburg v. Ohio* Updated," in *Perspectives on Freedom of Speech,* p. 136.
65. 414 U.S. 105 (1973).
66. *Id.* at 108.
67. *Id.*
68. 729 F. 2d 1270 (10th Cir., 1984), aff'd 470 U.S. 903 (1985).

cated, promoted, or encouraged public or private homosexual activity, if those statements were likely to come to the attention of students or co-workers. The appeals court invalidated the statute, pointing out that "the First Amendment does not permit someone to be punished for advocating illegal conduct at some indefinite future time."[69] The court noted that the statute would impermissibly allow the termination of a teacher who went before the state legislature and advocated a repeal of the Oklahoma antisodomy statute, although this type of advocacy is at the core of free speech protection.[70]

Courts have also followed the *Brandenburg* requirement that advocacy be *directed to* producing imminent lawless action, although the application of the rule has not always been sufficient to protect speech. In *United States v. Kelner*,[71] the defendant, a leader of the Jewish Defense League, made the following statement at a news conference:

> We have people who have been trained and who are out now and who intend to make sure that Arafat and his lieutenants do not leave this country alive. I am talking about justice . . . equal rights under the law. . . . Everything is planned in detail. . . . It's going to come off.[72]

Kelner was convicted for transmitting the threatened injury of another person in interstate commerce (the conference was covered by New York Channel WPIX, which has a three-state viewing area). The defendant claimed his statement was not intended to be a threat toward PLO leader Arafat, but was merely political hyperbole. The appeals court held that Kelner did have the intent required by the *Brandenburg* rule. The court upheld the jury's guilty verdict, because the jury must have found that the words are not political but express an intent to injure.

### THE *BRANDENBURG* RULE AND CONTEMPORARY COMMUNICATION

The clear and present danger cases you have read in this chapter all involved criminal prosecution, under which communicators were threatened with government sanction based on the harm their communication may have caused. In the past two decades, private citizens have also filed civil lawsuits alleging that various books, movies, and songs about violence have caused imitative violence. The courts have generally used the *Brandenburg* rule to deny recovery in these cases.[73]

For example, in *McCollum v. CBS, Inc.*,[74] the plaintiffs sued rock musician Ozzy Osbourne and CBS records because their nineteen-year-old son had shot

---

69. *Id.* at 1274.
70. *Id.*
71. 534 F. 2d 1020 (2nd Cir., 1976).
72. *Id.* at 1021.
73. Laura W. Brill, *The First Amendment and the Power of Suggestion: Protecting "Negligent" Speakers in Cases of Imitative Harm*, 94 Columbia Law Review 984, 995 (April 1994).
74. 249 Cal. Rptr. 187 (Ct. App. 1988).

himself in the head after repeatedly listening to an Osbourne song, "Suicide Solution."[75] The California appellate court held that the *Brandenburg* rule mandated the rejection of the plaintiff's claim. The court held that the music was not intended to cause "the imminent suicide of listeners."[76]

The film medium has also been accused of causing violence. Violence has broken out near theaters after the opening of films with violent or gang-related themes, such as *Boyz N the Hood, New Jack City,* and *Juice.*[77] In *Yakubowicz v. Paramount Pictures, Corp.,*[78] a father sued the filmmaker because his son had been stabbed to death by an attacker who had just seen *The Warriors.* The movie was replete with gang violence, and the perpetrator had uttered a line from the picture before committing the crime. The plaintiff argued that the *Brandenburg* standard had been met, but the Massachusetts court disagreed, noting that the movie "does not at any point exhort, urge, entreat, solicit, or overtly advocate or encourage unlawful or violent activity on the part of the viewers."[79]

Special circumstances have sometimes caused state courts not to follow the general trend to apply *Brandenburg.* In *Walt Disney Productions, Inc., v. Shannon,*[80] a suit was filed because an eleven-year-old had injured herself after imitating a television broadcast during which a sound effect was created by spinning a BB in a balloon. The Georgia Supreme Court ruled that the appropriate test was the *Schenck* clear and present danger rule, rather than *Brandenburg.*[81] The Georgia court may have invoked the lighter standard because the plaintiff was a child,[82] but despite applying the clear and present danger rule, the court denied recovery.[83]

Subliminal messages received less protection from a Nevada court in *Vance v. Judas Priest.*[84] The claim in *Vance* was that two teenagers had attempted suicide after being exposed to subliminal messages in the defendant's album. Although the defendant won the case, the Nevada judge ruled that the First Amendment did not apply, because the court did not believe that subliminal messages constituted "speech."[85]

---

75. The lyrics in question are:
  *Where to hide, Suicide is the only way out*
  *Don't you know what it's really about . . .*
  *Why try, why try*
  *Get the gun and try it*
  *Shoot, shoot, shoot*
Id. at 190–91, n. 5.
76. *Id.*at 193.
77. *Id.* at 985.
78. 536 N.E. 2d 1067 (Mass. 1989).
79. *Id.* at 1071.
80. 276 S.E. 2d 580 (Ga. 1981).
81. *Id.* at 582.
82. Brill, p. 1004–05.
83. 276 S.E. 2d at 583.
84. Cited in Brill, p. 1003. 1990 WL 130920 (Nev. Dist. Ct., Aug. 24, 1990).
85. *Id.* at 22–32.

# Rap Music as Incitement to Illegal Conduct

Rap artists may be the next defendants in incitement to illegal conduct cases. Police organizations demanded that Time-Warner stop distributing Ice-T's song "Cop Killer."[1] In several incidents at New York City swimming pools, young men taunted or assaulted young girls while chanting Tag Team's "Whoomp! (There It Is)."[2] Harlem pastor Calvin O. Butts III stated, "You get to the point where you are constantly hearing, over and over, talk about mugging people, killing women, beating women, sexual behavior. When young people see this—14, 15, 16 years of age—they think this is acceptable behavior."[3]

Would "hard core" rap music (glorifying crime, violence against women, and promiscuous sex) be protected by the *Brandenburg* standard? Should it make any difference if rap is particularly popular among minors? (Most of the speech in the incitement cases, from *Schenck* to *Brandenburg*, was directed primarily to adults.)

Are rappers significantly different from other news commentators? Public Enemy's Chuck D. argues that rap music is the Cable News Network of its audience,[4] and if sex, crime, and drugs are common themes in rap music, it is only because performers are describing the reality of many neighborhoods.

1. *Police Can't Budge Time on Ice-T's Song,* Fresno Bee (July 16, 1992), p. A4.
2. Michael Marriott, *Hard Core Rap Lyrics Stir Black Backlash,* The New York Times (August 15, 1993), p. 42.
3. *Id.*
4. *Id.*

◆◆◆

## SUMMARY

This chapter has considered the question of when speech should be protected by the First Amendment, despite the fact that such speech risks inciting people to commit crimes. The Supreme Court announced the clear and present danger test in its 1919 *Schenck* decision—the case wherein Justice Holmes contended that the First Amendment does not protect all speech, since one "cannot shout fire in a theatre, thereby causing a panic." Clear and present danger was the law of the land for fifty years, and the rule was often interpreted to allow for the conviction of speakers whose words had a mere "tendency" to cause illegal conduct. Beginning with the Holmes and Brandeis dissent in *Abrams,* some justices and commentators argued that the clear and present danger rule made it too easy to convict speakers whose only real crime was advocacy of an unpopular view. The persecution of Communists was a prime example of how the clear and present danger rule could be used to punish dissidents. Finally, in the 1969 *Brandenburg* decision, speakers were afforded additional protection. Nowadays, a speech that is alleged to incite illegal conduct cannot be punished unless the speaker intends to incite imminent lawless action and the advocacy is likely to produce such conduct.

# Chapter 5    Objectives

**After reading chapter 5,
you should understand
the following:**

◆ *The types of information that the government has attempted to censor on the grounds that secrecy is needed to preserve national security. The public's need for access to all relevant information about U.S. foreign policy, in order to make informed democratic decisions (a core goal of the First Amendment).*

◆ *The conflict between the societal goals of open, democratic decisions about U.S. foreign policy and optimal foreign policy (which may require secrecy).*

◆ *The judicial doctrines that have been used to resolve the conflict between democratic decision making and the need for secrecy in foreign policy.*

◆ *The heavy presumption against any prior restraint on the communication of information, even when the restraint is said to be justified by national security.*

◆ *The controversy over the executive branch's ability to prejudice the marketplace of ideas by selectively releasing secret foreign policy information to support its position on the issues.*

# 5 Is Freedom of Speech Inconsistent with National Security?

IN DEVELOPING THE marketplace of ideas metaphor for freedom of speech, we will study limits on the free exchange of certain ideas. These include obscenity, which threatens the perceived moral framework of the marketplace; and hate speech or fighting words, which threaten its order and structure. Suppose, however, we were to consider a threat to the *existence* of the marketplace, occasioned by a free exchange of ideas. For example, should military secrets be kept out on the grounds that without national security, a foreign power could destroy the marketplace of ideas along with all our other freedoms?

Before you answer, consider the following hypothetical. The President sends 500,000 U.S. troops to the former Yugoslavia, in support of the government of Bosnia. Reaction here is tumultuous. Some are appalled at the suffering of the people of Bosnia and believe the United States has a moral obligation to intervene. Others believe that not one drop of American blood is worth shedding on behalf of Bosnia. The pros and cons are argued in Washington, in small-town churches, and in neighborhood bars. A bill to cut off funding for this action and bring the troops home is introduced in the House of Representatives.

In the midst of this hypothetical situation, a State Department employee illicitly brings copies of classified information[1] to the *Washington Post*. These documents reveal the following:

1. The United States will undertake massive air attacks against Bosnian Serb strongholds within forty-eight hours.

---

1. Classified information is information that the executive branch of government wishes to keep secret. Under Executive Order 12,356, 3 C.F.R. 166 (1983), the executive branch can classify information as top secret, secret, and confidential. Although the Freedom of Information Act, 5 *U.S. Code*, Section 552 (1988) mandates that government information on many subjects must be made available to the public, there is an exemption for information the Executive opts to keep "secret in the interest of national defense or foreign policy" (*Id.*, Section 552 [b] [1] [A]).

A list of places to be attacked is included. These attacks constitute the strongest use of U.S. military force in the region to date.

2. A top-secret Defense Department study predicts that the United States would suffer at least 100,000 casualties before it could end fighting in Bosnia.

3. A memo from the secretary of state to the President suggests that the American people would never support an extended and unwinnable war on behalf of Bosnia. The secretary's suggestion is to send the troops over to the region as a bluff and attempt to negotiate a peaceful end to the conflict from that position of strength. The President has written "good idea" on the bottom of the memo.

A *Post* reporter, who owes the President a favor, calls the White House and says that the *Post* plans to publish these documents the next morning. The President's lawyers rush to federal court, and in a secret hearing, demand that the judge issue an injunction prohibiting the *Post* from running the story.

If you were the judge, would you block publication of the documents?

To make this decision, you would need to resolve the conflict between freedom of expression (including the public's right to know) and the need for national security. The First Amendment assumes that our society can make the best decisions when we have an unrestrained marketplace of ideas.[2] These classified documents in our hypothetical contain information that is highly relevant to an informed public decision about fighting a war in Bosnia, including how the war will be prosecuted, what level of casualties to expect, and which negotiating strategy the government intends to use.

The President might reply that publishing this information is somewhat like falsely shouting "Fire!" in a crowded theatre. She or he could say that it is the Commander-in-Chief's job to protect the security of the nation and to support our troops in the field. If the Bosnian Serbs know when and where air attacks are coming, they will be better prepared to fight, and U.S. casualties will be higher. Projections of high American casualties may bolster the opponent's morale, and the American negotiating position would be weakened if the Bosnian Serbs believed that the threatened invasion was a bluff. The President might also argue that publication of this information would strengthen domestic opposition to the war. The high level of protest in the United States during the Vietnam War arguably motivated the North Vietnamese to fight harder, knowing that America's patience with the war would erode.

This chapter examines how the Supreme Court has dealt with First Amendment and national security conflicts such as these. You will learn when existing case law allows, and disallows, censorship. The first section emphasizes the "Pentagon Papers" case—the landmark case on this subject—which arose when the *New York Times* and *Washington Post* attempted to publish secret

---

2. See, e.g., Justice Holmes's dissent in *Abrams*, in chapter 4 of this text.

government papers regarding the Vietnam War. The next section will consider subsequent contexts in which the federal courts have grappled with censorship in the name of national security. The final section considers how governmental control of information, in the name of national security, can limit the wares available to consumers in the marketplace of ideas.

## THE PENTAGON PAPERS: DO PRESIDENTIAL ASSERTIONS OF NATIONAL SECURITY JUSTIFY CENSORSHIP?

Most national security cases you will study involve government attempts to impose a prior restraint on the communication of information. In these cases, the government becomes aware of secret information that is to be published, and obtains a judicial injunction prohibiting publication. With the growth of the United States as a military power in the twentieth century, questions of when defense information could be censored began to receive increased judicial attention.

### *Near v. Minnesota:* Laying the Groundwork for Prior Restraint

*Near v. Minnesota*[3] did not involve national security. The issue was whether a Minnesota newspaper could be enjoined from publishing "scandalous and defamatory" matter[3a]—in this case, allegations that Minneapolis law enforcement agencies were derelict in their duty to arrest and punish gangsters.

Although the Court held that a prior restraint would be unconstitutional in this case, noting the historical importance of freedom to criticize public officials,[4] Chief Justice Charles Evans Hughes's majority opinion also argued that prior restraints could be acceptable in cases of national security. Hughes explained that prior restraints were not unconstitutional in every context:

> [T]he protection even as to previous restraints is not absolutely unlimited. But the limitation has been recognized only in exceptional cases. "When a nation is at war, many things that might be said in time of peace are such a hindrance to its effort that their utterance will not be endured so long as men fight and that no court could regard them as protected by any constitutional right" (*Schenck v. United States* [citations omitted]). No one would question but that a government might prevent actual obstruction to its recruiting service or the publication of the sailing dates of transports or the number and location of its troops.[5]

The nature of this exception to the constitutional ban on prior restraints did not become an issue in World War II or the Korean War. But during the highly divisive war in Vietnam, a landmark case was decided when two news-

3. 283 U.S. 697 (1931).
3a. Mason's Minn. Stat. 1927, 10, 123–1.
4. 283 U.S. at 716–19.
5. *Id.* at 716.

papers wanted to publish information that the government alleged would impair the national security.

### The Pentagon Papers Case Is Decided

*The Context of the Case.*   The Pentagon Papers consisted of classified documents that detailed the history of America's involvement in the Vietnam War. Daniel Ellsberg—who had worked for the Defense Department before becoming an activist against the war—copied the documents and gave them to the *New York Times*, and later to the *Washington Post* and other newspapers.

The documents contained information highly embarrassing to the government. For example, they showed that President Lyndon Johnson was secretly planning to escalate the war. At the same time, he was criticizing his 1964 opponent, Barry Goldwater, as a "hawk" who wanted to expand the conflict. The Pentagon Papers also showed that the government told the public that victory was in sight, while knowing that the opposite was true.[6]

The Nixon White House contended that publication of these documents would damage national security, jeopardize the safety of American prisoners of war, and harm U.S. foreign policy because other countries would perceive that the United States could not keep a secret.[7]

The government sought an injunction against publication of the documents. In New York, federal judge Murray Gurfein issued a temporary restraining order against the *Times*. This order marked the first instance in American history that a federal judge had issued a prior restraint against a specific newspaper article.[8] The case went to the Second Circuit Federal Court of Appeals, which ruled that the *New York Times* could publish the papers but that the *Times* must leave out any material the government found detrimental to national security. A similar legal battle was fought against the *Post* in Washington, culminating in an appeals court ruling against the government.[9]

*The Prior Restraint Is Unconstitutional.*   Both cases were appealed to the Supreme Court. By a six-to-three vote, the Court held that the injunctions against the *Times* and the *Post* were unconstitutional prior restraints. However, the justices could not agree on the rationale for their decision. After a short per curiam opinion, the members of the majority wrote six different opinions, none of which received the support of more than two justices. In addition, there were three dissenting opinions.

The First Amendment law to be learned from this case is that there is a heavy presumption against the use of prior restraint. Here, the government

---

6. Nat Hentoff, *The First Freedom, The Tumultuous History of Free Speech in America*, p. 192 (Delacorte Press, 1980).
7. *Id.* at 192–93. The President maintained that absolute confidentiality is often expected when leaders of foreign governments negotiate with the United States.
8. *Id.* at 193. Judge Gurfein lifted the order four days later, but the documents were not published while the issue was being appealed.
9. *United States v. Washington Post Co.*, 446 F. 2d 1327 (D.C. Cir., 1971).

did not overcome that presumption. This much can be found in the per curiam opinion. The concurring and dissenting opinions are also important because they provide examples of arguments for and against prior restraints, issued in the name of national security. Following are excerpts from several of these opinions. How do the justices propose that the following issues be resolved?

1. *Burden of proof.* All of the justices agree with the general rule that the government must meet a high standard of proof before a prior restraint is justified. Has the government met its burden in this case? Should the injunction against the newspapers be continued, at least temporarily, to give the government time to try and make a stronger case?

2. *Clash of values.* This case involves two conflicting values—the importance of a free flow of information about our government's foreign policy, and the right of the president to conduct that policy as he or she sees fit (which may include keeping some foreign policy information secret). Based on the intent of the Constitution's framers, and/or more modern judicial decisions, which value is more important? Should one value always take precedence?

3. *Pragmatic considerations.* How does society benefit by leaving the press free to publish information regarding foreign policy issues? What are the risks to society if such information is published?

### New York Times Co. v. United States,[10] 403 U.S. 713 (1971)

Per Curiam.

We granted certiorari in these cases in which the United States seeks to enjoin the *New York Times* and the *Washington Post* from publishing the contents of a classified study entitled "History of U.S. Decision-Making Process on Viet Nam Policy." (citation omitted).

"*Any system of prior restraints of expression comes to this court bearing a heavy presumption against its constitutional validity*" (emphasis added). *Bantam Books, Inc., v. Sullivan:* see also *Near v. Minnesota* (citations omitted). The Government "thus carries a heavy burden of proof for the imposition of such a restraint." . . . The District Court for the Southern District of New York in the *New York Times* case and the District Court for the District of Columbia and the Court of Appeals for the District of Columbia Circuit in the *Washington Post* case held that the Government had not met that burden. We agree. . . .

Mr. Justice Black, with whom Mr. Justice Douglas joins, concurring.

I believe that every moment's continuance of the injunctions against these newspapers amounts to a flagrant, indefensible, and continuing violation of the First Amendment. . . .

10. Together with *United States v. Washington Post Co.*

Our Government was launched in 1789 with the adoption of the Constitution. The Bill of Rights, including the First Amendment, followed in 1791. Now, for the first time in the 182 years since the founding of the Republic, the federal courts are asked to hold that the First Amendment does not mean what it says, but rather means that the Government can halt the publication of current news of vital importance to the people of this country. . . .

Madison and the other Framers of the First Amendment, able men that they were, wrote in language they earnestly believed could never be misunderstood: "Congress shall make no law . . . abridging the freedom . . . of the press. . . . " *Both the history and language of the First Amendment support the view that the press must be left free to publish news, whatever the source, without censorship, injunctions, or prior restraints* (emphasis added). . . .

Only a free and unrestrained press can effectively expose deception in government. And paramount among the responsibilities of a free press is the duty to prevent any part of the government from deceiving the people and sending them off to distant lands to die of foreign fevers and foreign shot and shell. In my view, far from deserving condemnation for their courageous reporting, the *New York Times,* the *Washington Post,* and other newspapers should be commended for serving the purpose that the Founding Fathers saw so clearly. In revealing the workings of government that led to the Vietnam war, the newspapers nobly did precisely that which the Founders had hoped and trusted they would do.

. . . [W]e are asked to hold that despite the First Amendment's emphatic command, the Executive Branch, the Congress, and the Judiciary can make laws enjoining publication of current news and abridging freedom of the press in the name of "national security." . . . To find that the President has "inherent power" to halt the publication of news by resort to the courts would wipe out the First Amendment and destroy the fundamental liberty and security of the very people the Government hopes to make "secure." . . .

The word "security" is a broad, vague generality whose contours should not be invoked to abrogate the fundamental law embodied in the First Amendment. The guarding of military and diplomatic secrets at the expense of informed representative government provides no real security for our Republic. *The Framers of the First Amendment, fully aware of both the need to defend a new nation and the abuses of the English and Colonial governments, sought to give this new society strength and security by providing that freedom of speech, press, religion, and assembly should not be abridged* (emphasis added). . . .

Mr. Justice Brennan, concurring.

. . . The entire thrust of the Government's claim throughout these cases has been that publication of the material sought to be enjoined "could," or "might," or "may" prejudice the national interest in various ways. But the First Amendment tolerates absolutely no prior judicial restraints of the press predicated upon surmise or conjecture that untoward consequences may result.

[I]n neither of these actions has the Government presented or even alleged that publication of items from or based upon the material at issue would cause the happening of an event of that nature [war or nuclear holocaust]. "[T]he chief purpose of [the First Amendment's] guaranty [is] to prevent previous restraints upon publication." *Near v. Minnesota*. . . . Thus, only governmental allegation and proof that publication must inevitably, directly, and immediately cause the occurrence of an event kindred to imperiling the safety of a transport already at sea can support even the issuance of an interim restraining order. In no event may mere conclusions be sufficient: for if the Executive Branch seeks judicial aid in preventing publication, it must inevitably submit the basis upon which that aid is sought to scrutiny by the judiciary. . . .

Mr. Justice White, with whom Mr. Justice Stewart joins, concurring.

I concur in today's judgments, but only because of the concededly extraordinary protection against prior restraints enjoyed by the press under our constitutional system. I do not say that in no circumstances would the First Amendment permit an injunction against publishing information about government plans or operations. Nor, after examining the materials the Government characterizes as the most sensitive and destructive, can I deny that revelation of these documents will do substantial damage to public interests. Indeed, I am confident that their disclosure will have that result. But I nevertheless agree that the United States has not satisfied the very heavy burden that it must meet to warrant an injunction against publication in these cases. . . .

What is more, terminating the ban on publication of the relatively few sensitive documents the Government now seeks to suppress does not mean that the law either requires or invites newspapers or others to publish them or that they will be immune from criminal action if they do. Prior restraints require an unusually heavy justification under the First Amendment; but failure by the Government to justify prior restraints does not measure its constitutional entitlement to a conviction for criminal publication. That the Government mistakenly chose to proceed by injunction does not mean that it could not successfully proceed in another way. . . .

The Criminal Code contains numerous provisions potentially relevant to these cases. . . . [For example], Section 793[11] makes it a criminal act for any unauthorized possessor of a document "relating to the national defense" either (1) willfully to communicate or cause to be communicated that document to any person not entitled to receive it or (2) willfully to retain the document and fail to deliver it to an officer of the United States entitled to receive it. . . .

Mr. Chief Justice Burger, dissenting.

. . . There is . . . little variation among the members of the Court in terms of resistance to prior restraints against publication. Adherence to this basic constitutional principle, however, does not make these cases simple. . . .

We do not know all the facts. No District Judge knew all the facts. No Court of Appeals judge knew all the facts. No member of this Court knows all the facts. . . .

Of course, the First Amendment right itself is not an absolute, as Justice Holmes so long ago pointed out in his aphorism concerning the right to shout

---

11. 18 *U.S. Code,* Section 793 (1976).

"fire" in a crowded theater if there was no fire. . . . Conceivably [exceptions to the First Amendment] may be lurking in these cases and would have been flushed if they had been properly considered in the trial courts, free from unwarranted deadlines and frenetic pressures. An issue of this importance should be tried and heard in a judicial atmosphere conducive to thoughtful, reflective deliberation, especially when haste, in terms of hours, is unwarranted in light of the long period the *Times*, by its own choice, deferred publication.[12]

It is not disputed that the *Times* has had unauthorized possession of the documents for three to four months, during which it has had its expert analysts studying them, presumably digesting them and preparing the material for publication. During all of this time, the *Times*, presumably in its capacity as trustee of the public's "right to know," has held up for publication purposes it considered proper and thus public knowledge was delayed. No doubt this was for a good reason; the analysis of 7,000 pages of complex material drawn from a vastly greater volume of material would inevitably take time and the writing of good news stories takes time. But why should the United States Government, from whom this information was illegally acquired by someone, along with all the counsel, trial judges, and appellate judges be placed under needless pressure? After these months of deferral, the alleged "right to know" has somehow become a right that must be vindicated instanter.

Would it have been unreasonable, since the newspaper could anticipate the Government's objections to release of secret material, to give the Government an opportunity to review the entire collection and determine whether agreement could be reached on publication? . . . To me, it is hardly believable that a newspaper long regarded as a great institution in American life would fail to perform one of the basic and simple duties of every citizen with respect to the discovery or possession of stolen property or secret government documents. . . .

The consequence of all this melancholy series of events is that we literally do not know what we are acting on. As I see it, we have been forced to deal with litigation concerning rights of great magnitude without an adequate record, and surely without time for adequate treatment either in the prior proceedings or in this Court. . . .

I would affirm the Court of Appeals for the Second Circuit and allow the District Court to complete the trial aborted by our grant of certiorari, meanwhile preserving the status quo in the *Post* case. We all crave speedier judicial processes but when judges are pressured as in these cases the result is a parody of the judicial function.

Mr. Justice Harlan, with whom The Chief Justice and Mr. Justice Blackmun join, dissenting.

These cases forcefully call to mind the wise admonition of Mr. Justice Holmes: . . .

---

12. As noted elsewhere, the *Times* conducted its analysis of the forty-seven volumes of Government documents over a period of several months and did so with a degree of security that a government might envy.

Great cases like hard cases make bad law. For great cases are called
great, not by reason of their real importance in shaping the law of the
future, but because of some accident of immediate overwhelming interest which appeals to the feelings and distorts the judgment. These
immediate interests exercise a kind of hydraulic pressure which makes
what previously was clear seem doubtful, and before which even well
settled principles of law will bend.

With all respect, I consider that the Court has been almost irresponsibly
feverish in dealing with these cases. . . .

But I think there is another and more fundamental reason why this judgment
cannot stand—a reason which also furnishes an additional ground for not reinstating the judgment of the District Court in the *Times* litigation, set aside by the Court
of Appeals. It is plain to me that the scope of the judicial function in passing upon
the activities of the Executive Branch of the government in the field of foreign affairs is very narrowly restricted. This view is, I think, dictated by the concept of sep-
aration of powers upon which our constitutional system rests.

In a speech on the floor of the House of Representatives, Chief Justice John
Marshall, then a member of that body, stated:

The President is the sole organ of the nation in its external relations,
and its sole representative with foreign nations. 10 *Annals of Cong.*
613 (1800).

From that time, shortly after the founding of the Nation, to this, there has
been no substantial challenge to this description of the scope of executive
power. . . .

From this constitutional primacy in the field of foreign affairs, it seems to me
that certain conclusions necessarily follow. Some of these were stated concisely by
President Washington, declining the request of the House of Representatives for
the papers leading up to the negotiation of the Jay Treaty:

The nature of foreign negotiations requires caution, and their successes
must often depend on secrecy; and even when brought to a conclusion a full disclosure of all the measures, demands, or eventual concessions which may have been proposed or contemplated would be extremely impolitic. . . .

[I]n my judgment the judiciary may not . . . redetermine for itself the probable impact of disclosure on the national security.

[T]he very nature of executive decisions as to foreign policy is political,
not judicial. Such decisions are wholly confided by our Constitution to
the political departments of the government, Executive and Legislative.
They are delicate, complex, and involve large elements of prophecy.
They are and should be undertaken only by those directly responsible
to the people whose welfare they advance or imperil. They are decisions of a kind for which the Judiciary has neither aptitude, facilities nor

responsibility and which has long been held to belong in the domain
of political power not subject to judicial intrusion or inquiry (citation
omitted).

. . . I can see no indication in the opinions of either the District Court or the
Court of Appeals in the *Post* litigation that the conclusions of the Executive were
given even the deference owing to an administrative agency, much less that owing
to a co-equal branch of the Government operating within the field of its constitutional prerogative. . . .

Pending further hearings in each case conducted under the appropriate
ground rules, I would continue the restraints on publication. I cannot believe that
the doctrine prohibiting prior restraints reaches to the point of preventing courts
from maintaining the *status quo* long enough to act responsibly in matters of such
national importance as those involved here.   ◆◆◆

We can glean two major points of consensus from the diverse opinions
written by the justices in the Pentagon Papers case. One is that the government has a heavy burden of proof before prior restraints are justified. The
other is the opposite side of this coin, namely, that only two justices (Black
and Douglas) took the viewpoint that news could never be subjected to prior
restraint. Justice Brennan's opinion emphasized that the government would
need a strong case to justify a prior restraint, but upon making this case, the
government could censor the press. Justice White's perspective posed an additional danger to the press—even in this case, where prior restraints were unjustified, there were a variety of laws under which the two newspapers could
be punished. The precedent set in *New York Times v. United States* was not sufficient to protect communicators in major cases that followed, as federal courts
opted to side with national security claims.

## FEDERAL COURTS GRAPPLE WITH COMPETING VALUES
## IN NATIONAL SECURITY CASES

### Prior Restraints on Government Employee Disclosure of Secret
### Information Are Justifiable

In the Pentagon Papers case, the question was whether a prior restraint
could be imposed on a third party (a newspaper), which had received classified information. In *United States v. Marchetti,*[13] the federal government sought
to restrain Marchetti, a former CIA agent, from writing about his experiences
as an agent. Marchetti had signed a contract promising not to divulge any
classified information, as well as a secrecy oath when he left the agency. That
oath bound him not to divulge any information relating to the national defense. The Fourth Circuit Court of Appeals ultimately decided the case, and

13. 466 F. 2d 1309 (4th Cir., 1972), *cert. den.,* 409 U.S. 1063 (1972).

ruled that a prior restraint was permissible but that only classified information could be so restrained.

### United States v. Marchetti, 466 F. 2d 1309 (4th Cir., 1972)

Marchetti claims that the present injunction is barred by the Supreme Court decision in the Pentagon Papers case because the Government has failed to meet the very heavy burden against any system or prior restraints on expression.

We readily agree with Marchetti that the First Amendment limits the extent to which the United States, contractually or otherwise, may impose secrecy requirements upon its employees and enforce them with a system of prior censorship. It precludes such restraints with respect to information which is unclassified or officially disclosed, but we are here concerned with secret information touching on the national defense and the conduct of foreign affairs, acquired by Marchetti while in a position of trust and confidence and contractually bound to respect it.

. . . Gathering intelligence information and the other activities of the [Central Intelligence] Agency, including clandestine affairs against other nations, are all within the President's constitutional responsibility for the security of the Nation as the Chief Executive and as Commander in Chief of our Armed forces. . . . Citizens have the right to criticize the conduct of our foreign affairs, but the Government also has the right and the duty to strive for internal secrecy about the conduct of governmental affairs in areas in which disclosure may reasonably be thought to be inconsistent with the national defense. . . .

Marchetti, by accepting employment with the C.I.A. and by signing a secrecy agreement, did not surrender his First Amendment right of free speech. The agreement is enforceable only because it is not a violation of those rights. We would decline enforcement of the secrecy oath signed when he left the employment of the C.I.A. to the extent that it purports to prevent disclosure of unclassified information, for, to that extent, the oath would be in contravention of his First Amendment rights.

Thus Marchetti retains the right to speak and write about the C.I.A. and its operations, and to criticize it as any other citizen may, but he may not disclose classified information obtained by him during the course of his employment which is not already in the public domain. . . ." ◆◆◆

At face value, the *Marchetti* opinion appears to be a compromise between the government's need to protect its secrets and the rights of Marchetti to criticize the CIA. But did the case provide too little protection for freedom of expression? In the Pentagon Papers case, the rationale was that the government needed to demonstrate a serious harm to national security before a prior restraint could be justified. In *Marchetti,* the federal appeals court held that any classified information possessed by the defendant could be censored, not merely classified information that would cause a clear and present danger to national security if disclosed. Is the public's need for information about their government any less merely because the information is possessed by a former employee rather than a newspaper? One commentator has suggested that government employees may know of information about our government that is vital to the public debate. David Topol writes:

> At times information may be classified because it reveals illegal acts or be-
> cause it will undermine administrative policies, and for the same reasons,
> leakers and reporters may be threatened with prosecution if they publish
> the information."[14]

## Prior Restraints on Nuclear Bomb Concepts Justified

*United States v. Progressive, Inc.*[15] is a case in which a federal court devoted considerable attention to an alleged harm that could justify a prior restraint. *The Progressive* magazine wanted to publish an article entitled "The H-Bomb Secret: How We Got It, Why We're Telling It." The government sought an injunction against publication, on the grounds that the information drawn together in the article could cause irreparable harm to the United States. As you read the opinion of the Wisconsin Federal District Court, analyze the danger that the court believes publication could cause. Also, decide whether the court's decision to place the threat to national security over freedom of speech is well reasoned.

### United States v. The Progressive, 467 F. Supp. 990 (W.D. Wisc., 1979)

Warren, District Judge.

. . . Does the article provide a "do-it-yourself" guide for the hydrogen bomb? Probably not. A number of affidavits make quite clear that a *sine qua non* to thermonuclear capability is a large, sophisticated industrial capacity coupled with a coterie of imaginative, resourceful scientists and technicians. One does not build a hydrogen bomb in the basement. However, the article could possibly provide sufficient information to allow a medium-size nation to move faster in developing a hydrogen weapon. It could provide a ticket to by-pass blind alleys.

The Morland piece [Morland authored the article for *The Progressive*] could accelerate the membership of a candidate nation in the thermonuclear club. Pursuit of blind alleys or failure to grasp seemingly basic concepts have been the cause of many inventive failures. . . .

The point has also been made that it is only a question of time before other countries will have the hydrogen bomb. That may be true. However, there are times in the course of human history when time itself may be very important. This time factor becomes critical when considering mass annihilation weaponry—wit-

---

14. David H. Topol, *United States v. Morison: A Threat to the First Amendment Right to Publish National Security Information*, 43 South Carolina Law Review 581, 600 (Spring 1992).
15. 467 F. Supp. 990 (W. D. Wisc., 1979), *dismissed*, 610 F. 2d 819 (7th Cir., 1979).

ness the failure of Hitler to get his V-1 and V-2 bombs operational quickly enough to materially affect the outcome of World War II. . . .

This case is different [from the Pentagon Papers case] in several important respects. In the first place, the study involved in the *New York Times* case contained historical data relating to events that occurred some three to twenty years previously. Secondly, the Supreme Court agreed with the lower court that no cogent reasons were advanced by the government as to why the article affected national security except that publication might cause some embarrassment to the United States. A final and most vital difference between these two cases is the fact that a specific statute is involved here. Section 2274 of The Atomic Energy Act prohibits anyone from communicating, transmitting or disclosing any restricted data to any person "with reason to believe such data will be utilized to injure the United States or to secure an advantage to any foreign nation." . . .

The Court is of the opinion that the government has shown that the defendants had reason to believe that the data in the article, if published, would injure the United States or give an advantage to a foreign nation. . . . What is involved here is information dealing with the most destructive weapon in the history of mankind, information of sufficient destructive potential to nullify the right to free speech and to endanger the right to life itself. . . . Faced with a stark choice between upholding the right to continued life and the right to freedom of the press, most jurists would have no difficulty in opting for the chance to continue to breathe and function as they work to achieve perfect freedom of expression. . . .

A mistake in ruling against *The Progressive* will seriously infringe cherished First Amendment rights. If a preliminary injunction is issued, it will constitute the first instance of prior restraint against a publication in this fashion in the history of the country, to this Court's knowledge. . . . A mistake in ruling against the United States could pave the way for thermonuclear annihilation for us all. In that event, our right to life is extinguished and the right to publish becomes moot. . . .

In light of these factors, this Court concludes that publication of the technical information on the hydrogen bomb contained in the article is analogous to publication of troop movements or locations in time of war and falls within the extremely narrow exception to the rule against prior restraint.     ◆◆◆


Judge Warren's opinion in this case exemplifies the ad hoc balancing doctrine discussed in chapter 1. He candidly compared the loss of First Amendment freedoms to an increased risk of a nuclear war, and ruled for the government because such a war would end the conditions which make free expression possible. Do you agree that the risk of nuclear war was high enough in this case to warrant a prior restraint?

*The Progressive* appealed the District Court's decision, but unlike the Pentagon Papers case, the appellate process was very slow. Despite the government's success in keeping the prior restraint for six months, it dropped its efforts in September 1979, because other newspapers had begun to publish information similar to that which *The Progressive* wanted to print. In addition, an ACLU researcher found the same type of information on the public shelves of the government atomic energy library in New Mexico.[16] The government's dropping of the case is not the equivalent of a legal victory on First Amendment grounds for *The Progressive*. Federal courts could accept prior restraints in the future if the government argues that publication of an article might result in a nuclear war.

### Limits on the Right to Know about the CIA

Prior restraints were also found acceptable in the case of *Snepp v. United States*.[17] Frank Snepp III, a former CIA agent, wrote a book describing CIA activities in South Vietnam. He did not obtain clearance from the Agency before publishing the book, although his contract provided that he would "not . . . publish . . . any information or material relating to the Agency, its activities or intelligence activities generally, either during or after the term of his employment . . . without specific prior approval by the Agency."[18]

The government sued Snepp for violating the agreement, and a federal district court issued an injunction requiring him to submit his future writings for prepublication review. The case ended up in the Supreme Court and resulted in a split decision. The issue was whether a prior restraint on Snepp was justified, even if the information he intended to publish was not classified. Do you think the danger to the United States was sufficient to justify a prior restraint in this case?

### *Snepp v. United States*, 444 U.S. 507 (1980)

Per Curiam.

. . . The government does not deny—as a general principle—Snepp's right to publish unclassified information. Nor does it contend—at this stage of the litigation—that Snepp's book contains classified material. The Government simply claims that, in light of the special trust reposed in him and the agreement that he signed, Snepp should have given the C.I.A. an opportunity to determine whether the material he proposed to publish would compromise classified information or sources. Neither of the Government's concessions undercuts its claim that Snepp's failure to submit to prepublication review was a breach of his trust. . . .

Undisputed evidence in this case shows that a C.I.A. agent's violation of his obligation to submit writings about the Agency for prepublication review impairs the C.I.A.'s ability to perform its statutory duties. Admiral Turner, Director of the C.I.A., testified without contradiction that Snepp's book and others like it have seriously impaired the effectiveness of American intelligence operations. He said:

---

16. Hentoff, p. 222.
17. 444 U.S. 507 (1980).
18. *Id.* at 508.

> Over the last six to nine months, we have had a number of sources dis-
> continue work with us. . . . We have had very strong complaints from a
> number of foreign intelligence services . . . who have questioned
> whether they should continue exchanging information with us, for fear
> it will not remain secret. I cannot estimate to you how many potential
> sources or liaison arrangements have never germinated because people
> were unwilling to enter into business with us. . . .

In view of this and other evidence in the record, both the District Court and
the Court of Appeals recognized that Snepp's breach of his explicit obligation to
submit his material—classified or not—for prepublication clearance has irreparably
harmed the United States Government. . . .

Mr. Justice Stevens, with whom Mr. Justice Brennan and Mr. Justice
Marshall join, dissenting.

In 1968, Frank W. Snepp signed an employment agreement with the C.I.A.
in which he agreed to submit to the Agency any information he intended to publish about it for prepublication review. The purpose of such an agreement . . . is
not to give the C.I.A. the power to censor its employees' critical speech, but rather
to ensure that classified, nonpublic information is not disclosed without the
Agency's permission. . . .

In this case Snepp admittedly breached his duty to submit the manuscript of
his book, *Decent Interval,* to the C.I.A. for prepublication review. However, the
Government has conceded that the book contains no classified, nonpublic material. Thus, by definition, the interest in confidentiality that Snepp's contract was designed to protect has not been compromised. . . .

Like an ordinary employer, the C.I.A. has a vital interest in protecting certain
types of information; at the same time, the C.I.A. employee has a countervailing interest in preserving a wide range of work opportunities (including work as an author)
and in protecting his First Amendment rights. *The public interest lies in a proper accommodation that will preserve the intelligence mission of the Agency while not abridging
the free flow of unclassified information* (emphasis added). When the Government
seeks to enforce a harsh restriction on the employee's freedom, despite its admission
that the interest the agreement was designed to protect—the confidentiality of classified information—has not been compromised, an equity court might well be persuaded that the case is not one in which the covenant should be enforced. . . .

[T]he Court seems unaware of the fact that its drastic new remedy has been
fashioned to enforce a species of prior restraint on a citizen's right to criticize the
government. Inherent in this prior restraint is the risk that the reviewing agency
will misuse its authority to delay the publication of a critical work or to persuade an
author to modify the contents of his work beyond the demands of secrecy. The
character of the covenant as a prior restraint on free speech surely imposes an especially heavy burden on the censor to justify the remedy it seeks. It would take
more than the Court has written to persuade me that that burden has been met.

I respectfully dissent.   ◆◆◆

## IS SUBSEQUENT PUNISHMENT A THREAT TO THE MARKETPLACE OF IDEAS?

Justice White's concurring opinion in the Pentagon Papers case made it clear that while a prior restraint could not be justified, there may be other ways in which the newspapers (or future communicators) could be punished, based on alleged threats to the national security.[19] In *United States v. Morison*,[20] a federal appeals court held that subsequent punishment for leaking classified information was not unconstitutional. Judge Russell's opinion found no First Amendment problems when a communicator is punished for disclosing information that the government has classified as secret. Judge Wilkinson's concurring opinion showed more concern with the First Amendment implications of the case, but also a reluctance to second-guess the government's decision to keep information secret.

### *United States v. Morison,* 844 F. 2d 1057 (4th Cir., 1988)

Russell, Circuit Judge:

The defendant is appealing his conviction . . . for violation . . . of two provisions of the Espionage Act, 18 U.S.C. 793(d) and (e). The violations of the Espionage Act involved the unauthorized transmittal of certain satellite secured photographs of Soviet naval preparations to "one not entitled to receive them" (count 1) and the obtaining of unauthorized possession of secret intelligence reports and the retaining of them without delivering them to "one entitled to receive them. . . .

The defendant was employed at the Naval Intelligence Support Center at Suitland, Maryland. . . . [He] saw, on the desk of another employee. . . , certain glossy photographs depicting a Soviet aircraft carrier under construction in a Black Sea naval shipyard. The photographs [were] produced by a KH-11 reconnaissance satellite photographing machine. . . . The photographs were stamped "Secret" and also had a "Warning Notice: Intelligence Sources of Methods Involved" imprinted on the borders of the photographs. . . . Unobserved, [Morison] picked the photographs up, secreted them, and, after cutting off the borders of the photographs which recorded the words "Top Secret" and the Warning Notice as well as any indication of their source, mailed them to Derek Wood [editor-in-chief of *Jane's Defence Weekly,* in London] personally. *Jane's Defence Weekly* published the photographs in its weekly edition a few days later and made the pictures available to other news agencies. One of these photographs was published on August 8, 1984 in the *Washington Post.* . . .

[The defendant] argues that, unless such an exemption [for leaks to the press] is read into these sections [of the Espionage Act] they will run afoul of the First Amendment. Actually we do not perceive any First Amendment rights to be implicated here. This certainly is no prior restraint case such as *New York Times v. United States,* and *United States v. [The] Progressive* (citations omitted). It is a pros-

19. *See* pp. 129, *supra.*
20. 844 F. 2d 1057 (4th Cir., 1988), *cert. denied,* 488 U.S. 908 (1988).

ecution under a statute, of which the defendant, who, as an employee in the intelligence service of the military establishment, had been expressly noticed of his obligations by the terms of his letter of agreement with the Navy. [The defendant] is being prosecuted for purloining from the intelligence files of the Navy national defense materials clearly marked as "Intelligence Information" and "Secret" and for transmitting [those] material[s] to "one not entitled to receive [them]." . . . We do not think that the First Amendment offers asylum under those circumstances, if proven, merely because the transmittal was to a representative of the press. . . .

[I]t seems beyond controversy that a recreant intelligence department employee who had abstracted from the government files secret intelligence information and had willfully transmitted or given it to one "not entitled to receive [them]" as did the defendant in this case, is not entitled to invoke the First Amendment as a shield to immunize his act of thievery. To permit the thief thus to misuse the Amendment would be to prostitute the salutary purposes of the First Amendment. . . .

Wilkinson, Circuit Judge, concurring:

. . . I do not think the First Amendment interests here are insignificant. Criminal restraints on the disclosure of information threaten the ability of the press to scrutinize and report on government activity. There exists the tendency, even in a constitutional democracy, for government to withhold reports of disquieting developments and to manage news in a fashion most favorable to itself. Public debate, however, is diminished without access to unfiltered facts. . . .

The First Amendment interest in informed popular debate does not simply vanish at the invocation of the words "national security." National security is public security, not government security from informed criticism. No decisions are more serious than those touching on peace and war, none are more certain to affect every member of society. Elections turn on the conduct of foreign affairs and strategies of national defense, and the dangers of secretive government have been well documented. Morison claims he released satellite photographs revealing construction of the first Soviet nuclear carrier in order to alert the public to the dimensions of a Soviet naval buildup. Although this claim is open to serious question, the undeniable effect of the disclosure was to enhance public knowledge and interest in the projection of Soviet sea power such as that revealed in the satellite photos.

The way in which those photographs were released, however, threatens a public interest that is no less important—the security of sensitive government operations. In an ideal world, governments would not need to keep secrets from their own people, but in this world much hinges on events that take place outside of public view. Intelligence gathering is critical to the formation of sound policy, and becomes more so every year with the refinement of technology and the growing threat of terrorism. Electronic surveillance prevents surprise attacks by hostile forces and facilitates international peacekeeping and arms control efforts. Confidential diplomatic exchanges are the essence of international relations.

None of these activities can go forward without secrecy. When the identities of our intelligence agents are known, they may be killed. When our electronic surveillance capabilities are revealed, countermeasures can be taken to circumvent them. When other nations fear that confidences exchanged at the bargaining table will only become embarrassments in the press, our diplomats are left helpless. When terrorists are advised of our intelligence, they can avoid apprehension and escape retribution. . . .

Courts have long performed the balancing task where First Amendment rights are implicated. . . . The aggressive balancing that courts have undertaken in other contexts is different from what would be required here. . . . [Q]uestions of national security and foreign affairs are "of a kind for which the Judiciary has neither aptitude, facilities, nor responsibility and which has long been held to belong in the domain of political power not subject to judicial intrusion or inquiry.". . .

[T]he judicial role must be a deferential one because the alternative would be grave. . . . Rather than enhancing the operation of democracy, as Morison suggests, this course would install every government worker with access to classified information as a veritable satrap. Vital decisions and expensive programs set into motion by elected representatives would be subject to summary derailment at the pleasure of one disgruntled employee.   ◆◆◆

Are the goals of the First Amendment satisfied when the government is given carte blanche to decide what information will be revealed to the American public? Withholding of government information is inimical to the concept of the marketplace of ideas. How can the American public make the best possible decision about the appropriate response to the threat posed by a foreign nation (e.g., the former Soviet Union in Morison's case) if they are denied relevant information about that nation's defense capabilities?

The power to keep information secret also gives the government the ability to manage public debate by prejudicing the marketplace of ideas. In the mid-1980s, when the United States was debating the wisdom of the Strategic Defense Initiative,[21] someone leaked classified information in favor of the project. Scientists who opposed the initiative could not feel safe in countering with leaks of their own.[22] Ray Kidder, a physicist at Livermore Laboratory, explained: "The public is getting swindled by one side that has access to classified information and can say whatever it wants and not go to jail, whereas we [the skeptics] can't say whatever we want. We would go to jail, that's the difference."[23]

Judge Wilkinson stated that courts lacked the competence to judge questions of national security. Can it be said that the executive branch lacks another important dimension of credibility: objectivity? After the Pentagon Papers were allowed to be published, executive branch predictions that the papers would cause grave harm, including the destruction of relations with

21. This proposal involved the United States attempting to place antimissile defenses in space, which could prevent nuclear warheads from reaching their target.
22. Topol, p. 601.
23. Flora Lewis, *A "Star Wars" Cover-Up,* New York Times (December 3, 1985), p. A31.

China, did not come true.[24] Yale Law professor Thomas Emerson has noted that "when national security claims are advanced there may well be a confusion of the interests of the administration in power with the interests of the nation."[25] Will a government in power, with an eye on re-election, be sufficiently public-spirited to release information that makes itself look bad?

## SUMMARY

At the beginning of this chapter, you were asked if the marketplace should allow free expression of secrets, even if their exposition threatened its existence. The tension between national security and free expression was exemplified by a hypothetical U.S. intervention in Bosnia. After reading this chapter, the implications of First Amendment law on this hypothetical information are evident. *Near v. Minnesota* indicates that disclosure of the location of the upcoming air attacks could likely be censored. Based on the Pentagon Papers case, the government would need to meet a very heavy burden of proof of harm to the nation, before prior restraints could be imposed on the disclosure of the Defense Department study and secretary of state's memo. The *Progressive* case shows the type of arguments the government would need to make in order to overcome its burden of proof. Because the information in the hypothetical was classified, however, the person who leaked the documents to the media could be punished, even if the facts were highly relevant to public debate on the intervention.

Have the courts struck an appropriate balance between the needs of the First Amendment and the national security? To answer that question, do not ask yourself whether censorship would be acceptable when a President you support withholds information about a war you believe in. Imagine instead a President (or candidate) whom you would never vote for, fighting a war you oppose. If you are comfortable with the President controlling the flow of information in either situation, you may agree that prior restraints are appropriate. If you would be troubled with the latter scenario (information controlled by a President you do not trust), you need a strong First Amendment.

24. Topol, p. 596.
25. Thomas I. Emerson, *National Security and Civil Liberties,* 9 Yale Journal of World Pub. Ord. 78, 80–81 (1982).

CHAPTER 6        *Learning Objectives*

**After reading chapter 6,
you should understand
the following:**

◆ *The categorical exceptions doctrine,
which holds that certain categories of expression are not protected by the First
Amendment.*

◆ *The fighting words exception, which
maintains that expression tending to incite immediate violence is not protected by
the First Amendment.*

◆ *The justification for exempting certain
categories of speech from the First Amendment, namely, that some words constitute
no essential part of any exposition of
ideas.*

◆ *The relation of the fighting words
doctrine to the theories of free speech that
were discussed in chapter 1.*

◆ *The evolution of the fighting words
definition, as it has narrowed and shifted
in focus from the content to the context of
expression.*

◆ *The unique contribution of* [**Cohen
v. California,**] *which recognized that the
emotive content of expression, as well as
the cognitive content, is protected by the
First Amendment.*

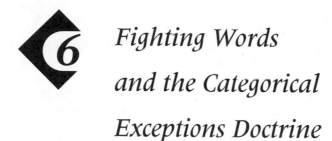

# Fighting Words and the Categorical Exceptions Doctrine

IN CHAPTER 1 we described several emerging legal doctrines that have altered the way we view freedom of expression in the United States. One of the more significant of these was the emerging doctrine of categorization, first suggested in the 1942 decision *Chaplinsky v. New Hampshire*. Historically this case is noteworthy because of its place in introducing categorization to First Amendment jurisprudence; but that is a long-range perspective. In a more immediate sense, the *Chaplinsky* case is also noteworthy because of its treatment of a *specific kind of categorization:* fighting words.

To understand the significance of labeling this kind of speech in exception to the First Amendment, let us consider the following scenario. As children, we may have been admonished by a parent for teasing a sibling—behavior that might promote a violent reaction. Or perhaps our teachers warned against taunting our classmates, again behavior that might precipitate verbal or physical retaliation.

When our parents reached back across the front seat of the family car, warning us with a wave of their finger, or our teachers admonished in class, they were really engaging the meaning of the fighting words doctrine. As children, our taunts had the potential of provoking a fight. Our words were *fighting words.* And by proscribing against them, our parents and our teachers were preserving a kind of harmony or domestic peace—but ultimately to what interest? And for whom?

One view suggests that our parents did this to preserve the peace, ostensibly because they couldn't trust their children to do this of their own accord, and in their own natural state, without parental supervision. A parental rule against fighting words, in this sense, is a tool for teaching and socializing children to what society sees as appropriate behavior.

Society also values preservation of the peace among adults. In chapter 3, you read that the British imposed restrictions on speech in the interest of preventing a breach of the peace.[1] American common law also punished speech that could provoke a violent response, based on a variety of theories.

These theories included breach of the peace, disorderly conduct, and nuisance. In Tennessee, a court ruled that obscene and vulgar words were indictable because they had a tendency to corrupt social morals, provoking violence and bloodshed.[2] A Kansas court sustained the conviction of a person using loud, profane, and indecent language, noting that "the peace of the city may have been disturbed" because the defendant called a man "a damn fool and a bastard."[3] A citizen who called a city council member a bootlegger at a meeting was convicted for disorderly conduct, because the words were uttered at a public meeting and labeled the member as a criminal. The court did note that a lesser insult, such as "souphead," would not have constituted disorderly conduct[4] And a Massachusetts court held that a nuisance conviction could be supported against a defendant who screamed profane words on a public highway, provided that the profane screaming was sufficient to upset all good citizens.[5]

Although American courts had long punished language that could provoke a disturbance of the peace, there was no uniform theory under which these words were punished. Furthermore, the question of whether the defendants' language in these cases could be protected by the First Amendment was not considered. In this chapter, you will study the fighting words doctrine as it was promulgated by the Supreme Court in its 1941 *Chaplinsky v. New Hampshire* decision and refined in later cases. You will also be introduced to another important theory articulated in *Chaplinsky*, the principle of categorical exceptions. This theory maintains that certain categories of expression, such as fighting words, do not constitute the type of speech that is protected by the Constitution.

## THE CATEGORICAL EXCEPTIONS AND FIGHTING WORDS DOCTRINES ARE ANNOUNCED IN *CHAPLINSKY*

Two questions facing the United States Supreme Court in 1941 were (1) could words that tend to provoke violence be prohibited under the First Amendment? and (2) if so, what criteria should the courts use to decide when words have this tendency? Although no federal case law or Supreme Court authority existed on the subject prior to this case, the Court was mindful of the influence of common law in cases like those mentioned earlier. The challenge for the Court was to fashion a rule protecting the state's interest in preventing violence without penalizing communicators' legitimate free expression rights.

1. See p. 3–46, *supra.*
2. *Bell v. State,* Swan 41 (1851).
3. *Topeka v. Heitman,* 47 Kan. 739 (1892).
4. *In Re Kirk,* 130 Atl. 569 (1925).
5. *Commonwealth v. Oaks,* 113 Mass. 8 (1873).

In 1942, the Supreme Court decided *Chaplinsky v. New Hampshire*, dealing with the application of a New Hampshire law aimed at preventing "offensive, derisive, or annoying" words in a public place. Walter Chaplinsky, a Jehovah's Witness, had been preaching and distributing literature on a streetcorner in Rochester, New Hampshire. Some local citizens complained to the City Marshall, Bowering, that Chaplinsky was denouncing all religion. Police officers later removed Chaplinsky—allegedly to protect him from an angry crowd. When he met Marshall Bowering near City Hall, Chaplinsky released a verbal fulmination which might seem tame by today's standards, but was considered outrageous and offensive at the time.

As you read the *Chaplinsky* decision, look for two important principles. First, it is important to comprehend why the Court held that fighting words were not protected by the First Amendment. Second, you should understand the Court's definition of fighting words. As you read the Court's analysis, decide whether the rules promulgated in *Chaplinsky* allow state and local governments to reduce the risk of violence in society without treading on the rights of communicators to express their ideas.

### *Chaplinsky v. New Hampshire,* 315 U.S. 568 (1942)

Mr. Justice Murphy (see Figure 6.1) delivered the opinion of the court.

Appellant, a member of the sect known as Jehovah's Witnesses, was convicted in the Municipal Court of Rochester, New Hampshire for violation of Chapter 378, Section 2 of the Public Laws of New Hampshire:

✳ No person shall address any offensive, derisive or annoying word to any other person who is lawfully in any street or other public place, nor call him by any offensive or derisive name, nor make any noise or exclamation in his presence or hearing with intent to deride, offend or annoy him, or to prevent him from pursuing his lawful business occupation.

The complaint charged the appellant, with force and arms, in a certain public place in said city of Rochester, to wit, on the public sidewalk of the easterly side of Wakefield Street, near unto the entrance of the City Hall, did unlawfully repeat, the words following, addressed to the complainant, that is to say, "You are a god damned racketeer" and "a damned Fascist and the whole government of Rochester are Fascists or agents of Fascists," the same being offensive, derisive and annoying words and names.

Upon appeal there was a trial in *de novo* of appellant before a jury in the Superior Court. He was found guilty and the judgment of conviction was affirmed by the Supreme Court of the State. . . .

By motions and exceptions, appellant raised the questions that the statute was invalid under the Fourteenth Amendment of the Constitution of the United States, in that it placed an unreasonable restraint on freedom of speech, freedom

*Figure 6.1. Justice Frank Murphy, formerly President Roosevelt's attorney general, was appointed to the Court in 1940. He authored the* Chaplinsky *opinion in 1942.*
(Harris & Ewing. Collection of the Supreme Court of the United States.)

of the press, and freedom of worship, and because it was vague and indefinite. These contentions were overruled and the case comes here on appeal. . . .

✦ Allowing the broadest scope to the language and purpose of the Fourteenth Amendment, it is well understood that the right of free speech is not absolute at all times and under all circumstances. There are certain well defined and narrowly limited classes of speech, the prevention and punishment of which have never been thought to raise any Constitutional problem. These include the lewd and obscene, the profane, the libelous, and the insulting or "fighting" words—those which by their very utterance inflict injury or tend to incite an immediate breach of the peace. *It has been well observed that such utterances are no essential part of any ex-* ✳ *position of ideas, and are of such slight value as a step to truth that any benefit that may be derived from them is clearly outweighed by the social interest in order and morality* (emphasis added). Resort to epithets or personal abuse is not in any proper sense communication of information or opinions safeguarded by the Constitution, and its punishment as a criminal act would raise no question under that instrument. . . .

On the authority of its earlier decisions, the state court declared that the statute's purpose was to preserve the public peace, no words being "forbidden except such as have a direct tendency to cause acts of violence by the persons to whom, individually, the remark is addressed." It was further said: "The word *offen-* ✳ *sive* is not to be defined in terms of what a particular addressee thinks. . . . The test

> is what men of common intelligence would understand would be words likely to cause an average addressee to fight. . . . The English language has a number of words and expressions which by general consent are *fighting words* when said without a disarming smile. . . . Such words, as ordinary men know, are likely to cause a fight. So are threatening, profane or obscene revilings. Derisive and annoying words can be taken as coming within the purview of the statute as heretofore interpreted only when they have this characteristic of plainly tending to excite the addressee to a breach of the peace. . . . The statute, as construed, does no more than prohibit the face-to-face words plainly likely to cause a breach of the peace by the addressee, words whose speaking constitutes a breach of the peace by the speaker—including classical fighting words, words in current use less classical but likely to cause violence, and other disorderly words, including profanity, obscenity and threats."
>
> We are unable to say that the limited scope of the statute as thus construed contravenes the Constitutional right of free expression. It is a statute narrowly drawn and limited to define and punish specific conduct lying within the domain of state power, the use in a public place of words likely to cause a breach of the peace. . . .
>
> Nor can we say that the application of the statute to the facts disclosed by the record substantially or unreasonably impinges upon the privilege of free speech. Argument is unnecessary to demonstrate that the appellations "damned racketeer" and "damned Fascist" are epithets likely to provoke the average person to retaliation, and thereby cause a breach of the peace. . . . ◆◆◆

Justice Murphy's conclusion that fighting words are not supported by the First Amendment is based on two premises. First, he defines the First Amendment's significance in terms of one of the justifications discussed in chapter 1, namely, its relationship to the promotion and attainment of *truth*. This is suggested in the passage describing categorical exceptions like fighting words possessing "slight social value as a step to truth. . . ." Justice Murphy's opinion fails to consider Walter Chaplinsky's interest in communicating his thoughts about a government official, using the language *he* believes will best express his viewpoint. To Murphy, fighting words may be excluded from the marketplace of ideas because they are not ideas. It is likely that Justice Murphy was influenced by the writings of legal scholar Zechariah Chafee (see Figure 6.2), who also described the function of free expression in this way (see p. 149).

The second premise supporting a fighting words exception to the First Amendment is based on the state's interest in promoting order and tranquility—what we described earlier as civility. By specifically referring to fighting words as those that "inflict injury or tend to incite an immediate breach of the peace," the Court here draws upon the previously described tendency at common law to limit expression and behavior that threatened the peace or was disorderly. Although this would be challenged and modified in later decisions, the Court here suggests that government has a key interest in controlling against this and

*Figure 6.2. Zechariah Chafee, Harvard Law professor, was never a member of the Supreme Court, but his writings proved influential in the Court's decisions involving the First Amendment.* (Courtesy of Harvard University Archives.)

promoting civility.[6] Combining his two premises, Justice Murphy suggests that speech that may incite a breach of the peace contributes little or nothing to finding the truth and therefore is unprotected by the First Amendment.

The *Chaplinsky* opinion also provided some insight into the criteria for determining when abusive language would rise to the level of fighting words and fall outside the scope of constitutional protection. The Court's opinion noted that fighting words "tend to incite an immediate breach of the peace." To the Court, it was obvious that Chaplinsky's insults would have this tendency because they would provoke the average person to retaliation. It was assumed that *men* of common intelligence knew what words were likely to cause a fight. When the Court revisited the fighting words doctrine in later decades, it would add more precision to its definition. But in 1942, the Court seemed to presume that males shared an implicit understanding of the meaning of fighting words, making further definition unnecessary.

The second prong of the Court's definition of fighting words, those that "by their very utterance inflict injury," was left unexplained. There was no evidence that Chaplinsky's words had inflicted any injury on Mr. Bowering. Was the Court thinking about words that cause hurt feelings? Or was the Court presuming words that could inflict deeper psychological scars?[7] Should the

6. For a discussion of this perspective, see *The Demise of the* Chaplinsky *Fighting Words Doctrine: An Argument for Its Interment,* 106 Harvard Law Review 1129, 1131 (1993).
7. One type of speech that can lead to significant psychological injury is hate speech. Examples of these injuries are provided in chapter 7.

# Chafee's Influence on the Chaplinsky *Opinion*

Of the many legal theorists and scholars whose writings and arguments have influenced the judiciary in this country, Harvard law professor Zechariah Chafee Jr. is perhaps the most significant. Chafee had published an article in the *Harvard Law Review* praising Justice Holmes's clear and present danger test in *Schenck*, and had good fortune to meet Holmes at social event hosted by Harvard colleague Harold Laski. Although Chafee's article had praised Holmes for the test, it had also admonished him for limiting its possibilities. Conceivably because of the impressions afforded Holmes in the face-to-face encounter, he later that year adopted Chafee's position while dissenting in the *Abrams* decision, discussed here in chapter 4.

It should come as no surprise, then, that Chafee would be cited later by Justice Murphy in *Chaplinsky* to support the proposition that certain categories of speech could be excluded from the First Amendment.[1] The actual citation in *Chaplinsky* is from Chafee's masterwork, *Free Speech in the United States.*[2] Interestingly, although Chafee was undoubtedly aware of instances in which fighting words had not been protected at common law, he cited no such cases. More likely, Chafee's view was guided by his perspective of the purpose behind free expression in our society:

> ✳ The true meaning of freedom of speech seems to be this. One of the most important purposes of society and government is *the discovery and spread of truth* on subjects of general concern. This is possible only through absolutely unlimited discussion, for . . . once force is thrown into the argument it becomes a matter of chance whether it is thrown on the false side or on the true, and truth loses all its natural advantages in the contest.[3]

In Chafee's calculus, freedom of speech and expression was critical because of its general connection to the attainment of truth. In this sense, he did not regard free expression as an absolute or natural right[4] but perhaps in a more utilitarian context, where truth was a necessary prerequisite to dealing with urgent and real social problems.[5] For Chafee, expression was "for the sake of discussion, and discussion was for the rational pursuit of truth."[6] Of the justifications provided for freedom of speech in chapter 1, which one(s) are consistent with Professor Chafee's views on the reasons for freedom of speech?

1. 315 U.S. at 572.
2. Zechariah Chafee Jr., *Free Speech in the United States* (Harvard Univ. Press, 1941).
3. *Id.*, p. 31.
4. Frances Canavan, *Freedom of Expression: Purpose as Limit*, p. 126 (Carolina Academic Press, 1984).
5. J. Prude, *Portrait of a Civil Libertarian: The Faith and Fear of Zechariah Chafee Jr.*, 60 Journal of American History 633, 642 (1973).
6. Canavan, p. 134.

◆◆◆

First Amendment permit any exception on the grounds that speech causes psychological damage? These questions are addressed later in this chapter and in chapter 7, on hate speech.

## THE FIGHTING WORDS DEFINITION IS REFINED IN *TERMINIELLO*

In 1949, the Court revisited the question of when communicators could be punished, either because their words tended to provoke violence or because they inflicted injury. In *Terminiello v. Chicago*,[8] the Court held that words could *not* be proscribed just because their content created a personal, emotional type of distress to one's sensibilities. In this case, the Court reviewed the constitutionality of a breach of the peace ordinance under which a suspended Catholic priest had been convicted. Father Terminiello had verbally lashed out at Jews and African Americans while addressing a veterans' group in a crowded Chicago auditorium. Outside the hall, more than a thousand angry demonstrators protested against the meeting. Some of the protesters threw ice picks and rocks at the police officers standing at the doors to the auditorium, and several windows were broken. Father Terminiello was later charged and convicted under a breach of the peace ordinance.

The trial court instructed the jury that Terminiello could be convicted for speech that "stirs the public to anger, invites dispute, brings about a condition of unrest, or creates a disturbance."[9] Based on this interpretation of the Chicago ordinance, the Supreme Court found the law unconstitutional because it prohibited speech that was protected by the First Amendment. Specifically, the Court noted that

> [A] function of free speech under our system of government is to invite dispute. It may indeed best serve its high purpose when it induces a condition of unrest, creates dissatisfaction with conditions as they are, or even stirs people to anger. Speech is often provocative and challenging. It may strike at prejudices and preconceptions and have profound unsettling effects as it presses for acceptance of an idea. That is why freedom of speech, though not absolute . . . is nevertheless protected against censorship or punishment, unless shown likely to produce a clear and present danger of a serious evil that rises far above public inconvenience, annoyance, or unrest.[10]

The holding in *Terminiello* refined the meaning of one prong of the *Chaplinsky* fighting words definition. Not all speech that provoked an emotional reaction or threatened some people's sensitivities would be unprotected by the First Amendment on the grounds that it "inflicts injury." The Court made it clear that the speech must induce a reaction greater than annoyance or unrest.

8. 337 U.S. 1 (1949).
9. *Id.* at 4.
10. *Id.*

The *Terminiello* opinion also recognized the value of free speech as an instrument of democratic government. An important premise in the Court's ruling against the Chicago ordinance was that debate on controversial issues would inevitably stir people's passions and sometimes induce anger between the participants. A rule that speech could be proscribed when it caused such effects would narrow the range of acceptable ideas in public debate to those that were not offensive to the dominant political group.[11]

What *Terminiello* did not firmly establish, however, was the resolution to another begging question, left over from *Chaplinsky*: namely, were these offensive terms to be evaluated as fighting words on the basis of *content* or *context*? The distinction is important, for a categorical exception based upon content would mean that government could sanction certain words because of their meaning alone, whereas an exception based upon context would require examining the situation in which the words were communicated to determine whether they were provocative.

To illustrate the difference between a content-based test and one based on context, let us contrast the circumstances surrounding Terminiello's speech with a private discussion at a coffee house. If a fighting words rule is based upon the content of the words, the court would reach the same result regardless of the surrounding circumstances. If the racist terms used by Terminiello would cause the average person to fight, they would be punishable as fighting words, regardless of whether they were delivered in the midst of two agitated groups of political enemies or in the serene atmosphere of a coffee house. If the communication context were analyzed to determine whether language constitutes fighting words, a different result would probably ensue. Racist language could be found likely to provoke violence in the context of Terminiello's actual speech. It would be much less likely to create a risk of violence in an environment where people tend to be more placid, particularly when no alcohol is being served.

## THE DEFINITION OF FIGHTING WORDS IS NARROWED

### *Cohen v. California*: Diverse Contributions to Freedom of Speech Doctrine

After *Terminiello*, more than two decades would pass before the Supreme Court gave further guidance on the question of whether context or content would determine when expressions were classified as fighting words.

***The Cohen Opinion.***   *Cohen v. California* was a very important case for freedom of speech. *Cohen* was decided in the midst of the war in Vietnam, and the four-letter word Mr. Cohen used to critique the draft often draws people's attention to the case. However, the implications of *Cohen* go well beyond the right of a communicator to use a popular expletive. In *Cohen*, the Court utilized a contextual fighting words analysis and ruled in favor of protecting speech.

11. *Id.* at 4–5.

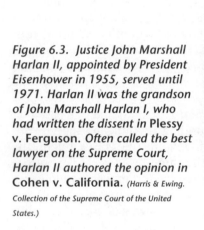

*Figure 6.3. Justice John Marshall Harlan II, appointed by President Eisenhower in 1955, served until 1971. Harlan II was the grandson of John Marshall Harlan I, who had written the dissent in* Plessy v. Ferguson. *Often called the best lawyer on the Supreme Court, Harlan II authored the opinion in* Cohen v. California. *(Harris & Ewing. Collection of the Supreme Court of the United States.)*

Justice Harlan's (see Figure 6.3) opinion also provided judicial validation of a concept that is highly salient to students of communication: the principle that the *emotive force* of a speaker's words may be the most essential element of his or her message.

### Cohen v. California, 403 U.S. 13 (1971)

Mr. Justice Harlan delivered the opinion of the Court.

Appellant Paul Robert Cohen was convicted in the Los Angeles Municipal Court of violating that part of California Penal Code Section 415 which prohibits "maliciously and willfully disturb[ing] the peace or quiet of any neighborhood or person . . . by . . . offensive conduct. . . . " He was given 30 days' imprisonment. The facts upon which his conviction rests are detailed as follows:

On April 26, 1968, the defendant was observed in the Los Angeles County Courthouse in the corridor outside of division 20 of the municipal court wearing a jacket bearing the words "Fuck the Draft" which were plainly visible. There were women and children present in the corridor. The defendant was arrested. The defendant testified that he wore the jacket knowing that the words were on the jacket as a means of informing the public of the depth of his feelings against the Vietnam War and the draft.

＊ The defendant did not engage in, nor threaten to engage in, nor did anyone as the result of his conduct in fact commit or threaten to commit any act of violence. The defendant did not make any loud or unusual noise, nor was there any evidence that he uttered any sound prior to his arrest.

. . . Throughout the proceedings below, Cohen consistently claimed that, as construed to apply to the facts of this case, the statute infringed his rights to freedom of expression guaranteed by the First and Fourteenth Amendments of the Federal Constitution. . . .

In order to lay hands on the precise issue which this case involves, it is useful first to canvass various matters which this record does not present.

. . . [T]he State certainly lacks power to punish Cohen for the underlying content of the message the inscription conveyed. At least so long as there is no showing of an intent to incite disobedience to or disruption of the draft, Cohen could not, consistently with the First and Fourteenth Amendments, be punished for asserting the evident position on the inutility or immorality of the draft his jacket reflected. . . .

＊ This Court has also held that the States are free to ban the simple use, without a demonstration of additional justifying circumstances, of so-called "fighting words," those personally abusive epithets which, when addressed to the ordinary citizen, are, as a matter of common knowledge, inherently likely to provoke violent reaction. *Chaplinsky v. New Hampshire*, 315 U.S. 568 (1942). *While the four-letter word displayed by Cohen in relation to the draft is not uncommonly employed in a personally provocative fashion, in this instance it was clearly not directed to the person of the hearer. No individual actually or likely to be present could reasonably have regarded the words on appellant's jacket as a direct personal insult.* (emphasis added). . . . There is, as noted above, no showing that anyone who saw Cohen was in fact violently aroused or that appellant intended such a result.

＊ Finally, in arguments before this Court much has been made of the claim that Cohen's distasteful mode of expression was thrust upon unwilling or unsuspecting viewers, and that the State might therefore legitimately act as it did in order to protect the sensitive from otherwise unavoidable exposure to appellant's crude form of protest. . . . [However], we have . . . consistently stressed that we are often "captives" outside the sanctuary of the home and subject to objectionable speech. The ability of government, consonant with the Constitution, to shut off discourse solely to protect others from hearing it is, in other words, dependent upon a showing that substantial privacy interests are being invaded in an essentially intolerable manner. Any broader view of this authority would effectively empower a majority to silence dissidents simply as a matter of personal predilections.

In this regard, persons confronted with Cohen's jacket were in a quite different posture than, say, those subjected to the raucous emissions of sound trucks blaring outside their residences. Those in the Los Angeles courthouse could effectively avoid further bombardment of their sensibilities simply by averting their eyes. . . .

   Against this background, the issue flushed by this case stands out in bold relief. It is whether California can excise, as "offensive conduct," one particular scurrilous epithet from the public discourse, either upon the theory of the court below
that its use is inherently likely to cause violent reaction or upon a more general assertion that the States, acting as guardians of public morality, may properly remove this offensive word from the public vocabulary.

   The rationale of the California court is plainly untenable. At most it reflects an
"undifferentiated fear or apprehension of disturbance [which] is not enough to
overcome the right to freedom of expression."

   . . . We have been shown no evidence that substantial numbers of citizens
are standing ready to strike out physically at [whomever] may assault their sensibilities with execrations like that uttered by Cohen. There may be some persons
about with such lawless and violent proclivities, but that is an insufficient base
upon which to erect, consistently with constitutional values, a governmental
power to force persons who wish to ventilate their dissident views into avoiding
particular forms of expression. The argument amounts to little more than the
self-defeating proposition that to avoid physical censorship of one who has not
sought to provoke such a response by a hypothetical coterie of the violent
and lawless, the States may more appropriately effectuate that censorship
themselves.

   Admittedly, it is not so obvious that the First and Fourteenth Amendments
must be taken to disable the States from punishing public utterance of this un-
seemly expletive in order to maintain what they regard as a suitable level of discourse within the body politic. We think, however, that examination and reflection
will reveal the shortcomings of a contrary viewpoint. . . .

   The constitutional right of free expression is powerful medicine in a society as
diverse and populous as ours. It is designed and intended to remove governmental
restraints from the arena of public discussion, putting the decision as to what views
shall be voiced largely into the hands of each of us, in the hope that use of such
freedom will ultimately produce a more capable citizenry and more perfect polity
and in the belief that no other approach would comport with the premise of individual dignity and choice upon which our political system rests. See Whitney v. California, 274 U.S. 357, 275–377 (1927) (Brandeis, J., concurring).

   ✳ To many, the immediate consequence of this freedom may often appear to
be only verbal tumult, discord, and even offensive utterance. These are, however,
within established limits, in truth necessary side effects of the broader enduring
values which the process of open debate permits us to achieve. That the air may at
times seem filled with verbal cacophony is, in this sense not a sign of weakness but
of strength. We cannot lose sight of the fact that, in what otherwise might seem a
trifling and annoying instance of individual distasteful abuse of a privilege, these
fundamental societal values are truly implicated. That is why "[w]holly neutral futil-
ities. . .come under the protection of free speech as fully as do Keats' poems or
Donne's sermons," and why "so long as the means are peaceful, the communication need not meet standards of acceptability" (citations omitted).

Against this perception of the constitutional policies involved, we discern certain more particularized considerations that peculiarly call for reversal of this conviction. First, the principle contended for by the State seems inherently boundless. How is one to distinguish this from any other offensive word? Surely the State has no right to cleanse public debate to the point where it is grammatically palatable to the most squeamish among us. Yet no readily ascertainable general principle exists for stopping short of that result were we to affirm the judgment below. For, while the particular four-letter word being litigated here is perhaps more distasteful than most others of its genre, it is nevertheless often true that one man's vulgarity is another's lyric. Indeed, we think it is largely because governmental officials cannot make principled distinctions in this area that the Constitution leaves matters of taste and style so largely to the individual.

Additionally, we cannot overlook the fact, because it is well illustrated by the episode involved here, that much linguistic expression serves a dual communicative function: it conveys not only ideas capable of relatively precise, detached explication, but otherwise inexpressible emotions as well. In fact, words are often chosen as much for their emotive as their cognitive force. We cannot sanction the view that the Constitution, while solicitous of the cognitive content of individual speech, has little or no regard for that emotive function which, practically speaking, may often be the more important element of the overall message sought to be communicated. Indeed, as Mr. Justice Frankfurter has said, "[o]ne of the prerogatives of American citizenship is the right to criticize public men and measures—and that means not only informed and responsible criticism but the freedom to speak foolishly and without moderation" (citation omitted).

Finally, and in the same vein, we cannot indulge the facile assumption that one can forbid particular words without also running a substantial risk of suppressing ideas in the process. Indeed, governments might soon seize upon the censorship of particular words as a convenient guise for banning the expression of unpopular views. We have been able, as noted above, to discern little social benefit that might result from running the risk of opening the door to such grave results.

It is, in sum, our judgment that, absent a more particularized and compelling reason for its actions, the State may not, consistently with the First and Fourteenth Amendments, make the simple public display here involved of this single four-letter expletive a criminal offense. Because that is the only arguably sustainable rationale for the conviction here at issue, the judgment below must be reversed.

◆◆◆

**Cohen** *and the Fighting Words Doctrine.*     Although Justice Harlan used a contextual analysis to review the facts of this case, his opinion did not clearly indicate that the Court was instituting a contextual test for fighting words.

The Court was sensitive to context when it noted that although Cohen's expletive was often employed in a personally provocative fashion, in this particular case it was not issued as a direct personal insult to any individual. The

Court also demonstrated an awareness that the word in question would produce different reactions, depending on the audience, because "one [person's] vulgarity is another's lyric."

However, the opinion also noted that the states would be free to ban the use of fighting words, which "when addressed to the ordinary citizen, are, as a matter of common knowledge, inherently likely to provoke violent reaction." The Court gave no indication of what gives fighting words their inherent quality; is it their content, or is it the context in which they are uttered?

**Cohen *and the Emotive Content of Speech.*** The most significant contribution of *Cohen* to freedom of speech comes from the Court's acknowledgment, for the first time, that there is value in speech such as Cohen's. Justice Harlan argued that language often has an emotive as well as a cognitive function. He recognized that words may be chosen "as much for their emotive as their cognitive force." Consequently, both functions of speech are valuable, and the First Amendment cannot and does not distinguish between them.

The words on Cohen's jacket exemplified how a communicator could rely on the emotive force of language to convey a message. Cohen discussed a political question, the desirability of a military draft. Using the word "fuck" on his jacket communicates a different message than "abolish the draft" or "the draft is not cool." The strong, and perhaps shocking, connotations of the word *fuck* reflect a uniquely high level of emotional intensity. If you imagine the word being used in 1971, when such expletives were less common in public discourse than they are today, the strength of Cohen's feelings against the draft are even more apparent. The fact that the word was shocking may also facilitate communication because it would draw the attention of viewers to the jacket.

The recognition of the emotive force of language very much challenges the *Chaplinsky* perspective, which evaluated the defendant's language in cognitive terms. Justice Murphy argued that words such as "racketeer" and "damned Fascist" are "no *essential* part of any exposition of ideas." The implication of this viewpoint is that Chaplinsky could have made the same point by calling the city marshall "an ineffectual civil servant." To Justice Murphy, the stronger language had no value as a step to the truth. Of course, this reasoning assumes that calm and rational argumentation is always the most effective way to express a viewpoint to an audience.

**Cohen *and Free Speech Theory.*** The *Cohen* decision is also significant because the Court gave credence to the diverse justifications for freedom of speech that were addressed in chapter 1.

Justice Harlan recognized the value of free speech to Mr. Cohen's autonomy as a human being. He explained that free speech protects not only responsible criticism but also "'the freedom to speak foolishly and without moderation.'" Harlan noted that the Constitution places the decision as to "what views shall be voiced largely into the hands of each of us." Justice Harlan also recognized the connection between free speech and democratic government, and he argued that it is a sign of strength when public debate is "filled with verbal cacophony."

The *Cohen* opinion is also consistent with the free marketplace of ideas metaphor and its corollaries. The principle that there is no such thing as a bad idea was exemplified by statements that "one [person's] vulgarity is another's lyric," and that peaceful communication "'need not meet standards of acceptability.'" The Court's fear of government control over the marketplace of ideas was addressed when the Court suggested that officials "cannot make principled distinctions" between acceptable and unacceptable words for public discourse. This fear was also evident in the argument that "governments might soon seize upon the censorship of particular words as a convenient guise for banning the expression of unpopular views."

The *Cohen* decision was rich in its defense of principles that maximize freedom of speech. This opinion represents a high-water mark for freedom of speech. When you read later cases about obscenity, abortion counseling and protest, and symbolic speech, consider whether the Court has remained loyal to the lessons taught in this case. Justice Harlan's opinion also suggested, without overtly expressing it, a preference for a contextual approach in fighting words cases. The next case you will study gives further guidance on this issue.

### *Gooding v. Wilson*: Rejection of the Average Person Test for Fighting Words?

In *Gooding v. Wilson*,[12] Johnny Wilson was arrested while picketing with other protesters at an army induction center. When police officers tried to remove the picketers, Wilson and others refused, and a scuffle ensued. Wilson committed assault and battery on the two officers involved. To one policeman he said, "White son of a bitch, I'll kill you," and "You son of a bitch, I'll choke you to death"; and to the other, "You son of a bitch, if you ever put your hands on me again, I'll cut you all to pieces."[13]

Wilson was convicted under a Georgia statute (Section 26-6303) providing that "[a]ny person who shall . . . use to or of another, and in his presence . . . opprobrious words or abusive language, tending to cause a breach of the peace . . . shall be guilty of a misdemeanor."[14] The case was appealed and ultimately reached the U.S. Supreme Court. Justice William Brennan wrote the majority opinion, which declared that the Georgia statute violated the First Amendment.

12. 405 U.S. 518 (1972).
13. *Id.* at 520.
14. *Georgia Code Ann.*, Section 26-6303 (1933).

Justice Brennan's opinion held that the Georgia statute was *overbroad*, because its proscription of speech included expression protected by the First Amendment. Brennan's explanation of why the law was overbroad constituted a context- rather than a content-based analysis of fighting words.

How did the Court address context and content? It reviewed earlier Georgia court decisions that had interpreted the requirement that fighting words must be "likely" to provoke a violent response. For example, in *Elmore v. State*,[15] the Georgia Court of Appeals had focused on the content of words that breach the peace, describing the "kind" or "character" of such words "inherently" likely to provoke violent reaction.

Justice Brennan rejected this approach, complaining that the Georgia courts had "applied Section 26-6303 to utterances where there was no likelihood that the person addressed would make an immediate response."[16] The shift in the Court's language was subtle—but definite. By referring to *"the person addressed,"* Justice Brennan was refining the *Chaplinsky* standard. He implied that the Court would no longer evaluate whether fighting words cause violence by looking to what the average, reasonable addressee would think, but rather by what the specific, actual addressee would think. He or she could only evaluate this in the context of his or her own experience and situation.

### *Cohen* and *Gooding* Are Used to Vacate Fighting Words Convictions

The court would use this contextual approach three more times in that same year. These cases are sometimes dubbed the "motherfucker" cases, because the use of that term in all three cases triggered fighting words laws against the user. The three cases were *Rosenfeld v. New Jersey*,[17] *Brown v. Oklahoma*,[18] and *Lewis v. City of New Orleans*.[19] In *Rosenfeld*, the appellant attended and addressed a public school board meeting, also attended by 150 people, including 40 children. In his address, he used the word *motherfucker* four separate times, describing teachers, the school board, his town and the country. He was later tried and convicted under a New Jersey law alleging that "any person who utters loud and offensive or profane or indecent language in any public street or other public place, public conveyance, or place to which the public is invited . . . [i]s a disorderly person."[20] Prior to Rosenfeld's prosecution, the New Jersey Supreme Court had limited this law to words "of such a nature as to be likely to incite the hearer to an immediate

---

15. 83 S.E. 799. (Ga. App. 1914)
16. 405 U.S. at 528.
17. 408 U.S. 901 (1972).
18. 408 U.S. 914 (1972).
19. 408 U.S. 913 (1972).
20. *N.J. Rev. Stat.*, Section 2A: 170–29(1) (1971).

breach of the peace or to be likely . . . to affect the sensibilities of the listener."[21]

In *Brown,* the appellant spoke to a large group of men and women gathered at the University of Tulsa chapel. In his question-and-answer period, he referred to some police officers as "motherfucking Fascist cops," and to a particular police officer as a "black motherfucking pig. . . . " Brown was convicted under an Oklahoma statute prohibiting the utterance of "obscene or lascivious language or word in any public place. . . . "[22]

In *Lewis,* police had been in the process of arresting the appellant's son on other grounds (not related to fighting words). Lewis tried to intervene, calling police officers "goddamned motherfucking police." She was arrested and tried and convicted under a New Orleans ordinance that stated, "It shall be unlawful and a breach of the peace for any person wantonly to curse or revile or to use obscene or opprobrious language toward or with reference to any member of the city police while in the actual performance of his duty."[23]

In all three cases, the Court simply vacated the conviction and **remanded**[24] the cases for reconsideration in light of both *Cohen* and *Gooding.* This had several effects, one of which was to continue the trend toward contextual evaluation of fighting words. Justice Powell's concurring opinion in *Lewis* provided a particularly good example of a contextual fighting words analysis:

❦ [W]ords may or may not be "fighting words," depending on the circumstances of their utterance. It is unlikely, for example, that the words said to have been used here would have precipitated a physical confrontation between the middle-aged woman and the police officer in whose presence they were uttered. . . . Moreover . . . a properly trained officer may reasonably be expected to exercise a higher degree of restraint than the average citizen, and thus be less likely to respond belligerently to "fighting words."[25]

Justice Powell employed this contextual analysis in a concurring opinion, which was not joined by other members of the Court. Hence the Court has not explicitly ruled in favor of a contextual framework in fighting words cases,[26] although some commentators have argued that cases such as *Lewis*

21. See *State v. Profaci,* 56 N.J. 346, 353 (1970).
22. 21 *Okla. Stat. Ann.,* Section 906 (1958).
23. *Code of City of New Orleans,* Section 49-7.
24. When a case is remanded, it is sent back to the court from which the appeal was taken. The lower court must reconsider the case, following the guidelines set forward by the higher court.
25. 415 U.S. at 135 (Powell, J., concurring).
26. *Id.* at 133. The majority opinion in *Lewis* left open the possibility that Ms. Lewis could have been punished for the use of these words under a narrowly drawn statute.

and *Gooding* indicate that the Court has adopted a contextual approach in fighting words cases.[27]

Regardless of whether the Court institutionalized a contextual analysis in its fighting words cases, there is no doubt that the Court was continuing a paradoxical trend begun in *Cohen*. The Court adhered to the idea that fighting words should be a categorical exception to the First Amendment, but paradoxically failed to find any state attempt at legislating against fighting words as constitutional.

### *R.A.V. v. CITY OF ST. PAUL:* FIGHTING WORDS AND CATEGORICAL EXCEPTIONS LIVE ON

### The *R.A.V.* Decision

The Court would not elaborate on the fighting words doctrine for two more decades. Finally, in 1991, the fighting words exception was reviewed in the context of hate speech restrictions.

The City of St. Paul had enacted the Bias Motivated Crime Ordinance,[28] which outlawed the use of symbols causing anger, alarm, or resentment based on factors such as race, religion, or gender. The Minnesota Supreme Court interpreted the phrase "anger, alarm, or resentment" to mean fighting words.

The defendant, R.A.V. (initials were used because the defendant was a juvenile), was accused of violating the St. Paul ordinance by burning a cross inside the yard of an African American family. R.A.V. challenged the constitutionality of the ordinance; the City of St. Paul defended the restriction, claiming that it applied only to fighting words, which are unprotected by the First Amendment. The Supreme Court's agreement to hear the case afforded an opportunity to revitalize or completely eliminate the fighting words doctrine. The case also raised the question of whether the categorical exceptions theory articulated in *Chaplinsky* should continue to be followed. Although we will reference this case in chapter 7 we present the opinion here since it impacted the categorization doctrine most directly. One major issue raised by the case is whether a symbol of racist oppression should be protected by the Constitution. But the case also has broad implications for the fighting words doctrine and other categorical exceptions. As you read the majority

---

✱ 27. See, e.g., Fran-Linda Kobel, *The Fighting Words Doctrine—Is There a Clear and Present Danger to the Standard?* 84 Dickinson Law Review 75, 88 (Fall 1979).

28. *St. Paul, Minn. Legis. Code,* Section 292.02 (1990). "Whoever places on public or private property a symbol, object, appellation, characterization or graffiti, including, but not limited to, a burning cross or Nazi swastika, which one knows or has reasonable grounds to know arouses anger, alarm or resentment in others on the basis of race, color, creed, religion, or gender commits disorderly conduct and shall be guilty of a misdemeanor."

*Figure 6.4. Justice Antonin E. Scalia, formerly a law professor, government official, and District of Columbia Circuit Court Judge, was appointed to the Supreme Court by President Reagan in 1986. Often referred to as brilliant but doctrinaire, Scalia authored the* R.A.V. v. City of St. Paul *opinion. (Joseph P. Lavenburg, National Geographic Society. Collection of the Supreme Court of the United States.)*

opinion, ask how the Court has changed the criteria for evaluating categorical exceptions.

### R.A.V. v. City of St. Paul, 112 S.Ct. 2538, 120 L.Ed. 2d 305 (1992)

Justice Antonin Scalia (see Figure 6.4) delivered the opinion of the Court. ✱ In the predawn hours of June 21, 1990, petitioner and several other teenagers allegedly assembled a crudely-made cross by taping together broken chair legs. They then allegedly burned the cross inside the fenced yard of a black family that lived across the street from the house where petitioner was staying. Although this conduct could have been punished under any of a number of laws, one of the two provisions under which respondent city of St. Paul chose to charge petitioner (then a juvenile) was the St. Paul Bias-Motivated Crime Ordinance. . . .

In construing the St. Paul ordinance, we are bound by the construction given to it by the Minnesota court. . . . Accordingly we accent the Minnesota Supreme

Court's authoritative statement that the ordinance reaches only those expressions that constitute "fighting words" within the meaning of *Chaplinsky*. . . .

The First Amendment generally prevents government from proscribing speech, . . . or even expressive conduct, . . . because of disapproval of the ideas expressed. Content-based regulations are presumptively invalid. . . . From 1791 to the present, however, our society, like other free but civilized societies, has permitted restrictions upon the content of speech in a few limited areas, which are "of such slight social value as a step to truth that any benefit that may be derived from them is clearly outweighed by the social interest in order and morality." . . . Our decisions since the 1960's have narrowed the scope of the traditional categorical exceptions for defamation, . . . and for obscenity, . . . but a limited categorical approach has remained an important part of our First Amendment jurisprudence.

We have sometimes said that these categories of expression are "not within the area of constitutionally protected speech," . . . or that the "protection of the First Amendment does not extend" to them. . . . Such statements must be taken in context, however, and are no more literally true than is the occasionally repeated shorthand characterizing obscenity "as not being speech at all." . . . What they mean is that these areas of speech can, consistently with the First Amendment, be regulated *because of their constitutionally proscribable content* (obscenity, defamation, etc.)—not that they are categories of speech entirely invisible to the Constitution, so that they may be made the vehicles for content discrimination unrelated to their distinctively proscribable content. Thus, the government may proscribe libel; but it may not make the further content discrimination of proscribing *only* libel critical of the government. . . .

Our cases surely do not establish the proposition that the First Amendment imposes no obstacle whatsoever to regulation of particular instances of such proscribable expression, so that the government "may regulate [them] freely." . . . That would mean that a city council could enact an ordinance prohibiting only those legally obscene works that contain criticism of the city government or, indeed, that do not include endorsement of the city government. Such a simplistic, all-or-nothing-at-all approach to First Amendment protection is at odds with common sense and with our jurisprudence as well. It is not true that "fighting words" have at most a *"de minimis"* expressive content, or that their content is *in all respects* "worthless and undeserving of constitutional protection," sometimes they are quite expressive indeed. We have not said that they constitute *"no* part of the expression of ideas," but only that they constitute "no *essential* part of any exposition of ideas." . . .

[T]he exclusion of the "fighting words" from the scope of the First Amendment simply means that, for purposes of that Amendment, the unprotected features of the words are, despite their verbal character, essentially a "non-speech" element of communication. Fighting words are thus analogous to a noisy sound truck; both can be used to convey an idea; but neither has, in and of itself, a claim upon the First Amendment. As with the sound truck, however, so also with fighting words: The government may not regulate use based on hostility—or favoritism—towards the underlying message expressed. . . .

The rationale of the general prohibition, after all, is that content discrimination "rais[es] the specter that the Government may effectively drive certain ideas or viewpoints from the marketplace.". . .

✳ Applying these principles to the St. Paul ordinance, we conclude that, even as narrowly construed by the Minnesota Supreme Court, the ordinance is facially unconstitutional. Although the phrase in the ordinance, "arouses anger, alarm or resentment in others," has been limited by the Minnesota Supreme Court's construction to reach only those symbols or displays that amount to "fighting words," the remaining, unmodified terms make clear that the ordinance applies only to "fighting words" that insult, or provoke violence, "on the basis of race, color, creed, religion or gender." Displays containing abusive invective, no matter how vicious or severe, are permissible unless they are addressed to one of the specified disfavored topics. Those who wish to use "fighting words" in connection with other ideas—to express hostility, for example, on the basis of political affiliation, union membership, or homosexuality—are not covered. The First Amendment does not permit St. Paul to impose special prohibitions on those speakers who express views on disfavored subjects. . . .

✳ In its practical operation, moreover, the ordinance goes even beyond mere content discrimination, to actual viewpoint discrimination. Displays containing some words—odious racial epithets, for example—would be prohibited to proponents of all views. But "fighting words" that do not themselves invoke race, color, creed, religion, or gender—aspersions upon a person's mother, for example—would seemingly be usable *ad libitum* in the placards of those arguing *in favor* of racial, color, etc. tolerance and equality, but could not be used by that speaker's opponents. One could hold up a sign saying, for example, that all "anti-Catholic bigots" are misbegotten; but not that all "papists" are, for that would insult and provoke violence "on the basis of religion." St. Paul has no such authority to license one side of debate to fight freestyle, while requiring the other to follow Marquis of Queensbury Rules. . . .

Finally, St. Paul and its *amici* defend the conclusion of the Minnesota Supreme Court that, even if the ordinance regulates expression based on hostility towards its protected ideological content, this discrimination is nonetheless justified because it is narrowly tailored to serve compelling state interests. Specifically, they assert that the ordinance helps to ensure the basic human rights of members of groups that have historically been subjected to discrimination, including the right of such group members to live in peace where they wish. We do not doubt that these interests are compelling, and that the ordinance can be said to promote them. But the "danger of censorship" presented by a facially content-based statute. . .requires that that weapon be employed only where it is necessary to serve the asserted compelling interest. . . . The dispositive question ✳ in this case, therefore, is whether content discrimination is reasonably necessary to achieve St. Paul's compelling interests; it plainly is not. An ordinance not limited to the favored topics, for example, would have precisely the same beneficial effect. . . .

Let there be no mistake about our belief that burning a cross in someone's front yard is reprehensible. But St. Paul has sufficient means at its disposal to prevent such behavior without adding the First Amendment to the fire.

The judgment of the Minnesota Supreme Court is reversed, and the case is remanded for proceedings not inconsistent with this opinion. ◆◆◆

### R.A.V.'s Impact on the Categorical Exceptions and Fighting Words Doctrines

*The Categorical Exceptions Theory Is Modified.* The *R.A.V.* majority indicated the Court's continuing commitment to the principle that certain categories of expression are not protected by the First Amendment. Although the scope of the exceptions has narrowed over time, Justice Scalia made it clear that "a limited categorical approach has remained an important part of our First Amendment jurisprudence."

One significant idea discussed in *R.A.V.* is the notion that categorical exceptions in general, and fighting words in particular, do have communicative value. Justice Scalia argued that "fighting words can be quite expressive indeed," and that although they may be outside the scope of constitutional protection, it is wrong to say that they are not speech. Instead, the Court allowed fighting words to be proscribed because they are not an *"essential* part of any exposition of ideas."

Is the *R.A.V.* decision consistent with *Cohen?* In *Cohen,* the Court upheld the freedom of the communicator to select the language that best expressed his or her message. In *R.A.V.,* the Court assumed that the government, not the individual, should judge whether words are essential to the expression of ideas. The *R.A.V.* opinion does not promote a free marketplace of ideas, because it permits government control of speech deemed to be nonessential as long as the controls do not discriminate against certain ideas. If the Court is committed to the fighting words doctrine, would it be better off candidly admitting that fighting words can be essential to the exposition of ideas? If fighting words do create a danger of violence, is there any reason this speech could not be regulated as incitement to illegal conduct under the *Brandenburg* test (see chapter 4)?

The second major influence of *R.A.V.* on the categorical exceptions doctrine is the holding that while states may restrict certain categories of speech, they *may not* do so in a content-selective manner. Here, the Court is concerned with the fourth dimension of free speech (see chapter 1)—the fear that government will have excessive influence on the marketplace of ideas.

Because the government "may not regulate [speech] based on hostility—or favoritism—towards the underlying message expressed," content-based regulations of speech are unconstitutional, even if the speech falls under a categorical exception. Justice Scalia indicted the St. Paul ordinance because it applied the doctrine "only to 'fighting words' that insult, or provoke violence, 'on the basis of race, color, creed, religion or gender.'" In Scalia's calculus, this limited the categorical exception only to these situations, while still allowing other fighting words, such as those based on political orientation, union membership, or sexuality.

In this way, Scalia suggested that the doctrine could be applied only in a general and content-neutral manner. To do this, an ordinance must prohibit an entire category of unprotected speech, or draw the line between protected and unprotected speech without reference to the content of the message (for example, an enhanced sentence in any fighting words case where the words lead to injury.)

*The Paradoxical Fighting Words Trend Is Continued.* In *R.A.V.*, the Court continued the paradoxical trend suggested earlier. The Court reaffirmed that fighting words are a valid category of speech excluded from the First Amendment. However, the Court again failed to hold that a state attempt to legislate against fighting words was constitutional.

Perhaps the reason that fighting words regulations fare so poorly before the Court is that government officials misunderstand the purpose of the doctrine. When a government is motivated to control speech, its tendency is to try and avoid First Amendment problems by fitting the regulation under a categorical exception. However, the speech to which the government objects may create little risk of a violent response. When juvenile thugs burn a cross in an African American family's yard, the parents' first priority will be protecting their children's safety. They will be unlikely to go outdoors and start a fight in which they are outnumbered. Politicians recognize the bad public relations that would result if they punched an angry constituent; hence, insults such as Chaplinsky's are unlikely to lead to fisticuffs. As Justice Powell suggested in *Lewis*, police officers should be trained to defuse tense situations, rather than applying their nightsticks to the heads of their critics. If the states are serious about restricting fighting words, they would be well advised to draft ordinances that are limited to speech contexts in which violence is highly likely.

### SUMMARY

In this chapter we have examined the origins of one of the more significant First Amendment doctrines pertaining to freedom of speech: categorization. As first enunciated by the Court in *Chaplinsky v. New Hampshire*, categorization referred to a wide number of possible exceptions to First Amendment protection: the exception applied in *Chaplinsky* was for fighting words. At common law, this doctrine included expressive words that were equated with breach of the peace, nuisance, or disorderly conduct. With the *Chaplinsky* opinion, however, the Court placed all such expression under the rubric of fighting words, those expressions "which by their very utterance inflict injury or tend to incite an immediate breach of the peace."

The theory underlying the fighting words exception (as well as the other categorical exceptions) is that words in these categories may be proscribed because they "are of slight value as a step to the truth" and are "no essential part of any exposition of ideas." Thus, the categorical exceptions theory is consistent with the truth-finding rationale for freedom of speech rather than the viewpoint that individual autonomy in communication should be preserved. This theory permits government intervention into the marketplace of ideas when the government determines that certain words are not helpful in society's quest for truth. The fighting words exception is also consistent with a communitarian perspective of free speech. It insists that we forgo a right to use language that is likely to breach the peace and security of our communities. Our responsibility to contribute to a safe and orderly society is of greater value than our right to express ourselves freely. In *Cohen*, the Court gave greater weight to the communicator's interest, suggesting that the individual ought to have the autonomy to select the message that best conveys his or her feelings on a subject.

The definition of fighting words has undergone considerable evolution since *Chaplinsky*. Initially, it was not clear exactly how the Court defined words that inflict "injury." Did this refer to real, physical injury? Psychological injury? In *Terminiello*, the Court suggested that the injury inflicted must be more than hurt feelings or a state of unrest.

That clarification did not end the definitional questions, however, for it was never—and still is not—clear what words would be inherently likely to provoke violence. Clearly, thresholds for violent reaction and intolerance can vary from individual to individual. Would future courts employ the fighting words doctrine by looking to the *content* of the words to determine if they were inherently likely to provoke violence, or to the *context* in which they were uttered?

In later opinions such as *Cohen, Gooding,* and *Lewis,* the Court suggested it was opting for a contextual interpretation of fighting words, meaning that future courts would evaluate whether certain expressions triggered the exception by considering the context in which they were uttered. However, the Court has not explicitly overturned the content-based standard, which allows language to be characterized as fighting words if the average person would be likely to respond violently.

In *R.A.V.*, the Court's holding added another condition that must be met before a fighting words (or other categorical exception) law can be constitutional: The government may not regulate a subset of any excepted category, based on hostility to the content of the messages in that subset.

The fighting words cases from *Cohen* to *R.A.V.* evidence a paradox about the doctrine. The Court uses language to express its support for a fighting words categorical exception to the First Amendment, but consistently fails to allow any state or local attempt at bringing this doctrine to legislation. This in turn raises another compelling question: Should we have a fighting words doctrine if the Court never approves any laws that apply the exception? It remains to be seen if the Court will one day free itself of this self-imposed paradox, and finally uphold a state or local attempt at codifying the doctrine.

CHAPTER 7        *Objectives*

**After reading chapter 7,**

**you should understand**

**the following:**

◆ *The reasons why attacks on im-mutable human characteristics, such as race or sex, have been argued to be un-worthy of First Amendment protection, particularly in the context of a society plagued by discrimination.*

◆ *The incidents of hate speech that led to the establishment of speech codes, par-ticularly in universities.*

◆ *The reasoning of the federal courts, which have consistently held speech codes unconstitutional and defended a market-place of ideas approach.*

◆ *The critique of the viewpoint that hate speech is protected by the First Amendment, and the arguments that have been advanced in favor of speech codes.*

◆ *The alternatives to existing speech codes, including reliance on more speech as an alternative to regulation.*

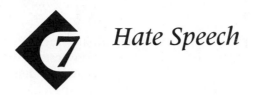 # 7 Hate Speech

IMAGINE A SITUATION in which two high school juniors, Jane and Stuart, are vying for the position of student body president. The competition between the two is particularly keen, with student support split fairly evenly. In the last week of campaigning, Stuart puts up new posters suggesting he is "the better man" for the job. Attached to the poster is a cartoon of both Jane and Stuart, showing each in a traditional three-piece, male-cut suit. Jane's hair is cut short in the picture. Quietly, Jane's supporters cry foul, arguing that Stuart is making a non-too-subtle reference to Jane's alleged sexuality, which had never been an issue before. Angry over the incident, Jane gives her final campaign speech at a student rally, accusing Stuart of "primitive jungle tactics." Stuart, who is African American, interprets these comments as racially based.

Both Jane and Stuart accuse one another of using language designed to call attention to race or sexual orientation as a means of drawing student votes. In each situation, however, the references are not as obvious as calling someone a name or using an overtly racial or homophobic insult. Should school officials sanction either student for his or her language?

Certain words and expressions carry more weight than others. At first glance this hardly seems a controversial statement, but if we rephrase it to suggest that some words or expressions—such as insults or epithets—carry a unique kind of negative weight, we do make a provocative statement. For that is one of the premises underlying the movement to restrict **hate speech.**

The regulation and attempted restriction of hate speech in our society have been difficult to execute and prove a vexing challenge for constitutional scrutiny. As this book has demonstrated, serious First Amendment problems arise anytime restrictions are targeted at speech because of the content of that message—and most attempts to control hate speech arise precisely because of disagreement with that content. But hate speech can pose serious problems for the recipient of the message. In recent years, judges and legal theorists have wrestled with this issue, attempting to balance the need for protecting First Amendment interests with the need for greater sensitivity to the damage hate speech can cause.

In this chapter we will examine the problems posed by hate speech, as well as the different solutions that have been attempted—or suggested—thus far. We will also consider whether the marketplace of ideas offers a better solution to the problem of hate speech than speech restrictions do.

## THE SPECIAL PROBLEMS RAISED BY HATE SPEECH

### Hate Speech Defined

As previously described, hate speech refers to insults, slurs, or epithets directed to a group of people, based on a shared characteristic of that group. Usually this is race, gender, or religion, but it can also include ethnicity, sexual orientation, disability, or even Vietnam-era veteran's status.

Of course, nearly all of us have been subjected to insults or slurs. Generally we have been raised to accept these as a part of life. Some of us may have been advised to have a "thicker skin" and not allow insults to unduly bother or disturb us. Some of us were probably also socialized to return these insults in kind. If such is the case, then why should we become concerned when the insults fall into the category of hate speech?

### Why Is Hate Speech Harmful?

*Hate Speech Targets Immutable Characteristics.* Perhaps one example of hate speech—the racially motivated variety—may support the argument that such words are more harmful than other insults. In racist hate speech, individuals are verbally attacked because of a shared characteristic that is *immutable*—meaning it cannot be changed. An individual has no choice, for example, in the selection of his or her race.

Critics argue that hate speech directed at immutable characteristics is harmful in several ways. It can lead to self-hatred as members of a nondominant minority are continually reminded of their alleged lack of worth;[1] and people thus stigmatized can exhibit low self-esteem and a diminished ability to enter into relationships—both with members of other racial groups and with their own.[2]

Victims of hate speech may also suffer physiological reactions, including difficulty breathing, nightmares, post-traumatic stress disorder, hypertension, and even suicide.[3] One study of African American males reported that they are prone to higher blood pressure because they repeatedly find themselves in social

1. See, e.g., Kenneth Clark, *Dark Ghetto: Dilemmas of Social Power*, p. 64 (Harper & Row, 1965).
2. See Richard Delgado, "Words That Wound: A Tort Action for Racial Insults, Epithets, and Name Calling," in *Words That Wound*, p. 91 (Westview, 1993).
3. Mari Matsuda, *Public Responses to Racist Speech: Considering the Victim's Story*, 87 Michigan Law Review 2320, 2332 (August 1989).

Figure 7.1. Justice Clarence Thomas, appointed to the Supreme Court in 1990 amid great controversy, has generally sided with Justices Scalia and Rehnquist—particularly in cases decided upon a more doctrinaire approach. His concurrence in R.A.V. suggested less tolerance for allegedly content-specific hate-crime regulations, but even Justice Thomas is not beyond the internal conflict many feel over hate speech and hate crime. His vigorous dissenting opinion in Dawson v. Delaware argued powerfully in favor of using membership in racist hate groups to demonstrate evidence of bad character, qualifying a defendant already convicted for murder to a sentence of death rather than life imprisonment.

(Joseph H. Bailey, National Geographic Society. Collection of the Supreme Court of the United States.)

positions and situations in which they are attacked—but are required to suppress their feelings of hostility.[4] In some instances the victims of hate speech seek escape through alcohol, drugs, or various forms of antisocial behavior.[5]

This is not to claim that *hate speech* is the cause of this kind of oppression: racism is. Hate speech in this context is the expression of this core cause. Nevertheless, it is a medium that by many accounts carries far more impact than an ordinary insult.

### Hate Speech Occurs in the Context of Prejudice

At the root of these words and expressions is their historical, political, and social context.[6] This is a context from which the targeted recipient finds it difficult to escape. The *R.A.V. v. City of St. Paul* decision, discussed in chapter 6, illustrates this point well. In *R.A.V.*, the appellant had constructed a cross from broken chair legs and then set fire to it inside the yard of an African American family. Although the Court did not go to great lengths to discuss this, the *context* of this expressive conduct and symbol should not be missed (see Figure

---

4. Ernest Harburg, et al., *Socio-Ecological Stress, Suppressed Hostility, Skin Color, and Black-White Male Blood Pressure: Detroit,* 35 Psychosomatic Medicine 276, 277–78 (July–August 1973).
5. Delgado, *Words that Wound,* p. 91.
6. See, e.g., Matsuda, *Public Responses to Racist Speech,* p. 2331–35.

*Figure 7.2. A burning cross surrounded by members of the Ku Klux Klan conveys a message of white supremacy and membership in a specific group. But for those targeted to receive a burning cross in their yard or near vicinity, the message is deeply contextual—especially for many in the African American community, for whom the message is associated with a history of racial violence and death, often by lynching.*(New York Times (July 9, 1963). (c) 1963 New York Times *Pictures. Reprinted by Permission*)

7.1). The history of the burning cross—especially in close proximity to the homes of African Americans—suggests a direct connection to the activity of groups like the Ku Klux Klan (see Figure 7.2): lynching, arson, and racist-fueled terror. Historically—contextually—we know these things occurred in the not too distant past. African Americans, regardless of their economic status or political leanings, are aware of this—and painfully reminded by the sight of the burning cross. The deeper contextual meaning cannot be escaped lightly.

In another example, members of the National Socialist Party of America—contemporary representatives of the old Nazi Party from Hitler's Germany—wished to march through Skokie, Illinois—home to many Jewish Americans.[7] The presence of Nazi swastikas and uniforms, even *without* oral or written messages denying or justifying the Holocaust, would still have a specific historic, political, and social context for Jews. As with the burning cross, that context is not easily dismissed.

Hate speech can occur anywhere in American society—from city streets to suburban yards to offices.[8] Most settings have specific rules for behavior that facilitate certain interests— civility, harmony, efficiency, the ability to do one's job. What happens, then, if the forum for hate speech is a school?

In a college or university, higher learning theoretically occurs when students are exposed to as many different ideas as possible. Can this purpose of higher education coexist in an environment where hate speech is present? Equally so, does it suffer if restrictions against hate speech are imposed?

### The Problem of Hate Speech on Campus

Schools in our society enjoy a special kind of protection where the First Amendment is concerned. As Justice Brennan, writing for the majority in *Keyishian v. Board of Regents*,[9] observed:

> Our nation is deeply committed to safeguarding academic freedom which is of transcendent value to all of us and not merely to the teachers concerned. That freedom is therefore a special concern of the First Amendment, which does not tolerate laws that cast a pall of orthodoxy over the classroom. The vigilant protection of Constitutional freedoms is nowhere more vital than in the community of American schools. . . . The classroom is particularly the "marketplace of ideas."[10] ◆◆◆

Academic freedom, in Justice Brennan's words, is significant for both students and teachers in our school system—especially in colleges and universities, where students mature and develop the skills to reason, advocate, and learn. Although these settings are designed to be arenas for enlightened thought, they can also reflect the real attitudes and prejudices of the societies they serve, and consequently exhibit the kind of intolerance and hatred present in the general community.

For example, the University of Wisconsin system has been the site of numerous examples of racist and discriminatory language and conduct. In one instance, a fraternity held a party that featured a "Harlem room," where fried

---

7. See, e.g., *Collin v. Smith*, 578 F.2d 1197 (7th Cir. 1978) *cert. denied*, 439 U.S. 916 (1978). While the Court of Appeals here affirmed a district court decision declaring Skokie's ordinances (which had blocked the Nazi demonstration) unconstitutional, it did admit that many observers would find the demonstration "seriously disturb[ing], emotionally and mentally" (578 F.2d at 1206).
8. See, e.g., *Contreras v. Crown Zellerbach Inc.*, 565 P. 2d 1173 (1977) (en banc). Here, a Mexican American employee was subjected to a campaign of verbal racial abuse by co-workers.
9. 385 U.S. 589 (1966). The *Keyishian* case is excerpted and analyzed in chapter 12.
10. *Id.* at 603.

chicken and watermelon punch were served. The students there all wore blackface as a joke. Yet another fraternity used a large cardboard caricature depicting a black man to announce a party with the theme of "Fiji Island." At a different fraternity, racist name-calling led to a fight. Other Wisconsin incidents included a mock slave auction and abusive epithets written on mirrors and on the walls of private living quarters.[11]

The problems exist at other campuses around the country. Spouting the rhetoric of white supremacy, Ku Klux Klan (KKK) members spoke at a rally at Kansas University,[12] allegedly distributed white supremacist flyers at Northwest Missouri State University, and distributed material pertaining to the Invisible Empire at Stockton State College in New Jersey.[13] Aryan Resistance literature was distributed at Stanford University in California.[14]

A 1989 incident at Arizona State University was even more telling. An African American student became entangled in a violent altercation with a white member of Sigma Alpha Epsilon (SAE) fraternity. The African American student later told police that the SAE student had said, "Fuck you, nigger," precipitating their violent exchange and attracting some two dozen SAE members, who similarly chanted, "Coons, nigger, porch monkey." Police broke up the confrontation, but noted that the instigator—the SAE member—continued making "racial slurs and threats," including a threat to "get those niggers" and "kill them."[15]

Several hours later, just after midnight, police were summoned back to the same fraternity. The same SAE member had confronted two other African American ASU students. Their attacker now declared, "Those are the niggers! They're back!" A mob of nearly two thousand fraternity members from nearby houses surrounded the two as ten to fifteen white students beat them. Ironically—but perhaps not surprisingly—the victims were handcuffed, taken into custody, and later released.

These incidents are not limited to students. At Dartmouth University, an African American professor was called a "cross between a welfare queen and a bathroom attendant,"[16] while at Purdue a university counselor found the words "Death, Nigger" scratched into her door.[17]

In 1991, Colorado law professor Richard Delgado wrote that nearly two hundred campuses had experienced racial unrest serious or graphic enough to be reported to the press.[18] A study by the National Institute Against Prejudice

11. Patricia Hodulick, *Prohibiting Discriminatory Harassment by Regulating Student Speech: A Balancing Test of First Amendment and University Interests,* 16 Journal of College and University Law 573, 574 (1990).
12. *Klanwatch Intelligence Report # 42* (February 1988).
13. *Id.*
14. *Id.*
15. J. Weiner, *Free Speech for Campus Bigots?* 250 The Nation 272, 273 (February 26, 1990).
16. Charles Lawrence III, *If He Hollers Let Him Go: Regulating Racist Speech on Campus,* 1990 Duke Law Journal 431, 432.
17. *Id.*
18. Richard Delgado, *Campus Antiracism Rules: Constitutional Narratives in Collision,* 85 Northwestern Law Review 343 (Winter 1991).

and Violence found that in the course of one academic year, twenty percent of all minority students would suffer physical or verbal abuse motivated by prejudice.[19] Evidence that the problem is not going away continues to mount. The Southern Poverty Law Center's *Klanwatch* report documented more than 270 occurrences of hate crimes during 1992 in schools and colleges—a figure likely to be low because victims and schools frequently do not report such incidents.[20] Howard Erlich, research director for the National Institute Against Prejudice and Violence, noted that "every single indicator we have suggests that ethnoviolence incidents are at least steady, if not increasing."[21]

On campus, the result of such expression may be a "disruption of an equal learning environment"[22] as African American students are forced to hear that "they belong hanging from trees"[23] and Asian students are subjected to taunts such as "Die, Chink" or "Hostile Americans want your yellow hide."[24] Women on campus have been called "fat housewives"[25] and "fucking cunts."[26] Such demeaning expression can damage students' self-image and self-confidence as well as alienating them from their school.[27] In an academic environment, hate speech undoubtedly hinders learning and participation both inside and outside the classroom.

## ✳ The Campuses Respond

Fueled by increased public awareness and scrutiny, college and university administrators began responding to hate speech. By 1992, more than one hundred colleges had adopted speech codes.[28]

The University of Michigan sought to regulate hate speech by adopting the following language as part of its *Policy on Discrimination and Discriminatory Conduct*, to the effect that persons would be subject to discipline for

1. Any behavior, verbal or physical, that stigmatizes or victimizes an individual on the basis of race, ethnicity, religion, sex, sexual orientation, creed, national origin, ancestry, age, marital status, handicap or Vietnam era veteran status, and that

19. Ellen Lange, *Racist Speech on Campus*, 64 Southern California Law Review 105, 129 (November 1990).
20. John O'Neil, *A New Generation Confronts Racism*, 50 Educational Leadership 60, 61 (May 1993).
21. *Id.*
22. "First Amendment—Racist and Sexist Expression on Campus," 103 *Harvard Law Review*, 1397, 1399 (April 1990).
23. *Campus Blacks Feel Racism's Nuances*, New York Times p. A1 (April 17, 1988).
24. 103 *Harvard Law Review*, p. 1400.
25. Project on the Status and Education of Women, Association of American Colleges, *The Classroom Climate: A Chilly One for Women?*, p. 5 (1982).
26. *See* Complaint Number 2, University of Wisconsin—Eau Claire, as cited in *UWM v. Board of Regents*, 774 F. Supp. 1163, 1167 (E.D. Wisc. 1991).
27. See e.g., Richard Delgado, *Words That Wound: A Tort Action for Racial Insults, Epithets, and Name Calling*, 17 Harvard Civil Rights-Civil Liberties Law Review 133 (Spring 1982).
28. Louis Freedberg, *Stanford, U.C. Unruffled by Hate Speech Ruling*, San Francisco Chronicle A15 (June 29, 1992).

(a) Involves an express or implied threat to an individual's academic efforts, employment, participation in University sponsored
extra-curricular activities or personal safety; or
(b) Has the purpose or reasonably foreseeable effect of interfering with an individual's academic efforts, employment, participation in University sponsored extra-curricular activities or personal safety; or
(c) Creates an intimidating, hostile, or demeaning environment
for educational pursuits, employment or participation in University sponsored extra-curricular activities."[29]

Sanctions for violating the Michigan policy could include a formal repri-
mand; community service; sensitivity classes; payment of restitution; removal
from university housing; suspension from courses and activities; suspension;
and expulsion. The latter two remedies could be imposed only for violent or
dangerous acts, repeated offenses, or a willful failure to comply with lesser
sanctions. If a complaint was filed and supported by sufficient evidence, a
hearing would be held before a panel consisting of four students and a
tenured faculty member. The university president could set aside or reduce
any sanction the panel imposed.[30]

Although most concerned groups acknowledged Michigan's attempt to
redress the problems with hate speech, not all were comfortable with the language of the policy. In *Doe v. University of Michigan*, an anonymous graduate
student (simply titled John Doe) in psychology and biopsychology brought
suit against the university, alleging that the policy might have a chilling effect
on his right to discuss potentially controversial theories of biology in class.
This was to be the first of several legal challenges to speech codes, discussed in
the next section of this chapter.

## DO SPEECH CODES VIOLATE THE FIRST AMENDMENT?

### The University of Michigan Policy—No First Amendment Exception for Offensive Speech

Doe's challenge to the Michigan code was heard in a federal district
court. The court's opinion, written by Judge Cohn, concluded that the code
was unconstitutionally vague and overbroad. After reviewing the facts of the
case, Judge Cohn drew the line between speech and behavior that the university could regulate and expression that was protected from university sanction
by the First Amendment. He then explained how the Michigan policy reached
protected expression, and hence was unconstitutional. As you read the *Doe*
opinion, decide whether the speech that the University of Michigan sought to
regulate should be protected by the First Amendment.

---

29. *Doe v. University of Michigan*, 721 F.Supp. 852, 856 (E.D. Mich. 1989). Section 1c was withdrawn before this policy was ultimately adjudicated in federal court.
30. *Id.* at 857.

### *Doe v. University of Michigan,* 721 F. Supp 852 (E.D. Mich. 1989)

Cohn, District Judge.

I. Introduction

It is an unfortunate fact of our constitutional system that the ideals of freedom and equality are often in conflict. The difficult and sometimes painful task of our political and legal institutions is to mediate the appropriate balance between these two competing values. Recently, the University of Michigan at Ann Arbor (the University) . . . adopted a Policy on Discrimination and Discriminatory Harassment of Students in the University Environment (the Policy) in an attempt to curb what the University's governing Board of Regents (Regents) viewed as a rising tide of racial intolerance and harassment on campus. . . .

II. Facts Generally

According to the University, in the last three years incidents of racism and racial harassment appeared to become increasingly frequent at the University. For example, on January 27, 1987, unknown persons distributed a flier declaring "open season" on blacks, which it referred to as "saucer lips, porch monkeys, and jigaboos." On February 4, 1987, a student disc jockey at an on-campus radio station allowed racist jokes to be broadcast. At a demonstration protesting these incidents, a Ku Klux Klan uniform was displayed from a dormitory window. . . .

On March 5, 1987, the Chairperson of the State House of Representatives Appropriations Subcommittee on Higher Education held a public hearing on the problem of racism at the University in Ann Arbor. Forty-eight speakers addressed the subcommittee and an audience of about 600. The speakers were uniformly critical of the University's response to racial incidents and accused it of generally ignoring the problems of minority students. At the close of the hearing, the Chairperson was quoted as stating:

> Michigan legislators will not tolerate racism on the campus of a state institution. . . . [The subcommittee] will make our decision [on appropriations for the University] during their budget discussions of the next few weeks. . . . Holding up funds as a club may be part of our response, but that will predicate on how the university responds.

Following the hearing, the United Coalition Against Racism (UCAR), a campus anti-discrimination group, announced that it intended to file a class action civil rights suit against the University "for not maintaining or creating a non-racist, non-violent atmosphere" on campus. . . .

At the January 15, 1988 meeting of the Regents, the Acting President informed the Board that he been working on a proposed policy on student discipline dealing with racial harassment. . . . He stated that he was taking this action in response to widespread complaints that the University could not or would not enforce its existing regulations concerning racial harassment.

Following the January meeting, the Acting President appointed the Director of the University Office of Affirmative Action (Director) to draft a policy. The proposed policy went through twelve drafts. . . . At the April 14, 1988 Regents meeting, the Policy was unanimously adopted. . . .

III. The University of Michigan Policy on Discrimination and Discriminatory Harassment

[At this point, the court printed the Michigan policy verbatim. Relevant portions of the code have already been discussed previously in this chapter. The court went on to describe a guide to the policy that the university had distributed.]

Shortly after the promulgation of the policy in the fall of 1988, the University Office of Affirmative Action issued an interpretive guide (Guide) entitled *What Students Should Know about Discrimination and Discriminatory Harassment by Students in the University Environment.* The Guide purported to be an authoritative interpretation of the Policy and provided examples of sanctionable conduct. These included:

    A flyer containing racist threats distributed in a residence hall.

    Racist graffiti written on the door of an Asian student's study carrel.

    A male student makes remarks in class like "Women just aren't as good in this field as men," thus creating a hostile learning atmosphere for female classmates.

    Students in a residence hall have a floor party and invite everyone on their floor except one person because they think she might be a lesbian.

    A black student is confronted and racially insulted by two white students in a cafeteria.

    Male students leave pornographic pictures and jokes on the desk of a female graduate student.

    Two men demand that their roommate in the residence hall move out and be tested for AIDS. . . .

According to the University, the Guide was withdrawn at an unknown date in the winter of 1989, because "the information in it was not accurate." The withdrawal had not been announced publicly as of the date this case was filed.

IV. Standing

Doe is a psychology graduate student. His specialty is in the field of biopsychology, which he describes as the interdisciplinary study of the biological bases of individual differences in personality traits and mental abilities. Doe said that certain controversial theories positing biologically based differences between sexes and races might be perceived as "sexist" and "racist" by some students, and he feared that discussion of such theories might be sanctionable under the Policy. He asserted that his right to freely and openly discuss these theories was impermissibly chilled, and he requested that the Policy be declared unconstitutional and enjoined on the grounds of vagueness and overbreadth. . . .

## V. Vagueness and Overbreadth . . .

### A. Scope of Permissible Regulation

Before inquiring whether the policy is impermissibly vague and overbroad, it would be helpful to first distinguish between verbal conduct and verbal acts that are generally protected by the First Amendment and those that are not. It is the latter class of behavior that the University may legitimately regulate.

Although the line is sometimes difficult to draw with precision, the Court must distinguish at the outset between the First Amendment protection of so-called "pure speech" and mere conduct. As to the latter, it can be safely said that most extreme and blatant forms of discriminatory conduct are not protected by the First Amendment, and indeed are punishable by a variety of state and federal criminal laws and subject to civil actions. . . .

While the University's power to regulate so-called pure speech is far more limited,. . .certain categories can be generally described as unprotected by the First Amendment. It is clear that so-called "fighting words" are not entitled to First Amendment protection. . . . Under certain circumstances racial and ethnic epithets, slurs, and insults might fall within this description and could constitutionally be prohibited by the University. In addition, such speech may also be sufficient to state a claim for common law intentional infliction of emotional distress. . . . Finally, the University may subject all speech and conduct to reasonable and nondiscriminatory time, place and manner restrictions which are narrowly tailored and which leave open ample alternative means of communication. . . . If the Policy had the effect of only regulating in these areas, it is unlikely that any constitutional problem would have arisen.

What the University could not do, however, was establish an anti-discrimination policy which had the effect of prohibiting certain speech because it disagreed with ideas or messages sought to be conveyed. . . . As the Supreme Court stated in *West Virginia State Board of Education v. Barnette:*

> If there is any star fixed in our constitutional constellation, it is that no official, high or petty, can prescribe what shall be orthodox in politics, nationalism, religion, or other matters of opinion or force citizens to confess by word or act their faith therein.

Nor could the University proscribe speech simply because it was found to be offensive, evenly gravely so, by large numbers of people. . . . As the Supreme Court noted in *Street v. New York:*

> It is firmly settled that under our Constitution the public expression of ideas may not be prohibited merely because the ideas are themselves offensive to some of their hearers . . .

These principles acquire a special significance in the university setting, where the free and unfettered interplay of competing views is essential to the institution's educational mission. . . . With these general rules in mind, the Court can now consider whether the Policy sweeps within its scope speech which is otherwise protected by the First Amendment.

## B. OVERBREADTH

. . . A law regulating speech will be deemed overbroad if it sweeps within its ambit a substantial amount of protected speech along with that which it may legitimately regulate. . . . [T]he state may not prohibit broad classes of speech, some of which may indeed be legitimately regulable, if in so doing a substantial amount of constitutionally protected conduct is also prohibited. This was the fundamental infirmity of the Policy.

The University repeatedly argued that the Policy did not apply to speech that is protected by the First Amendment. It urged the Court to disregard the Guide as "inaccurate" and look instead to "the manner in which the Policy has been interpreted and applied by those charged with its enforcement." However, as applied by the University over the past year, the Policy was consistently applied to reach protected speech. . . .

On December 7, 1988, a complaint was filed against a graduate student in the School of Social Work alleging that he harassed students based on sexual orientation and sex. The basis for the sexual orientation charge was apparently that in a research class, the student openly stated his belief that homosexuality was a disease and that he intended to develop a counseling plan for changing gay clients to straight. . . .

Although the student was not sanctioned over the allegations of sexual orientation harassment, the fact remains that the Policy Administrator—the authoritative voice of the University on these matters—saw no First Amendment problem in forcing the student to a hearing to answer for allegedly harassing statements made in the course of academic discussion and research. . . .

A second case, which was formally resolved, also demonstrated that the University did not exempt statements made in the course of classroom academic discussions from the sanctions of the policy. On September 28, 1988, a complaint was filed against a student in an entrepreneurship class in the School of Business Administration for reading an allegedly homophobic limerick during a scheduled class public-speaking exercise which ridiculed a well known athlete for his presumed sexual orientation. The Policy Administrator was able to persuade the perpetrator to attend an educational "gay rap" session, write a letter of apology to the *Michigan Daily,* and apologize to his class and the matter was dropped. No discussion of the possibility that the limerick was protected speech appears in the file or in the Administrator's notes.

A third incident involved a comment made in the orientation session of a preclinical dentistry class. The class was widely regarded as one of the most difficult for second year dentistry students. To allay fears and concerns at the outset, the class was broken up into small sections to informally discuss anticipated problems. During the ensuing discussion, a student stated that "he had heard that minorities had a difficult time in the course and that he had heard that they were not treated fairly." A minority professor teaching the class filed a complaint on the grounds that the comment was unfair and hurt her chances for tenure. Following the filing of the complaint, the student was "counseled" about the existence of the policy and agreed to write a letter apologizing for making the comment without adequately verifying the allegation, which he said he had heard from his room-mate, a black former denistry student.

The manner in which these three complaints were handled demonstrated that the University considered serious comments made in the context of classroom discussion to be sanctionable under the Policy. . . . The University could not seriously argue that the policy was never interpreted to reach protected conduct. It is clear that the policy was overbroad both on its face and as applied.

C. VAGUENESS

Doe also urges that the policy be struck down on the grounds that it is impermissibly vague. A statute is unconstitutionally vague when "men of common intelligence must necessarily guess at its meaning. . . . " A statute must give adequate warning of the conduct which is to be prohibited and must set out explicit standards for those who apply it. . . .

Looking at the plain language of the Policy, it was simply impossible to discern any limitation on its scope or any conceptual distinction between protected and unprotected conduct. . . . The operative words in the cause section required that language must "stigmatize" or "victimize" an individual. However, both of these terms are general and elude precise definition. . . .

The first of the "effects clauses" stated that in order to be sanctionable, the stigmatizing and victimizing statements had to "involve an express or implied threat to an individual's academic efforts, employment, participation in University sponsored extra-curricular activities or personal safety." It is not clear what kind of conduct would constitute a "threat" to an individual's academic efforts. . . .

Moving to the second "effect clause," a stigmatizing or victimizing comment is sanctionable if it has the purpose or reasonably foreseeable effect of interfering with an individual's academic efforts, etc. Again, the question is what conduct will be held to "interfere" with an individual's academic efforts. The language of the policy alone gives no inherent guidance. The one interpretive resource the University provided was withdrawn as "inaccurate," an implicit admission that even the University itself was unsure of the precise scope and meaning of the Policy.

✳ During the oral argument, the Court asked the University's counsel how he would distinguish between speech which was merely offensive, which he conceded was protected, and speech which "stigmatizes or victimizes" on the basis of an invidious factor. Counsel replied "very carefully." The response, while refreshingly candid, illustrated the plain fact that the university never articulated any principled way to distinguish sanctionable from protected speech. Students of common understanding were necessarily forced to guess at whether a comment about a controversial issue would later be found to be sanctionable under the Policy. The terms of the Policy were so vague that its enforcement would violate the due process clause. . . .

VI. Conclusion

[A 1975 Yale University] report concluded that "freedom of expression is a paramount value, more important than civility or rationality" (*New York Times,* Sept. 22, 1986, at B4). Writing about [a case of hate speech on the Yale campus,] Professor Woodward observed:

It simply seems unnatural to make a fuss about the rights of a speaker who offends the moral or political convictions passionately held by a majority. The far more natural impulse is to stop the nonsense, shut it up, punish it—anything but defend it. But to give rein to that inclination would be to make the majority the arbiters of truth for all. Furthermore, it would put the universities into the business of censorship (*New York Times,* Oct. 15, 1986, at A27).

While the Court is sympathetic to the University's obligation to ensure equal educational opportunities for all of its students, such efforts must not be at the expense of free speech. Unfortunately, this was precisely what the University did. . . .
◆◆◆

After reading this case, do you feel the issue is as simple as Judge Cohn suggests? At one level, Cohn's opinion plainly uses vagueness and overbroad analysis to reject the Michigan policy. By arguing that the policy could punish pure speech that, however offensive, is protected by the First Amendment, Cohn reasoned that the Michigan rules were unconstitutionally overbroad. And by asserting that average students (even "reasonable students") would find it impossible to discern any difference between protected and unprotected conduct, he was claiming that the policy was also vague.

Although Cohn's opinion had no binding effect outside his own district, it was nevertheless influential in other courts through the federal system. Any university administrator or counsel probing the opinion for guidance might likely conclude that a campus speech code needed to be narrowly tailored and clear (thereby evading overbreadth and vagueness) to pass constitutional muster.

Such a cursory reading of this case, however, would potentially miss a more significant aspect of legal analysis by Judge Cohn—for in this case he also discussed the doctrine we have referred to as *categorization* to reject the Michigan policy. In describing the various categorical exceptions to the First Amendment, he concluded that the policy did not limit its definition of hate speech to words that fit any of these categories (e.g., fighting words or obscenity); he very clearly inferred that if the code had done so, "it is very unlikely that any constitutional problem would have arisen."[31]

The message was clear: Draft a response to hate speech that is grounded in a categorical exception, and the Court will likely permit the restriction. Other universities attempted to argue that their speech codes were constitutional, because the expression they forbade fell within these exceptions to the First Amendment.

31. *Id.* at 863.

### The University of Wisconsin Policy—Not Saved by the Categorical Exceptions Theory

The University of Wisconsin thought that its hate speech policy was limited to categorical exceptions to the First Amendment. Wisconsin's rule allowed the University to discipline students

> (2) (a) For racist or discriminatory comments, epithets or other expressive behavior directed at an individual or on separate occasions at several individuals, or for physical conduct, if such comments, epithets or expressive behavior or physical conduct intentionally:
>
> > 1. Demean the race, sex, religion, color, creed, disability, sexual orientation, national origin, ancestry or age of the individual or individuals; and
> > 2. Create an intimidating, hostile or demeaning environment for education, university-related work, or other university-authorized activity.[32]

The Wisconsin rule was challenged in federal court on First Amendment grounds in the case of *UWM Post, Inc. v. Board of Regents of the University of Wisconsin System*,[33] presided over by federal district court Judge Warren. University administrators argued that by limiting their rule to racist or discriminatory comments, epithets, or other expressive behavior, they had sufficiently narrowed the class of proscribed speech to that with "minimum social value" and that which was "likely to cause violent response."[34] In other words, the university believed that its rule only applied to speech that the *Chaplinksy*[35] doctrine left unprotected.

The federal district court rejected the university's analysis. Citing *Gooding v. Wilson*,[36] Judge Warren noted that fighting words include "only words which tend to incite an immediate breach of the peace."[37] The Wisconsin code prohibited all language directed at an individual when the words created a hostile educational environment by demeaning individuals on the basis of characteristics such as race or sex. The university attempted to argue that such speech always constituted fighting words:

> [I]t is understandable to expect a violent response to discriminatory harassment, because such harassment demeans an immutable characteristic which is central to the person's identity. . . . [T]he victim will feel compelled to respond, not just for his own dignity, but for the dignity of his brothers and sisters of color, national origin or creed."[38]

---

32. *Wisc. Admin. Code,* Section UWS 17.06(2).
33. 774 F.Supp. 1163 (E.D. Wis. 1991).
34. *Id.* at 1169.
35. 315 U.S. 568 (1942). The categories of speech that were held to be unprotected in *Chaplinsky* are found in Chapter 6, page 146, of this text.
36. 405 U.S. 518 (1972). The *Gooding* case is discussed in Chapter 6, beginning on p. 157.
37. 774 F.Supp. at 1171.
38. *Id.* at 1173.

The district court rejected the university's analysis, and concluded instead that "it is unlikely that all or nearly all . . . expressive behavior which creates an intimidating, hostile, or demeaning environment tends to provoke a violent response."[39] Because the Wisconsin policy applied in part to speech that was not likely to provoke a breach of the peace, it did not meet the fighting words exception.

The federal court also declined the university's invitation to classify hate speech as a new category of unprotected speech, above and beyond the categories identified in *Chaplinsky*. Judge Warren reasoned that *Chaplinsky* did not ask lower courts to create additional categorical exception. Furthermore, the court was not persuaded that hate speech, like fighting words, lacked social utility. The opinion recognized that students who used hateful terms probably were attempting "to inform their listeners of their racist or discriminatory views."[40] However, this did not strip them of First Amendment protection. Under *Cohen*,[41] the emotive function of speech is protected, and hate speech expresses students' feelings about persons of a different race, gender, or religion. Furthermore, even if a majority of persons would agree that racist views are wrong, the First Amendment does not require that the correct viewpoints will win out in the marketplace of ideas.[42]

The *UWM Post* decision echoed the opinion of the U.S. district court in *Doe*. In the university context, an uninhibited marketplace of ideas was to be maintained, even when it led to speech that was highly offensive to some or all of its listeners. Speech codes could only promote communitarian values, such as civility on campus and respect for other members of the university community, if the restrictions were limited to speech that met a categorical exception to the First Amendment. Within two months of the *UWM Post* decision, a federal district court in Virginia taught George Mason University a similar lesson.

### George Mason University—Offensiveness Is Not a Valid Grounds for Controlling Expression

The principle that freedom of speech demands tolerance of ideas, no matter how repugnant they are to many people, was put to the test in the case of *Iota Xi Chapter of Sigma Chi v. George Mason University*.[43] The expression in question took place on the campus of George Mason University, a state institution, during a week-long social event called Derby Days. One Derby Days activity, held in the cafeteria of the student union, was called "Dress a Sig." In this contest, fraternity brothers dressed as caricatures of "ugly women." At the 1991 event, "one participant dressed in black face, used pillows to represent

39. *Id.*
40. *Id.* at 1175.
41. 403 U.S. 13 (1971). The *Cohen* case is discussed in Chapter 6, beginning on p. 151.
42. 774 F.Supp. at 1175.
43. 773 F.Supp. 792 (E.D. Va. 1991).

breasts and buttocks and wore a black wig with curlers."[44] Several student leaders, offended by the racial and sexual stereotypes perpetuated by the contest, demanded that Sigma Chi be sanctioned. The dean of student services barred the fraternity from holding social and sports activities for a two-year probationary period, and the fraternity took their case to federal court, claiming the university had violated their First Amendment rights.

The federal district court agreed, and enjoined the university from imposing any discipline on Sigma Chi as a result of the "Dress a Sig" contest. The court held that "a state university may not suppress expression because it finds that expression offensive,"[45] as there are no First Amendment exceptions for bigoted or racist views.

The district court agreed that the university had a right to pursue its educational mission, and that goals such as enhancing the education of women and minorities and promoting a diverse student body were part of that mission. However, the university offered no specific proof of any harm to those goals. Conversely, the court ruled that the fraternity's action was "consistent with GMU's educational mission in conveying ideas and promoting the free flow and expression of those ideas."[46]

The U.S. district court in Virginia was consistent with its counterparts in Michigan and Iowa, in that it reaffirmed that offensiveness cannot be a justification for suppressing speech on campus. However, the *Sigma Chi v. George Mason* opinion, authored by district court Judge Hilton, raised other issues as well. First, the court noted that the university had offered no proof of any harm to goals such as promoting diversity and improving the learning environment of women and minorities. Would the outcome of the case have been different if the university could prove that students had sought medical treatment or dropped out of the university because the contest had been so traumatizing? The court left that question open, but later in this chapter we will discuss the argument that speech that causes such effects should be regulated.

A second line of analysis developed by the court was the contention that freedom of speech does not merely benefit the individual communicators. In addition, the court opined, the educational mission of a university is promoted when there is a free flow of ideas. In other words, freedom of speech has a communitarian dimension as well as an individual one. The university may do its best job of educating in an environment where no idea is too offensive to be expressed. George Mason University obviously thought that preserving diversity was more important to its educational mission than protecting all speech on campus, no matter how offensive. The dichotomy between promoting diversity and preventing censorship of expression forces any university to make a value judgment when it considers a speech code. The federal court in *Sigma Chi* was convinced that the Constitution had already made this value

44. *Id.* at 793.
45. *Id.* at 795.
46. *Id.* at 794.

judgment (against regulation of speech) for the university. Would you want your university to react as George Mason's administration did, or do you agree with the federal district court?

## Summary of the Federal Court Decisions on Speech Codes

Three different federal district courts have upheld challenges to university regulation of hate speech on First Amendment grounds. A municipal restriction of hate speech was also found unconstitutional in the *R.A.V.* decision, discussed in chapter 6. Although *R.A.V.* did not consider a university speech code, the Supreme Court's reasoning in that case was highly consistent with that of the lower courts in *Doe, UWM Post,* and *Sigma Chi.* The courts will not allow hate speech to be regulated when the justification for restriction is that such speech is highly offensive.

Nevertheless, the courts that have considered hate speech have left open the possibility that carefully written speech codes may be found constitutional. *R.A.V.* reaffirmed the validity of the categorical approach to the First Amendment, and *Doe* and *UWM Post* specifically noted that a university could restrict speech that fits a categorical exception. If a university restricts a category highlighted in *Chaplinsky,* such as fighting words or libel, and the restriction meets *R.A.V.*'s edict not to discriminate on the basis of content,[47] a speech code would have a much greater chance of being found constitutional by a federal court. This is not to say that universities necessarily should adopt speech codes, but it is important to understand the possibility that some speech codes may pass judicial muster in the future.

Do you agree with the reasoning of the federal courts that have found speech codes unconstitutional? Would you support some form of speech code for your university or community? These are important decisions for all members of a democratic society to consider. The next section will offer differing viewpoints on these issues.

## THINKING CRITICALLY ABOUT HATE SPEECH REGULATION

We present three issues for you to consider in this section. First is the question of the reasoning in the judicial opinions holding that speech codes are unconstitutional. In the previous section of this chapter, you studied the reasoning of the federal courts, which have consistently agreed that hate speech restrictions violate the First Amendment. The reasoning of the courts (and civil libertarians who oppose speech codes) has been critiqued by commentators. In the interest of taking a balanced approach to this issue, we will review their positions. Second, we will address the desirability of basing speech codes on the fighting words doctrine. Even if speech codes are desir-

---

47. Speech codes that only applied to racist fighting words or to anti-Catholic libel would be examples of restrictions that discriminate on the basis of content.

able, should these rules be predicated on the assumption (made by the University of Wisconsin in *UWM Post*) that hate speech constitutes fighting words? We will conclude this section by discussing the marketplace of ideas. Would a marketplace approach to hateful speech be superior to a prohibition of such discourse?

### Are Speech Codes Constitutional? The Critics Respond

Claims that speech codes violate the First Amendment have been critiqued by scholars who support restrictions on hate speech. Some of the major contentions they develop are summarized here. After reading these viewpoints and contrasting them with the reasoning of the federal courts (see the previous section), do you agree that codes restricting hate speech should be held to violate the First Amendment?

***Bad Ideas Do Exist and Can Be Regulated.*** The argument that "there is no such thing as a false idea"[48] is a central premise in the case against government regulation of hate speech. Under this view, the worth of ideas is determined in the marketplace of ideas, rather than by government officials with the power to prohibit expression of "bad" ideas.

Defenders of speech codes argue that certain ideas, such as assertions that one race or sex is genetically inferior to another, are undeniably bad ones. How can we determine that certain ideas are bad? A consensus of the world's diverse cultures is one standard that has been advocated. For example, Professor Richard Delgado notes that 104 states have signed the *International Convention on the Elimination of All Forms of Racial Discrimination*. Article 4 of this Convention states that the signatories "condemn all propaganda and all organizations which are based on ideas or theories of superiority of one race or group of persons of one colour or ethnic origin."[49] UCLA law professor Mari Matsuda contends that human experience teaches us that certain ideas are wrong. Presumably we would all agree that slavery, the Holocaust, and apartheid are evil.[50] On issues such as these, advocates of codes contend, opposing viewpoints do not need a hearing in the marketplace of ideas.

***The First Amendment Should Not Trump the Fourteenth Amendment.*** The Fourteenth Amendment to the U.S. Constitution includes the guarantee that "no state shall . . . deny to any person within its jurisdiction the equal protection of the laws." Proponents of speech codes argue that there is no valid reason to assume that the First Amendment should always prevail when

---

48. *Gertz v. Robert Welch, Inc.*, 418 U.S. 323, 339 (1974).
49. Richard Delgado, *Campus Antiracism Rules: Constitutional Narratives in Collision*, 85 Northwestern Law Review 343, 363 (Winter 1991). The United States signed, but did not ratify, the Convention on September 28, 1966. *Id.*, n. 154.
50. Mari J. Matsuda, *Public Response to Racist Speech: Considering the Victim's Story*, 87 Michigan Law Review 2320, 2359 (August 1989).

it conflicts with the Fourteenth.[51] Instead, the First Amendment interests of the perpetrator of hate speech should be balanced against the equal protection interests of the target of that speech. For example, verbal harassment (and the fear of verbal harassment) on a college campus can have a devastating effect on the victims' academic performance.[52] Why should the victim's right to equal educational opportunity be subordinated to a racist's free speech right?

Hate speech might perpetuate inequality in society, as well as in the university setting. Racist speech may sustain racist attitudes,[53] whereas prohibition of racist speech might weaken the impulse to engage in racist behavior.[54] Hateful speech can create an environment in which society is less likely to worry about the human needs of those who are targeted. In the words of feminist scholar Catharine MacKinnon, "there is a relation . . . between the use of the epithet 'nigger' and the fact that a disproportionate number of children who go to bed hungry every night in this country are African-American."[55]

***Hate Speech Is Not a Mere Insult.*** In each hate speech case that has been discussed in this chapter, the court has held that speech cannot be banned on the grounds that it is offensive. Advocates of regulation counter that hate speech is not the equivalent of an everyday insult. Physical and psychological harms of hate speech, which are hardly limited to hurt feelings, were noted earlier in this chapter. Hate speech functions as a verbal "slap in the face," telling another person that he or she is not a human being and often producing physical symptoms.[56] Ethnic slurs occur in the context of a society plagued by racism, and can "cause long term emotional pain" by "intensifying the effects of the stigmatization, labeling, and disrespectful treatment that the victim has previously undergone."[57] It is argued that members of the dominant culture cannot fully understand the impact of hate speech, because they have no analogous experience from which to empathize.[58] But to members of the target groups, the injury experienced is all too painful and real.

***Hate Speech Silences Others' Voices.*** In chapter 1, we noted that one justification for restricting speech is the argument that some speech operates to inhibit others from expressing their right to freedom of speech. Defenders of speech codes have argued that hate speech is particularly likely to have this effect. Hate speech occurs in the context of a society where the efforts of women, minorities, and homosexuals to exercise their rights have caused them to be fired, publicly humiliated, and even lynched. Stanford law professor Lawrence argues that to the target of hate speech, the use of insulting epi-

---

51. See, e.g., Catharine A. MacKinnon, *Only Words,* p. 71 (Harvard Univ. Press, 1993).
52. Lawrence in *Words That Wound,* pp. 75–76.
53. Matsuda, *Public Response to Racist Speech,* p. 2339.
54. Delgado, *Campus Antiracism Rules,* p. 374.
55. MacKinnon, *Only Words,* p. 74.
56. Lawrence in *Words That Wound,* p. 68.
57. Delgado in *Words That Wound,* p. 60.
58. See, e.g., Lawrence in *Words That Wound,* p. 72.

thets is effectively a threat. Members of the target group are silenced because they recognize a connection between hateful speech and subsequent violent acts.[59]

In summary, one reaction to judicial decisions that speech codes are unconstitutional is a critique of the premises underlying these opinions. Critics have decried the marketplace assumption that there is no such thing as a bad idea and the claim that hate speech causes no greater harm than the hurt feelings produced by everyday insults all of us encounter daily. These critics also argue that the Fourteenth Amendment interest in equality can outweigh society's interest in protecting racist, sexist, and homophobic expression, and that any gains in freedom of speech to those who use hate speech are outweighed by the chilling effect of hate speech on its victims. Rather than attacking the premises of hate speech cases and advocating their reversal, a second alternative for opponents of hate speech would be to develop policies that are consistent with the case law on speech codes.

### Developing Speech Codes That Are Consistent with First Amendment Doctrine

*A Speech Code Prohibiting Fighting Words?* Although the courts reviewing speech codes have suggested that a policy directed only at fighting words would be a constitutional means to regulate hate speech, this approach raises some problems.

First is the fact that within the legal and academic community there is widespread disagreement as to what ultimate force the doctrine of fighting words carries. As evidenced in our chapter on fighting words and the reference to the *R.A.V.* case, every fighting words conviction heard by the U.S. Supreme Court since it narrowed the rule (disregarding the original *Chaplinsky* language of words "which by their very utterance inflict injury" and replacing it with a requirement that words must "tend to incite an immediate breach of the peace") has been overturned. This is the paradox mentioned in chapter 6. The Court wants this categorical exception—but almost never enforces it. Should the prevention of hate speech be based on a doctrine with this track record?

Second and equally critical is the fact that we cannot always say that the normal response to fighting words *today* is a violent response. The fighting words doctrine assumes a level playing field—one in which the target of the speech feels free, unfettered and courageous enough to react with violence. The reality of a society tainted by bigotry, however, is that we do *not* always operate on such a field; more often than not, the grounds are *uneven*. Even within a utopia such as a college or university, minorities are likely to be overwhelmed by the sheer numerical superiority of the dominant culture and merely succumb to the speech and move along.

---

59. Lawrence, *id.*, p. 79.

We can only imagine what passed through the minds of two African American students at Arizona State University who were threatened with blatantly racist, hateful invective; were later surrounded by some two thousand individuals; and beaten by another fifteen or so. Regardless of the courage or character of these students, would it be reasonable to assume that they would have stayed for the beating if not trapped by the crowd? More to the point, even assuming a smaller crowd size, would other minority students or other targets of hate speech reasonably be expected to stay and fight in this situation?

Third, the fighting words doctrine assumes very much a gender-biased perspective. Many would argue that women in our society have not been socialized to respond to insults by using violence—yet the assumption underlying this doctrine is that the recipient of this speech will react in just this way. Notwithstanding the earlier point about uneven playing fields, even if minority men did feel comfortable with a violent response, can we necessarily say the same of minority women?

For these reasons, it may not make much sense to base rules for hate speech upon a categorical exception like fighting words. How, then, would we deal with hate speech? Perhaps the answer lies in a second categorical exception, suggested by Judge Cohn in the *Doe* case.

### A Speech Code Prohibiting Intentional Infliction of Emotional Distress?

Victims of messages that are calculated to cause severe emotional damage have been able to sue in civil court, relying on the **tort** law of intentional infliction of emotional distress. This tort assumes a situation in which the speaker intends to harm the recipient of the message by causing a stressful reaction. The *Second Restatement of the Law of Torts* indicates when there is civil liability for intentional infliction of emotional distress:

> One who by extreme and outrageous conduct intentionally or recklessly causes severe emotional distress to another is subject to liability for such emotional distress, and if bodily harm to the other results from it, for such bodily harm.[60]

Virtually all states now recognize this tort as defined by the *Second Restatement*. Prohibition of this conduct, rather than fighting words, could form the basis of a university speech code.

According to the *Second Restatement*, extreme and outrageous conduct occurs when "the recitation of the facts to an average member of the community would arouse his [or her] resentment against the actor, and lead him [or her] to exclaim 'Outrageous!'"[61] The decision of whether particular conduct rises to

---

60. *Restatement (Second) of the Law of Torts*, Section 46, p. 71 (American Law Institute, 1965).
61. *Id.* p. 73.

the level of outrage is made by the trier of fact on a case-by-case basis, usually taking into account changing social conditions and the plaintiff's own susceptibility.[62]

Hate speech can constitute extreme and outrageous conduct. Although at one time courts referred to racist language as "merely" offensive, rather than outrageous,[63] judicial decisions have begun to maintain that hate speech is not necessarily a "mere insult." For example, in *Bailey v. Binyon*, an employer called Mr. Bailey a "nigger," followed him into the kitchen, and repeated the insult. After Bailey asked to be treated like a human being, Binyon replied "you're not a human being, you're a nigger." The court noted that it would not characterize Binyon's remarks as "mere insults."[64] In response to derogatory remarks made by co-workers to a Mexican American employee, the Supreme Court of Washington noted: "Racial epithets which were once part of common usage may not now be looked upon as 'mere insulting language.' Changing sensitivity in society alters the acceptability of former terms."[65]

A university disciplinary regulation against the intentional infliction of emotional distress might reduce problems inherent in speech codes based on fighting words. One advantage is that intentional infliction of emotional distress combats the actual harm caused by hate speech. By targeting outrageous conduct resulting in severe distress, the regulation applies when the harm to the victim is the greatest. When fighting words are prohibited, words that cause little long-term damage to the victim can be forbidden on the grounds that a fight may ensue, whereas very hateful messages are tolerated if they are not uttered in a context where the victim is likely to fight back. Moreover, intentional infliction of emotional distress is only applicable when distress does result. A lesson of the *UWM Post* decision is that university regulations will be deemed overbroad if they apply to situations where the harm (e.g., violence) may not occur. Finally, the language of the *Restatement's* definition is **content neutral.** The perpetrator is liable when the effect of the message on its victim is sufficiently severe. There is no prohibition of messages on any particular subject; hence, it would be less suspect in the eyes of a reviewing court.

Although a speech code based on the language of the intentional infliction of emotional distress tort would avoid some of the problems inherent in the fighting words approach, the code would not resolve all the difficulties inherent in the regulation of hate speech.

First, this standard, like codes based on fighting words, presumes a level playing field as a starting place. To feel comfortable about responding to hate

62. See, e.g., *Alcorn v. Ambro Engineering Inc.*, 2 Cal.3d 493 (1970).
63. Shawna Yen, *Redressing the Victim of Racist Speech After* R.A.V. v. City of St. Paul, 26 Columbia Journal of Law and Social Problems 589, 596–97 (Summer 1993).
64. *Bailey v. Binyon*, 583 F.Supp. 923, 934 (N.D. Ill. 1984).
65. *Contreras v. Crown Zellerbach Corporation*, 565 P. 2d 1173, 1177 (Wash. 1977).

speech by using a lawsuit to recover damages, one would first have to feel comfortable and confident with the legal system. Given the historical treatment of women and minorities in our legal system, can we honestly say this inspires such confidence?

Second, and problematic for the First Amendment, is yet another potential vagueness problem. Under the *Restatement* definition, a hate speaker might be liable if his or her words constitute outrageous conduct. The *Doe* court found terms such as "victimize" and "stigmatize" vague. How is a speaker any more likely to know that his or her words rise to the level of "outrageous" than that his or her speech stigmatized or victimized another person?

Finally, there are difficulties with proof of harm in cases involving emotional distress. What would serve as evidence of stress? If a victim told university administrators that he or she had suffered severe distress, should that be a sufficient basis for punishing speech? If so, any offensive speech could be punished. And how would university disciplinary authorities be expected to filter out the other aspects of general bigotry in society to know that a sufficient proportion of a victim's stress was caused by the perpetrator's hate speech?

The questions raised by speech codes, whether they are based on fighting words or emotional distress, have led to suggestions that universities look for answers to the problems of discrimination that do not rely on suppressing speech.

## A Marketplace of Ideas Remedy for Hate Speech

In *Sigma Chi*, Judge Hilton noted that promoting the free flow of ideas, not limiting them, was consistent with the university's mission.[66] This approach is consistent with Justice Brandeis's call for more speech as a response to speech we abhor.[67] When a person tells a joke that sounds racist or sexist or homophobic, students and faculty could indicate their distaste for such jokes, even if members of the target group are not present. In classroom discussions, professors and students can challenge assumptions that are based on stereotypes about a class of persons. Rather than shouting down a speaker who is being politically incorrect, participants can challenge that speaker to provide evidence supporting his or her views.

Is the marketplace of ideas the best remedy for hate speech? Or are the harms to the individual victims and the university community too great to allow such words to go unpunished? In formulating an answer, rely on your first-hand experience on campus and elsewhere, as well as what you have read. Although students and faculty may be powerless to change the course of the law of libel or obscenity, the members of the university community will ultimately decide the fate of hate speech on campus.

66. 773 F. Supp. at 794.
67. *Whitney v. California*, discussed in chapter 4 of this text.

## SUMMARY

Without question, hate speech—abusive insults, epithets, and expressive conduct targeted at individuals on the basis of immutable characteristics like race, ethnicity, or gender—creates a serious problem for our society. Hate speech can stigmatize, leading to serious psychological and even physical damage. Because it is contextually based, it can promote ugly stereotypes and the sorts of images that perpetuate such practices as racism or homophobia.

This has proven to be a particularly difficult problem for schools—especially at the college and university level—where students are expected to participate in a free and open exchange of ideas. Campus administrators have tried various remedies aimed at ridding the academy of hate speech—but not all validate the contextually based suffering of victims or accomplish this goal without also encroaching on speech protected by the First Amendment. Although courts and legal theorists continue to develop theories and models for proscribing this kind of speech, no single contemporary effort completely escapes practical—or constitutional—problems.

Future efforts at regulating hate speech in schools will likely make use of categorical exceptions to the First Amendment (e.g., fighting words) but could also include more novel exceptions such as intentional infliction of emotional distress. Whether these will actually diminish hate speech is at best unclear.

An alternative response to hate speech is reliance on the marketplace of ideas. Regardless of whether a speech code is in place at a university, students and faculty can respond to any incidents of racism and prejudice with more speech. If members of the university community use their voices to advocate tolerance and diversity, rather than relying on their power to silence opposing views, they might gain far greater results than any speech code could hope to achieve.

CHAPTER *8*    *Objectives*

**After reading chapter 8,**
**you should understand**
**the following:**

◆ *How* **defamatory** *statements expose a person's reputation to attack or ridicule, and what types of statements are typically at issue in defamation cases.*

◆ *The landmark Supreme Court decision in* New York Times v. Sullivan, *and the meaning of the* **actual malice** *standard the court employed to decide the case.*

◆ *The defamation cases following* New York Times v. Sullivan *that defined the* **meaning** *and* **applicability** *of the actual malice rule.*

◆ *A fundamental justification for protecting defamatory statements about* **public officials** *and* **public figures** *that are not made with actual malice, which is preserving a robust marketplace of ideas on issues of public concern.*

◆ *The justification for a lower standard of protection for defamatory statements about* **private citizens,** *who have less ability to respond in the marketplace of ideas.*

◆ *The question of how the right to know about matters of public concern should be balanced with a news subjects'* **right to privacy.**

# 8 *Defamation of Character and Related Issues*

Surely no American in recent times has labored more diligently and heroically against reason and rational thinking than Rush Limbaugh has.[1]

She [Hillary Clinton] is a bitch, whispers Kathleen Gingrich to Connie Chung, quoting her son Newt.[2]

IF RUSH LIMBAUGH READS THESE WORDS, should he feel insulted? Publicly humiliated? If Mrs. Clinton sees the television interview in which Newt Gingrich's mother calls her a bitch, should she feel as if her character and name have been publicly sullied? Does it matter that Mrs. Clinton, although not an elected official, is nevertheless a political figure? Does it matter that Mr. Limbaugh, although not necessarily a political figure, is nevertheless a public figure? If Mrs. Clinton and Mr. Limbaugh were ordinary private citizens, would they have a greater right to be sensitive to these comments?

In modern discourse, it is common to hear or read hostile, caustic character assassinations such as the above. When it is alleged that a person did something bad, or *is* bad, the target of the message may fight back by filing a **defamation** suit. Defamation, as defined by **common law,** is language that tends to expose another to hatred, shame, ridicule, ostracism, or disgrace.[3] This language must be directed to at least one person, not including the target of the claim. At common law, defamation was divided into **libel** (the printed word) and **slander** (the spoken word), but this distinction is not significant in modern case law. When a plaintiff wins a defamation lawsuit, he or she is entitled to money damages. Compensatory damages provide the victim with

---

1. Maria Falbo, *Rush to Ignorance*, 54 The Humanist 6 (July–August 1994).
2. David Maraniss, *The First Lady of Paradoxes*, Washington Post National Weekly Edition 6 (January 23–29, 1995).
3. 50 *American Jurisprudence*, p. 520 (Bancroft-Whitney, 2nd ed 1970).

money that is equal to the harm she or he has suffered.[4] In some jurisdictions, a jury may also award punitive damages—a penalty above and beyond the actual loss suffered by the victim, intended to deter similar acts in the future.

When the government allows the target of defamatory speech to recover damages, it is discouraging that speech from entering the marketplace of ideas. As you remember from chapter 6, defamation is one of the categories deemed "worthless" in *Chaplinsky*. The basis for placing a low value on such speech is that *falsehoods* about another person do not contribute to society's search for *truth*. From a communitarian perspective, it can be argued that we have a duty to our fellow citizens not to damage their reputations with lies.

Jury verdicts show society's intolerance of defamation. A public prosecutor sued a television station after it ran an unflattering series. The jury voted $58 million in damages against the station. *Business Week* published an article in which it described a lawyer as "arrogant"; the magazine lost a $1,637,000 jury verdict.[5]

With huge verdicts such as these at stake, defendants in defamation cases ordinarily fight hard to prevail. One typical defense is the claim that the alleged defamation is true. For example, if Joe Jones files a defamation suit against a newspaper for running a story indicating that he is a murderer, and Jones has been convicted of murder, there is no defamation. A second defense is that the defendant's words should be protected by the First Amendment, *even if they are false*. This chapter will focus on this latter defense.

The question of whether the First Amendment should protect defamation focuses on how our society should balance two conflicting goals—preservation of robust debate on leading issues of the day and protection of a person's right to preserve his or her good name. In most of the cases you will study in this chapter, it is assumed that a false, defamatory statement about the plaintiff has been communicated by the defendant. The issue to be decided is whether, in some circumstances, the First Amendment should protect a communicator, even one who has made a false statement about another person.

### *NEW YORK TIMES V. SULLIVAN:* THE ACTUAL MALICE RULE

As Americans, we highly value our right to criticize elected leaders. Should we make it easy for public officials to recover money damages by winning lawsuits against individuals who cannot verify their statements about politicians? Would there be vigorous and uninhibited political debate in the United States if citizens had to guarantee the truth of the claims they make about their leaders? The Supreme Court considered these questions in *New York Times v. Sullivan*,[6] and announced the modern-day test for First Amendment protection of false statements about public officials.

4. Id., p. 869–70. Compensatory damages include general damages, which are presumed to be the natural result of publication; and special damages, which are not assumed to be inevitable but have been proven.
5. Barbara Dill, "Libel Law Doesn't Work, but Can It Be Fixed?" in *At What Price? Libel Law and Freedom of the Press*, p. 36. (Twentieth Century Fund Paper, 1993).
6. 376 U.S. 254 (1964).

*Figure 8.1. Justice William J. Brennan Jr., was nominated to the Court in 1956 by President Eisenhower. Brennan was always willing to answer the objections of his brethren on the Court whenever drafting an opinion, a quality which endeared him to Chief Justice Warren, and enabled him to draft many majority opinions for the Warren Court. Brennan's majority-authored opinion in* New York Times v. Sullivan *follows.* (Ken Heinen, National Geographic Society. Collection of the Supreme Court of the United States.)

### *New York Times Co. v. Sullivan*, 376 U.S. 254 (1964)

Mr. Justice Brennan (see Figure 8.1) delivered the opinion of the Court.

We are required in this case to determine for the first time the extent to which the constitutional protections for speech and press limit a State's power to award damages in a libel action brought by a public official against critics of his official conduct.

Respondent L.B. Sullivan is one of the three elected Commissioners of the City of Montgomery, Alabama. He testified that he was "Commissioner of Public Affairs" and [his] duties [include] supervision of the Police Department. . . . He brought this civil libel action against the four individual petitioners, who are Negroes and Alabama clergymen, and against petitioner, the New York Times Company. . . . A jury in the Circuit Court of Montgomery County awarded him damages of $500,000, the full amount claimed, against all the petitioners, and the Supreme Court of Alabama affirmed (citation omitted).

Respondent's complaint alleged that he had been libeled by statements in a full page advertisement that was carried in the *New York Times* on March 29, 1960.[7]

---

7. The insert was signed by the Committee to Defend Martin Luther King. Under the appeal "Your Help Is Urgently Needed . . . NOW!!" were listed sixty-four names, including Marlon Brando, Nat King Cole, Langston Hughes, Jackie Robinson, and Eleanor Roosevelt.

Of the 10 paragraphs in the text in the advertisement, the third and a portion of the sixth were the basis of respondent's claim of libel. They read as follows:

> Third paragraph: "In Montgomery, Alabama, after students sang My
> Country, 'Tis of Thee on the State Capitol steps, their leaders were ex-
> pelled from school, and truckloads of police armed with shotguns and
> tear gas ringed the Alabama State College Campus. When the entire
> student body protested to state authorities by refusing to re-register,
> their dining hall was padlocked in an attempt to starve them into sub-
> mission." Sixth paragraph: "Again and again the Southern violators
> have answered Dr. King's peaceful protests with intimidation and vio-
> lence. They have bombed his home almost killing his wife and child.
> They have assaulted his person. They have arrested him seven times—
> for 'speeding,' 'loitering' and similar 'offenses.'" . . .

Although neither of these statements mentions respondent by name, he
contended that the word "police" in the third paragraph referred to him as the
Montgomery Commissioner who supervised the Police Department. . . . As to the
sixth paragraph, he contended that since arrests are ordinarily made by the police,
the statement "They have arrested [Dr. King] seven times" would be read as referring to him; he further contended that the "they" who did the arresting would be
equated with the "Southern violators." . . .

It is uncontroverted that some of the statements contained in the two paragraphs were not accurate descriptions of events which occurred in Montgomery. . . . Although nine students were expelled by the State Board of Education, this was not for leading the demonstration at the Capitol, but for demanding
service at a lunch counter in the Montgomery County Courthouse on another
day. . . . The campus dining hall was not padlocked on any occasion. . . . Although
the police were deployed near campus in large numbers on three occasions, they
did not at any time "ring" the campus, and they were not called to the campus in
connection with the demonstration on the State Capitol steps, as the third paragraph implied. Dr. King had not been arrested seven times, but only four. . . . Although Dr. King's home had in fact been bombed twice when his wife and child
were there, both of these occasions antedated respondent's tenure as Commissioner, and the police were not only not implicated in the bombings, but had
made every effort to apprehend those who were. . . .

Under Alabama law as applied in this case, a publication is "libelous per se" if
the words "tend to injure a person . . . in his reputation" or to "bring [him] into
public contempt." . . . *The question before us is whether this rule of liability, as applied to an action brought by a public official against critics of his official conduct,
abridges the freedom of speech and of the press that is guaranteed by the First and
Fourteenth Amendments* (emphasis added). . . .

The general proposition that freedom of expression upon public questions is
secured by the First Amendment has long been settled by our decisions. . . . "It is a
prized American privilege to speak one's mind, although not always with perfect
good taste, on all public institutions," and this opportunity is to be afforded for

"vigorous advocacy" no less than "abstract discussion" (citations omitted). Thus we consider this case against the background of a profound national commitment to the principle that debate on public issues should be uninhibited, robust, and wide-open, and that it may well include vehement, caustic, and sometimes unpleasantly sharp attacks on government and public officials. . . .

The present advertisement, as an expression of grievance and protest on one of the major public issues of our time, would seem clearly to qualify for the constitutional protection. The question is whether it forfeits that protection by the falsity of some of its factual statements and by its alleged defamation of respondent.

Authoritative interpretations of the First Amendment guarantees have consistently refused to recognize an exception for any test of truth, whether administered by judges, juries, or administrative officials—and especially not one that puts the burden of proving truth on the speaker. . . . The constitutional protection does not turn upon the "truth, popularity, or social utility of the ideas and beliefs which are offered" *N.A.A.C.P. v. Button,* 371 U.S. 415, 445. . . .

In *Cantwell v. Connecticut,* 310 U.S. 296, 310, the Court declared:

> . . . To persuade others to his own point of view, the pleader, as we know, at times, resorts to exaggeration, to vilification of men who have been, or are, prominent in church or state, and even to false statement. But the people of this nation have ordained in the light of history, that, in spite of the probability of excesses and abuses, these liberties are, in the long view, essential to enlightened opinion and right conduct on the part of the citizens of a democracy.

. . . [E]rroneous statement is inevitable in free debate, and . . . it must be protected if the freedoms of expression are to have the "breathing space" that they need . . . to survive.

. . . A rule compelling the critic of official conduct to guarantee the truth of all his factual assertions—and to do so on pain of libel judgments virtually unlimited in amount—leads to . . . self censorship. . . . Under such a rule, would-be critics of official conduct may be deterred from voicing their criticism, even though it is believed to be true and even though it is in fact true, because of doubt whether it can be proved in court or fear of the expense of having to do so. They tend to make only statements which "steer far wider of the unlawful zone" (citation omitted). The rule thus dampens the vigor and limits the variety of public debate. It is inconsistent with the First and Fourteenth Amendments.

*The constitutional guarantees require, we think, a federal rule that prohibits a public official from recovering damages for a defamatory falsehood relating to his official conduct unless he proves that the statement was made with "actual malice"—that is, with knowledge that it was false or with reckless disregard of whether it was false or not* (emphasis added). . . .

[T]he facts do not support a finding of actual malice. The statement by the *Times'* Secretary that, apart from the padlocking allegation, he thought the advertisement was "substantially correct," affords no constitutional warrant for the Alabama Supreme Court's conclusion that it was a "cavalier ignoring of the falsity of

*Figure 8.2. Montgomery, Alabama, Police Commissioner L.B. Sullivan.* *(Associated Press/World Wide Photo. May 25, 1961. Reprinted by permission.)*

the advertisement [from which] the jury could not have but been impressed with the bad faith of The *Times* . . . That opinion [of the secretary] was at least a reasonable one, and there was no evidence to impeach the witness' good faith in holding it. . . .

[T]here is evidence that the *Times* published the advertisement without checking its accuracy against the news stories in the *Times'* own files. . . . With respect to the failure of [the *Times'* personnel] to make the check, the record shows that they relied upon their knowledge of the good reputation of many of those whose names were listed as sponsors of the advertisement, and upon the letter from A. Philip Randolph, known to them as a responsible individual, certifying that the use of the names was authorized. . . .

The judgment of the Supreme Court of Alabama is reversed and the case is remanded to that court for further proceedings not inconsistent with this opinion.

◆◆◆

The result of *New York Times v. Sullivan* (see Figure 8.2) is that there is no liability for statements relevant to the official conduct of public servants, even if the statements are *false,* unless **actual malice** is proven. What is actual malice? The Court defined it as making a statement that one *knows* to be false, or making a statement with **reckless** disregard for the truth of the statement.

The *New York Times v. Sullivan* rule provided more protection for false statements about public officials' conduct than did the common law. The Court was concerned that without an actual malice rule, communicators who believed information about their representatives to be true would be deterred from discussing public issues. In other words, some false statements about public officials must be tolerated in the marketplace of ideas to avoid the greater evil of *inhibiting* statements that are not defamatory from entering the marketplace. A key premise of the *Sullivan* holding is that society is better served by having more information about its public servants (even if some of it is false) than by having the limited pool of information that would result if the Alabama law of defamation were enforced.

A landmark Supreme Court decision such as *New York Times v. Sullivan* changes the philosophical underpinnings of our freedom of speech law. However, landmark decisions do not directly apply to subsequent cases that are factually different from the precedent-setting case. The courts must decide how the philosophy behind the landmark decision applies in differing factual contexts. We will focus on two important aspects of the actual malice doctrine that needed to be refined in the aftermath of *Sullivan*. One issue was deciding whether there were other contexts in which proof of actual malice should be required before defamed persons could recover damages. Should the rule be limited to false criticism of elected officials, or should erroneous criticisms of other noteworthy persons (for example, Hillary Clinton or Michael Jackson) also be protected? A second issue dealt with the concept of actual malice. What criteria would be used to determine whether an individual had recklessly disregarded the truth, and who would have the burden of proof on this issue? The next two sections of this chapter will discuss these issues.

## THE *NEW YORK TIMES* RULE: WHO NEEDS TO PROVE ACTUAL MALICE?

### The Court Defines Public Officials and Official Conduct

*Who Is a Public Official?*    The Court needed to establish guidelines for determining who is a public official. In the *Sullivan* case, the rule was applied to a city police commissioner. Would the rule also apply to the assistant commissioner or a rank-and-file police officer? What if the plaintiff were a custodian for the police department?

*Rosenblatt v. Baer*[8] involved an alleged libel of Baer, who had supervised the Belknap County (New Hampshire) Recreation Area, used primarily as a ski resort. Rosenblatt had contributed a column to the local newspaper, the Laconia *Evening Citizen,* and Baer claimed that the column libeled him by implying that he had been a corrupt manager.[9]

---

8. 383 U.S. 75 (1966).
9. The column indicated that under the leadership of Baer's replacement, the ski area was thriving financially. Rosenblatt asked, "When consider[ing] that last year was [an] excellent snow year, that season started because of more snow, months earlier last year, one can only ponder the following question: 'What happened to all the money last year? and every other year?'" *Id.* at 78.

To decide whether Baer was obligated to show actual malice on the part of Rosenblatt, the Court needed to settle upon an appropriate definition of *public official.* Justice Brennan's opinion held that this definition should be consistent with the rationale of *New York Times v. Sullivan.* The important principle in *Sullivan* was protecting wide-open debate on public issues. For such debate to be free, criticism of those responsible for government operations would have to be free. Therefore, the Court held that

> [T]he "public official" designation applies at the very least to those among the hierarchy of government employees who have, or appear to the public to have, substantial responsibility for or control over the conduct of governmental affairs.[10]

The case was **remanded** for further proceedings in the state courts of New Hampshire. The trial judge was directed to decide whether Baer was a public official, and if so, to retry the case with a jury that was instructed about the need to find actual malice on the part of Rosenblatt.

***What Is Official Conduct?***   The *Sullivan* case ruled that actual malice must be proven in order to recover damages for a false statement about a public official's "official conduct." The question of where to draw the line between a politician's official conduct and his or her private life is highly controversial. This issue is debated each time a political figure is reported to be an unfaithful marriage partner or to have experimented with marijuana in college.

The Supreme Court's definition of official conduct is broad, meaning the actual malice rule applies to a wide variety of claims that a communicator might want to make about a politician. *Garrison v. Louisiana*[11] involved claims that Jim Garrison, the New Orleans district attorney,[12] had libeled Louisiana state court judges by accusing them of inefficiency and laziness.[13] He was convicted for violating Louisiana's criminal defamation statute. The Louisiana Supreme Court upheld the conviction, reasoning that these statements were attacks on the personal integrity of judges, rather than their official conduct.

The U.S. Supreme Court held that the actual malice test should have been followed in Garrison's case. The Court held that because the goal of the *New York Times v. Sullivan* rule is protecting the free flow of information about public servants, "anything which might touch on an official's fitness for office is relevant."[14] Justice Brennan's majority opinion noted that few

---

10. Id. at 85.
11. 379 U.S. 64 (1964).
12. Garrison did not investigate only judicial corruption. His inquiry into the John F. Kennedy assassination was dramatized in Oliver Stone's movie *J.F.K.*
13. Garrison said, "The judges have now made it eloquently clear where their sympathies lie in regard to aggressive vice investigations by refusing to authorize use of the DA's funds to pay for the cost of closing down the Canal Street clip joints. . . . This raises interesting questions about the racketeer influences on our eight vacation minded judges." 379 U.S. at 66.
14. Id. at 77.

characteristics are more relevant to fitness for office "than dishonesty, malfeasance, or improper motivation." Because the Court believed that Garrison's statements did pertain to the judges' official conduct, and that the Louisiana law did not require proof of actual malice, Garrison's conviction was reversed.

In *Monitor Patriot Co. v. Roy*,[15] the alleged defamation occurred in a New Hampshire newspaper column that referred to Alphonse Roy, a candidate for Senator in the Democratic primary election, as a "former small time bootlegger." The column was run three days before the primary, and, after losing the election, Roy sued the newspaper for libel.

The jury was instructed that no proof of actual malice was required unless "it was more probable than otherwise" that the information in the column would be relevant to a candidate's fitness for office. After deliberations, the jury rendered a $20,000 verdict for Roy.

The Supreme Court reversed the judgment. The Court reasoned that "a charge of criminal conduct, no matter how remote in time or place, can never be irrelevant to an official's or a candidate's fitness for office" for purposes of the *New York Times v. Sullivan* rule.[16] The Court reasoned that since candidates put before the voters "every conceivable aspect" of their public and private lives that may create a good impression in the minds of the electorate, they cannot "cry ['Foul!'] when an opponent or an industrious reporter attempts to demonstrate the contrary."[17] If the jury based its evaluation of actual malice on whether the information was "not relevant," they would be given "far more leeway to act as censors than is consistent with the protection of the First and Fourteenth Amendments in the setting of a political campaign."[18]

In *New York Times v. Sullivan* and the cases that followed, the Supreme Court made it clear that false statements about public officials (and candidates for office) deserved strong First Amendment protection in the form of the actual malice rule. What if a person is not a public official or seeking elective office? Does the First Amendment require the same level of protection for false speech about those who do not aspire to public office? The cases that follow will give insight into these questions.

---

15. 401 U.S. 265 (1971).
16. Id. at 277.
17. Id. at 274.
18. Id. at 275–76. The rule announced in *Monitor Patriot Co.* was followed in another case decided the same day, *Ocala Star-Banner Co. v. Damron* (401 U.S. 295 [1971]). In this case, the defendant had printed a story claiming that Leonard Damron, the mayor of Crystal River, Florida, had been indicted for perjury by a federal grand jury and arrested by federal marshals. In reality, it was the plaintiff's brother, James Damron, who had been indicted. A jury awarded Leonard Damron $22,000. The Florida District Court upheld the verdict, holding that Damron was not required to prove actual malice on the part of the *Star-Banner*, because his official conduct was not the basis of the inaccuracy. (The alleged perjury occurred when Damron was testifying as a witness in an auto accident case.) The U.S. Supreme Court reversed the judgment, holding that "under any test we can conceive, the charge that a local mayor and candidate for a county elective post has been indicted for perjury in a civil rights suit is relevant to his fitness for office." *Id.* at 301.

## The Court Extends the Actual Malice Rule to Public Figures

*The* **Butts** *and* **Walker** *Decisions.*    Three years after deciding *Sullivan,* the Court was presented with two successful, well-known defamation plaintiffs who were not public officials. One was Wally Butts, the former athletic director at the University of Georgia. The *Saturday Evening Post* published an article alleging that Butts had called Alabama's football coach (the legendary Paul "Bear" Bryant) and outlined Georgia's offensive plays and defensive game plan.[19] Butts sued the publisher for libel and won $460,000 in damages.[20] The jury in the *Butts* case had not been instructed that proof of actual malice was necessary before Butts could be awarded damages.

Edwin Walker was a private citizen at the time he was allegedly libeled. He had enjoyed a long, honorable career in the Army, rising to the rank of general. After resigning from the armed forces, he became politically active against the use of U.S. troops as a means to force states to follow federal law.[21] His statements on the issue received wide publicity and earned him a group of followers named "Friends of Walker."

Walker's lawsuit was based on a news dispatch describing events at the University of Mississippi, where riots broke out after a federal court decree had ordered the enrollment of James Meredith, an African American. The Associated Press reported that Walker had taken command of the violent crowd and personally led a charge against federal marshals who were sent in to enforce the court decree. The report also contended that Walker had encouraged the rioters to use violence, and gave them technical advice about how to mitigate the effects of tear gas.

Walker sued the Associated Press for libel. He received $500,000 in compensatory damages and $300,000 in punitive damages. The trial judge reversed the award of punitive damages, on the grounds that no actual malice was proven. But the judge upheld the $500,000, maintaining that actual malice was not required to support such a result.

The Supreme Court's decision in *Curtis Publishing Co. v. Butts*[22] resolved the issues raised in the Butts and Walker cases. The fundamental question was whether a private (albeit noteworthy) citizen would be subject to the same actual malice rule as public official plaintiffs. The Supreme Court held that public figures did need to meet the *New York Times* standard. Chief Justice War-

---

19. The article, entitled "The Story of a College Football Fix," was prefaced by a note from the editors that stated, "Not since the Chicago White Sox threw the 1919 World Series has there been a sports story as shocking as this one." *Curtis Publishing Co. v. Butts,* 388 U.S. 130, 136 (1967), The University of Alabama won the football game.
20. Id. at 138.
21. In 1957, Walker had commanded federal troops who enforced school desegregation in Little Rock, Arkansas.
22. 388 U.S. 130 (1967).

ren's concurring opinion provides the reasons why public figures must prove actual malice in defamation cases.[23]

After reading the Chief Justice's opinion, you will also read the opinion of Justice Black in this case. When reading the latter opinion, ask yourself why Justice Black objects to the actual malice rule itself (for public officials and public figures). What rule does Justice Black advocate in these defamation cases?

### Curtis Publishing Co. v. Butts, 388 U.S. 130, 162 (1967)

Mr. Chief Justice Warren, concurring in the result:

. . . In the New York Times case, we held that a State cannot, consistently with the First and Fourteenth Amendments, award damages to a "public official" for a defamatory falsehood relating to his official conduct unless the verdict is based on proof of "actual malice." . . . The present cases involve not "public officials," but "public figures" whose views and actions with respect to public issues and events are often of as much concern to the citizen as the attitudes and behavior of "public officials" with respect to the same issues and events.

All of us agree that the basic considerations underlying the First Amendment require that some limitations be placed on the application of state libel laws to "public figures," as well as "public officials." Similarly, the seven members of the Court who deem it necessary to pass upon the question agree that the respondents in these cases are "public figures" for First Amendment purposes. . . .

To me, differentiation between "public figures" and "public officials" and adoption of separate standards of proof for each have no basis in law, logic, or First Amendment policy. Increasingly in this country, the distinctions between governmental and private sectors are blurred. Since the depression of the 1930s and World War II there has been a rapid fusion of economic and political power, a merging of science, industry, and government, and a high degree of interaction between the intellectual, governmental, and business worlds. . . . While these trends and events have occasioned a consolidation of governmental power, power has also become much more organized in what we have commonly considered to be the private sector. . . .

This blending of positions and power has also occurred in the case of individuals so that many who do not hold public office at the moment are nevertheless

---

23. In later cases, the Supreme Court has acknowledged that the principles for which the *Butts* and *Walker* decisions stand come from Justice Warren's concurring opinion. See, e.g., *Gertz v. Robert Welch, Inc.*, 418 U.S. 323, 336 n.7 (1974). Only three justices joined in Justice Harlan's plurality opinion. On the other hand, Chief Justice Warren's contention that the *New York Times* holding reaches public figures as well as public officials was supported by justices Brennan and White, 388 U.S. at 172 (Brennan, J., concurring in the result in *Walker* and dissenting in *Butts*); and also by justices Douglas and Black, 388 U.S. at 170 (Black, J., concurring in the result in *Walker*, and dissenting in *Butts*). For a noteworthy legal scholar's analysis of this complex legal result, see H. Kalven's discussion in "You Can't Tell the Players without a Score Card," 1967 *Supreme Court Review* 267, 275.

intimately involved in the resolution of important public questions, or by reasons of their fame, shape events in areas of concern to society at large.

Viewed in this context, then, it is plain that although they are not subject to the restraints of the political process, "public figures," like "public officials," often play an influential role in ordering society. And surely as a class these "public figures" have as ready access as "public officials" to mass media of communication, both to influence policy and to counter criticism of their views and activities. Our citizenry has a legitimate and substantial interest in the conduct of such persons, and freedom of the press to engage in uninhibited debate about their involvement in public issues and events is as crucial as it is in the case of "public officials." The fact that they are not amenable to the restraints of the political process only underscores the legitimate and substantial nature of the interest, since it means that public opinion may be the only instrument by which society can attempt to influence their conduct.

I therefore adhere to the *New York Times* standard in the case of "public figures" as well as "public officials." It is a manageable standard, readily stated and understood, which also balances to a proper degree the legitimate interests traditionally protected by the law of defamation. . . .

Mr. Justice Black, with whom Mr. Justice Douglas joins, concurring in the result in No. 150 (Walker) and dissenting in No. 37 (Butts).

I would reverse this case [*Walker*] first for the reasons given in my concurring opinion in *New York Times Co. v. Sullivan,* and my concurring and dissenting opinion in *Rosenblatt v. Baer* (citations omitted), but wish to add a few words.

These cases illustrate, I think, the accuracy of my prior predictions that the *New York Times* constitutional rule concerning libel is wholly inadequate to save the press from being destroyed by libel judgments. Here the Court reverses the case of *Associated Press v. Walker,* but affirms the judgment of *Curtis Publishing Co. v. Butts.* The main reason for this quite contradictory action, so far as I can determine, is that the Court looks at the facts in both cases as though it were a jury and reaches the conclusion that the *Saturday Evening Post,* in writing about Butts, was so abusive that its article is more of a libel at the constitutional level than is the one by the Associated Press. That seems a strange way to erect a constitutional standard for libel cases. If this precedent is followed, it means that we must in all libel cases hereafter weigh the facts and hold that all papers and magazines guilty of gross writing or reporting are constitutionally liable, while they are not if the quality of the reporting is approved by a majority of us. . . .

I think it is time for this Court to abandon *New York Times Co. v. Sullivan* and adopt the rule to the effect that the First Amendment was intended to leave the press free from the harassment of libel judgment. ◆◆◆

## Cases Define the Nature of a Public Figure

Although the *Butts* case reflected a divergence of opinion regarding the use of the actual malice rule in defamation cases involving public figures, the

Supreme Court agreed that both Butts and Walker were public figures.[24] Justice Harlan's plurality opinion gave some reasons why both plaintiffs were classified in that way:

> Butts may have attained that status by position alone and Walker by his purposeful activity amounting to a thrusting of his personality into the "vortex" of an important public controversy, but both commanded sufficient continuing public interest and had sufficient access to the means of counterargument to be able "to expose through discussion the falsehood and fallacies" of the defamatory statements.

A public figure may also be a person who is active on the local level. The plaintiff in *Greenbelt Cooperative Publishing Assn., Inc., et al., v. Bresler*[25] was a real estate developer who had been negotiating with the Greenbelt, Maryland, City Council to gain permission to build high-density housing. A small local newspaper, the Greenbelt *News Review*, characterized Bresler's negotiating position as "blackmail." Bresler sued the newspaper, claiming he had been defamed as one who had committed the crime of blackmail. Because Bresler had been "deeply involved" in the development of Greenbelt, had sought favors from the city in the form of zoning ordinances, and had negotiated with the city to sell a tract of his land for the purpose of building a school, the Supreme Court agreed that "Bresler's status clearly fell within even the most restrictive definition of 'public figure.'"[26]

Butts, Walker, and Bresler were all found to be public figures, but there was no line of demarcation between public and private figures given in these cases. To gain insight into the differences between public figures and private citizens, we will next discuss several cases in which the plaintiff was not held to be a public figure.

The case of *Gertz v. Robert Welch*[27] provided one example of a person who was not deemed a public figure. The plaintiff, Elmer Gertz, was an attorney who represented the Nelson family in a civil suit against a Chicago police officer, Richard Nuccio. The officer had shot the Nelsons' son and been convicted for murder in separate criminal proceedings. Robert Welch, publisher of the John Birch Society monthly, *American Opinion*, ran an article entitled "Frame Up: Richard Nuccio and the War On Police." The article implied that Gertz had a criminal record and had been an official of the "Marxist League for Industrial Democracy"; it further labeled Gertz a "Communist-fronter." There was no evidence these statements were true. The defendant argued that Gertz should be classified as a public figure.

The Supreme Court disagreed with the labeling of attorney Gertz as a public figure. First, the Court noted that there are two types of public figures:

24. 388 U.S. 162–63 (Warren, C.J., concurring).
25. 398 U.S. 6 (1970).
26. Id. at 8–9.
27. 418 U.S. 323 (1974).

Chapter Eight

In some instances an individual may achieve such pervasive fame or notoriety that he becomes a public figure for all purposes and in all contexts. More commonly, an individual voluntarily injects himself or is drawn into a particular public controversy and thereby becomes a public figure for a limited range of issues. In either case such persons assume special prominence in the resolution of public questions.[28]　◆◆◆


The Supreme Court held that Gertz was not a public figure, although he had served as an officer of local civic groups and professional organizations and published several legal writings. Gertz was not a general purpose public figure, because, while well known in some circles, he had not achieved general fame in the community.[29] His involvement as an attorney in the case against Nuccio did not make him a limited purpose public figure. Gertz was not involved in the criminal prosecution of Nuccio. He never discussed the case with the press, and did not attempt to engage the public's attention in an attempt to influence its outcome.[30]

This distinction between public and private figures was followed in subsequent cases. In *Time, Inc. v. Firestone*,[31] the alleged defamation was an item in *Time* magazine's "Milestones" section, stating that Mary Alice Sullivan Firestone's husband, Russell Firestone (heir to the Firestone Tire fortune), had been granted a divorce on grounds of extreme cruelty and adultery.[32] The Florida Supreme Court had labeled the divorce proceedings as a "cause celebre," but the U.S. Supreme Court held that one did not become a public figure simply by being involved in a controversy that may interest members of the public (e.g., a divorce involving a wealthy family). Ms. Firestone did not meet the public figure test, because she had not freely chosen to publicize issues concerning her married life and had not assumed any special prominence in the resolution of public questions.[33]

*Hutchinson v. Proxmire*[34] arose out of Senator William Proxmire's "Golden Fleece Awards," given to people who (in the senator's opinion) have wasted government funds. The plaintiff, Hutchinson, had received federal research grants to study animal aggression. Mr. Proxmire sent out a newsletter suggest-

---

28. Id. at 351.
29. Id. at 352. None of the jurors called at the trial had ever heard of Mr. Gertz before this case was commenced.
30. Based on these criteria, an attorney who "tried his or her case in the media" would be at least a limited purpose public figure with respect to issues raised by that case.
31. 424 U.S. 448 (1976).
32. The actual judgment of the Palm Beach, Fla., Circuit Court noted that Russell Firestone had filed a counterclaim for divorce, on the grounds of extreme cruelty and adultery. The actual finding of the court was that neither party was a faithful marriage partner, and that therefore the marriage should be dissolved. Id. at 450–51.
33. Id. at 454–55.
34. 443 U.S. 111 (1979).

ing that Hutchinson's research was nonsense.[35] The Supreme Court held that Dr. Hutchinson was not a public figure. He had not assumed any broad, public role in the debate on the size of the federal budget. His only coverage in the local media had been reports indicating that he had obtained government grants, and his response to the Golden Fleece Award.[36]

### An Actual Malice Rule for Private Citizen Plaintiffs?

In two major cases, the Supreme Court considered the possibility of extending the actual malice rule to plaintiffs who were neither public officials nor public figures. First, in *Rosenbloom v. Metromedia*,[37] and then in the *Gertz*[38] decision, the Supreme Court wrestled with the conflict between freedom of the press and the rights of a defamed private individual to recover damages for assaults on his or her good name. As you read these two opinions, analyze the costs and benefits of extending the actual malice rule. Decide for yourself whether the Court decision in *Gertz* is in our society's best interest.

The issue in *Rosenbloom* was whether the actual malice rule should apply when the plaintiff is a private individual but was involved in an event of public interest. The plaintiff, Rosenbloom, was a distributor of nudist magazines. He was arrested during a police crackdown on the dissemination of obscene publications. Philadelphia radio station WIP broadcasted a report of the arrest, noting that the police believed they had hit the supply of a main distributor of obscene material. Later news reports described a legal action by Rosenbloom against the police and the media, claiming that a federal judge may order the defendants to "lay off the smut literature racket." Rosenbloom was acquitted of criminal obscenity charges; he sued for defamation and won a $250,000 judgment. The judgment was reversed by a federal appeals court, which ruled that Rosenbloom should have been required to prove actual malice.

The Supreme Court let the appellate court ruling against Rosenbloom stand, but the five justices in the majority were divided on the reasons why. Thus, the decision did not set a precedent. Nevertheless, the plurality opinion is worth considering to gain an understanding of the arguments for extending actual malice.

Justice Brennan, joined by Chief Justice Burger and Justice Blackmun, held that Rosenbloom needed to prove actual malice. Justice Brennan wrote

---

35. Proxmire's statement included the following: "The funding of this nonsense makes me angry enough to scream and kick. . . . [T]he good doctor has made a fortune from his monkeys and in the process has made a monkey out of the American taxpayer. . . . In view of the transparent worthlessness of Hutchinson's study of jawgrinding and biting by angry or hard-drinking monkeys, it is time we put a stop to the bite Hutchinson and the bureaucrats who fund him have been taking of the taxpayer." Id. at 116.
36. Id. at 133–36. Chief Justice Burger's majority opinion argued that a defendant could not, after an alleged libel, turn a plaintiff into a public figure by publicizing the case.
37. 403 U.S. 29 (1971).
38. See p. 207

that when the *topic* of a news report is of public interest, it is irrelevant whether the person involved in the event is a public or private figure. In Rosenbloom's case, the plurality argued, the community had two important interests: making certain that criminal obscenity laws were being properly enforced, and making sure that obscenity laws were not being used to suppress protected expression. Therefore, Justice Brennan argued in favor of extending the actual malice rule to all communication involving matters of public concern, to honor the commitment to robust debate on public issues.[39]

Three years later, in 1974, a majority of the Court came to a different consensus and rejected application of the *New York Times* rule to private citizens. Earlier in this chapter, you read the reasons the Court gave for finding that attorney Elmer Gertz was a private citizen. In *Gertz*, a five-justice majority also rejected the plurality decision in *Rosenbloom*, establishing the rule that private defamation plaintiffs do not need to prove actual malice.

### *Gertz v. Robert Welch, Inc.,* 418 U.S. 323 (1974)

Mr. Justice Powell delivered the opinion of the Court. . . .

Under the First Amendment there is no such thing as a false idea. However pernicious an opinion may seem, we depend for its correction not on the conscience of judges and juries but on the competition of other ideas. But there is no constitutional value in false statements of fact. . . .

Although the erroneous statement of fact is not worthy of constitutional protection, it is nevertheless inevitable in free debate. . . . And punishment of error runs the risk of inducing a cautious and restrictive exercise of the constitutionally guaranteed freedoms of speech and press. . . .

The legitimate State interest underlying the law of libel is the compensation of individuals for the harm inflicted on them by defamatory falsehood. We would not lightly require the State to abandon this purpose, for, as Mr. Justice Stewart has reminded us, the individual's right to the protection of his own good name "reflects no more than our basic concept of the essential dignity and worth of every human being—a concept at the root of any decent system of ordered liberty."[40] . . .

[W]e believe that the *New York Times* rule states an accommodation between this concern [protecting the press] and the *limited* state interest present in the context of libel actions brought by public persons. *For the reasons stated below, we conclude that the state interest in compensating injury to the reputation of private individuals requires that a different rule should obtain with respect to them* (emphasis added).

. . . The first remedy of any victim of defamation is self-help—using available opportunities to contradict the lie or correct the error and thereby minimize its adverse impact on reputation. Public officials and public figures usually enjoy signifi-

---

39. 403 U.S. at 43–44.
40. *Rosenblatt v. Baer,* 383 U.S. 75, 92 (1966) (Stewart, J., concurring).

cantly greater access to the channels of effective communication and hence have a more realistic opportunity to counteract false statements than private individuals normally enjoy. Private individuals are therefore more vulnerable to injury, and the state interest in protecting them is correspondingly greater.

More important than the likelihood that private individuals will lack effective opportunities for rebuttal, there is a compelling normative consideration underlying the distinction between public and private defamation plaintiffs. An individual who decides to seek governmental office must accept certain necessary consequences of that involvement in public affairs. He runs the risk of closer public scrutiny than might otherwise be the case. . . .

Those classed as public figures stand in a similar position. Hypothetically, it might be possible for someone to become a public figure through no purposeful action of his own, but the instances of truly involuntary public figures must be exceedingly rare. For the most part those who attain this status have assumed roles of especial prominence in the affairs of society. Some occupy positions of such persuasive power and influence that they are deemed public figures for all purposes. More commonly, those classed as public figures have thrust themselves to the forefront of particular public controversies in order to influence the resolution of the issues involved. In either event, they invite attention and comment. . . .

For these reasons we conclude that the States should retain substantial latitude in their efforts to enforce a legal remedy for defamatory falsehood injurious to the reputation of a private individual. The extension of the *New York Times* test proposed by the *Rosenbloom* plurality would abridge this legitimate state interest to a degree that we find unacceptable. . . . We hold that, so long as they do not impose liability without fault,[41] the states may define for themselves the appropriate standard of liability for a publisher or broadcaster of defamatory falsehood injurious to a private individual.   ◆◆◆

In *Gertz*, the Supreme Court declined to extend the actual malice rule to defamation cases involving private persons. The marketplace of ideas philosophy provided a rationale for this holding. The Court assumed public officials and public figures could gain access to the marketplace and use the preferred approach of *more speech* as a response to "bad speech." Conversely, the Court acknowledged that many citizens lack the access to effective means of communication. These persons would be unable to use more speech to counter attacks on their reputation. For information about private citizens, the Court decided that it would be preferable to have a smaller marketplace of ideas rather than a marketplace that only gave us one side of the story—the attacks on a person's character.

---

41. If liability were imposed without fault, it would mean that a publisher of false information is always liable for damages, even if he or she has acted conscientiously and professionally in investigating the truth of a story. After *Gertz*, private plaintiffs must at least prove that the publisher was negligent. Negligence occurs when one does not behave as a reasonably prudent person would perform under the circumstances of a case.

### THE PROCESS OF PROVING ACTUAL MALICE

The previous section covered the cases that settled the principle that public figures and public officials must prove actual malice before they can prevail in defamation lawsuits. This section will discuss the concept of actual malice. The First Amendment influences two categories of issues: substantive and procedural. **Substantive** questions deal with the meaning of actual malice—in other words, what facts does the First Amendment require a judge or jury to find before a verdict of actual malice can be supported? **Procedural** questions relate to the mechanics of proving these facts are true. Our discussion of these issues will analyze how the First Amendment impacts procedural rules regarding actual malice, such as the burden of proof.

#### The First Amendment and Substantive Actual Malice Issues

*An Evil Motive Does Not Prove Actual Malice.*   Based on the ordinary meaning of the term *malice,* you might assume that actual malice is established if a communicator hopes that a false statement will hurt the person who is targeted. However, in *Garrison v. Louisiana,*[42] the Supreme Court held that the only basis for finding actual malice is if a communicator knew a statement was false or acted with reckless disregard for the truth. Justice Brennan explained why a nefarious motive would be an insufficient basis for finding actual malice:

> Debate on public issues will not be uninhibited if the speaker must run the risk that it will be proved in court that he spoke out of hatred; even if he did speak out of hatred, utterances honestly believed contribute to the free interchange of ideas and the ascertainment of truth."[43]   ◆◆◆

*Failure to Investigate a Source Does Not Necessarily Prove Actual Malice.* In *St. Amant v. Thompson,*[44] the defendant (St. Amant) made a political speech, falsely charging deputy sheriff Herman Thompson with criminal conduct in connection with an allegedly corrupt labor union leader.[45] St. Amant based his claim on the affidavit of a union member, J. D. Albin. The defendant had no personal knowledge about Thompson's activities, and he did not attempt to verify the information with persons in the union office.

The Supreme Court held that St. Amant had not acted with the reckless disregard for the truth needed to support a finding of actual malice. The Court would not accept a finding of recklessness predicated on the fact that a reasonably prudent person would have investigated before publishing. Instead, "there must be sufficient evidence to permit the conclusion that the defendant in fact entertained serious doubts as to the truth of his publication."[46] The

---

42. 379 U.S. 64 (1964). The facts of this case were discussed earlier in this chapter.
43. Id. at 73.
44. 390 U.S. 727 (1968).
45. St. Amant had alleged that his political opponent had ties to an allegedly corrupt union leader, E. G. Partin. He further asserted that Partin had ties to the sheriff's office through deputy Thompson, and that money had passed hands between Partin and Thompson. Id. at 728–29.
46. Id. at 731.

Court explained that the stake of the citizenry in knowing about the conduct of public officials is so great that "neither the defense of truth nor the standard of ordinary care[47] would protect against self-censorship and thus adequately implement First Amendment policies."[48]

*Inaccurate Paraphrasing Is Not Necessarily Actual Malice.* The alleged defamation in *Time, Inc. v. Pape*[49] was a *Time* magazine story contending that the Chicago police broke through two doors at the Monroe house at 5:45 A.M. and awakened James Monroe and his wife with flashlights. The description of this incident was part of *Time*'s discussion of the U.S. Commission on Civil Rights report, *Justice*. *Time* also noted that the report "carries a chilling text about police brutality in both the South and the North."[50]

Pape was the deputy chief of detectives who had led the raid on the Monroe apartment. He sued for defamation, because the *Time* article made it appear that the Civil Rights Commission had concluded that these facts about the raid were true. In reality, the Commission report had noted that these facts were alleged in a lawsuit filed by the Monroe family.

The Supreme Court found that *Time* had not acted with actual malice in their summary of the Commission's findings. Justice Potter Stewart's opinion pointed out that unless a publisher is going to provide full and direct quotations of the words of the source, there are many possible choices for describing the findings of a report. The Court noted that the Civil Rights Commission report did not make it clear whether it found each of the examples true.[51] Justice Stewart's opinion concluded that *Time*'s interpretation of the report, although perhaps reflecting a misconception, was not sufficient to support a finding of actual malice. If liability could be found when the source of information is as ambiguous as the Commission report, "it is hard to imagine a test of 'truth' that would not put the publisher virtually at the mercy of the unguided discretion of the jury."[52]

## The First Amendment and Procedural Issues Pertaining to Actual Malice

*Does the First Amendment Limit Discovery Regarding a Reporter's State of Mind?* Before civil cases are brought to trial, the attorneys for both sides ordinarily engage in discovery. During this process, the attorneys take depositions from witnesses on the other side of the case. Federal rules permit the

---

47. Under a standard of ordinary care, the publisher of a falsehood could be liable for damages if he or she did not act as a reasonably prudent person would have done before publishing the information.
48. Id. at 732.
49. 401 U.S. 279 (1971).
50. Id. at 281.
51. Id. at 286. For example, the heading of the chapter read, in large type, "UNLAWFUL POLICE VIOLENCE." Yet, in the text of the chapter, the Commission noted that it was describing alleged facts. Then, the Commission also reported "that the allegations appeared substantial enough to justify discussion in this study." Id. at 287.
52. Id. at 291.

discovery of any information "relevant to the subject matter involved in the pending action."[53]

Anthony Herbert was a retired Army officer who had accused his superiors of covering up war crimes in Vietnam. In *Herbert v. Lando*,[54] the purported defamation was a CBS news program produced by Lando, claiming that Herbert was a liar who had made up the war crimes charges to explain the fact that he had been relieved from his command. Herbert sued for defamation; however, as a public figure he could only recover if Lando had published with actual malice.

During discovery, Herbert attempted to find out whether Lando did have actual malice. Herbert wanted to ask questions about Lando's investigative process, such as why he had decided to pursue certain leads and not others, and ask for Lando's conclusions with respect to the veracity of the people he had interviewed.[55] Lando claimed that the First Amendment protected him from inquiries into his state of mind.

The Supreme Court refused to grant a constitutional **privilege**[56] to the editorial process of a media defendant. The Court reasoned that such a privilege "would constitute a substantial interference with the ability of a defamation plaintiff to establish the ingredients of malice as required by *New York Times*."[57] The Court was also troubled by creating a situation in which defamation defendants can testify that they believed their writing was true, and cannot be challenged regarding the basis of those beliefs.

*Does the First Amendment Require Appellate Courts to Scrutinize a Jury's Actual Malice Finding?*   In our system of justice, it is normally the jury's duty to make the findings of fact in a trial, and these factual determinations are rarely overturned. For example, the Federal Rules of Civil Procedure provide that "[f]indings of fact shall not be set aside unless clearly erroneous, and due regard shall be given to the opportunity of the trial court to judge the credibility of witnesses."[58] However, the cases in this chapter have shown that the Supreme Court is very concerned about the effect of defamation lawsuits on the press, particularly when the alleged victims are public officials or public figures.

How much deference should be given to a jury verdict on the actual malice issue? The Supreme Court considered the question in *Bose Corp. v. Consumers Union of the United States, Inc.*[59] An article in *Consumer Reports* had re-

53. *Fed. Rule Civ. Proc.* 26(b).
54. 441 U.S. 153 (1979).
55. Id. at 157, n. 2.
56. In this case, the privilege of not testifying about the editorial process that a reporter went through in preparing a story. Another example is the attorney-client privilege. Based on this privilege, if a client reveals incriminating information to his or her attorney, that information cannot be used against the client in court.
57. Id. at 170.
58. *Fed. Rule Civ. Proc.* 52(a).
59. 466 U.S. 485 (1984).

ported that the Bose 901 speaker system played strange music—"worse, individual instruments heard through the Bose system seemed to grow to gigantic proportions and tended to wander about the room."[60] The trial court held that this was a false statement, made with actual malice. The Supreme Court disagreed, noting that "the choice of such language, though reflecting a misconception, does not place the speech beyond the outer limits of the First Amendment's broad protective umbrella. . . . [T]he difference between hearing violin sounds move around the room and hearing them wander back and forth fits easily into the breathing space that gives life to the First Amendment."[61] The Court noted that in any case governed by *New York Times*, "appellate judges must exercise independent judgment and determine whether the record establishes actual malice with convincing clarity."[62]

*Who Has the Burden of Proof Regarding a Statement's Falsity?* At common law it was presumed that an individual had a good reputation. Consequently, when a defamatory statement was made about a person, it was up to the defendant to prove that the statement was true. The Supreme Court reversed that presumption, when the speech was of public concern, in the case of *Philadelphia Newspapers, Inc. v. Hepps*.[63] The *Philadelphia Inquirer* had published articles suggesting a pattern of interference in state government by a legislator on behalf of Hepps and Thrifty, a convenience store chain.[64] In addition, it was reported that federal "investigators found connections between Thrifty and underworld figures."[65]

The Supreme Court held that Hepps needed to bear the burden of proving that these defamatory statements were false. Justice O'Connor wrote that when the evidence of falsity is ambiguous, the burden of proof is likely to be decisive. If the burden is assigned to the plaintiff, some false speech will be protected in ambiguous cases. Conversely, if the defense must prove their statements are true, defendants may be punished for writing true statements in such cases. Justice O'Connor argued that when the scales are in an uncertain balance, "we believe that the Constitution requires us to tip them in favor of protecting true speech." Therefore, the common law presumption of falsity must be reversed "when a plaintiff seeks damages against a media defendant for speech of public concern."[66]

Thus, in the 1980s the Supreme Court gave priority to freedom of expression when resolving procedural issues in *Bose* and *Hepps*. Defamation plaintiffs must convincingly prove that false statements were made with ac-

60. Id. at 488.
61. Id. at 513.
62. Id. at 514.
63. 475 U.S. 767 (1986).
64. Thrifty was a chain of stores, where beer, soft drinks, and snacks were sold. Hepps was principal stockholder in G.P.I., the corporation that franchised Thrifty.
65. 475 U.S. at 769.
66. Id. at 776–77.

tual malice, and appellate courts are to scrutinize any jury finding of such malice. However, in *Herbert v. Lando,* the Court refused to curtail the discovery process, thereby preserving a means for defamation plaintiffs to attempt to meet their heavy burden of proving actual malice.

## OTHER DEFAMATION ISSUES

### Group Defamation

Each case reviewed in this chapter dealt with an alleged defamation of a specific person or company. But what if the defamatory words are directed to an entire class of people, as with racist, sexist, and homophobic expression? Such prejudiced statements have been the subject of laws and regulations directed against hate speech, discussed in chapter 7. However, a defamation lawsuit would be another means by which a target of prejudiced speech might seek redress. If a communicator defames an entire class of people, when are his or her words protected by the First Amendment?

Twelve years before the *New York Times v. Sullivan* decision, the Supreme Court ruled on the question of group libel. Joseph Beauharnais, president of the White Circle League in Chicago, had passed out leaflets filled with racist invective. In the leaflet, it was noted that "if persuasion and the need to prevent the white race from becoming mongrelized by the negro will not unite us, then the aggressions . . . rapes, robberies, knives, guns, and marijuana of the negro, surely will" (ellipses in the original).[67] Beauharnais was convicted under an Illinois law forbidding publications that portray "depravity, criminality, unchastity, or lack of virtue of a class of citizens of any race" and expose those citizens to contempt or derision.[68]

Beauharnais appealed his conviction, claiming that the Illinois statute violated his First Amendment rights. The U.S. Supreme Court upheld the conviction. The Court noted that *Chaplinsky* stood for the proposition that libelous words are not safeguarded by the Constitution, and reasoned that since a state can punish defamation of an individual, the state should not be denied the right to punish the same defamatory utterance when directed at a group. The only caveat was that the penal law could not be unrelated to the peace and well-being of the state.[69]

The Court found a rational basis[70] for this law, noting a long history of racial tension in Illinois, dating back to the murder of abolitionist Elijah Lovejoy. The majority refused to second-guess the legislature's use of defamation

---

67. *Beauharnais v. People,* 343 U.S. 250, 252 (1952).
68. *Illinois Criminal Code,* Ch. 38, Sec. 471 (1949).
69. 343 U.S. at 257–58.
70. If legislation does not conflict with constitutionally protected rights, the Court uses the rational basis test when the law is challenged. As we noted in chapter 1, this test gives great deference to the legislature's decision, because if there could be a rational basis for the policy, it is held to be constitutional.

# Critical Thinking about the Actual Malice Rule: Has It Served Its Purpose?

The goal of the actual malice rule, as announced by Justice Brennan in *New York Times v. Sullivan*, is to provide "breathing space" for freedom of expression. Justice Black's concurring opinion in the *New York Times* case warned that the actual malice rule would not prevent juries from awarding million-dollar verdicts, thereby deterring criticism of public officials.[1] Has the actual malice rule operated to protect freedom of the press?

Defamation litigation is very costly to the press. The $58 million jury verdict noted at the beginning of this chapter is not the only multimillion-dollar judgment. A San Francisco television station paid $2.3 million in damages after reporting suspicions that an antiques dealer was dealing in stolen goods. A $34 million judgment was returned against the *Philadelphia Inquirer,* and a Niagara Falls restaurant owner was awarded $15.4 million in a lawsuit against WKBW-TV in Buffalo, New York.[2] Although sixty percent to seventy percent of the judgments against libel defendants are reversed on appeal, the attorney fees needed to defend these cases are substantial. In the average litigated case, defense costs are about $150,000, and many of these cases are won by the defense without ever going to trial.[3] The need to research the question of actual malice (facilitated by the discovery process allowed in the *Herbert v. Lando* decision), combined with preparation to prove the truth or falsity of the statement at issue, generates many hours of costly legal work before the trial even begins.[4] If the case goes to trial and the result is appealed, expenses are much higher.

Because plaintiffs who allege defamation rarely win, and defendants are faced with high costs even when they do win, one commentator has suggested that the system only works well for trial lawyers who charge by the hour.[5]

The Iowa Libel Research Project has considered the possibility of alternatives to litigation in defamation cases. The Iowa researchers found that a majority of *plaintiffs* say that their main objective is correcting alleged falsehoods rather than receiving money.[6] Errors are bound to occur in journalism, an industry that operates under tight deadlines, using information from a wide variety of sources. Nevertheless, many newsrooms are defensive about allegations of factual errors. The Iowa researchers found that even news editors told them that the press is rude and arrogant, and does not respond well to complaints.[7]

Could defamation rules be changed to make it easier for plaintiffs to win an admission or a judicial ruling that the defendant had made a false statement, without adding to the costs incurred by the defendant? With the actual malice rule in effect, the issue of a statement's veracity often falls by the wayside. If a plaintiff has no proof of actual malice, she or he loses the case, even if the statement could be proven false.

Defamation rules could be changed to entitle the plaintiff to a judicial determination of the veracity of the defendant's statement. This would help restore the defendant's good name, even if no money damages were awarded.[8] A similar proposal would require a defendant to admit that she or he had made a false statement, or at least was uncertain about the truth of the statement, before allowing the lack of actual malice to be a defense.[9] Such rules could be supplemented by limitations on recoverable money damages. One suggestion is a $1 million limit, because no final judgment in a libel case has exceeded that figure. To provide more protection for smaller media outlets, the limit could be proportional to the size of the defendant's business.[10]

After reading the cases involving the actual malice rule, and the above analysis of the implications of the rule, do you think that *New York Times v. Sullivan* was a good decision? Do you believe most defamation plaintiffs would be satisfied if the media would correct false statements? Would the media spend less energy fighting defamation charges if losing the case merely meant printing a retraction rather than owing millions of dollars in damages? Which interest groups would fight the solutions discussed in this section of the text?

1. 376 U.S. at 294–95 (Black, J., concurring).
2. Dill, in *At What Price*, p. 37.
3. Henry R. Kaufman, "Trends in Damage Awards, Insurance Premiums and the Cost of Media Libel Litigation," in *The Cost of Libel: Economic and Policy Implications*, p. 7 (Columbia Univ. Press, 1989).
4. Id., p. 8.
5. Dill, p. 40.
6. Randall P. Bezanson, Gilbert Cranberg, and John Soloski, in "The Economics of Libel: An Empirical Assessment," *The Cost of Libel*, p. 33.
7. Id., at 27. Former *Wall Street Journal* editor Vermont Royster noted that newspapers will print a correction if they gave the wrong date for a school board meeting, but most are reluctant to admit publishing stories that are "basically wrong or misleading or unfair." Id. at 30.
8. Richard A. Epstein, "Was *New York Times v. Sullivan* Wrong?" in *The Cost of Libel*, p. 148.
9. Mark S. Nadel, "Refining the Doctrine of *New York Times v. Sullivan*," in *The Cost of Libel*, p. 162.
10. Epstein, p. 149.

◆◆◆

law as a remedy. Because libelous words do not constitute protected speech, there was no need to ask whether Beauharnais's words had created a clear and present danger.[71]

Although the *Beauharnais* decision has not been explicitly overruled, it is doubtful that a similar group libel case would prevail in the aftermath of *New York Times v. Sullivan*. Under the actual malice test, it would need to be shown that a communicator made a false statement of fact and that she or he made the statement with reckless disregard for the truth. Professor Franklyn

71. 343 U.S. at 266.

Haiman has argued that defamatory utterances about groups are expressions of prejudiced opinion, rather than false statements of fact.[72] It would also be difficult to prove that a communicator knew that his or her insult was false. Prejudiced persons often come from a culture in which stereotypes are voiced on a regular basis. They do not have the type of interactions with persons different from themselves that would cause them to reflectively think about their prejudices.

### Defamation and Statements of Opinion

In *Milkovich v. Lorain Journal Co.*,[73] the Supreme Court considered the question of whether defamatory statements of *opinion* (as contrasted with statements of fact) were entitled to absolute First Amendment protection. Michael Milkovich was a wrestling coach, whose Maple Heights High School team had been involved in a post-match altercation with another team; there were injuries. The Ohio High School Athletic Association had ruled that Milkovich's team was ineligible for the state tournament; the ban was challenged in court, and the judge issued a temporary injunction against the athletic association's ruling. Milkovich testified in that judicial proceeding.

The day after the court issued the injunction, a column in the *Lorain Journal* ran under the headline, "Maple beat the law with the 'big lie.'" After contending that students learn by observing educators' conduct outside of class, as well as through classroom activities, the columnist noted that students at Maple Heights had learned such a lesson. The column read:

> It [the lesson] is simply this: If you get in a jam, lie your way out. If you're successful enough, and powerful enough, and can sound sincere enough, you stand an excellent chance of making the lie stand up, regardless of what really happened.
>
> The teachers responsible were mainly head Maple wrestling coach, Mike Milkovich, and former superintendent of schools H. Donald Scott. . . .
>
> [B]y the time the hearing before Judge Martin rolled around, Milkovich and Scott apparently had their version of the incident polished and reconstructed, and the judge apparently believed them. . . .
>
> Anyone who attended the meet . . . knows in his heart that Milkovich and Scott lied at the hearing after each had given his solemn oath to tell the truth.
>
> But they got away with it.[74]

---

72. Franklyn Haiman, *Speech and Law in a Free Society*, p. 95 (University of Chicago Press, 1981). Haiman asks how one could prove the falsity of an insult such as "dumb Poles." What percentage of Poles need to be smart before the generalization becomes a lie? By what criteria does one decide who is smart and who is not?
73. 497 U.S. 1 (1990).
74. Id. at 9–10, n. 2.

The Ohio courts that reviewed Milkovich's defamation action had concluded that the column was expressing an "opinion," rather than a fact, and
therefore was protected by the First Amendment.[75] The U.S. Supreme Court
disagreed with this analysis, declining to create a defamation exception for
opinions. Chief Justice Rehnquist's majority opinion argued that expressions
of "opinion" may often imply an assertion of objective fact. For example, if a
speaker says, "In my opinion, John Jones is a liar," he implies that he knows
facts that support this claim. This statement could cause just as much damage
to Jones's reputation as the statement "Jones is a liar."[76]

In the case of the Milkovich column, the Court noted that factual issues
had been raised, which the plaintiff could prove to be false. For example, a
jury could conclude that the statements assert that Milkovich had committed
perjury in a judicial proceeding. Milkovich could disprove this claim, based on
his own testimony as well as evidence taken from other witnesses.[77] Therefore, the case was remanded for further proceedings on the question of
whether a defamation had occurred.

### INVASION OF PRIVACY

The communication of information about a person's private life is related
to the issue of defamation. This personal information may not be defamatory,
either because it may be true or because it is a false statement that does not
expose one to ridicule or disgrace. In these cases, the argument is not that
claims should be left unsaid because they damage a person's reputation. Instead, the argument is that the information should be kept secret because *it is
none of the public's business.*

### Disclosure of Personal Information

One cause of action for invasion of privacy pertains to the disclosure of
true but embarrassing information. For example, suppose that a news report
had broadcast truthful information about a person's sexual or bathroom
habits. Could the subject of the report win an invasion of privacy lawsuit? The
courts will look to several criteria in such a case.[78]

One question is whether the information is highly offensive. For example, College of Alameda student body president Toni Ann Diaz was able to win

---

75. Id. at 10. Two arguments from an earlier case involving the same column give insight into the
suggestion that the author had expressed an opinion rather than a factual claim: (1) the caption
"TD Says" at the start of the column indicates that the article is the author's opinion; and (2) the
article appeared on the sports page, a traditional location for invective and hyperbole, and therefore would be construed as opinion rather than fact. Id. at 9–10.
76. Id. at 18–19.
77. Id. at 21.
78. See, e.g., Barbara Dill, *The Journalist's Handbook on Libel and Privacy,* pp. 158–59 (Free Press,
1986).

an invasion of privacy lawsuit against *The Oakland Tribune*, which truthfully revealed that Diaz had undergone a sex change operation.[79]

A second requirement is that the information must not be newsworthy. Medical information about a private citizen is unlikely to be information that the public needs to know. Even if facts about a health condition or treatment procedure are informative, the name of the patient could be withheld. By contrast, the President's health is a matter of public concern. Hence, a detailed description of surgery on the President's colon (complete with a diagram) would likely be found newsworthy.

A third question is whether the information is truly private. If a person has communicated a fact to the world at large, that information is no longer private. For example, a *San Francisco Chronicle* column noted that the ex-Marine who thwarted an assassination attempt on President Ford was gay. This was not found to be an invasion of privacy. The hero testified that he had openly acknowledged his sexual orientation.[80] If information is contained in a *public record* it is also not private. In *Cox Broadcasting Corporation v. Cohn*,[81] the Supreme Court denied the invasion of privacy claim of the family of a young victim of rape and murder. Justice White's majority opinion indicated that at a minimum, the First and Fourteenth Amendments will not allow sanctions for the publication of "truthful information contained in official court records open to public inspection."[82]

### False Light Invasions

Suppose that a writer makes a calculated decision to report false facts about another person, but those facts are not defamatory because they do not expose the target to shame or ridicule. The information may not be embarrassing, but it may still disturb the subject of the story because she or he does not like to be placed in a false light. The Supreme Court considered this issue in *Time, Inc. v. Hill*.[83]

The Hill family had been held hostage by escaped convicts. The convicts had been courteous and nonviolent during the ordeal. Later, a novel and a play were written about a hostage incident based on the Hills' experience and that of other hostages. Although the Hills had moved away and were attempting to prevent further publicity about their ordeal, *Life* magazine published an article entitled "True Crime Inspires Tense Play." The article indicated that the story had been *reenacted* in a novel and a Broadway play, and included pictures depicting the son as being roughed up by a convict.

---

79. *Diaz v. Oakland Tribune*, 188 Cal. Rptr. 762 (Cal. App. 1983). Her sex change operation was found not to be newsworthy because it was not relevant to her fitness for office. Id. at 773.
80. Dill, *The Journalist's Handbook*, p. 138.
81. 420 U.S. 469 (1975).
82. Id. at 495.
83. 385 U.S. 374 (1967).

The Hills sued, contending that *Life* knowingly gave the false impression that the play accurately represented their hostage experience. A jury awarded $30,000 in damages, and the case reached the Supreme Court. The Court held that false reports of *newsworthy* facts were protected by the Constitution, unless there was proof that the publisher acted with actual malice.[84] The Court noted that the information in the article about a new play, linked to a real-life incident, was a matter of public interest. The Court feared a chilling effect on newsworthy information if the press needed to guarantee the certainty of facts in news articles.[85]

However, the Court also concluded that a calculated falsehood deserved no immunity. Calculated falsehoods "are of slight social value as a step to the truth" and do not enjoy constitutional protection.[86] Therefore, the case was remanded so that a jury could determine whether *Life* had innocently or negligently misstated facts about the Hills' ordeal, or had acted with actual malice in writing the article.

Judicial decisions on claims of invasion of privacy indicate that there is no absolute First Amendment protection for communicating true private information, or false nonembarrassing information. Nevertheless, when information about an individual is newsworthy, the courts will give greater weight to the public's right to know than to that person's right to be left alone.

## SUMMARY

In this chapter, we have examined what happens when defamatory statements (attacks on a person's character or reputation) are made. We questioned whether such statements belong in the marketplace of ideas. Defenders of this form of expression explain its connection to criticism of government, a linchpin of participatory democracy. Detractors counter that this type of expression does not belong in the marketplace because it only promotes false and potentially damaging accusations and innuendo.

Courts have allowed the recovery of damages for this form of expression, but only after the communicator has been proven sufficiently blameworthy. The leading case on this issue is *New York Times v. Sullivan,* in which the Court held that public officials can win defamation lawsuits for false reports on matters relevant to their official conduct only if the communicator acted with actual malice. Actual malice was defined to mean statements made with knowledge that they are false, or with reckless disregard for their truth. The actual malice rule also applies to public figures, those persons who have general fame in society or thrust themselves into the vortex of a particular controversy.

The rationale for imposing such a high standard of proof on public officials and figures is that they accept a higher threshold of potentially scurrilous

84. Id. at 390.
85. Id. at 388–89.
86. Id. at 390.

criticism as part of the price they pay for governance and high profile. They also have greater access to the marketplace of ideas, and can use *more speech* to counter the alleged defamation. The threshold diminishes as we move from public figures to limited purpose public figures to private individuals. Those citizens who are not public figures have less access to the marketplace of ideas, and may be denied the chance to tell their side of the story.

In addition to refining the substantive law of actual malice, the Supreme Court has ruled on the procedures to be followed in defamation cases. Freedom of expression has been enhanced by requiring the defendant to prove the falsity of defamatory statements on issues of public concern, and by facilitating appellate review of jury findings that defendants acted with actual malice. However, defamation plaintiffs may use discovery to gain information that may prove that a defendant acted with actual malice.

Finally, although the Court has been determined to protect the free flow of information about newsworthy events to the public, a zone of privacy has been maintained. Embarrassing, secret facts about individuals may not be freely published unless they are newsworthy. Furthermore, even newsworthy reports may not include calculated lies about their subjects.

CHAPTER 9      *Objectives*

**After reading chapter 9,
you should understand
the following:**

◆ *The reasons why the Supreme Court
considers obscene expression to be worthless in the marketplace of ideas.*

◆ *The Court's struggle to find a workable definition of obscenity.*

◆ *The current First Amendment standard for regulations against obscenity,
which was articulated in* Miller v. California.

◆ *The question of whether the context in
which obscene materials are read or
viewed should be relevant to determining
the level of constitutional protection.*

◆ *The arguments of conservative and
liberal critics in support of greater restrictions on erotic works.*

◆ *The arguments of civil libertarians in
favor of greater protection for erotic
works.*

# 9  *Obscenity*

My ancestors were Puritans from England, [who] arrived here in 1648 in the hope of finding greater restrictions than were permissible under English law at the time." Garrison Keillor[1]

IN THE CONTEXT OF freedom of speech, obscenity comprises expression that appeals to the prurient (erotic) interest. The question of whether such speech should be protected by the First Amendment has been highly controversial in the second half of this century.[2] Given the diversity of opinion about sexual morality in the United States, the controversy should come as no surprise. Obscene speech has been characterized as having low value and no worth in the marketplace of ideas. Such expression has also been argued to cause harm to society. The political right claims that obscene material is contrary to the appropriate moral values of society, particularly when the sexual behavior depicted is "unconventional." Left-wing criticism is based on the allegation that exposure to obscene material engenders attitudes that favor subordination and violation of women. In Berkeley, California, one small but popular diner recently attempted to prohibit the reading of pornographic magazines by patrons on diner property. A patron had read *Playboy* magazine at the counter, causing discomfort to women in the diner—especially those who worked there. The women felt that such a magazine, although not as graphic as other publications, could be prohibited since it met their definition of obscenity. Could the diner prohibit this? Could the city of Berkeley pass an ordinance restricting the viewing of this "obscene" material within the diner?

1. Nadine Strossen, *Defending Pornography: Free Speech, Sex, and the Fight for Women's Rights,* p. 37 (Scribner's, 1995). Keillor was testifying in support of the National Endowment for the Arts, under attack for funding works such as Robert Mapplethorpe's homoerotic photographs.
2. See *Roth v. United States,* 354 U.S. 479 (1957), p. 226, *infra.* Efforts to suppress obscene speech began to intensify more than one hundred years ago, with the antivice campaign of Anthony Comstock (see chapter 3). However, the Supreme Court did not directly address the First Amendment implications of obscene material until 1957.

You will study four major topics in this chapter. First is the Supreme Court's rationale for holding that obscenity is not protected by the First Amendment. The second topic is the complex issue of defining obscenity. Third, we will consider contextual differences and the law regarding obscenity. The final part of this chapter will examine the arguments for and against suppression of obscene speech. After examining the evidence for each side of the debate, you can decide for yourself if you agree with the Supreme Court's doctrine in obscenity cases.

## OBSCENITY IS NOT PROTECTED BY THE FIRST AMENDMENT

The Supreme Court directly addressed the issue of First Amendment protection for obscene speech in *Roth v. United States*. Samuel Roth was a publisher and bookseller in New York; his inventory included titles such as *Photo and Body* and *American Aphrodite*. He was convicted for mailing obscene circulars and an obscene book in violation of the federal obscenity statute.[3] Roth appealed, contending that the statute violated the First Amendment. The Supreme Court upheld Roth's conviction, ruling that obscenity was not protected expression.

### Roth v. United States, 354 U.S. 479 (1957)

Mr. Justice Brennan delivered the opinion of the Court.

. . . The dispositive question is whether obscenity is utterance within the area of protected speech and press. Although this is the first time the question has been squarely presented to this Court, . . . expressions found in numerous opinions indicate that this Court has always assumed that obscenity is not protected by the freedoms of speech and press. . . .

The guarant[e]es of freedom of expression in effect in 10 of the 14 States which by 1792 had ratified the Constitution, gave no absolute protection for every utterance. Thirteen of the 14 States provided for the prosecution of libel, and all of those States made either blasphemy or profanity, or both, statutory crimes. As early as 1712, Massachusetts made it criminal to publish "any filthy, obscene, or profane song, pamphlet, libel or mock sermon" in imitation or mimicking of religious services. . . .

The protection given speech and press was fashioned to assure unfettered interchange of ideas for the bringing about of political and social changes desired by the people. . . .

All ideas having even the slightest redeeming social importance—unorthodox ideas, controversial ideas, even ideas hateful to the prevailing climate of opinion—have the full protection of the guarant[e]es, unless excludable because they encroach upon the limited area of more important interests. *But implicit in the history of the First Amendment is the rejection of obscenity as utterly without redeeming*

---

3. The relevant portion of the statute read: "Every obscene, lewd, lascivious, or filthy book, pamphlet, picture, paper, letter, writing, print, or other publication of an indecent character . . . [i]s declared to be nonmailable matter and shall not be conveyed in the mails or delivered from any post office or by any letter carrier . . ." (354 U.S. at 479, n. 1).

*social importance* (emphasis added). This rejection for that reason is mirrored in the universal judgment that obscenity should be restrained, reflected in the international agreement of over 50 nations, in the obscenity laws of all of the 48 States, and in the 20 obscenity laws enacted by the Congress from 1842 to 1956. This is the same judgment expressed by this Court in *Chaplinsky v. New Hampshire:*

> There are certain well defined and narrowly limited classes of speech,
> the prevention and punishment of which have never been thought to
> raise any Constitutional problem. These include the lewd and obscene.

We hold that obscenity is not within the area of constitutionally protected speech or press.

It is strenuously urged that these obscenity statutes offend the constitutional guarantees because they punish incitation to impure sexual thoughts, not shown to be related to any overt antisocial conduct which is or may be incited in the persons stimulated to such thoughts. . . .

It is insisted that the constitutional guarantees are violated because convictions may be had without proof either that the obscene material will perceptibly create a clear and present danger of antisocial conduct, or will probably induce its recipients to such conduct. But, in light of our holding that obscenity is not protected speech, the complete answer to this argument is in the holding of this Court in *Beauharnais v. Illinois* (citations omitted):

> Libelous utterances not being within the area of constitutionally protected speech, it is unnecessary either for us or for the State courts to consider the issues behind the phrase clear and present danger. Certainly no one would contend that obscene speech, for example, may be punished only upon a showing of such circumstances.  ◆◆◆

You are free to apply your critical thinking skills to decide whether obscenity has any value in the marketplace of ideas. The Court placed obscenity at the bottom of the hierarchy of speech, and consequently did not require the government to prove that such speech was dangerous to society. Since *Roth,* Supreme Court majorities have consistently adhered to this rule. However, the Court has experienced far more difficulty in reaching a consensus on the meaning of obscenity.

### 1957–1973: THE COURT STRUGGLES WITH THE MEANING OF OBSCENITY

### The *Roth* Test for Obscenity

In *Roth,* Justice Brennan attempted to make a distinction between sexually oriented material that has social value and that which does not. Only the latter would not be protected by the First Amendment. Read the continuation of the majority opinion in *Roth,* and decide whether the Court provided a good test for distinguishing worthless and worthwhile expression regarding sex.

### *Roth v. United States,* 354 U.S. 476, 487 (1957)

[S]ex and obscenity are not synonymous. Obscene material is material which deals with sex in a manner appealing to prurient interest. The portrayal of sex, e.g., in art, literature and scientific works, is not itself sufficient reason to deny material the constitutional protection of freedom of speech and press. Sex, a great and mysterious motive force in human life, has indisputably been a subject of absorbing interest to mankind through the ages; it is one of the vital problems of human interest and public concern. As to all such problems this Court said in *Thornhill v. Alabama* (citations omitted):

> The freedom of speech and of the press guaranteed by the Constitution embraces at the least the liberty to discuss publicly and truthfully *all matters of public concern* without previous restraint or fear of subsequent punishment.

The fundamental freedoms of speech and press have contributed greatly to the development and well being of our free society and are indispensable to its continued growth. Ceaseless vigilance is the watchword to prevent their erosion by Congress or by the States. The door barring federal and state intrusion into this area cannot be left ajar; it must be kept tightly closed and opened only the slightest crack necessary to prevent encroachment upon more important interests. It is therefore vital that the standards for judging obscenity safeguard the protection of freedom of speech and press which does not treat sex in a manner appealing to the prurient interest.

The early leading standard of obscenity allowed material to be judged merely by the effect of an isolated excerpt upon particularly susceptible persons (*Regina v. Hicklin* [1868]). . . . Some American courts adopted this standard but later decisions have rejected it and substituted this test: *whether to the average person, applying contemporary community standards, the dominant theme of the material taken as a whole appeals to prurient interest* (emphasis added). The *Hicklin* test, judging obscenity by the effect of isolated passages upon the most susceptible persons, might well encompass material legitimately treating with sex, and so it must be rejected as unconstitutionally restrictive of the freedoms of speech and press. On the other hand, the substituted standard provides safeguards adequate to withstand the charge of constitutional infirmity. ◆◆◆

### Court Attempts to Clarify Obscenity After *Roth*

After reaching a majority consensus on the meaning of obscenity in *Roth,* the Court had a very difficult time reaching a similar consensus in future cases.

**Jacobellis v. Ohio.**[4] In this case, the appellant, theater manager Nico Jacobellis, was convicted for exhibiting a French film called *Les Amants* (The lovers). Six justices agreed that the conviction should be overturned, but these

---

4. 378 U.S. 184 (1964).

justices produced four different opinions.[5] Although the result was helpful to Mr. Jacobellis, the case could not function as precedent.

Justices Black and Douglas took the absolutist approach, contending that the First Amendment did not permit the conviction of anyone for exhibiting a motion picture.[6] Justices Brennan and Goldberg believed that convictions that met the *Roth* test for obscenity could be sustained, but that this film was not obscene under *Roth*. Justice Brennan described the plot: A woman, bored with her life and marriage, abandons her family for a young archaeologist. Justice Brennan noted that a single explicit love scene near the end of the film was the basis for Ohio's objection to the film, and that the film had been favorably reviewed in some national publications. Therefore, Justice Brennan wrote, the *Roth* test was not satisfied.[7]

The most memorable opinion in *Jacobellis* was delivered by Justice Potter Stewart. He opined that the First Amendment limited valid criminal obscenity laws to those that deal with hard-core pornography. Justice Stewart then described the difficulty of defining such material:

I shall not today attempt further to define the kinds of material I understand to be embraced within that shorthand description; and perhaps I could never succeed in intelligibly doing so. *But I know it when I see it* (emphasis added), and the motion picture involved in this case is not that.[8]  ◆◆◆

***Memoirs v. Massachusetts.*[9]**   John Cleland's 1750 novel, *Memoirs of a Woman of Pleasure* (commonly known as *Fanny Hill*), provided the subject matter for another obscenity case, again resulting in a wide divergence of Court opinions. *Memoirs* deals with the experiences of a London prostitute, who ultimately renounces that career and marries her first lover. An earlier edition, apparently containing erotic illustrations to supplement the prose, had been suppressed in 1821.[10] The later proceeding against the book involved an appeal from a civil judgment that it was obscene.[11]

The U.S. Supreme Court reversed this judgment, but as in *Jacobellis*, the justices could not reach an agreement on their reasons for decision. Justice Brennan wrote a plurality opinion (joined by Chief Justice Warren and Justice Fortas), which noted that the Massachusetts Supreme Judicial Court had misinterpreted the *Roth* test. The Massachusetts court had held that the "social importance" criterion of *Roth* did not mean that a book had to be

5. Id. at 196. Justice White, who concurred, did so without issuing an opinion.
6. Id. (Black, J., concurring).
7. 378 U.S. at 195–96.
8. Id. at 197 (Stewart, J., concurring).
9. 383 U.S. 413 (1966).
10. 383 U.S. at 424–25 (Douglas, J., concurring). The earlier case was *Commonwealth v. Holmes*, 17 Mass. 336 (1821).
11. *Massachusetts General Laws*, Chapter 272, Section 28C. In addition to provisions for criminal penalties against distributors of obscene books, state law allowed for civil proceedings in which the attorney general could attempt to have a book declared obscene.

unqualifiedly worthless before it could be deemed obscene. Justice Brennan's opinion disagreed with this premise, noting that to be obscene, a book must be *utterly* without redeeming social value.[12] Because Massachusetts had applied *Roth* incorrectly in this case, the obscenity finding was reversed; but Justice Brennan argued that in the future, a court could properly judge that *Memoirs* was obscene.[13]

Only Justice Douglas (see Figure 9.1) aggressively defended the literary merit of *Fanny Hill*. In addition to writing his own opinion (see following excerpt), he attached an appendix to his decision—an article by the Reverend John Graham of the First Universalist Church of Denver. Rev. Graham defended *Memoirs,* arguing that it makes a serious point: There are far worse ways to degrade people than either being or visiting a prostitute. Wrote Graham, "If our society collapses, it will not be because people read a book such as *Fanny Hill*. It will fall, because we have refused to understand it."[14]

### *Memoirs v. Massachusetts,* 383 U.S. 413, 424 (1966)

Mr. Justice Douglas, concurring in the judgment.

*Memoirs of a Woman of Pleasure,* or, as it is often titled, *Fanny Hill,* concededly is an erotic novel. It was first published in about 1749 and has endured to this date, despite periodic efforts to suppress it. The book relates the adventures of a young girl who becomes a prostitute in London. At the end, she abandons that life and marries her first lover, observing:

> Thus, at length, I got snug into port, where, in the bosom of virtue, I gather'd the only uncorrupt sweets: where, looking back on the course of vice I had run, and comparing its infamous blandishments with the infinitely superior joys of innocence, I could not help pitying, even in point of taste, those who, immers'd in gross sensuality, are insensible to the delicate charms of VIRTUE, than which even PLEASURE has not a greater friend, nor than VICE a greater enemy.

[E]ven applying the prevailing view of the *Roth* test, reversal is compelled by this record which makes clear that *Fanny Hill* is not "obscene." The prosecution made virtually no effort to prove that this book is "utterly without redeeming social importance." The defense, on the other hand, introduced considerable and impressive testimony to the effect that this was a work of literary, historical, and social importance.[15]

---

12. 383 U.S. at 419.
13. Id. at 420. Justice Brennan noted that the book could be found to be utterly devoid of social value if the book's advertising only discussed sexually provocative aspects of the book.
14. Id. at 439.
15. Justice Douglas enumerates: "The defense [witnesses included]: Fred Holly Stocking, Professor of English . . . , Williams College; John M. Bullitt, Professor of English . . . , Harvard College; Robert H. Sproat, Associate Professor of English Literature, Boston University. . . . In addition, the defense introduced into evidence reviews of impartial literary critics. These are, in my opinion, of particular significance since their publication indicates that the book is of sufficient significance as to warrant serious critical comment."

*Figure 9.1. Justice William O. Douglas was appointed to the Court in 1939 and served until 1975. Known as a fiercely independent thinker who often fashioned his own concurring or dissenting opinions, Douglas was at the time of his appointment only forty years old. One example of his thinking can be seen in his concurring opinion in* Memoirs v. Massachusetts. *(Harris & Ewing. Collection of the Supreme Court of the United States.)*

. . . If there is to be censorship, the wisdom of experts on such matters as literary merit and historical significance must be evaluated. On this record, the Court has no choice but to reverse the judgment of the Massachusetts Supreme Judicial Court, irrespective of whether we would include *Fanny Hill* in our own libraries.

◆◆◆

The Court's analysis of obscenity in the aftermath of *Roth* was not limited to disputes over the definition of the term. The Court also questioned whether a defendant's techniques for advertising a publication could be a criteria for determining obscenity.

### *Ginzburg v. U.S.*[16]

In *Ginzburg,* the Court used a different approach to reach the conclusion that certain publications were obscene. Ralph Ginzburg had been convicted in federal court for mailing three publications—*EROS, Liaison,* and *The Housewife's Handbook on Selective Promiscuity*—in violation of the federal obscenity statute.[17] The prosecution admitted that these works, standing alone, were not neces-

16. 383 U.S. 463 (1966).
17. 18 U.S.C. Section 1461.

sarily obscene. Instead, the theory of their case was that the materials were obscene, given the context of their production, advertising, and sale. The Supreme Court resolved this issue in favor of the prosecution. As you read Justice Brennan's opinion, ask yourself whether it is appropriate to conclude that a book is obscene because a publisher's advertising made it appear so.

### Ginzburg v. United States, 383 U.S. 463 (1966)

Mr. Justice Brennan delivered the opinion of the Court.

Besides testimony as to the merit of the material, there was abundant evidence to show that each of the accused publications was originated or sold as stock in trade of the sordid business of pandering—"the business of purveying textual or graphic matter openly advertised to appeal to the erotic interest of their customers." *EROS* early sought mailing privileges from the postmasters of Intercourse and Blue Ball, Pennsylvania. The trial court found the obvious, that these hamlets were chosen only for the value their names would have in furthering petitioner's efforts to sell their publications on the basis of salacious appeal; the facilities of the post offices were inadequate to handle the anticipated volume of mail, and the privileges were denied. Mailing privileges were than obtained from the postmaster of Middlesex, New Jersey. . . .

The "leer of the sensualist" also permeates the advertising for the three publications. The circulars sent for *EROS* and *Liaison* stressed the sexual candor of the respective publications, and openly boasted that the publishers would take full advantage of what they regarded as an unrestricted license allowed by law in the expression of sex and sexual matters. . . .

This evidence, in our view, was relevant in determining the ultimate question of obscenity and, in the context of this record, serves to resolve all ambiguity and doubt. The deliberate representation of petitioners' publications as erotically arousing, for example, stimulated the reader to accept them as prurient; he looks for titillation, not for saving intellectual content. . . .

We perceive no threat to First Amendment guarantees in thus holding that in close cases evidence of pandering may be probative with respect to the nature of the material in question and thus satisfy the *Roth* test. . . . [T]he fact that each of these publications was created or exploited entirely on the basis of its appeal to prurient interests strengthens the conclusion that the transactions here were sales of illicit merchandise, not sales of constitutionally protected matter.   ◆◆◆

Justice Douglas disagreed with the majority's analysis. He contended that sex is used to sell a wide variety of products, from liquor to autos to tires. To him, "a book should stand on its own, irrespective of the reasons why it was written or the wiles used in selling it."[18] He questioned whether a portion

18. Id. at 482 (Douglas, J., dissenting).

of the *Bible* could become obscene, depending on how stanzas 7 and 8 of the Song of Solomon[19] were marketed.

*Interstate Circuit, Inc. v. City of Dallas.*[20]  In *Interstate Circuit*, a majority of the Court was able to reach the conclusion that a Dallas city ordinance, which allowed movies to be classified as unsuitable for children under sixteen, unconstitutional. One of the criteria under which a film could be deemed unsuitable was that it portrayed "sexual promiscuity or extra-marital or abnormal sexual relations in such a manner as . . . likely to incite or encourage delinquency or sexual promiscuity on the part of young persons. . . . " The Court noted that the term *sexual promiscuity* was too vague, opining that "it could extend, depending on one's moral judgment, from the obvious to any sexual contacts outside a marital relationship."[21]

Justice Harlan wrote an opinion in which he concurred in part and dissented in part from the majority. His opinion highlighted the difficulties that continued to plague the Court.

### *Interstate Circuit v. Dallas,* 390 U.S. 676, 706 (1968)

Mr. Justice Harlan, concurring and dissenting.

Most of the present Justices who believe that "obscenity" is not beyond the pale of governmental control seemingly consider that the *Roth-Memoirs-Ginzburg* tests permit suppression of material that falls short of so-called "hard core pornography," on equal terms as between federal and state authority. Another view is that only "hard core pornography" may be suppressed, whether by federal or state authority. And still another view, that of this writer, is that only "hard core pornography" may be suppressed by the Federal Government, whereas under the Fourteenth Amendment States are permitted wider authority to deal with obnoxious matter than might be justifiable under a strict application of the *Roth-Memoirs-Ginzburg* rules.

. . . The upshot of all this divergence in viewpoint is that anyone who undertakes to examine the Court's decisions since *Roth* which have held particular material obscene or not obscene would find himself in utter bewilderment. From the standpoint of the Court itself the current approach has required us to spend an inordinate amount of time in the absurd business of perusing and viewing the miserable stuff that pours into the Court, mostly in state cases, all to no better end than second-guessing state judges.  ◆◆◆

19. The Song of Solomon depicts King Solomon's efforts to win the heart of a beautiful girl, who remains faithful to the common shepherd who loves her. Benson Y. Landis, *An Outline of the Bible,* p. 57 (Barnes & Noble, 1963). In stanzas 7 and 8, the anatomy of the young girl is praised in language that most would consider mild compared to words commonly used in contemporary film and song.

20. 390 U.S. 676 (1968).

21. Id. at 687.

## A MAJORITY REACHES AGREEMENT ON OBSCENE MATERIAL

### The Court Announces the *Miller* Test

By 1973, the Supreme Court was ready to make another effort to resolve the obscenity question. The membership of the Court had changed. Liberal Chief Justice Earl Warren had been replaced by the more conservative Warren Burger (see Figure 9–2). William Rehnquist, who would later be appointed Chief Justice, had also been added to the Court. In an opinion authored by Chief Justice Burger, five justices agreed upon an obscenity test. As you read this opinion, consider these four important questions:

1. What is the new test for determining when expression may be suppressed because it is obscene?

2. Do the examples provided by the Court in *Miller* effectively clarify the elements of the test?

3. Does the *Miller* test enable the majority to achieve its objective of "carefully limiting" obscenity laws to "hard-core pornography"?

4. Why does the Court reject a rule requiring the use of national standards to define obscenity?

*Figure 9.2. Chief Justice Warren Burger was nominated to the Court in 1969 by President Nixon. Although Burger was commonly perceived as intending to undo much of Earl Warren's constitutional judicial activism, no major Warren opinion was overturned during Burger's tenure. The Burger Court decided many significant First Amendment cases including* **Miller v. California.** *(Robert S. Oakes, National Geographic Society. Collection of the Supreme Court of the United States.)*

## Miller v. California, 413 U.S. 15 (1973)

Mr. Chief Justice Burger delivered the opinion of the Court.

Appellant conducted a mass mailing campaign to advertise the sale of illustrated books, euphemistically called "adult" material. After a jury trial, he was convicted of violating California Penal Code Section 311.2(a), a misdemeanor, by knowingly distributing obscene matter. . . .

The brochures [sent through the mail by Miller] advertise four books entitled "Intercourse," "Man-Woman," "Sex Orgies Illustrated," and "An Illustrated History of Pornography," and a film entitled "Marital Intercourse." While the brochures contain some descriptive printed material, primarily they consist of pictures and drawings very explicitly depicting men and women in groups of two or more engaging in a variety of sexual activities, with genitals often prominently displayed. . . .

Apart from the initial formulation in the *Roth* case, no majority of the Court has at any given time been able to agree on a standard to determine what constitutes obscene, pornographic material subject to regulation under the States' police power. . . .

This much has been categorically settled by the Court, that obscene material is unprotected by the First Amendment. . . . We acknowledge, however, the inherent dangers of undertaking to regulate any form of expression. State statutes designed to regulate obscene materials must be carefully limited. As a result, we now confine the permissible scope of such regulation to works which depict or describe sexual conduct. . . .

The basic guidelines for the trier of fact must be: *(a) whether "the average person, applying contemporary community standards" would find that the work, taken as a whole, appeals to the prurient interest; (b) whether the work depicts or describes, in a patently offensive way, sexual conduct specifically defined by the applicable state law; and (c) whether the work, taken as a whole, lacks serious literary, artistic, political, or scientific value* (emphasis added). We do not adopt as a constitutional standard the "*utterly* without redeeming social value" test of *Memoirs v. Massachusetts* (citation omitted); that concept has never commanded the adherence of more than three Justices at one time. . . .

We emphasize that it is not our function to propose regulatory schemes for the States. That must await their concrete legislative efforts. It is possible, however, to give a few plain examples of what a state statute could define for regulation under part (b) of the standard announced in this opinion, *supra:*

(a) Patently offensive representations or descriptions of ultimate sexual acts, normal or perverted, actual or simulated.

(b) Patently offensive representations or descriptions of masturbation, excretory functions, and lewd exhibition of the genitals.

Sex and nudity may not be exploited without limit by films or pictures exhibited or sold in places of public accommodation any more than live sex and nudity can be exhibited or sold without limit in such public places. At a minimum, prurient, patently offensive depiction or description of sexual conduct must have serious literary, artistic, political, or scientific value to merit First Amendment protection. . . .

For example, medical books for the education of physicians and related personnel necessarily use graphic illustrations and descriptions of human anatomy. . . .

Under the holdings announced today, no one will be subject to prosecution for the sale or exposure of obscene materials unless these materials depict or describe patently offensive "hard core" sexual conduct specifically defined by the regulating state law, as written or construed. We are satisfied that these specific prerequisites will provide fair notice to a dealer in such materials that his public and commercial activities may bring prosecution. . . . If the inability to define regulated materials with ultimate, god-like precision altogether removes the power of the States or the Congress to regulate, then "hard core" pornography may be exposed without limit to the juvenile, the passerby, and the consenting adult alike, as indeed, Mr. Justice Douglas contends. . . . In this belief, however, Mr. Justice Douglas now stands alone. . . .

It is certainly true that the absence, since Roth, of a single majority view of this Court as to proper standards for testing obscenity has placed a strain on both state and federal courts. But today, for the first time since Roth was decided in 1957, a majority of this Court has agreed on concrete guidelines to isolate "hard core" pornography from expression protected by the First Amendment. . . .

Under a National Constitution, fundamental First Amendment limitations on the powers of the States do not vary from community to community, but this does not mean that there are, or should be, fixed, uniform national standards of precisely what appeals to the "prurient interest" or is "patently offensive." These are essentially questions of fact, and our nation is simply too big and too diverse for this Court to reasonably expect that such standards could be articulated for all 50 States in a single formulation, even assuming the prerequisite consensus exists. . . . To require a State to structure obscenity proceedings around evidence of a *national* "community standard" would be an exercise in futility. . . .

It is neither realistic nor constitutionally sound to read the First Amendment as requiring that the people of Maine or Mississippi accept public depiction of conduct found tolerable in Las Vegas, or New York City. . . .

The dissenting Justices sound the alarm of repression. But, in our view, to equate the free and robust exchange of ideas and political debate with commercial exploitation of obscene material demeans the grand conception of the First Amendment and its high purposes in the historic struggle for freedom. . . .

There is no evidence, empirical or historical, that the stern 19th century American censorship of public distribution and display of material relating to sex . . . in any way limited or affected expression of serious literary, artistic, political, or scientific ideas. On the contrary, it is beyond any question that the era following Thomas Jefferson to Theodore Roosevelt was an "extraordinarily vigorous period," not just in economics and politics, but in *belles lettres* and in "the outlying fields of social and political philosophies." . . .

The judgment of the Appellate Department of the Superior Court, Orange County, California, is vacated and the case remanded to that court for further proceedings not inconsistent with the First Amendment standards established by this opinion. ◆◆◆

# ◄ 2 Live Crew Meets the Miller Test

In response to citizen complaints, a Broward County (Florida) sheriff's deputy listened to six of the songs on rap group 2 Live Crew's *As Nasty As They Wanna Be* recording. The deputy then obtained a ruling from a county judge stating there was probable cause that the recording was obscene. The sheriff's office warned retail stores in Broward County, and soon the recording could not be bought anywhere in the county.

The lyrics of *Nasty* included references to the male and female genitalia, oral sex, group sex, sadomasochism, and sexual intercourse. When Skyywalker Records, Inc. (a company owned by 2 Live Crew member Luther Campbell) filed suit in federal court challenging the obscenity finding, the *Miller* test had to be applied. As District Judge Jose Gonzalez Jr. framed the issue, "today this court decides whether the First Amendment permits one to yell another 'F' word [the first 'f' word was fire, as in a theatre] anywhere in the community when combined with graphic sexual descriptions.[1]

***The Prurient Interest.***    According to Judge Gonzalez, 2 Live Crew was appealing to the prurient interest in *Nasty*. Gonzalez held that

> the frequency and graphic description of the sexual lyrics evinces a clear intention to lure hearers into this activity. The depictions of ultimate sexual acts are so vivid that they are hard to distinguish from seeing the same conduct described in the words of a book, or in pictures. . . . 2 Live Crew itself testified that the *Nasty* recording was made to be listened and danced to. The evident goal of this particular recording is to reproduce the sexual act through musical lyrics. It is an appeal directed to "dirty" thoughts and the loins, not to the intellect and the mind.[2]

***Patently Offensive.***    The judge also found that the work was patently offensive. He noted:

> The recording depicts sexual conduct in graphic detail. The specificity of the descriptions makes the audio message analogous to a camera with a zoom lens, focusing on the sights and sounds of various ultimate sex acts. Furthermore, the frequency of the sexual lyrics must be considered. With the exception of part B on Side 1, the entire *Nasty* recording is replete with sexual lyrics. This is not a case of subtle references or innuendo, nor is it just "one particular scurrilous epithet," as in *Cohen v. California*.[3]

***Serious Social Value.***    Judge Gonzalez also found social value to be lacking. He opined:

---

1. *Skyywalker Records, Inc. v. Navarro,* 739 F. Supp. 578 (S.D. Fla. 1990).
2. Id. at 591.
3. Id. at 592.

The plaintiffs themselves testified that neither their music nor their lyrics were created to convey a political message. The only witness testifying at trial that there was political content in the *Nasty* recording was Carlton Long, who was qualified as an expert on the culture of black Americans. . . . Long identifies three cultural devices evident in this work here: "call and response," "doing the dozens," and "boasting." The court finds none of these arguments persuasive.

The only examples of "call and response" in the *Nasty* recording are portions where males and females yell, in repetitive verse, "Tastes Great— Less Filling," . . . merely a phrase lifted from a beer commercial.

The device of "doing the dozens" is a word game composed of a series of insults escalating in their satirical content. The "boasting" device is a way for persons to overstate their virtues such as sexual prowess.

While this court does not doubt that both "boasting" and "doing the dozens" are found in the culture of black Americans, these devices are also found in other cultures. . . .

The plaintiffs stress that *Nasty* has value as comedy and satire. . . . It cannot be reasonably argued that the violence, perversion, abuse of women, graphic depictions of all forms of sexual conduct, and microscopic descriptions of human genitalia contained on this recording are comedic art.[4] . . .

## "OBSCENITY? YES!"[5]

Do you agree with Judge Gonzalez? Did he correctly apply the elements of the *Miller* test? If you have listened to *As Nasty As They Wanna Be*, would you agree that sales of the record should have been banned?

2 Live Crew appealed the district court's obscenity finding. In *Luke Records, Inc. v. Navarro*,[6] a federal appeals court held that *Nasty* was not legally obscene. In a per curiam opinion, the appellate court held:

> The Sheriff concedes that he has the burden of proof to show that the recording is obscene. Yet, he submitted no evidence to contradict the testimony that the work had artistic value. A work cannot be held obscene unless each element of the *Miller* test has been met. We reject the argument that simply by listening to this musical work, the judge could determine that it had no serious artistic value."[7]

4. Id. at 594–95.
5. Id. at 596.
6. 960 F. 2d 134 (11th Cir., 1992).
7. Id. at 138–39.

◆◆◆

## Subsequent Cases Apply the *Miller* Test

For more than twenty years, *Miller* has remained the law of the land for determining the constitutionality of obscenity statutes. Unlike the cases decided in the aftermath of *Roth*, *Miller* did not spawn a generation of cases in which no majority of the Court could agree on the meaning of the new obscenity test. There were, however, several cases in which the Court elaborated on the components of the *Miller* test.

### Sexual Themes and Occasional Nudity Do Not Render a Film "Patently Offensive"

#### Jenkins v. Georgia, 418 U.S. 153 (1974)

Mr. Justice Rehnquist delivered the opinion of the Court.

Appellant was convicted in Georgia of the crime of distributing obscene material. His conviction, in March 1972, was for showing the film "Carnal Knowledge" in a movie theatre in Albany, Georgia. . . .

There is little to be found in the record about the film "Carnal Knowledge" other than the film itself. However, appellant has supplied a variety of information and critical commentary, the authenticity of which appellee does not dispute. . . . We believe that the following passage from a review which appeared in the *Saturday Review* is a reasonably accurate description of the film:

> [It is basically a story] of two young college men, roommates and lifelong friends forever preoccupied with their sex lives. Both are first met as virgins. [Jack] Nicholson is the more knowledgeable and attractive of the two; speaking colloquially, he is a burgeoning bastard. Art Garfunkel is his friend, the nice but troubled guy. . . . He falls in love with the lovely Susan (Candice Bergen) and unknowingly shares her with his college buddy. As the "safer" one of the two, he is selected by Susan for marriage.

. . . [I]t would be a serious misreading of *Miller* to conclude that juries have unbridled discretion in determining what is "patently offensive." . . . [W]e made it plain that under that holding "no one will be subject to prosecution for the sale or exposure of obscene materials unless these materials depict or describe patently offensive hard core sexual conduct."

. . . Our own viewing of the film satisfies us that "Carnal Knowledge" could not be found under the *Miller* standards to depict sexual conduct in a patently offensive way. Nothing in the movie falls within either of the two examples given in *Miller* of material which may constitutionally be found to meet the "patently offensive" element of those standards, nor is there anything sufficiently similar to such material to justify similar treatment. While the subject matter of the picture is, in a broader sense, sex, and there are scenes in which sexual conduct including "ultimate sexual acts" is to be understood to be taking place, the camera does not focus on the bodies of the actors at such times. There is no exhibition whatever of the actors' genitals, lewd or otherwise, during these scenes. There are occasional scenes of nudity, but nudity alone is not enough to make material legally obscene under the *Miller* standards.

. . . We hold that the film could not, as a matter of constitutional law, be found to depict sexual conduct in a patently offensive way, and that it is therefore not outside the protection of the First and Fourteenth Amendments because it is obscene. ◆◆◆

*States Have Wide Latitude in Determining the Community Whose Standards Will Be Applied.* In *Kaplan v. California*,[22] decided the same day as *Miller*, the defendant was convicted after selling the book *Suite 69* to an undercover police officer. The book consisted entirely of descriptions of "almost every conceivable variety of sexual conduct, homosexual and heterosexual." At the defendant's trial, the police officer testified that he had extensive experience with pornographic materials, and opined that "applying contemporary standards," *Suite 69* went "substantially beyond the customary limits of candor" in the State of California. The Supreme Court held that "the contemporary community standards of California, as opposed to 'national standards,' are constitutionally adequate to establish whether a work is obscene."[23]

In *Jenkins*, the Court clarified even further the latitude given states to define the relevant community. In that case, the judge had directed jurors to apply community standards, but failed to specify what community. The Supreme Court indicated that a state could define obscenity in terms of "community standards" without further specification, or provide more precise geographic terms.[24]

*The Examples of Permissible State Laws in* **Miller** *Are Not Exhaustive.* The *Miller* opinion had given examples of sexual conduct that might be found patently offensive in part (b) (see p. 235). In *Ward v. Illinois*,[25] the defendant was convicted for selling obscene sadomasochistic materials. On appeal, Ward argued that the Illinois obscenity law did not specifically ban such materials, and this type of sexual conduct had not been given as an example of what states could ban in *Miller*.

The Supreme Court upheld Ward's conviction. Justice White's opinion noted that the examples in part (b) of *Miller* "were not intended to be exhaustive." Furthermore, the opinion pointed out that nothing in *Miller* could be read as extending constitutional protection to flagellatory materials. The Court also rejected the claim that the Illinois obscenity statute needed to explicitly forbid sadomasochism. Ward was ruled to have been given sufficient notice, on the grounds that the Illinois Supreme Court had already ruled that "sadism and masochism" were obscene under the Illinois law.[26]

*Expert Testimony Is Not Required to Show That Material Lacks Social Value.* Another basis for the appeal in the *Kaplan* case was that the prosecution had introduced no expert testimony that the book, *Suite 69*, was utterly without redeeming social importance; whereas the defense had brought in expert testimony to the contrary. The Court reiterated that the First Amendment does not require expert testimony to prove obscenity once the material itself is entered into evidence. Because the prosecution had entered *Suite 69* into evidence, the jury could base a finding of obscenity on the book alone.[27]

22. 413 U.S. 115 (1973).
23. Id. at 121.
24. Id. at 157.
25. 431 U.S. 767 (1977).
26. Id. at 771.
27. 413 U.S. at 121.

## DOES CONTEXT INFLUENCE CONSTITUTIONAL PROTECTION?

In many cases, the context in which a message is delivered may influence constitutional protection. For example, a lie about a politician, broadcast in the heat of a political campaign, receives more constitutional protection than a lie told about your neighbor's private life. In chapter 10, you will read about how limits on expression that apply only to certain times or places may be constitutional. This section of chapter 9 deals with a similar question in obscenity cases. Should the right to send or receive obscene communications vary, depending on the context? Supreme Court decisions indicate that the right does vary.

### Private Possession of Obscene Material Is Protected

In *Stanley v. Georgia*,[28] law enforcement agents had entered Stanley's home armed with a warrant to search for evidence of illegal bookmaking. While conducting that search, the agents discovered three reels of film. The officers found a projector in the home and viewed the films. An officer concluded that the films were obscene and arrested the defendant for knowing possession of obscene matter (a violation of Georgia law). Although it may have been possible to decide this case on illegal search and seizure grounds,[29] the majority decided to expand the protection of the Constitution in a different manner.

#### *Stanley v. Georgia,* 394 U.S. 557 (1969)

Mr. Justice Marshall delivered the opinion of the Court.

[Georgia] contends that since "obscenity is not within the area of constitutionally protected speech or press," . . . the States are free to the limits of other provisions of the Constitution, . . . to deal with it any way deemed necessary, just as they may deal with possession of other things thought to be detrimental to the welfare of their citizens. If the [State] can protect the body of a citizen, may it not, argues Georgia, protect his mind? . . .

None of the statements cited by the Court in *Roth* for the proposition that "this Court has always assumed that obscenity is not protected by the freedoms of speech and press" were made in the context of a statute punishing mere private possession of obscene material; the cases cited deal for the most part with use of the mails to distribute objectionable material or with some form of public distribution or dissemination. . . .

In this context, we do not believe that this case can be decided simply by citing *Roth. Roth* and its progeny certainly do mean that the First and Fourteenth Amendments recognize a valid governmental interest in dealing with the problem of obscenity. But the assertion of that interest cannot, in every context, be insulated from all constitutional protections. . . .

---

28. 394 U.S. 557 (1969).
29. Id. at 569 (Stewart, J., concurring). A concurring opinion written by Justice Stewart, and joined by Justices Brennan and White, contended that the Court should have based its reversal on the illegal search and seizure issue.

✳ It is now well established that the Constitution protects the right to receive information and ideas. "This freedom of [speech and press] . . . necessarily protects the right to receive. . . ." This right to receive information and ideas, regardless of their social worth, . . . is fundamental to our free society. Moreover, in the context of this case—a prosecution for mere possession of printed or filmed matter in the privacy of a person's own home—that right takes on an added dimension. For also fundamental is the right to be free, except in very limited circumstances, from unwanted governmental intrusions into one's privacy. . . .

These are the rights that appellant is asserting in the case before us. He is asserting the right to read or observe what he pleases—the right to satisfy his intellectual and emotional needs in the privacy of his own home. He is asserting the right to be free from state inquiry into the contents of his library. . . . If the First Amendment means anything, it means that a State has no business telling a man, sitting alone in his own house, what books he may read or what films he may watch. Our whole constitutional heritage rebels at the thought of giving government the power to control men's minds. . . .

And yet, in the face of these traditional notions of individual liberty, Georgia asserts the right to protect the individual's mind from the effects of obscenity. We are not certain that this argument amounts to anything more than the assertion that the State has the right to control the moral content of a person's thoughts. To some, this may be a noble purpose, but it is wholly inconsistent with the philosophy of the First Amendment. . . . Its [the First Amendment's] guarantee is not confined to the expression of ideas that are conventional or shared by a majority. . . . And in the realm of ideas it protects expression which is eloquent no less than that which is unconvincing. . . . Whatever the power of the state to control public dissemination of ideas inimical to the public morality, it cannot constitutionally premise legislation on the desirability of controlling a person's private thoughts. . . .

We hold that the First and Fourteenth Amendments prohibit making mere private possession of obscene material a crime.   ◆◆◆

✳

### An Extension of the *Stanley* Rationale to Adults-Only Theatres Is Rejected

If it is permissible to observe obscene material while sitting at home alone, it is reasonable to ask whether it should also be acceptable to experience the same material, while in the company of other consenting adults, in an "adults-only" theatre? Based on the *Stanley* decision, you might expect that the Court would conclude that a desire to "purify" the viewers' minds would be an insufficient basis for limiting obscenity in adults-only theatres, and that to justify regulation, the state would need to show some tangible harm from viewing obscene films in that setting. Nevertheless, in *Paris Adult Theatre I v. Slaton*,[30] decided on the same day as *Miller*, the Supreme Court held that there was no First Amendment right to exhibit obscene works in an adult theatre.

---

30. 413 U.S. 49 (1973).

Because obscenity is not considered protected speech for First Amendment purposes, the Supreme Court gave considerable deference to the Georgia legislature's judgment about the effects of obscenity in adult theatres. As you read the Court's opinion, decide how strong the arguments are in favor of regulating obscenity in this context.

### Paris Adult Theatre I v. Slaton, 413 U.S. 49 (1973)

Mr. Chief Justice Burger delivered the opinion of the Court.

Petitioners are two Atlanta, Georgia, movie theaters and their owners and managers, operating in the style of "adult" theaters. On December 28, 1970, respondents . . . filed civil complaints alleging that petitioners were exhibiting to the public for paid admission two allegedly obscene films. . . . The two films in question, "Magic Mirror" and "It All Comes Out in the End," depict sexual conduct characterized by the Georgia Supreme Court as "hard core pornography" leaving "little to the imagination." . . .

We categorically disapprove the theory, apparently adopted by the trial judge, that obscene, pornographic films acquire constitutional immunity from state regulation simply because they are exhibited for consenting adults only. . . . Although we have often pointedly recognized the high importance of the state interest in regulating the exposure of obscene materials to juveniles and unconsenting adults, this Court has never declared these to be the only legitimate state interests permitting regulation of obscene material. . . . In an unbroken series of cases extending over a long stretch of this Court's history, it has been accepted as a postulate that "the primary requirements of decency may be enforced against obscene publications." . . .

In particular, we hold that there are legitimate state interests at stake in stemming the tide of commercialized obscenity, even assuming it is feasible to enforce effective safeguards against exposure to juveniles and to passersby. . . . These include the interest of the public in the quality of life and the total community environment, the tone of commerce in the great city centers, and possibly, the public safety itself. The Hill-Link Minority Report of the Commission on Obscenity and Pornography indicates that there is at least an arguable correlation between obscene material and crime. . . .

As Mr. Chief Justice Warren stated, there is a "right of the Nation and of the States to maintain a decent society. . . ."

But, it is argued, there are no scientific data which conclusively demonstrate that exposure to obscene material adversely affects men and women or their society. It is urged on behalf of the petitioners that, absent such a demonstration, any kind of state regulation is "impermissible." We reject this argument. It is not for us to resolve empirical uncertainties underlying state legislation, save in the exceptional case where that legislation plainly impinges upon rights protected by the Constitution itself. . . . Mr. Justice Brennan . . . said "We do not demand of legislatures scientifically certain criteria of legislation. . . . Although there is no conclusive proof of a connection between antisocial behavior and obscene material, the legislature of Georgia could quite reasonably determine that such a connection does or might exist. . . .

If we accept the unprovable assumption that a complete education requires the reading of certain books, . . . and the well nigh universal belief that good books, plays, and art lift the spirit, improve the mind, enrich the human personality, and develop character, can we then say that a state legislature may not act on the corollary assumption that commerce in obscene books, or public exhibitions focused on obscene conduct, have a tendency to exert a corrupting and debasing impact leading to antisocial behavior? . . . Nothing in the Constitution prohibits a State from reaching such a conclusion and acting on it legislatively simply because there is no conclusive evidence or empirical data. . . .

[I]t is unavailing to compare a theater open to the public for a fee, with the private home of *Stanley v. Georgia,* . . . and the marital bedroom of *Griswold v. Connecticut.* . . . This Court has, on numerous occasions, refused to hold that commercial ventures such as a motion-picture house are "private" for the purpose of civil rights litigation and civil rights statutes. . . .

Our prior decisions recognizing a right to privacy guaranteed by the Fourteenth Amendment included "only personal rights that can be deemed fundamental or implicit in the concept of ordered liberty." This privacy right encompasses and protects the personal intimacies of the home, the family, marriage, motherhood, procreation, and child rearing. . . . Nothing, however, in this Court's decisions intimates that there is any "fundamental" privacy right "implicit in the concept of ordered liberty" to watch obscene movies in places of public accommodation. . . .

It is also argued that the State has no legitimate interest in "control [of] the moral content of a person's thoughts," . . . and we need not quarrel with this. But we reject the claim that the State of Georgia is here attempting to control the minds or thoughts of those who patronize theatres. Preventing unlimited display or distribution of obscene material, which by definition lacks any serious literary, artistic, political, or scientific value as communication . . . is distinct from a control of reason and the intellect. . . .

Finally, petitioners argue that conduct which directly involves "consenting adults" only has, for that sole reason, a special claim to constitutional protection. Our Constitution establishes a broad range of conditions on the exercise of power by the States, but for us to say that our Constitution incorporates the proposition that conduct involving consenting adults only is always beyond state regulation, is a step we are unable to take. Commercial exploitation of depictions, descriptions, or exhibitions of obscene conduct on commercial premises open to the adult public falls within a State's broad power to regulate commerce and protect the public environment.

. . . In this case we hold that the States have a legitimate interest in regulating commerce in obscene material and in regulating exhibition of obscene material in places of public accommodation, including so-called "adult" theaters from which minors are excluded.   ◆◆◆

*Paris Adult Theatre* refused to extend the holding of *Stanley* to the realm of the adults-only theatre. The Court's opinion is an example of deference. The Chief Justice required little proof that the state would benefit by regulating obscenity in adults-only theatres; he explicitly noted that empirical proof of harm was not required.

Do *Paris Adult Theatre* and *Stanley* reflect a consistent position on obscenity questions? We can make a case for a heightened privacy right in the home, compared to a privacy right in a theatre that is open to all adults. Can other points of the *Stanley* and *Paris Adult Theatre* opinions be squared? If obscenity lacks social value, and therefore can be banned without leading to mind control (see p. 244), how can the *Stanley* majority maintain that prohibition of similar material in the home would be mind control? If any given obscene work is "worthless speech" when exhibited in a theatre, how does it become any less worthless when observed in the home? The claim that anti-obscenity laws are justified as a crime-fighting tool is similarly suspect. If the connection between exposure to obscene material and antisocial behavior is strong enough to justify censorship in theatres, would not the same risk come about when obscene matter is read in the home?

## CRITICAL THINKING ABOUT THE OBSCENITY ISSUE

The obscenity question has generated diverse viewpoints, above and beyond analysis and criticism of existing Supreme Court doctrine. Obscenity has been attacked by the political right on moral grounds, as well as by members of the left, on the basis that it constitutes discrimination against women. Both groups would agree that there is a sufficient link between obscene material and sex crimes to justify regulation of obscenity. Civil libertarians take an entirely different approach, contending that obscenity should not be exempted from the First Amendment and that the evidence linking obscenity to illegal action is weak. The final section of this chapter provides evidence offered by proponents of all three perspectives and lets you draw your own conclusions.

## The Conservative Viewpoint: Obscenity Is Immoral

A traditional line of argument, that obscenity may be regulated to protect the morals of society, was advanced by Anthony Comstock in the 1870s and continues to be used by conservative opponents of obscenity today. This rationale was held to be a sufficient justification for obscenity statutes in *Paris Adult Theatre*.[31]

Advocates of this viewpoint believe that the purpose of sex is procreation, and that gratification is a less defensible reason for engaging in the act, particularly if the partners are out of wedlock. It is argued that rules of behavior were laid down by God, and they do not change as society changes:

> What was wrong yesterday is still wrong today and will be wrong tomorrow. Prohibitions against homosexuality, adultery, and promiscuity in the

31. 413 U.S. at 57–60.

interest of preserving heterosexual fidelity, marriage, and the family reflect enduring and immutable values.[32]

From this perspective, ideas about promiscuity or infidelity should not be spread. They may prove too tempting to those who are exposed to them, and destroy moral values.[33]

Opponents of obscenity on the political right (as well as the left) would argue that there is a causal link between exposure to such materials and anti-social acts. One relatively recent document endorsing this viewpoint was the report of a commission headed by Ronald Reagan's attorney general, Edwin Meese.[34]

### Obscenity Is Violence Against Women

Another anti-obscenity approach focuses on the harms obscenity causes to women rather than the moral harm it causes society. Advocates of this proposition ordinarily use the term *pornography* (defined as sexually explicit material that is dehumanizing or degrading to women) rather than *obscenity* (as defined by the Supreme Court) to refer to the sexually explicit material that they find objectionable. Two spokespersons most commonly identified with this viewpoint are University of Michigan law professor Catharine Mac-Kinnon and author Andrea Dworkin.

Advocates of this viewpoint argue that pornography itself constitutes violence against women. According to Catharine MacKinnon:

> [O]ne can also say simply that pornography violates women. Perhaps this is what the woman had in mind who testified at our hearings. . . . "Porn is already a violent act against women. It is our mothers, our daughters, our sisters, and our wives that are for sale for pocket change at the newsstands in this country."[35]

This attack on pornography also maintains that there is a causal connection to sexual assaults. In Mills College sociology professor Diana Russell's model, for example, pornography is viewed as undermining males' internal inhibitions against acting out rape desires. She argues that pornography does this in many ways, such as objectifying women, so that males don't perceive them as human beings.[36] The Canadian case of *R. v. Wagner* also reached the conclusion that social harm does result "from repeated exposure to both violent pornography and non-violent dehumanizing pornography."[37]

---

32. Daniel Linz and Neil Malamuth, *Pornography*, p. 7 (Sage, 1993).
33. Id.
34. Department of Justice, *Attorney General's Commission on Pornography, Final Report* (Washington D.C., U.S. Government Printing Office, 1986).
35. Catharine A. MacKinnon, "Pornography, Civil Rights and Speech," in *Pornography: Women, Violence, and Civil Liberties*, p. 483 (Oxford Univ. Press, 1992).
36. Diana E. H. Russell, "Pornography and Rape: A Causal Model," in *Pornography: Women, Violence, and Civil Liberties*, p. 323.
37. James V. P. Check, "Legal Implications: A Canadian Perspective," id., p. 354.

Another key argument is that pornography causes men to believe that women are inferior, and promotes sexist attitudes and gender discrimination. Catharine MacKinnon argues that pornography eroticizes acts of dominance, such as rape, sexual harassment, and child sexual abuse. It makes hierarchy seem sexy, and "constructs what a woman is as what men want from sex."[38] Andrea Dworkin argues that pornography dehumanizes women by making them commodities to be bought and sold rather than human beings. The attitude that women are not fully human facilitates discrimination.[39]

The marketplace of ideas is viewed as an inadequate remedy to the harms of pornographic speech. It is argued that publishers and editors often refuse to print critiques of the unequal allocation of power between men and women, thereby denying equal access to the marketplace of ideas. Marketplace control dictates the result of the public debate, as there is no fair competition between rival perspectives on the gender inequality question.[40] Pornography also *silences* the cries of victims of sexual abuse by creating a false perception in society that women consent to—and even gain pleasure from—the abuse depicted in pornography.[41]

### The Civil Libertarian Perspective

Civil libertarians argue that obscenity deserves greater constitutional protection than the Supreme Court has afforded it. They contend that obscene works are not "worthless speech," deny the causal link between obscenity and adverse behavior or attitudes, and argue that obscenity laws will be abused to punish the speech of powerless members of society.

Is it correct to say that obscenity has no value in the marketplace of ideas? Justice Black in his dissent in *Ginzburg,* took exception to the assumption that communication about sex is worthless speech:

> Sex is a fact of life. Its pervasive influence is felt throughout the world and it cannot be ignored. . . . I would follow the course which I believe is required by the First Amendment, that is, recognize that sex at least as much as any other aspect of life is so much a part of our society that its discussion should not be made a crime.[42]  ◆◆◆

Nadine Strossen, president of the American Civil Liberties Union, argues that obscenity laws will be used to suppress speech with political connotations. She suggests that it is impossible to separate political and sexual speech, and cites the example of performing artists who were denied NEA grants because their works were alleged to be indecent or obscene. The work of these

---

38. MacKinnon, id., p. 461.
39. Andrea Dworkin, "Against the Male Flood," id., p. 527.
40. Catharine A. MacKinnon, *Only Words,* pp. 77–78 (Harvard Univ. Press, 1993).
41. See generally, id., pp. 4–10.
42. 383 U.S. at 481–82 (Black, J., dissenting).

artists addressed important social issues, such as domestic violence, homophobia, and sexism.[43] Ms. Strossen also emphasizes the fact that the subjective nature of the *Miller* test gives jurors considerable latitude to suppress speech simply because they are offended by its content. For example, white middle-class jurors may be turned off by erotic rap lyrics, and heterosexual jurors may be "grossed out" by Robert Mapplethorpe's gay erotica.[44]

Civil libertarians cite research that obscene material does not cause sex crimes. One major research effort, the 1970 Presidential Commission on Obscenity and Pornography, concluded that "on the basis of the available data . . . it is not possible to conclude that erotic material is a significant cause of crime."[45] More recent research can also be cited. For example, Berl Kutchinsky, a Senior Lecturer at the Institute of Criminal Science, University of Copenhagen, studied the incidence of rape in Denmark, Sweden, West Germany, and the United States, and concluded that there was no relationship between the availability of pornography and rape rate in the four countries.[46]

The claim that pornography breeds sexist attitudes has also been challenged. Strossen argues that the most significant causes of discrimination are factors such as sexist concepts of marriage, discrimination in education, and lack of day-care services. She contends that when pro-censorship feminists make the argument that pornography is a central cause of discrimination, it deflects attention from these more important causes of discrimination.[47]

In chapter 1, we noted that *even if certain speech did result in harm,* regulation may be unjustified because of the potential for abuse. In *American Booksellers Association, Inc. v. Hudnut,*[48] the Seventh Circuit Court of Appeals concluded that even if pornography caused sexist attitudes, it could not be censored. The court feared the implications of allowing the government to decide what speech could be censored on the grounds of falsity. In striking down an Indianapolis antipornography ordinance, which applied to the "sexually explicit subordination of women," the court concluded:

> [T]he Constitution does not make the dominance of truth a necessary condition for freedom of speech. To say that it does would be to confuse an outcome of free speech with a necessary condition for the application of [the First] [A]mendment. A power to limit speech on the ground that truth has not yet prevailed and is not likely to prevail implies the power to declare truth. At some point the government must be able to say (as Indianapolis has said): "We know what the truth is, yet a free exchange of speech has not driven out the falsity, so that we must now prohibit falsity."

43. Strossen, pp. 56–57.
44. Id., p. 55.
45. Presidential Commission on Obscenity and Pornography, *Technical Report of the Presidential Commission on Obscenity and Pornography,* p. 243 (U.S. Government Printing Office, 1970).
46. Linz and Malamuth, p. 33.
47. Strossen, pp. 266–67.
48. 771 F. 2d 323 (7th Cir., 1985).

> If the government may declare the truth, why wait for the failure of speech? Under the First Amendment, however, there is no such thing as a false idea. . . .

Civil libertarians have not convinced their opponents on the political left or right that obscene speech deserves protection. Obscenity is likely to remain a divisive moral issue in the United States.

### SUMMARY

In this chapter, we examined a significant categorical exception to the First Amendment: obscenity. The Supreme Court has viewed obscene speech as unnecessary in the marketplace of ideas because it lacks value as a step to the truth.

In the United States, obscene expression has been defined as that which appeals to a prurient or deviant interest in sex, perhaps owing to a lingering Victorian obsession over the issue. Courts have not defined the term in other ways (e.g., expression that glorifies female subordination or violence).

After sixteen years of struggling to find a workable definition of obscenity, the Court reached a definitional consensus in *Miller v. California*. Under *Miller*, the First Amendment does not protect speech that (1) appeals to the prurient interest (according to contemporary community standards) when taken as a whole, (2) depicts (in a patently offensive way) sexual conduct specifically defined by state law, and (3) lacks serious literary, artistic, political, or scientific value.

The Court perceived that the *Miller* test would restrict only what it called hard-core pornography. This "middle ground" test has not pleased either side in the obscenity debate. Civil libertarians argue that obscene speech should not be categorized as worthless. They contend that any harm created by obscene works is either negligible or impossible to legislate against without opening the floodgates of censorship. Opponents view obscenity either as a major contributor to the decline in moral values in society or a leading cause of sex discrimination. Both conservative and liberal critics argue that there is a causal relationship between obscenity and sex-related crimes. The Supreme Court may be standing alone in the middle of an ideological stream, with political currents pulling hard both to the left and to the right.

It is also debatable whether the *Miller* test can draw a bright line between hard-core and presumably less offensive obscenity. In a society where sexually oriented expression is increasingly evident, what is left of contemporary community standards? Is it possible to find some literary, artistic, political, or scientific value even in hard-core obscenity? This issue is complex, and we will revisit it when we consider government funding for the arts in chapter 12.

CHAPTER 10    *Objectives*

**After reading chapter 10, you**
**should understand the**
**following:**

◆ *How* time, place, or manner *rules emphasize limits on the* **context** *in which a message is delivered, rather than constraints on the* **content** *of a message.*

◆ *The* **evolution** *of time, place, or manner rules, beginning with the theory that government ownership of public property justifies government control of expression, and moving to the theory that public forums belong to the citizens, who may use them for communicating their ideas.*

◆ *The current* **doctrine** *for the constitutionality of time, place, and manner restrictions: that such laws must be narrowly tailored to serve a significant governmental interest and leave open alternative channels of communication.*

◆ *How time, place, or manner restrictions can be* **applied** *to the detriment of First Amendment values, including access to effective means of communication, government neutrality in the marketplace of ideas, and the communicator's autonomy to express him or herself as she or he believes would be best.*

◆ *The question of whether protection of expression in forums that have* **historically** *been open for public expression provides communicators with sufficient access to their target audience in modern society.*

◆ *How time, place, and manner rules have been employed in major* **social controversies** *such as Nazi marches and abortion protests.*

# 10 Time, Place, or Manner Restrictions

IN PREVIOUS CHAPTERS, we addressed the issue of freedom of speech by focusing on the content, meaning, or motivation behind the intended expression. Excluding the categorical exceptions—considered nonspeech for First Amendment purposes—we can generally say that restrictions aimed at expression because of its content, meaning, or motivation will be suspect. Suppose, however, that we shifted our focus, dealing less with content and more with context. As suggested in chapter 6, it is possible that people ascribe certain meanings to so-called fighting words, ranging from a friendly insult to an invitation to fight. We can analyze context in other ways, including the manner by which a message is expressed, when it is expressed—and most significantly, *where* it is expressed.

To see how free speech rights may vary depending on where they are exercised, we shall modify an oft-stated First Amendment hypothetical. Ann is sitting in her living room alone, watching a television war drama. On screen, a trio of attack jets descend upon an unsuspecting battleship captained by her favorite movie star. Suddenly, the screen displays the ship's guns trained on the jets, and Ann yells out, "Fire!" There is no question as to the meaning of *fire* here; but what if Ann had been a live observer at a standoff between armed police sharpshooters and kidnappers inside a diner? The definition of *fire* (discharge a weapon) is similar in both instances, but given the context, Ann's utterance of this word in the privacy of her home has far different implications from a similar exclamation amid the tension of an armed standoff. The context of "fire" has conditioned our acceptance or rejection of Ann's use of the word. Why? Because in the first example, Ann's utterance was made only for the benefit of her television and out of earshot of anyone else. More to the point, anyone watching Ann as she observed the television would not likely confuse her exclamation with anything else. In the second example, however, different things could motivate Ann's use of the word (perhaps she observed a fire in the diner's kitchen), but her expression would likely be interpreted in the context of the standoff, encouraging one or many of the participants of the event to discharge a weapon.

In consideration of societal interests such as public safety, the Supreme Court has allowed rules that might limit what we may say—not because of a message's *content* but because of its *context*. Rules that regulate when, where, and how a message is expressed are called **time, place, or manner restrictions**. Each component of context has a different meaning. *Time* can refer to the specific chronological date, time, or period when an utterance is made or events occur. *Place* refers to the forum or site of the expression; in plain terms, the location. *Manner*, conversely, refers to medium, the means by which the expression occurs, whether through expressive conduct, words, or the use of symbols.

In this chapter, we will examine time, place, or manner restrictions, beginning with their historical development (including the reasons why the Supreme Court has held that the First Amendment places limits on these regulations). Second, we will cover the traditional test for determining the constitutionality of such restrictions. Third, we will summarize the public forum theory, which has been used to determine the contexts in which these restrictions will be subject to judicial scrutiny. Finally, we will present cases dealing with significant time, place, or manner controversies.

## HISTORICAL DEVELOPMENT

The United States Supreme Court did not develop significant doctrine concerning *time, place, or manner* until the late 1930s. Before this time, governments were given a free hand to control expression on state and local public property. This philosophy was exemplified by the 1897 *Davis v. Massachusetts*[1] decision. *Davis* dealt with an attempt to preach in a public place—called the Boston Common—contravening a rule requiring a permit for such an occasion. The United States Supreme Court ruled against Davis, agreeing with the Massachusetts State Court's opinion that "for the legislature absolutely or conditionally to forbid public speaking in a highway or public park is no more an infringement of the rights of a member than for the owner of a private house to forbid it in his house."[2] The high Court added that the discretionary power for issuing permits "may be fairly claimed to be a mere administrative function vested in the mayor to effectuate the purpose for which the commons was maintained and by which its use was regulated."[3] The Supreme Court thus sided with the mayor and City of Boston, finding that the power to grant permits for speech in public places did not vest too much authority in the hands of government officials, with the great potential for abuse.

1. 167 U.S. 43 (1896).
2. See *Commonwealth v. Davis*, 140 Mass. 485.
3. 167 U.S. at 48.

*Davis* was good precedent for more than four decades, until the Supreme Court reconsidered the issue in the late 1930s. Then, a doctrine began to emerge from cases such as *Hague v. C. I. O.*,[4] *Schneider v. State*,[5] *Cantwell v. Connecticut*,[6] and *Cox v. State of New Hampshire*.[7] These cases were significant for two reasons: first, they represented a departure from the tradition of *Davis*, which had deferred to the authority of government to regulate expression in public places; second, in these cases could be found the roots for the present-day test for time, place, and manner restrictions.

In *Hague*, the Court reviewed the application of a New Jersey ordinance, which had been used to deny certain individuals (many of them in unincorporated labor organizations) the right to lease property for public meetings, on the grounds they were Communists or represented Communist organizations. The ordinance was also said to be used to prevent these individuals from distributing leaflets, handouts, newspapers, or books. Justice Roberts' opinion claimed not to overturn or invalidate the use of *Davis* in reviewing the New Jersey law, but effectively did so anyway. In rejecting the view that government title to property legitimized its control of expression on that property, the Court held that

> Wherever the title of streets and parks may rest, they have immemorially been held in trust for the use of the public and, time out of mind, have been used for purposes of assembly, communicating thoughts between citizens, and discussing public questions. Such use of the streets and public places has from ancient times, been a part of the privileges, immunities and liberties of citizens. The privilege of a citizen of the United States to use streets and parks for communication of views on national questions may be regulated in the interest of all; it is not absolute, but relative and must be exercised in subordination to the general comfort and convenience, and in consonance with peace and good order; but it must not, in the guise of regulation, be abridged or denied.[8]   ◆◆◆

The *Hague* opinion was sensitive to the fact that certain kinds of property have been important marketplaces of ideas throughout history. The Court left open the possibility that the government could regulate communication on public land but could not do so in a manner constituting an "arbitrary suppression of free expression."[9] The door for limiting and defining time, place, or manner restrictions had been opened.

The Court revisited this issue a few months later, as it decided the *Schneider* case. In *Schneider*, the justices reviewed four different cases that had been

4. 307 U.S. 496 (1939).
5. 308 U.S. 147 (1939).
6. 310 U.S. 296 (1940).
7. 312 U.S. 569 (1941).
8. 301 U.S. at 515–16.
9. Id. at 516.

consolidated for one opinion. Because all four dealt with the same issue,[10] the Court agreed to review them simultaneously. As you read Justice Roberts's opinion, decide whether the Court adequately preserved government neutrality in the marketplace of ideas.

### *Schneider v. State,* 308 U.S. 147 (1939)

Justice Roberts delivered the opinion of the Court:

. . . Municipal authorities, as trustees for the public, have the duty to keep the community's streets open and available for movement of people and property, the primary purpose to which the streets are dedicated. So long as legislation to this end does not abridge the constitutional liberty of one rightfully upon the street to impart information through speech or the distribution of literature, it may lawfully regulate the conduct of those using the streets. For example, a person could not exercise this liberty by taking his stand in the middle of a crowded street, contrary to traffic regulations, and maintain his position to the stoppage of all traffic; a group of distributors could not insist upon a constitutional right to form a cordon across the street and to allow no pedestrian to pass who did not accept a tendered leaflet; nor does the guarantee of freedom of speech or of the press deprive a municipality of power to enact regulations against throwing literature broadcast in the streets. . . .

In every case, therefore, where a legislative abridgement of the rights is asserted, the courts should be astute to examine the effect of a challenged legislation. Mere legislative preferences or belief respecting matters of public convenience may well support what regulation directed at other personal activities, but be insufficient to justify such as diminishes the exercise of rights so vital to the maintenance of democratic institutions. And so, as cases arise, the delicate and difficult task falls upon the courts to weight the circumstances and to appraise the substantiality of the reasons advanced in support of the regulation of the free enjoyment of the rights. . . .

The motive of the legislation under attack . . . is held by the courts below to be the prevention of littering of the streets. . . . We are of opinion that the purpose to keep the streets clean and of good appearance is insufficient to justify an ordinance which prohibits a person rightfully on a public street from handing literature to one willing to receive it. Any burden imposed upon the city authorities in cleaning and caring for the streets as an indirect consequence of such distribution results from a constitutional protection of the freedom of speech and press. This constitutional protection does not deprive a city of all power to prevent street littering. There are obvious methods of preventing littering. Amongst these is the punishment of those who actually throw papers on the streets. . . .

[T]he Irvington ordinance [one of the four municipal ordinances at issue in this case] . . . affects all those, who, like the petitioner, desire to impart informa-

---

10. All dealt with municipal ordinances for Los Angeles, Milwaukee, Worcester, and Irvington— that forbade distribution of literature on the street or other public places. Three of these ordinances purported to control "littering."

tion and opinion to citizens at their homes. . . . It bans unlicensed communication of any views or the advocacy of any cause from door-to-door, and prevents canvassing only subject to the power of a police officer to determine, as a censor, what literature may be distributed from house-to-house and who may distribute it. The applicant must submit to that officer's judgement evidence as to his good character and as to the absence of fraud in the "project" he purposes to promote or the literature he intends to distribute, and must undergo a burdensome and inquisitorial examination, including photographing and fingerprinting. In the end, his liberty to communicate with the residents of the town at their homes depends upon the exercise of the officer's discretion.

As said in *Lovell v. City of Griffin,* pamphlets have proved most effective instruments in the dissemination of opinion. And perhaps the most effective way of bringing them to a notice of individuals is the distribution at the homes of the people. On this method of communication the ordinance imposes censorship, abuse of which engendered the struggle in England, which eventuated in the establishment of the doctrine of the freedom of the press embodied in our Constitution. To require a censorship through license which makes impossible the free and unhampered distribution of pamphlets strikes at the very heart of the Constitutional guarantees.

Conceding that fraudulent appeals may be made in the name of charity and religion, we hold a municipality cannot, for this reason, require all who wish to disseminate ideas to present them first to police authorities for their consideration and approval, with the discretion in the police to say some ideas may, while others may not, be carried to the homes of citizens; some persons may, while others may not, disseminate information from house to house. Frauds may be denounced as offenses and punished by law. Trespasses may similarly be forbidden. If it is said that these means are less efficient and convenient than bestowal of power on police authorities to decide what information may be disseminated from house-to-house, and who may impart the information, the answer is that considerations of this source do not empower a municipality to abridge freedom of speech and press.

We are not to be taken as holding that commercial soliciting and canvassing may not be subjected to such regulation as the ordinance requires. Nor do we hold that the town may not fix reasonable hours when canvassing may be done by persons having such objects as a petitioner. Doubtless there are other features of such activities which may be regulated in the public interest without prior licensing or other invasion of constitutional liberty. . . . ◆◆◆

Whereas *Hague* was important for breaking with *Davis, Schneider* was pivotal in laying the foundation for the modern test of time, place, and manner restrictions. It did this in three ways. First, it implied in the closing paragraph that cities *could* regulate speech but that limitations must be *reasonable*. An ordinance banning all door-to-door canvassing between 10 P.M. and 8 A.M. may well be found reasonable, because many people sleep during this time, and solicitors would be allowed to bring their message to people's homes through-out the day. The reasonability criteria would lay the groundwork for what we would later term *reasonable* time, place, and manner restrictions.

Second, by arguing that prevention of littering was insufficient interest to justify suppression of speech, the Court was suggesting that only a more substantial interest could validate the rule. Third, and equally important, by suggesting there may be other means to prevent littering (such as arresting the litterer), the Court was beginning to develop a rule that is very important in modern civil liberties cases: that courts should evaluate whether the as-serted state interest could be advanced in a manner that places less burden on the constitutional right in question.

One year later in 1940, Justice Roberts wrote the majority opinion in *Cantwell v. Connecticut* and added new criteria for First Amendment challenges to time, place, and manner rules. The *Cantwell* case began when three Jeho-vah's Witnesses—Newton Cantwell and his sons, Jesse and Russell—were convicted for violating a Connecticut law prohibiting solicitation for alleged religious purposes without approval of the county secretary of public welfare. Reaffirming the right of any state or locality to regulate expression by reason-able time, place, and manner restrictions, Justice Roberts nevertheless re-versed the Cantwells' convictions. The Court was willing to recognize a valid state interest in preventing fraud from solicitation based upon religion, but clearly felt that this ordinance, which vested the decision to issue permits in the country secretary, would not accomplish this interest. Justice Roberts wrote:

> Nothing we have said is intended to even remotely imply that, under the cloak of religion, persons may, with impunity, commit frauds upon the public. Cer-tainly penal laws are available to punish such conduct. . . . Without a doubt a state may protect its citizens from fraudulent solicitation by requiring a stranger in the community, before permitting him publicly to solicit funds for any purpose, to es-tablish his identity and his authority to act for the cause which he purports to rep-resent. . . . But to condition the solicitation of aid for perpetuation of religious views or systems upon a license, the grant of which rests in the exercise of a deter-mination by state authority as to what is a religious cause, is to lay a forbidden bur-den upon the exercise of liberty protected by the Constitution.[11]  ◆◆◆

In this opinion, unlike the *Schneider* case, Roberts suggested that the state interest (preventing solicitation-based fraud) was valid and substantial, but the ordinance at issue was not drawn narrowly enough to achieve this goal, since it left a county secretary with limitless power to decide what is—or is not—a valid religious cause.

---

11. 310 U.S. at 306–07.

Cox v. New Hampshire[12] provided an example of the type of time, place, or manner restriction that would survive constitutional scrutiny. At issue was a parade by Jehovah's Witnesses down several sidewalks in the Manchester, New Hampshire, business district. The Jehovah's Witnesses were convicted because they had not obtained a license from their municipal board, as required by New Hampshire law. The case was appealed to the Supreme Court.

The Court upheld the constitutionality of the statute. After noting that there were valid justifications for requiring parade permits (for example, to avoid overlapping parades), Chief Justice Hughes argued that Manchester's procedure for allocating permits did not violate the First Amendment. The Chief Justice noted that cities "cannot be denied authority to give consideration, without unfair discrimination, to time, place, and manner in relation to the other proper uses of the streets."[13] In this case, there was no evidence that the ordinance had been administered in a discriminatory manner.

In Cox, the Court also held the city's license fee, which could range from $0 to $300, to be nondiscriminatory. The cost of policing different parades would vary, and it was reasonable to charge a fee proportional to the city's cost for the parade that had been licensed.

With these cases as a primary foundation, the roots for our present-day understanding of time, place, or manner restrictions would be set.

## THE MODERN TIME, PLACE, OR MANNER TEST

Today the Court employs a three-pronged test for determining the constitutionality of time, place, or manner restrictions that limit the use of public forums to disseminate messages. Although the roots for these prongs were suggested in the cases referenced above, it was not until the 1970s that the Court congealed these into one statement of the issue. Reasonable time, place, or manner restrictions will be upheld if

1. they are justified without reference to the content of the regulated speech;

2. they are narrowly tailored to serve a significant governmental interest; and

3. they leave open ample alternative channels for communication of the information.[14]

### What Constitutes a Reasonable Time, Place, or Manner Restriction?

An example of how the Court evaluates the reasonableness of such a regulation can be found in Justice Thurgood Marshall's (see Figure 10.1)

---

12. 312 U.S. 569 (1941).
13. Id. at 576.
14. See, e.g., Ward v. Rock Against Racism, 491 U.S. 781, 791 (1989).

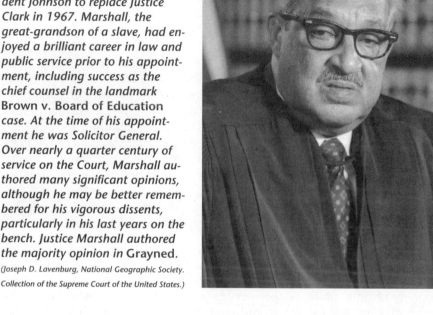

*Figure 10.1. Justice Thurgood Marshall was nominated by President Johnson to replace Justice Clark in 1967. Marshall, the great-grandson of a slave, had enjoyed a brilliant career in law and public service prior to his appointment, including success as the chief counsel in the landmark* **Brown v. Board of Education** *case. At the time of his appointment he was Solicitor General. Over nearly a quarter century of service on the Court, Marshall authored many significant opinions, although he may be better remembered for his vigorous dissents, particularly in his last years on the bench. Justice Marshall authored the majority opinion in* **Grayned.**

(Joseph D. Lavenburg, National Geographic Society. Collection of the Supreme Court of the United States.)

opinion in *Grayned v. City of Rockford*.[15] As you read this decision, decide whether you agree that Rockford's antinoise ordinance is reasonable. Near the end of the opinion, Justice Marshall also touches on each component of the three-prong test we have described.

### Grayned v. City of Rockford, 408 U.S. 104 (1971)

Mr. Justice Marshall delivered the opinion of the Court.

Appellant Richard Grayned was convicted for his part in a demonstration in front of West Senior High School in Rockford, Illinois. Negro students at the school had first presented their grievances to school administrators. When the principal took no action on crucial complaints, a more public demonstration of protest was planned. On April 25, 1969, approximately 200 people—students, their family members, and friends—gathered next to the school grounds. Appellant, whose brother and twin sisters were attending the school, was part of this group. The demonstrators marched around on a sidewalk about 100 feet from the school building, which was set back from the street. Many carried signs which summarized the grievances: "Black cheerleaders to cheer too"; "Black history with black

15. 408 U.S. 104 (1971).

teachers"; "Equal rights, Negro counselors." Others, without placards, made the "power to the people" sign with their upraised and clenched fists. . . .

After warning the demonstrators, the police arrested 40 of them, including appellant. For participating in the demonstration, Grayned was tried and convicted of violating two Rockford ordinances, hereinafter referred to as the "anti-picketing"[16] ordinance and the "antinoise" ordinance. . . .

The antinoise ordinance reads, in pertinent part, as follows:

> [N]o person, while in public or private grounds adjacent to any build-
> ing in which a school or any class thereof is in session, shall wilfully
> make or assist in the making of any noise or diversion which disturbs or
> tends to disturb the peace or good order of such school session or class
> thereof. . . .

. . . Although appellant does not claim that, as applied to him, the antinoise ordinance has punished protected expressive activity, he claims that the ordinance is overbroad on its face. Because overbroad laws, like vague ones, deter privileged activity, our cases firmly establish appellant's standing to raise an overbreadth challenge. The crucial question, then, is whether the ordinance sweeps within its prohibitions what may not be punished under the First and Fourteenth Amendments. Specifically, appellant contends that the Rockford ordinance unduly interferes with First and Fourteenth Amendment rights to picket on a public sidewalk near a school. We disagree. . . .

Clearly, government has no power to restrict such activity because of its message. Our cases make equally clear, however, that reasonable "time, place and manner" regulations may be necessary to further significant governmental interests, and are permitted. For example, two parades cannot march on the same street simultaneously, and government may allow only one. . . . A demonstration or parade on a large street during rush hour might put an intolerable burden on the essential flow of traffic, and for that reason could be prohibited. . . . If overamplified loudspeakers assault the citizenry, government may turn them down. . . .

The nature of a place, "the pattern of its normal activities, dictate the kinds of regulations of time, place, and manner that are reasonable." Although a silent vigil may not unduly interfere with a public library, . . . making a speech in the reading room almost certainly would. That same speech should be perfectly appropriate in a park. The crucial question is whether the manner of expression is basically incompatible with the normal activity of a particular place at a particular time. Our cases make clear that in assessing the reasonableness of a regulation, we must weigh heavily the fact that communication is involved; the regulation must be narrowly tailored to further the State's legitimate interest. Access to the "streets, sidewalks, parks, and other similar public places . . . for the purpose of exercising [First Amendment rights] cannot constitutionally be denied broadly. . . . " Free expression "must not, in the guise of regulation, be abridged or denied."

16. The Court held that the antipicketing ordinance was unconstitutional because it discriminated, based on the content of the message. We will focus on the Court's analysis of the antinoise ordinance, which addresses all three prongs of the time, place, or manner test.

In light of these general principles, we do not think that Rockford's ordinance is an unconstitutional regulation of activity around a school. . . .

We would be ignoring reality if we did not recognize that the public schools in a community are important institutions, and are often the focus of significant grievances. Without interfering with normal school activities, daytime picketing and handbilling on public grounds near a school can effectively publicize those grievances to pedestrians, school visitors, and deliverymen, as well as to teachers, administrators, and students. Some picketing to that end will be quiet and peaceful, and will in no way disturb the normal functioning of the school. For example, it would be highly unusual if the classic expressive gesture of the solitary picket disrupts anything related to the school, at least on a public sidewalk open to pedestrians. On the other hand, schools could hardly tolerate boisterous demonstrators who drown out classroom conversation, make studying impossible, block entrances, or incite children to leave the schoolhouse.

✳ Rockford's antinoise ordinance . . . is narrowly tailored to further Rockford's compelling interest in having an undisrupted school session conducive to the students' learning, and does not unnecessarily interfere with First Amendment rights. Far from having an impermissibly broad prophylactic ordinance, Rockford punishes only conduct which disrupts or is about to disrupt normal school activities. That decision is made, as it should be, on an individualized basis, given the particular fact situation. Peaceful picketing which does not interfere with the ordinary functioning of the school is permitted. And the ordinance gives no license to punish anyone because of what he is saying.

. . . Rockford's modest restricting on some peaceful picketing represents a considered and specific legislative judgment that some kinds of expressive activity should be restricted at a particular time and place, here in order to protect the schools. Such a reasonable regulation is not inconsistent with the First and Fourteenth Amendments.   ◆◆◆

In evaluating the reasonableness of any time, place, or manner restriction, Justice Marshall advocated a *basic incompatibility* test. To be reasonable, regulations must restrict expression that is not compatible with the normal activity of a given place at a given time. Because loud noises near campus disrupt the educational mission of a school, the Court found it reasonable to regulate noise while school was in session.

Although the three-pronged test for reasonable time, place, and manner rules is referenced in different places in the *Grayned* opinion, we can summarize them as follows. To decide the constitutionality of an ordinance, the Court must inspect to see if the ordinance is (a) content neutral and (b) narrowly drawn to serve or further a significant governmental interest, while (c) still leaving open adequate alternative channels for communication of information. How has the Court applied each of these three components of the test? Let us consider how each was used in *Grayned* and subsequent time, place, or manner decisions.

### Application of the Three-Pronged Time, Place, or Manner Test

*Is the Regulation Content Neutral?*    Content neutrality is the first prong of the test, primarily because a regulation's status as either content neutral or content based is key to determining the level of scrutiny the Supreme Court will employ in evaluating the constitutionality of the regulation. By content neutral, the Court means that the purpose or motivation behind the regulation is unrelated to the content of the restricted message. For example, the Rockford antinoise ordinance was found content neutral because it gave "no license to punish anyone because of what he is saying." Any noise that disturbed the peace was prohibited. *Content based* means that the purpose of the regulation is to restrict a certain message content. For example, in the *Schneider* decision, the Court was concerned with time, place, or manner ordinances allowing a city official to say that some *ideas* could be carried to the homes of citizens, while others could not. If the Rockford ordinance had allowed loud classical music to be played near campus while forbidding equally loud rap music, the rule would probably not have been found content neutral.

The justification for content neutrality in time, place, and manner cases is similar to the rationale of the hate speech cases you studied in chapter 7. The government should not abandon its neutrality in the marketplace of ideas. When the government allows a forum to be used for approved messages while denying use of the same forum for opposing views, it gives the favored idea an unfair advantage in the battle for public acceptance. Public property belongs to the public, not the government. If the First Amendment is to serve its historic role as a vehicle for dissent against the government, the government should not be able to give a public forum to supporters while taking that same forum away from critics.

*Is the Regulation Narrowly Tailored to Further a Substantial Governmental Interest?*    To understand this prong of the time, place, and manner test, we must ask three questions: (1) is the regulation *narrowly* tailored? (2) does it further or facilitate a government interest? and (3) is this government interest a significant or substantial one? Let us consider each of these in turn.

To determine whether a regulation is *narrowly* drawn, we see how closely a regulation comes to meeting its objective, while exerting the minimum impact on any rights of expression.

One test is the *least restrictive means* analysis. This questions whether the regulation or ordinance furthers government interest with the least possible restriction of expression. If other, less burdensome alternatives exist to further that interest, the Court could find the restriction not drawn narrowly enough. However, if the ordinance itself were the least restrictive means possible, it would satisfy this part of the analysis.

The *Schneider* case provides a good example of a least restrictive means analysis. As Justice Roberts wrote, "There are obvious methods of preventing littering. Amongst these is the punishment of those who actually throw papers on the streets." By suggesting an alternative (arresting litterers instead of preventing people from passing out leaflets), Roberts was suggesting that the city could meet the goal of preventing litter without having to suppress expression.

The Court has not been consistent in using a least restrictive means analysis to determine if a regulation is narrowly tailored. In some cases, the Court simply looked to the legislative history behind a rule, and, finding evidence that government had considered the ordinance to be the least restrictive means, simply deferred to the government.[17] In truth, the least restrictive means analysis has been called a subjective form of examination, which the Court could use to facilitate whatever conclusion it desired.[18]

The least restrictive means analysis was dealt a serious blow in *Ward v. Rock Against Racism*.[19] There, the Court noted,

Lest any confusion on the point remain, we reaffirm today that a regulation of the time, place or manner of protected speech must be narrowly tailored to serve the government's legitimate, content-neutral interests, but that it need not be the least restrictive or least intrusive means of doing so.[20]   ◆◆◆

Rather, suggested the Court, the test should be whether a "regulation promotes a significant government interest that would be achieved less effectively absent the regulation."[21] Thus, Justice Kennedy shifted the discussion of narrowness away from whether alternative policies would be less intrusive to expression, and instead asked if alternative regulations would achieve the interest *less effectively*.

The implication of *Ward* is that time, place, and manner restrictions will more likely be found narrowly tailored in the future. For example, suppose the *Ward* rationale had been employed in the *Schneider* antilittering ordinance case. The Court could easily have concluded that since keeping leaflet distributors off the streets would attack the litter problem at the source, a ban on passing out leaflets would be more effective than only banning recipients from throwing leaflets on the ground. From that premise, the Court could have reasoned that the ban on leaflet distribution was narrowly tailored.

Once a restriction is determined to be narrowly drawn, the next question is, does the ordinance further or facilitate a government interest? In many respects, this is a factual and not a normative question; it simply seeks to examine, on a factual basis, whether a restriction (*A*) furthers an interest (*B*). The logic here is compelling: if *A* does *not* further *B*, then regardless of however significant an interest *B* is, or how narrowly drawn *A* is, the ordi-

17. See, e.g., Justice Stevens' opinion in *Regan v. Time, Inc.* 468 U.S. 641, 696 (1984): "Congress' attempt to reconcile the competing interest . . . is entitled to great respect."
18. See, e.g., *Illinois State Bd. of Elections v. Socialist Workers Party*, 440 U.S. 173 (1979).
19. 491 U.S. 781 (1989).
20. Id. at 798.
21. Id. at 799.

nance cannot pass muster, since the restriction does not meet the need it was designed to solve.

This is the logic. However, in recent years, the Court has been less rigorous in its application of this portion of the test. In *Ward*, the Court reviewed a New York City rule governing the volume of amplified music from concerts held at Central Park's Naumberg Acoustic Bandshell. Justice Kennedy, writing for the Court, described the interest furthered by this rule:

> The principal justification for the sound-amplification guideline is the City's desire to control noise levels at bandshell events, in order to retain the character of the sheep meadow, and its more sedate activities, and to avoid undue intrusion into residential areas and other areas of the park.[22]   ◆◆◆

The rule in question required that any concert in the amphitheater use sound-amplification equipment and a sound technician provided by the City. In showing that the rule *furthered* the City's interest in noise control, Justice Kennedy declared,

> It is undeniable that the City's substantial interest in limiting sound volume is served in a direct and effective way by the requirement that the City's sound technician control the mixing board during performances. Absent this requirement, the City's interest would have been served less well, as is evidenced by the complaints about excessive volume generated by respondent's past concerts.[23]   ◆◆◆

Justice Kennedy calls this conclusion undeniable—but is it really? By looking only to see if noise complaints have decreased, he implies that any rule in New York City that achieved the same effectiveness of noise control might be acceptable. However, as Justice Marshall dissented in *Ward*, the "effectiveness rule" also robs the Court of ample analytical tools when free expression is threatened by the rule.[24] If other means are available—such as punishing someone for excessive noise—why would the City's rule necessarily further the interest in the most effective way?

Justice Kennedy's twist on the rule seems to answer these questions by suggesting that to meet the time, place, and manner test, the restriction need not be the most effective—or the only effective—means of furthering the interest; rather, it need merely be effective. Presumably, whether there are other means is irrelevant.

The final question implicated in the second prong of the time, place, and manner test is whether the government interest is *significant* or substantial.

22. Id. at 792.
23. Id. at 800.
24. Id. at 806 (Marshall, J., dissenting).

The idea behind this question is simple: It is not enough for government to further any whimsical or silly interest by restricting speech—the interest must be significant to justify this. This much is logical. However, the Court has been inconsistent in its criteria for measuring significance. Part of this uncertainty has been compounded by the fact that the Court has used different language to describe the required strength of the interest, including the terms *significant*,[25] *substantial*,[26] and even *legitimate*.[27] Although *significant* and *substantial* are similar, they do not *share* meaning—nor are they consonant with—*legitimate*. A government interest might be substantial but it might not be significant. The same is true for legitimacy. For example, if an ordinance proscribed the distribution of leaflets at a busy streetcorner in a city of 200,000 people, we might say that the city's size made its interest in controlling traffic substantial. But if leaflets were only given out on one streetcorner in a remote part of town, would the interest necessarily be significant? Would it be legitimate?

When the Court does not carefully consider the importance of the government interest furthered by a time, place, or manner restriction, its decision making process resembles the *ad hoc balancing* test described in chapter 1. Freedom of expression is not presumed to be a weightier interest than public order or public convenience. Instead, it can easily be trumped by an interest that is lower in the constitutional hierarchy, such as the right to a quiet day in the park.

*Are There Adequate Alternate Channels of Communication?*   The third and final prong of the test asks whether the restrictive law or ordinance leaves the speaker with any alternative forms of communication; in effect, if the restriction is imposed, is there any other way to effectively get one's message across? Historically, the Court has imposed this prong of the test because it believed that if the expression could be communicated in other contexts, time, place, or manner restrictions would not greatly burden freedom of speech.

If alternative channels of communication are effectively limited, the Court is more likely to find a restrictive ordinance unconstitutional. Conversely, if alternatives exist, the Court is less likely to find a restriction in violation of the First Amendment.

The problem with employing this form of analysis—particularly in the past decade—has been the Court's failure to account for two critical and relevant aspects of communication. First, merely suggesting that alternative modes of communication can still get a message out may not redress the serious diminution of speech suffered by imposition of a restrictive rule, because alternative modes may not necessarily be as effective as the proscribed mode.

25. 491 U.S. at 791.
26. Id. at 799.
27. Id. at 798.

For example, if a city were to impose a restriction against all public speeches at a busy intersection—but suggested that alternatives were available, since people could still engage in one-to-one conversations on the curbs of the same intersection—the reality of the alternative would not necessarily be adequate. A speaker can reach many more individuals—sometimes with greater efficiency and force—in a public address. Thus, even though the conversational option exists to "get the message out," it is not at all equal to the original mode.

Second, and equally compelling: Sometimes the mode itself has communicative or expressive value. As Marshall McCluhan's eponymous work of several decades ago suggested, the medium is the message.[28] This is particularly true when the mode or medium of communication has special symbolic value. In chapter 6, you read the *Cohen* decision, in which the Court held that the emotive content of words may be as important to the message as their cognitive content. Is the Court being consistent with the *Cohen* rationale when it assumes that words will have the same meaning regardless of the context in which they are delivered?

The case of *Clark v. Community for Creative Nonviolence* provides a good example of the latter point. *Clark* also provides an example of how the Rehnquist Court has applied the three prongs of the time, place, or manner test. The dissenting opinion, authored by Justice Marshall, challenges the prevailing application of the test. After you have read the two opinions, decide whether the National Park Service regulations at issue were a reasonable effort to preserve the unique purpose of national parks in urban Washington, D.C., or an unreasonable restriction on freedom of expression.

### The "Time, Place, or Manner" Test in Operation—*Clark v. CCNV.*

### *Clark, Secretary of the Interior, v. Community for Creative Non-Violence,* 468 U.S. 288 (1984)

Justice White delivered the opinion of the Court.

The issue in this case is whether a National Park Service regulation prohibiting camping in certain parks violates the First Amendment when applied to prohibit demonstrators from sleeping in Lafayette Park and the Mall in connection with a demonstration intended to call attention to the plight of the homeless. . . .

The Interior Department, through the National Park Service, is charged with responsibility for the management and maintenance of the National Parks and is authorized to promulgate rules and regulations for the use of the parks in accordance with the purposes for which they were established. . . . The network of National Parks includes the National Memorial-core parks, Lafayette Park and the Mall, which are set in the heart of Washington, D.C., and which are unique resources that the Federal Government holds in trust for the American people. . . .

28. See Marshall McCluhan & Quentin Fiore, *The Medium Is the Massage* (Bantam, 1967).

Lafayette Park . . . is a "garden park with a . . . formal landscaping of flowers and trees, with fountains, walks, and benches. . . . " The Mall is a stretch of land running westward from the Capitol to the Lincoln Memorial some two miles away. It includes the Washington Monument, a series of reflecting pools, trees, lawns, and other greenery. . . .

✱   Under the regulations involved in this case, camping in National Parks is permitted only in campgrounds designated for that purpose. . . . Demonstrations for the airing of views or grievances are permitted in the memorial-core parks, but for the most part only by Park Service permits. . . . Temporary structures may be erected for demonstration in Lafayette Park and the Mall for the purpose of demonstrating the plight of the homeless. The permit authorized the erection of two symbolic tent cities. . . . The Park Service, however, relying on the above regulations, specifically denied CCNV's request that demonstrators be permitted to sleep in the symbolic tents. . . .

We need not differ with the view of the Court of Appeals that overnight sleeping in connection with the demonstration is expressive conduct protected to some extent by the First Amendment. . . . [B]ut this assumption only begins the inquiry. Expression, whether oral or written or symbolized by conduct, is subject to reasonable time, place, or manner restrictions. We have often noted that restrictions of this kind are valid provided that they are justified without reference to the content of the regulated speech, that they are narrowly tailored to serve a significant governmental interest, and that they leave open ample alternative channels for communication of the information. . . .

The requirement that the regulation be content-neutral is clearly satisfied. The courts below accepted that view, and it is not disputed here that the prohibition on camping, and on sleeping specifically, is content-neutral, and is not being applied because of disagreement with the message presented.

Neither was the regulation faulted, nor could it be, on the ground that without overnight sleeping the plight of the homeless could not be communicated in other ways. The regulation otherwise left the demonstration intact, with its symbolic city, signs, and the presence of those who were willing to take their turns in a day-and-night vigil. Respondents do not suggest that there was, or is, any barrier to delivering to the media, or to the public by other means, the intended message concerning the plight of the homeless.

It is also apparent to us that the regulation narrowly focuses on the Government's substantial interest in maintaining the parks in the heart of our Capital in an attractive and intact condition, readily available to the millions of people who wish to see and enjoy them by their presence. To permit camping—using these areas as living accommodations—would be totally inimical to these purposes, as would be readily understood by those who have frequented the National Parks across the country and observed the unfortunate consequences of the activities of those who refuse to confine their camping to designated areas.

It is urged by respondents . . . that if the symbolic city of tents was to be permitted and if the demonstrators did not intend to cook, dig, or engage in aspects of camping other than sleeping, the incremental benefit to the parks could not justify the ban on sleeping, which was here an expressive activity said to enhance the message concerning the plight of the poor and homeless. We cannot agree. . . . Without a permit to sleep, it would be difficult to get the poor and homeless to participate or to be present at all. This much is apparent from the permit application filed by respondents: "Without the incentive of sleeping space or a hot meal, the homeless would not come to the site." . . . The sleeping ban, if enforced, would thus effectively limit the nature, extent, and duration of the demonstration and to that extent ease the pressure on the parks. . . .

We do not believe . . . that . . . the time, place, or manner decisions assign to the judiciary the authority to replace the Park Service as the manager of the nation's parks or endow the judiciary with the competence to judge how much protection of park lands is wise and how that level of conservation is to be attained. Accordingly, the judgment of the Court of Appeals [for CCNV] is reversed.   ◆◆◆

Justice Marshall, with whom Justice Brennan joins, dissenting.
✳  . . . The proper starting point for analysis of this case is a recognition that the activity in which respondents seek to engage—sleeping in a highly public place, outside, in the winter for the purpose of protesting homelessness—is symbolic speech protected by the First Amendment. . . .

In late autumn of 1982, respondents sought to begin their demonstration on a date full of ominous meaning to any homeless person: the first day of winter. Respondents were similarly purposeful in choosing demonstration sites. . . . missing from the majority's descriptions is any inkling that Lafayette Park and the Mall have served as the sites for some of the most rousing political demonstrations in the Nation's history. . . . [T]hese areas constitute, in the Government's words, "a fitting and powerful forum for political expression and political protest."

✳ The primary purpose for making *sleep* an integral part of the demonstration was "to re-enact the central reality of homelessness," and to impress upon public consciousness, in as dramatic a way as possible, that homelessness is a widespread problem, often ignored, that confronts its victims with life-threatening deprivations. As one of the homeless men seeking to demonstrate explained: "Sleeping in ✳ Lafayette Park or on the Mall, for me, is to show people that conditions are so poor for the homeless and poor in this city that we would actually sleep *outside* in the winter to get the point across." . . .

Although sleeping in the context of this case is symbolic speech protected by the First Amendment, it is nonetheless subject to reasonable time, place, and manner restrictions. . . .

According to the majority, the significant Government interest advanced by denying respondents' request to engage in sleep-speech is the interest in "maintaining the parks in the heart of our Capital in an attractive and intact condition readily available to the millions of people who wish to see and enjoy them by their presence." . . . That interest is indeed significant. However, neither the Government nor the majority adequately explains how prohibiting respondent's planned activity will substantially further that interest. . . .

The majority fails to offer any evidence indicating that the absence of an absolute ban on sleeping would present administrative problems to the Park Service that are substantially more difficult than those it ordinarily confronts. A mere apprehension of difficulties should not be enough to overcome the right to free expression. . . .

The majority cites no evidence indicating that sleeping engaged in as symbolic speech will cause *substantial* wear and tear on park property. Furthermore, the Government's application of the sleeping ban in the circumstances of this case is strikingly underinclusive. The majority acknowledges that a proper time, place, and manner restriction must be "narrowly tailored." Here, however, the tailoring requirement is virtually forsaken inasmuch as the Government offers no justification for applying its absolute ban on sleeping yet is willing to allow respondents to engage in activities—such as feigned sleeping—that [are] no less burdensome. . . .

The disposition of this case impels me to make two additional observations. First, in this case, as in some others involving time, place, and manner restrictions, the Court has dramatically lowered its scrutiny of governmental regulations once it has determined that such regulations are content-neutral. . . . By narrowly limiting its concern to whether a given regulation creates a content-based distinction, the Court has seemingly overlooked the fact that content-neutral restrictions are also capable of unnecessarily restricting protected expressive activity. The Court . . . has transformed the ban against content distinctions from a floor that offers all persons at least equal liberty under the First Amendment into a ceiling that restricts persons to the protection of the First Amendment equality—but nothing more. The consistent imposition of silence upon all may fulfill the dictates of an evenhanded content-neutrality. But it offends our "profound national commitment to the principle that debate on public issues should be uninhibited, robust, and wide open."

Second, the disposition of this case reveals a mistaken assumption regarding the motives and behavior of Government officials who create and administer content-neutral regulations. The Court's salutary skepticism of governmental decision making in First Amendment matters suddenly dissipates once it determines that a restriction is not content-based. The Court evidently assumes that the balance struck by officials is deserving of deference so long as it does not appear to be trained by content discrimination. What the Court fails to recognize is that public officials have strong incentives to overregulate even in the absence of an intent to censor particular views. This incentive stems from the fact that of the two groups whose interest officials must accommodate—on the one hand, the interests of the general public and, on the other, the interests of those who seek to use a particular forum for First Amendment activity—the political power of the former is likely to be far greater than that of the latter. . . .

For the foregoing reasons, I respectfully dissent.   ◆◆◆


In *Clark,* the Court encountered what the majority deemed a content-neutral restriction imposed on a restricted public forum. Justice White felt comfortable upholding the constitutionality of the Park Service regulations, since they appeared to be narrowly tailored to serve the government's interests in protecting the parks and making them available to all who wished to use them. The argument that the protesters had other alternatives—since the park rules prohibited only sleeping and camping—seems powerful and compelling. Justice White was correct in assuming that the protesters can still have their displays, still make speeches—and express their angst over the plight of the homeless.

But as Justice Marshall eloquently argued, the Court's insistence that alternatives existed ignored the symbolic value of a demonstration about homelessness in our nation's capital, with the seats of the rich and powerful government in the foreground. It also ignored the communicative value of the mode of expression—sleeping at night, on the first day of winter. The most common form of death for the homeless is exposure; and sleeping outside, exposed to the cold, is a powerful reminder of this message. Would an alternative all-night protest necessarily make the same point? Here, the medium was the message.

The *Clark* decision completes our discussion of the three-pronged test for time, place, or manner restrictions, but it does not complete our inquiry. A different question involves the identification of public forums. As the *Hague* decision explained, the places where access may not be denied are those *immemorially held in trust for purposes of public assembly*. How do courts determine which places are held in trust for the public? We will consider this question in the following section.

## THE FORUMS HELD IN TRUST FOR PUBLIC EXPRESSION

### Public Forums Defined by Historical Usage

The case of *U.S. v. Grace*[29] exemplifies traditional public forum analysis. Appellee Mary Grace stood on the sidewalk in front of the Supreme Court building in 1980, and displayed a large sign containing a verbatim text of the First Amendment. Two years earlier, appellee Thaddeus Zywicki had positioned himself in a similar location and distributed leaflets regarding the removal of unfit judges from the bench. Both Grace and Zywicki were told that federal law prohibited "the display [of] any flag, banner, or device designed or adapted to bring into public notice any party, organization, or movement"[30] in the U.S. Supreme Court building or on its grounds. They were warned that they would be arrested if they did not leave the grounds. Grace and Zywicki sued in federal court, seeking a judgment that the law in question was unconstitutional. The case was appealed to the Supreme Court.

29. 461 U.S. 171 (1983).
30. 40 *U.S. Code*, Section 13k.

## United States v. Grace, 461 U.S. 171 (1983)

Justice White delivered the opinion of the Court.

. . . There is no doubt that as a general matter peaceful picketing and leafleting are expressive activities involving "speech" protected by the First Amendment. . . .

It is also true that "public places" historically associated with the free exercise of expressive activities, such as streets, sidewalks, and parks, are considered, without more, to be "public forums. . . . " In such places, the government's ability to permissibly restrict expressive conduct is very limited: the government may enforce reasonable time, place, and manner regulations as long as the restrictions "are content-neutral, are narrowly tailored to serve a significant governmental interest, and leave open ample alternative channels of communication. . . . " Additional restrictions such as an absolute prohibition on a particular type of expression will be upheld only if narrowly drawn to accomplish a compelling governmental interest.

Publicly owned or operated property does not become a "public forum" simply because members of the public are permitted to come and go at will. . . . Although whether the property has been "generally opened to the public" is a factor to consider in determining whether the government has opened its property to the use of the people for communicative purposes, it is not determinative of the question. We have regularly rejected the assertion that people who wish "to propagandize protests or views have a constitutional right to do so whenever and however and wherever they please." . . . There is little doubt that in some circumstances the government may ban the entry [on to] public property that is not a "public forum" of all persons except those who have legitimate business on the premises. The government, "no less than a private owner of property, has the power to preserve the property under its control for the use to which it is lawfully dedicated." . . .

The prohibitions imposed by Section 13k technically cover the entire grounds of the Supreme Court. . . . That section describes the Court grounds as extending to the curb of each of the four streets enclosing the block on which the building is located. Included within this small geographical area, therefore, are not only the building, the plaza and surrounding promenade, lawn area, and steps, but also the sidewalks. The sidewalks comprising the outer boundaries of the Court grounds are indistinguishable from any other sidewalks in Washington, D.C., and we can discern no reason why they should be treated any differently. Sidewalks, of course, are among those areas of public property that traditionally have been held open to the public for expressive activities and are clearly within those areas of public property that may be considered, generally without further inquiry, to be public forum property. . . . Traditional public forum property occupies a special position in terms of First Amendment protection and will not lose its historically recognized character for the reason that it abuts government property that has been dedicated to a use other than as a forum for public expression. Nor may the government transform the character of the property by the expedient of including it within the statutory definition of what might be considered a nonpublic forum parcel of property. The public sidewalks forming the perimeter of the Supreme Court grounds, in our view, are public forums and should be treated as such for First Amendment purposes.  ◆◆◆

After establishing that the sidewalks were a public forum, Justice White applied the three-pronged test for time, place, or manner restrictions. He concluded that Section 13k was unconstitutional because it did not sufficiently serve the government's asserted interests, such as protecting the Court building and maintaining proper decorum in the Court.

### Is a Property's Historical Function the Best Criterion For Determining a Public Forum?

In *Grace*, Justice White determined the public forum status of the Supreme Court sidewalks by looking to the historical role of sidewalks. If sidewalks had not been a typical forum for public protest throughout our history, Section 13k would have been given a less exacting scrutiny, and the Court may well have deferred to the government's judgment that the regulation was necessary.

Why is it necessary that property be the *traditional* place for public communication before applying the three-pronged test? Communicators who are denied access to the place where they believe they can best disseminate their message can justifiably wonder why historical usage should be the deciding factor. Should the courts demand a better justification from the government than "historically this property has not been available for public expression" before regulations will be sustained?

Justice Marshall's analysis in *Grayned* provides an alternative approach for determining public forum status. He suggested that a reasonable restriction forbade only expression that was "basically incompatible with the normal activity of a particular place at a particular time."[31] If expression on public property is not incompatible with that property's regular use, the government should be forced to justify any restriction, even if that public property is not a historical forum.

California courts have held that the basic incompatibility test is required by the *California* constitution's free expression clause.[32] Thus, protesters were allowed to distribute antinuclear literature at the Lawrence Livermore Laboratory's visitor center, a facility run by the University of California. Far from concluding that the protesters' actions were incompatible with the purpose of the visitor center, the Court reasoned that the center should accommodate a

---

31. *See* p. 258.
32. "Every person may freely speak, write, and publish his or her sentiments on all subjects, being responsible for the abuse of this right. A law may not restrain or abridge liberty of speech or press." *Cal. Consti.*, Art. 1, Sec. 2.

meaningful exchange of views instead of only presenting the government line.[33] In another case, the California constitution was interpreted to allow the Prisoners Union (an organization concerned with the welfare of prisoners and their families) to set up a card table in the visitors' parking lot and distribute literature there.[34] Neither of these cases involved historical public forums, but a basic incompatibility analysis preserved the communicators' right to select an optimal forum to disseminate their message.

### TIME, PLACE, OR MANNER RULES: NOTEWORTHY CONTROVERSIES

Time, place, or manner restrictions have been imposed in a wide variety of communication contexts. Our goal in this chapter has been to focus on the rules for determining the constitutionality of such restrictions, rather than to report every federal lawsuit challenging these rules. Each professor will undoubtedly cover cases on the issues that he or she finds most salient. The final section of this chapter will highlight several of the more noteworthy controversies with respect to time, place, or manner regulations.

### The Nazi March in Skokie, Illinois

In 1977 the National Socialist Party of America (described by its leader, Frank Collin, as a Nazi party) planned to march in Skokie, Illinois. During their marches, the Nazis often wore uniforms reminiscent of those worn by German Nazis during the Third Reich, and displayed a swastika on their flags. As we mentioned in chapter 7, the population of Skokie was predominantly Jewish, and included several thousand survivors of Nazi atrocities. The Village of Skokie passed a parade ordinance, which required applicants to obtain $350,000 in insurance. It also required village officials to deny a permit if the assembly would "incite violence, hatred, abuse or hostility toward a person or group of persons by reason of reference to religious, racial, ethnic, national or regional affiliation."[35] Village officials also prohibited public demonstrations by members of political parties while wearing military style uniforms.[36]

In *Collin v. Smith*,[37] the Seventh Circuit Court of Appeals held that the Skokie ordinance violated the First Amendment. Judge Pell noted that the NSPA demonstration could be subjected to reasonable time, place, or manner restrictions. However, the Skokie regulations were not content neutral. The

---

33. *U.C. Nuclear Weapons Labs Conversion Project v. Lawrence Livermore Laboratory*, 201 Cal. Rptr. 837, 847 (Cal. App. 1st Dist. 1984).
34. *Prisoner's Union v. California Department of Corrections*, 185 Cal. Rptr. 634 (1982).
35. Village of Skokie, Ordinance No. 77-5-N-994, Section 27-56 (c).
36. Id., No. 77-5-N-996, Section 28.42.1.
37. 578 F.2d 1197 (7th Cir., 1978), *cert. den.* 439 U.S. 916 (1978).

village was attempting to limit the demonstration because it objected to the content of Nazi views and symbols.[38]

The Seventh Circuit recognized that the demonstration would be extremely disturbing to residents of Skokie, and also expressed the opinion that Nazi beliefs are repugnant to the values of most Americans. Nevertheless, the court employed a marketplace philosophy when it noted that even the identification "with a regime whose record of brutality and barbarism is unmatched in modern history" could not be considered a bad idea under the First Amendment.[39] The fact that we protect unpopular minorities from government harassment under our Constitution distinguishes the United States from the Third Reich.[40]

### Freedom of Speech in the Public Schools

Suppose the public land in question was used for the education of our young? In 1969, the Supreme Court ruled in favor of free speech rights for public school students in *Tinker v. Des Moines School District*.[41] *Tinker* involved the constitutionality of a policy by Des Moines school principals that prohibited students from wearing black armbands (which were understood to be a symbol of opposition to the Vietnam War). The Supreme Court held that the restriction was unconstitutional. Justice Fortas reasoned that teachers and students do not "shed their constitutional rights to freedom of speech or expression at the schoolhouse gate."[42] Consequently, where there is no proof that engaging in the forbidden conduct would "materially and substantially interfere with the requirements of appropriate discipline in the operations of the school," a restriction on speech could not be sustained.[43] In this case, there was no proof that a disruption would result if students wore armbands; hence the policy was unconstitutional.

The Supreme Court reached a different outcome seventeen years later in *Bethel School District v. Fraser*.[44] The expression at issue in this case was student Matthew Fraser's nominating speech for a student government candidate at a high school assembly. Mr. Fraser's address contained sexual innuendo,[45] and as a result he was suspended for three days and forbidden from speaking at graduation. The Supreme Court ruled that the school did not violate Fraser's First Amendment rights. Chief Justice Burger opined

---

38. Id. at 1201–02.
39. Id. at 1203.
40. Id. at 1201.
41. 393 U.S. 503 (1969).
42. Id. at 506.
43. Id. at 509.
44. 478 U.S. 675 (1986).
45. Id. at 687 (Brennan, J., concurring). Fraser's address included claims that the candidate is "firm in his pants," a man who will "take an issue and nail it to the wall," and "go to the very end—even the climax, for each and every one of you."

that "freedom to advocate unpopular and controversial views in schools and classrooms must be balanced against the society's countervailing interest in teaching students the boundaries of socially appropriate behavior."[46] Mr. Fraser's inappropriate behavior was deemed to include the use of offensive expressions in public debate and the glorification of male sexuality.

The *Fraser* opinion gave school officials additional tools for controlling student expression. *Tinker* allowed expression to be penalized if it resulted in a material and substantial disruption of school operations. Under *Fraser*, schools may also limit speech in the name of teaching the boundaries of socially appropriate behavior, even when such speech does not cause a disruption. The federal Court of Appeals, which heard the case (and held for Fraser) before it was appealed to the Supreme Court, feared that school officials would cement "white, middle-class standards for determining what is acceptable and proper speech and behavior in our public schools."[47] Regardless of the extent that you think school authorities *ought* to control student speech, it is clear that public schools are a *place* where speech can be controlled without proof of its imminent danger.

### Free Expression Rights of Abortion Protesters

Abortion rights have been a highly controversial subject in American political debate. Opponents of legalized abortion believe that the practice constitutes murder, while supporters believe that the right to choose (or decline) to have an abortion should be a fundamental freedom of every pregnant woman. Few Americans would question the First Amendment right of abortion protesters to argue that abortion is murder or to advocate a reduction in abortion rights. However, when loud and angry protests are directed to patients about to enter an abortion clinic, the question becomes more complicated. Can time, place, or manner restrictions be used to limit such protest without violating the First Amendment?

In *Madsen v. Women's Health Center, Inc.*,[48] the Supreme Court considered the constitutionality of a Florida state court injunction against abortion protesters. This injunction restrained the defendants (antiabortion groups such as Operation Rescue) from "congregating, picketing, patrolling, demonstrating or entering that portion of public right-of-way or private property within [36] feet of the property line of the [Women's Health Center],[49] a clinic where abortions are performed."

The Supreme Court held that the injunction was content neutral because it was directed at the *conduct* of the defendants (repeatedly violating court orders not to impede public access to the clinic), rather than at their

---

46. Id. at 681.
47. 755 F.2d 1356, 1363 (9th Cir. 1985).
48. 129 L.Ed. 2d 593 (1994).
49. Id. at 604.

antiabortion message.[50] But because a judicial injunction carried a particularly high risk of censorship, the Court imposed a more stringent standard than that imposed in typical time, place, or manner cases. The test was whether "the challenged provisions of the injunction burden no more speech than necessary to serve a significant government interest."[51]

The majority held that the injunction in question was constitutional because it met this more stringent test. Significant government interests included "a woman's freedom to seek lawful medical or counseling services in connection with her pregnancy" and "promoting the free flow of traffic on public streets and sidewalks."[52] The Court believed that a thirty-six-foot buffer zone to protect clinic access and maintain an orderly flow of traffic burdened no more speech than necessary.[53]

It may be difficult to consider the First Amendment implications of this case without reference to your position on the abortion issue. Nevertheless, the Court's reasoning transcends this particular controversy. People picket and protest a wide variety of enterprises. The same rule that limits abortion protest today can be used tomorrow to limit protests against a restaurant that practices racial discrimination. When you decide how the Court should rule in cases such as these, consider this fundamental question: To what extent should the First Amendment allow communicators to attempt to reach their target audience?

### Can the Government Require the *Inclusion* of an Organization in a Public Parade?

In the cases discussed so far in this chapter, the government has attempted to limit the ability of certain communicators to express their message. What if the government is attempting to compel the *inclusion* of an organization in a parade? A private association, the South Boston Allied War Veterans Council, had sponsored a St. Patrick's Day parade since 1947. In 1992, the Irish-American Gay, Lesbian, and Bisexual Group of Boston (GLIB) was denied the right to participate in the parade by the Veterans Council. The GLIB members, who were of Irish descent, wanted to express pride in their heritage. In 1993, the parade sponsor again refused to allow the GLIB to participate, prompting a lawsuit. A Massachusetts state court held that the Veterans Council violated a state law banning discrimination based on sexual orientation in a place of public accommodation.

But in *Hurley v. Irish-American Gay, Lesbian, and Bisexual Group of Boston,*[54] the Supreme Court held that this application of Massachusetts law violated

50. Id. at 606.
51. Id. at 608.
52. Id. at 609.
53. Id. at 611.
54. 132 L. Ed. 2d 487 (1995).

the parade sponsor's First Amendment rights. Writing for a unanimous Court, Justice Souter opined that in this case, the state law was being used to require the Veterans Council to alter the expressive content of their parade. Yet under the Constitution, "a speaker has the autonomy to choose the content of his own message."[55]

How did the Court view the rights of GLIB to gain access to the marketplace of ideas on a day that was significant to them as persons of Irish descent? Justice Souter did note that "GLIB presumably would have had a fair shot (under neutral criteria developed by the city) at obtaining a parade permit of its own."[56] The issue of Boston's criteria for awarding a parade permit was not before the Court; thus it is not known whether the city's rules would be found neutral. If both the Veterans Council and GLIB requested a parade permit for the same time and location on a future St. Patrick's Day, how would you decide who should receive a permit? This time, place, or manner question may be revisited by the Court at a later date.

### SUMMARY

Until the 1930s, the government had considerable power to control expression on public property. As exemplified by *Davis v. Massachusetts*, the government owned such property and could limit speech, much as a homeowner could on private property.

Beginning with the 1939 case of *Hague v. C.I.O.*, a new doctrine evolved. The Court recognized that certain types of public property had been used since time immemorial for public assembly and communication. In such *public forums*, the government could impose reasonable limitations on speech, but it could not forbid expression.

How is a restriction on the time, place, or manner of expression determined to be constitutional? The Court has established a three-pronged test to determine constitutionality, requiring that the regulation must be content neutral, be narrowly drawn to serve a significant governmental interest, and leave open adequate alternative channels for communication. In theory, this three-pronged test does not adversely affect the marketplace of ideas because viewpoints may be expressed in any context not covered by the regulation, and because the content neutrality rule prevents the government from favoring advocates on one side of an issue. However, as Justice Marshall's dissent in *Clark* (and our discussion of the three prongs of the time, place, or manner test) pointed out, the test is being interpreted to the detriment of dissident viewpoints.

Another issue in time, place, or manner cases is whether a limited definition of a public forum can narrow the options for effective communication.

55. Id. at 503.
56. Id. at 506

An analysis of whether the proposed expression is incompatible with the purpose of any given public property would benefit communicators more than a requirement that a public forum must be a place that has been used for public address and interaction.

As we have indicated in our analysis of the Nazi protest in Skokie, the unconventional expression by public school students, abortion protest, and the Boston St. Patrick's Day parade controversy, time, place, and manner issues touch on many vital public issues. The marketplace of ideas cannot remain truly free if courts grant too much deference to the government when reviewing these restrictions.

*Learning Objectives*

**After reading chapter 11, you should understand the following:**

◆ *The meaning of symbols in communication, and the fact that symbols are conveyed through verbal and nonverbal means.*

◆ *The diverse **methods** by which communicators have used nonverbal symbols to express their viewpoints on public issues.*

◆ *The **doctrine** of **symbolic speech**, which is used by the judiciary to determine when nonverbal expression will be protected by the First Amendment.*

◆ *The **differences** in the rules for First Amendment protection of symbolic speech and the rules protecting verbal expression.*

◆ *The **question** of whether the symbolic speech doctrine creates an optimal balance between the values of free expression and the government's interest in regulating symbolic conduct.*

◆ *The **controversy** over flag burning as an act of symbolic expression, and the relationship between argumentation on the constitutionality of flag burning and arguments on other free speech topics such as hate speech and obscenity.*

# 11 *Symbolic Expression and the First Amendment*

A CLOTHING MANUFACTURER has produced men's jockey shorts with the stars and stripes printed upon them, and marketed them with full-size highway billboard advertisements. Suppose a federal prosecutor elects to prosecute the manufacturer for degrading the United States Flag, in violation of federal law. Could such a prosecution pass constitutional muster? Before you answer, think about the flag for a moment; is it a special symbol of our country? If so, does it deserve a special kind of protection? Might other kinds of symbols merit special status—or restriction—by our government?

In previous chapters we discussed many cases in which verbal expression came into conflict with real or perceived societal interests, and the courts determined whether the expression was constitutionally protected. What happens, however, in a situation where the expression takes a *nonverbal* form? How is the First Amendment applied when the expression is derived from the symbolic meaning of some action or conduct—for example, the burning of an American flag?

Communicators have long recognized that actions can speak louder than words. The Boston Tea Party, which antedates the Bill of Rights, is an example of symbolic protest. Speech communication scholars also recognize the communicative power of nonverbal symbols.[1] When a message source uses such symbols to convey meaning, should we apply the same First Amendment rules that protect verbal expression?

This chapter will address symbolic speech or expression, terms that legal scholars often apply to nonverbal communication. In this chapter, you will read how the Supreme Court's acknowledgment of the communicative nature of actions has evolved. You will also study the principles that govern First Amendment protection of nonverbal expression, and see how they differ from the rules for verbal expres-

1. See, e.g., Mark Knapp, *Nonverbal Communication in Human Interaction* (Holt, 1978).

*Figure 11.1. In this photo a young man burns his selective service notification, a form of symbolic protest very common during the conflict in Vietnam.* (New York Times, October 17, 1969. (c) 1969 New York Times *Pictures. Reprinted by permission.*)

sion discussed up to this point in the text. The flag-burning controversy will be analyzed as an example of how symbolic speech doctrine is applied by the Court. Before studying these issues, however, it is worth reviewing how non-verbal symbols are an important part of communication (see Figure 11.1).

## NONVERBAL SYMBOLS AS COMMUNICATION

### What Are Symbols?

A dictionary might define a symbol as something taken or standing for something else, suggesting that the symbol can have more than one interpretation. For the purposes of expression, however, symbols are conceptually better understood when viewed in the context of their role in communication.

Communication between human beings involves the transmission of messages between *sources* and *receivers*.[2] Sources form messages and attempt to communicate them to others. When they transform their ideas and emotions

2. Communication may be more accurately characterized as an interaction in which both source and audience are engaged in sending and receiving messages. First Amendment analysis of symbolic speech is more consistent with a linear model of communication, however, as the cases you will study assume that one party to a communication transaction is the message source, while other people are message receivers.

into words, sounds, or actions, they are *encoding*. Receivers process those messages, attempting to react verbally and nonverbally to them. When receivers translate and transform these symbols into understandable ideas and feelings, they are *decoding* the message.

Symbols are key to this process, since they provide the means by which ideas or feelings can be expressed through words, sounds, or conduct. When we speak to others, we select certain words to convey certain meanings. However, the language we select only constitutes part of the message we communicate. Our nonverbal actions are likely to convey even more meaning to an audience.[3] Public speakers often use body movements such as gestures, eye contact, and facial expression to express themselves. Other common nonverbal codes include the use of space, physical appearance, touch, voice, time, and artifacts.[4] Artifacts are particularly common in symbolic political protest, and many of the cases you will study in this chapter involve this means of communication.

Symbols, thus, are the key to the way we communicate. Words themselves are symbols, as are nonverbal expressions. From the perspective of the Court and Constitution, however, "symbolic expression" has usually been used to refer only to the nonverbal form of expression described above.

### When Should Nonverbal Acts Be Classified as Expression?

Although an infinite variety of nonverbal conduct may be used to express meaning, it does not necessarily follow that all nonverbal conduct should be treated as expression for First Amendment purposes. A person may rob a bank, motivated only by a desire to obtain money. After the fact, she or he could claim that the robbery was a symbolic expression of protest against the bank's poor service, and thereby protected by freedom of speech. Unless every act is to be treated as speech, there must be criteria to use in determining when nonverbal conduct will fall under the scope of the First Amendment. Three factors that relate to whether conduct could be considered expression are intent, context, and relativity.

*Intent.* Does the person who employs a symbol intend for it to be interpreted in a particular way? If there is no such intent, the case for treating the act as communication is weak. What if a person conveys a symbolic meaning without *intending* to do so? For example, suppose you engage in nonverbal behavior such as walking on a sidewalk, intending only to go from point A to point B. This is against the law, but you do not know it; do you in your ignorance make a symbolic protest of this rule by walking on the sidewalk? Or, be-

3. See, e.g., Gary Cronkhite, *Communication and Awareness*, p. 295 (Cummings, 1976). "Most researchers agree that the nonverbal channels carry more social meaning than do the verbal channels"; and Ray L. Birdwhistell, *Introduction to Kinesics* (Univ. of Louisville Press, 1952). More than 700,000 signals can be sent through bodily movement.
4. Judee K. Burgoon, "Nonverbal Signals," in *Handbook of Interpersonal Communication*, pp. 349–50 (Sage, 1985).

fore your conduct should be considered symbolic, must you know this is unlawful and intend that observers will consider your act to be a protest? Some
speech communication theorists distinguish message behavior from nonmes-
sage behavior on the basis of intentionality,[5] others believe that all behavior is
communication if it is interpreted by someone in a meaningful way.[6] Since
some observers could perceive that almost any act is communicative,[7] the
issue of intent must be approached with caution or all action would be considered speech.

*Context.* Regardless of intent, nonverbal behavior may have different
consequences for symbolic value when considered in different contexts. For
our purposes, context here refers to both geography and chronology. To extend our earlier example: If you walk the street in the midst of many people,
the symbolic value of your action would be very different from a situation in
which you walked the same street quietly with others who carried signs
protesting working conditions at the factory on the corner. If you walked with
these people in their circular chain, never carrying a sign yourself, your action
might still have very different symbolic interpretation precisely because of the
context—your timing and location in relation to the activity.

*Relativity.* It may be argued that regardless of intention or context,
symbolic expression is still at best an amorphous act precisely because of its
relative effects; different people may see and interpret the same action in entirely different ways. Does nonverbal behavior require uniform interpretation
of some form of message to make the behavior "expression"? Historically, our
courts have not been clear about this. The way we, as receivers, interpret the
messages we receive is a relative consideration. Each of us may indeed look at
the same act and see things entirely differently.

Although the Supreme Court did not provide a definitive answer to the
questions of intent, context, and relativity, the justices began to acknowledge
the communicative power of nonverbal symbols in the 1930s and 1940s.
However, specific criteria for determining when symbolic expression would
receive First Amendment protection would not be formulated until the turbu-
lent 1960s.

5. Emmert and Emmert, *Interpersonal Communication* (William Brown Publishing, 1984) p. 47.
6. This viewpoint is described in Steven W. Littlejohn, *Theories of Human Communication*, pp. 5–7.
(Wadsworth, 1983).
7. Many theorists would maintain that one "cannot not communicate." See P. Watzlawick et al,
*Pragmatics of Human Communication* (W.W. Norton, 1967) pp. 212–14. But see Michael T. Motley,
*On Whether One Can (not) Not Communicate: An Examination Via Traditional Communication Postulates*,
54 Western Journal of Speech Communication (Winter 1990), 1, 18. Motley writes, "While it is
probably the case that there are no behaviors inherently irrelevant to communication, it remains
the case that there are behaviors which do not meet the conditions for classification as communication, at least according to certain traditional assumptions about communication.

## DIVERSE MEANS OF COMMUNICATION CAN BE THE EQUIVALENT OF SPEECH

The Supreme Court first noted the possibility that a nonverbal symbol could be the equivalent of speech in *Stromberg v. California*.[8] Yetta Stromberg was a supervisor at a Young Communist League summer camp. She directed the campers through a daily ritual in which a camp-made reproduction of the flag of Soviet Russia was raised. The children recited a pledge of allegiance to the workers' red flag. Stromberg was convicted of violating the California penal code, which provided that "any person who displays a red flag . . . as a sign, symbol or emblem of opposition to organized government . . . is guilty of a felony." The Supreme Court reversed the conviction because the statute was vague. The Court noted that any display of a red flag as a symbol of opposition to organized government could be punished, even if the message conveyed peaceful and orderly opposition to government by legal means. This reasoning implicitly recognized that the nonverbal act of flying a flag could communicate ideas about our government, even though the Court did not directly address the question of when the First Amendment protects communication through nonverbal symbols.

The Court directly held that nonverbal communication was a form of speech in *West Virginia State Board of Education v. Barnette*.[9] Marie and Gathie Barnette were Jehovah's Witnesses. The Witnesses' religious beliefs, based on a literal reading of Exodus 20:4–5, maintained that the flag salute constitutes worship of an idol.[10] A West Virginia Board of Education resolution required that schoolchildren salute the flag (a stiff arm salute, with the right hand raised and the palm turned up), and provided that failure to conform would result in expulsion. The expelled child could be treated as a delinquent, and the child's guardians could be jailed based on the child's enforced absence from school. The Barnettes sought an injunction restraining the enforcement of these laws against Jehovah's Witnesses.

In *Barnette*, the Court explicitly recognized that a symbol could serve the same function as a verbal message. The *Barnette* opinion is also important for three additional reasons. First, it recognized the First Amendment problems raised by communication that is compelled, rather than censored. Second, it afforded the Court an opportunity to vehemently denounce government compulsion of what to believe about topics such as politics, nationalism, and religion. This condemnation of government control has been a fundamental premise in many subsequent judicial opinions that ruled in favor of freedom of speech,[11] and it is a vital principle if free speech is to function as a vehicle

---

8. 283 U.S. 359 (1931).
9. 319 U.S. 624 (1943).
10. A 1935 speech by the American head of the Jehovah's Witnesses noted that "Witnesses do not 'Heil Hitler' or any other creature." *The Bill of Rights*, 14 Life 62 (Fall 1991).
11. See, e.g., *Texas v. Johnson*, 491 U.S. 397 (1989), quoted on p. 298, *infra*.

for democratic political change. Finally, the Court reinforced the principle that adding more speech to the marketplace of ideas is the preferred remedy for communication perceived to be dangerous.

### *Barnette v. West Virginia State Board of Education,* 319 U.S. 624 (1943)

Mr. Justice Jackson delivered the opinion of the Court:

. . . There is no doubt that, in connection with the pledge, the flag salute is a form of utterance. Symbolism is a primitive but effective way of communicating ideas. The use of an emblem or flag to symbolize some system, idea, institution, or personality, is a short cut from mind to mind. . . .

Over a decade ago, Chief Justice Hughes led this Court in holding that the display of a red flag as a symbol of opposition by peaceful and legal means to organized government was protected by the free speech guarantees of the Constitution. . . . Here it is the State that employs a flag as a symbol of adherence to government as presently organized. It requires the individual to communicate by word and sign his acceptance of the political ideas it.thus bespeaks. Objection to this form of communication *when coerced* is an old one, well known to the framers of the Bill of Rights (emphasis added). . . .

It is now a commonplace that censorship or suppression of expression of opinion is tolerated by our Constitution only when the expression presents a clear and present danger of action of a kind the State is empowered to prevent and punish. It would seem that involuntary affirmation could be commanded only on even more immediate and urgent grounds than silence. But here the power of compulsion is invoked without any allegation that remaining passive during a flag salute creates a clear and present danger that would justify an effort even to muffle expression. . . .

It was said that the flag-salute controversy confronted the Court with "the problem which Lincoln cast in a memorable dilemma: 'Must a government of necessity be too strong for the liberties of its people or too weak to maintain its own existence?'" . . . It may be doubted whether Mr. Lincoln would have thought that the strength of government to maintain itself would be impressively vindicated by our confirming power of the state to expel a handful of children from school. . . .

Government of limited power need not be anemic government. Assurance that rights are secure tends to diminish fear and jealousy of strong government, and by making us feel safe to live under it makes for its better support. Without promise of a limiting Bill of Rights it is doubtful if our Constitution could have mustered enough strength to enable its ratification. To enforce those rights today is not to choose weak government over strong government. It is only to adhere as a means of strength to individual freedom of mind in preference to officially disciplined uniformity for which history indicates a disappointing and disastrous end. . . .

National unity as an end which officials may foster by persuasion and example is not in question. The problem is whether under our Constitution compulsion as here employed is a permissible means for its achievement.

Struggles to coerce uniformity of sentiment in support of some end thought essential to their time and country have been waged by many good as well as by evil men. . . . As first and moderate methods to attain unity have failed, those bent on its accomplishment must resort to an ever increasing severity. As governmental pressure toward unity becomes greater, so strife becomes more bitter as to whose unity it shall be. . . . Ultimate futility of such attempts to compel coherence is the lesson of every such effort from the Roman drive to stamp out Christianity as a disturber of its pagan unity, the Inquisition, as a means to religious and dynastic unity, the Siberian exiles as a means to Russian unity, down to the fast failings of our present totalitarian enemies. Those who begin coercive elimination of dissent soon find themselves exterminating dissenters. Compulsory unification of opinion achieves only the unanimity of the graveyard.

It seems trite but necessary to say that the First Amendment to our Constitution was designed to avoid these ends by avoiding these beginnings. There is no mysticism in the American concept of the State or of the nature of the origin of its authority. We set up government by consent of the governed, and the Bill of Rights denies those in power any legal opportunity to coerce that consent. Authority here is to be controlled by public opinion, not public opinion by authority. . . .

[F]reedom to differ is not limited to things that do not matter very much. That would be a mere shadow of freedom. The test of its substance is the right to differ as to things that touch the heart of the existing order.

*If there is any fixed star in our constitutional constellation, it is that no official, high or petty can prescribe what shall be orthodox in politics, nationalism, religion, or other matters of opinion, or force citizens to confess by word or act their faith therein*[12] (emphasis added). . . . ◆◆◆

The controversies of the 1960s provided the Court with further opportunity to recognize symbolic nonverbal acts as expression. *Brown v. Louisiana*[13] involved a case against five African Americans who entered a segregated library in Louisiana and silently waited for fifteen minutes. They refused to leave when the sheriff asked them to, and they were convicted for breach of the peace. Justice Fortas's plurality opinion noted that "we need not assume that petitioner Brown and his friends were in search of a book for night reading. We instead rest on the manifest fact that they intended to and did stage a demonstration, with no intent to provoke a breach of the peace."[14] The opinion held that First Amendment rights are not confined to verbal expression. They include appropriate types of action and certainly include the right to

---

12. Justice Jackson's statement that no government official may prescribe what is acceptable in politics, nationalism, religion, or other matters of conscience has served as a rationale against regulation of expression in a variety of contexts. See, e.g., *Texas v. Johnson* (this chapter), *American Booksellers Assn. v. Hudnut* (chapter 9), and *Doe v. University of Michigan* (chapter 7).
13. 383 U.S. 131 (1966).
14. Id. at 139–40.

peacefully protest the unconstitutional segregation of public facilities in a place where the protesters had every legal right to be.

Protest against the Vietnam War was the backdrop in the case of *Tinker v. Des Moines School District*.[15] Mary Beth Tinker, John Tinker, and Christopher Eckhardt wore black armbands to school in protest of American policy in Vietnam. The principals of Des Moines' public schools had adopted a policy that any student wearing an armband to school would be asked to remove it; refusal would mean suspension. The students were sent home until they were willing to come back without the armbands. The Supreme Court found no justification for the Des Moines restriction. The majority noted that wearing an armband for the purpose of expressing views is closely akin to pure speech, which is entitled to comprehensive protection under the First Amendment. Where there is "no showing that the forbidden conduct would materially and substantially interfere with the requirements of appropriate discipline," the restriction on expression could not be sustained.

*Stromberg, Barnette, Brown,* and *Tinker* were important cases because the Court recognized that specific nonverbal symbols could constitute speech for purposes of the First Amendment. But the doctrine of "symbolic speech" (the common phrase used in the legal field to denote nonverbal conduct that may have a communicative element) was far from developed. One unsettled question was what criteria should be used to determine when nonverbal action constituted speech. A second was what test(s) should be used to determine when conduct will be protected by the First Amendment, if such action is classified as expression. The next section of this chapter will discuss these questions.

## THE COURT DEVELOPS A DOCTRINE OF SYMBOLIC EXPRESSION

### A Definition of Expressive Conduct Premised on Source-Receiver Understanding

*The Court's Expressive Conduct Test.* *Spence v. Washington*[16] considered the right of a college student to hang an upside-down American flag from the window of his apartment, with a peace symbol made of black tape attached to the flag. The student, Spence, was convicted under a Washington statute prohibiting improper use of the U.S. flag.[17] He argued that his action, which occurred shortly after American forces had invaded Cambodia and four students had been killed during a protest at Kent State University, conveyed the message that the American flag should be associated with peace rather than war and violence.

15. 393 U.S. 503 (1969). The *Tinker* case is also significant because it established a standard for analyzing when constitutional rights could not be denied to students. (See chapter 10).
16. 418 U.S. 405 (1974).
17. "No person shall . . . expose to public view any . . . [U.S. or Washington State] flag . . . to which shall have been attached, appended, affixed or annexed any such word, figure, mark, picture, design, drawing, or advertisement . . ." (*Washington Rev. Code* 9.86.0101, *Id.* at 407).

In *Spence*, the Supreme Court held that this conduct was expressive because there was an "intent to convey a particularized message," and "in the surrounding circumstances the likelihood was great that the message would be understood by those who viewed it."[18] In the context of intense public concern over the Cambodian incursion and the Kent State tragedy, the Court noted that "it would have been difficult for the great majority of citizens to miss the drift of [Spence's] point at the time that he made it."[19] Because Spence's act was protected expression, and there was no proof that any valid state interest was impaired by his display, the conviction was overturned.

**Implications of the Court's Expressive Conduct Test.** In *Spence* the Court used the concepts of intent, context, and relativity to fashion a rule to determine when conduct would be considered expressive. First, intentionality is a necessary condition for expressive conduct. The communicator must intend to convey a particularized message. Second, the context in which a symbol is used helps determine whether the symbol constitutes expression. Finally, if the message's meaning is highly relative, it will not constitute expression. The receivers of the message must be likely to correctly decode the source's intended message. The Court reasoned that in 1971, shortly after Cambodia and Kent State, the message would be understood, whereas by 1974, Spence's flag may have been interpreted as nothing more than bizarre behavior.[20]

The *Spence* definition was not the most expansive conception of nonverbal communication that could have been selected. Because intentionality is required, when the actor does not intend to convey a specific message through his or her action, it will be unprotected—even if the action has great meaning to observers. For example, suppose that outside an abortion clinic, a protester is silently praying for abortions to stop and a patient ignores a crowd of antiabortion protesters and marches into the clinic. If the protester or the patient do not intend to communicate a particular message to others by their actions, their conduct would not likely be deemed expressive, even if the acts were very inspirational to some observers.

In most symbolic expression cases that have reached the Supreme Court, the issue of whether conduct constitutes expression has not been the decisive factor. Often (as in the *O'Brien* case you will read in this chapter) the Court assumes for purpose of argument that the challenged conduct is expression. In a leading flag-burning case,[21] the state of Texas conceded that this action was expressive.

By contrast, an example of how the *Spence* criteria can operate to restrict communication is found in the Second Circuit Court of Appeals decision in *Young v. New York City Transit Authority*.[22] In *Young*, the Second Circuit rejected

18. Id. at 410–11.
19. Id. at 410.
20. Id.
21. *Texas v. Johnson*, p. 298 of this chapter.
22. 903 F. 2d 146 (2nd Cir. 1990), *cert. den.* 111 S.Ct. 516 (1990).

the claim that begging or panhandling in the New York City subways constitutes expressive conduct. Relying on *Spence*, the court held that begging was not intertwined with a particularized social or political message. Even if a person asking for money intended this action to communicate a concept such as "government benefits are inadequate" or "I am homeless," the court opined that there was no great likelihood that subway passengers would discern the particularized message.[23] Your opinion of the Second Circuit's decision will probably depend on your feelings about the purpose of the First Amendment. The *Young* holding denies some of the poorer members of society access to the means of effective communication. Conversely, it can be argued that the privacy rights of subway commuters should entitle them not to be approached by persons asking for money.

Even when the communicator can prove that his or her actions were symbolic expression, a second hurdle remains before the expression will be protected. As Justice Holmes's "fire in a theatre" example reminds us, free speech rights are not absolute, and other government interests may outweigh the First Amendment. When communication occurs through expressive conduct, does it receive the same protection as verbal expression? That question was resolved in another case involving symbolic protest against the Vietnam War.

## The Test for Constitutional Protection of Symbolic Expression

The doctrine of symbolic speech protection was established in the seminal decision provided in *U.S. v. O'Brien*,[24] a case involving a popular form of Vietnam War protest, the burning of draft registration certificates.

### United States v. O'Brien, 391 U.S. 367 (1968)

Mr. Chief Justice Warren (see Figure 11.2) delivered the opinion of the Court (see Figure 11.3):

On the morning of March 31, 1966, David Paul O'Brien and three companions burned their Selective Service registration certificates on the steps of the South Boston Courthouse. A sizable crowd, including several agents of the Federal Bureau of Investigation, witnessed the event. . . .

For this act, O'Brien was indicted, tried, convicted, and sentenced in the United States District Court for the District of Massachusetts. He did not contest the fact that he had burned the certificate. He stated in argument to the jury that he burned the certificate publicly to influence others to adopt his antiwar beliefs, as he put it, "so that other people would reevaluate their positions with Selective Service, with the armed forces, and reevaluate their place in the culture of today, to hopefully consider my position." . . .

23. Id. at 153–54.
24. 391 U.S. 367 (1968).

*Figure 11.2. Chief Justice Earl Warren was nominated to the high Court by President Eisenhower. Warren had been a successful district attorney and a somewhat conservative Governor of California. When Eisenhower nominated Warren, he had no idea how judicially active the Chief Justice and the "Warren Court" would come to be. Warren's strength was seen in his leadership, demonstrated in his shepherding of the Court through numerous cases, which literally rewrote the law on a number of Constitutional issues, including Freedom of Speech. Yet for his activism, his majority-authored opinion in* United States v. O'Brien *struck many as overly deferential to the government and the military.* (Robert S. Oakes, National Geographic Society. Collection of the Supreme Court of the United States.)

[In 1965, Congress amended a 1948 law[25] prohibiting many different abuses involving selective service registration certificates. The provision here at issue creates criminal liability not only for one who "forges, alters, or in any manner changes" but also one who "knowingly destroys, [or] knowingly mutilates" a certificate.] We note at the outset that the 1965 Amendment plainly does not abridge free speech on its face, and we do not understand O'Brien to argue otherwise. [The amendment,] on its face deals with conduct having no connection with speech. It prohibits the knowing destruction of certificates issued by the Selective Service System, and there is nothing necessarily expressive about such conduct. . . .

O'Brien first argues that the 1965 Amendment is unconstitutional as applied to him because his act of burning his registration certificate was protected "symbolic speech" within the First Amendment. His argument is that the freedom of expression which the First Amendment guarantees includes all modes of "communication of ideas by conduct," and that his conduct is within this definition because he did it in "demonstration against the war and against the draft."

25. 62 *Stat.* 604. The 1965 Amendment prohibiting destruction of a registration certificate, which was at issue in this case, is found in Section 12(b) (3) of the Act.

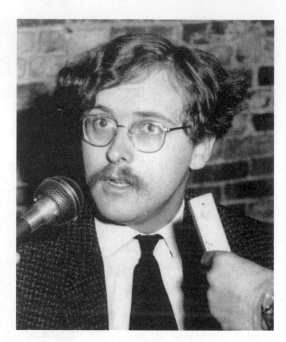

*Figure 11.3. David P. O'Brien is shown talking to reporters just after the Supreme Court announced its decision in his case.* (Associated Press/World Wide Photo. May 27, 1968. Reprinted by permission.)

We cannot accept the view that an apparently limitless variety of conduct can be labeled "speech" whenever the person engaging in the conduct intends thereby to express an idea. However, even on the assumption that the alleged communicative element in O'Brien's conduct is sufficient to bring into play the First Amendment, it does not necessarily follow that the destruction of a registration certificate is constitutionally protected activity. This Court has held that when "speech" and "nonspeech" elements are combined in the same course of conduct, a sufficiently important governmental interest in regulating the nonspeech element can justify incidental limitations on First Amendment freedoms. To characterize the quality of the governmental interest which must appear, the Court has employed a variety of descriptive terms: compelling; substantial; subordinating; paramount; cogent; strong. Whatever imprecision inheres in these terms, we think it clear that *a government regulation is sufficiently justified if it is within the constitutional power of the Government; if it furthers an important and substantial government interest; if the governmental interest is unrelated to the suppression of free expression; and if the incidental restriction on alleged First Amendment freedoms is no greater than is essential to the furtherance of that interest* (emphasis added). We find that the 1965 Amendment to Section 12 (b) (3) of the Universal Military Training and Service Act meets all of these requirements, and consequently that O'Brien can be constitutionally convicted for violating it.

The constitutional power of Congress to raise and support armies and to make all laws necessary and proper to that end is broad and sweeping. . . . The power of Congress to classify and conscript manpower for military service is "beyond question. . . . " Pursuant to this power, Congress may establish a system of registration for individuals liable for training and service, and may require such individuals within reason to cooperate in the registration system. . . .

. . . Many of [the purposes of the registration certificate] would be defeated by the certificates' destruction or mutilation. Among these are:

1. The registration certificate serves as proof that the individual described thereon has registered for the draft. . . . [T]he availability of the certificates for such display relieves the Selective Service System of the administrative burden it would otherwise have in verifying the registration and classification of all suspected delinquents.

2. The information supplied on the certificates facilitates communication between registrants and local boards. . . . [E]ach certificate bears the address of the registrant's local board, an item unlikely to be committed to memory. Further, each card bears the registrant's Selective Service number, and a registrant who has his number readily available so that he can communicate it to his local board when he supplies or requests information can make simpler the board's task in locating his file.

3. Both certificates carry continual reminders that the registrant must notify his local board of any change of address, and other specified changes in his status. The smooth functioning of the system requires that local boards be continually aware of the status and whereabouts of registrants. . . .

4. The regulatory scheme involving Selective Service certificates includes clearly valid prohibitions against the alteration, forgery, or similar deceptive misuse of certificates. The destruction or mutilation of certificates obviously increases the difficulty of detecting and tracing abuses such as these. Further, a mutilated certificate might itself be used for deceptive purposes. . . .

We think it apparent that the continuing availability to each registrant of his Selective Service certificates substantially furthers the smooth and proper functioning of the system that Congress has established to raise armies. We think it also apparent that the Nation has a vital interest in having a system for raising armies that functions with maximum efficiency and is capable of easily and quickly responding to continually changing circumstances. For these reasons, the Government has a substantial interest in assuring the continuing availability of issued Selective Service certificates.

It is equally clear that the 1965 Amendment specifically protects this substantial governmental interest. We perceive no alternative means that would more precisely and narrowly assure the continuing availability of issued Selective Service certificates than a law which prohibits their wilful mutilation or destruction. . . . The

1965 Amendment prohibits such conduct and does nothing more. In other words, both the governmental interest and the operation of the 1965 Amendment are limited to the noncommunicative aspect of O'Brien's conduct. The governmental interest and the scope of the 1965 Amendment are limited to preventing harm to the smooth and efficient functioning of the Selective Service System. When O'Brien deliberately rendered unavailable his registration certificate, he wilfully frustrated this governmental interest. For this noncommunicative impact of his conduct, and for nothing else, he was convicted. . . . ◆◆◆

The Court's test for constitutional protection of symbolic speech has been in place—and never seriously challenged or modified—since 1968. A government regulation that restricts symbolic expression will be justified if (a) it is within the constitutional power of government; (b) if it furthers an important or significant government interest; (c) if the government interest is unrelated to the suppression of free expression; and (d) if the incidental restriction is no greater than is necessary to further the interest.

Each part of this test must be met—although at times the Court has appeared more interested in one than another. Parts (a) and (b) question whether the government's restriction is within its lawful power and in pursuit of some kind of important interest. It would appear that the Court routinely glosses over (a), but looks very carefully at (b). A problem for the Court, however, has been its occasional difficulty with identifying exactly what the state interest is. *Barnes v. Glen Theatre, Inc.,*[26] dealing with the regulation of establishments featuring nude dancing, is a case in point. In *Barnes,* the constitutionality of an Indiana statute proscribing nudity was called into question. Justice Rehnquist wrote: "It is impossible to discern, other than from the text of the statute, exactly what governmental interest the Indiana legislators had in mind when they enacted this statute. . . . "[27] Later the Court presumed that interest to be one of "protecting social order and morality. . . . "[28]

Once an interest is identified, that interest "trumps" freedom of expression. The Court does not ask whether the benefits achieved by the regulation are worth the cost, in terms of diminished free speech. As long as the regulation is unrelated to the suppression of expression (in other words, if it is content neutral), it meets part (c) of the *O'Brien* test, even if it has the effect of restricting the communication of ideas.

On the question of content neutrality, the Court has often been deferential to the government. For example, in the *Clark* case, examined in the previous chapter on time, place, or manner restrictions, a key issue concerned whether "sleeping" in Lafayette Park or the Mall was symbolic expression that

26. 111 S.Ct. 2456 (1991).
27. Id. at 2461.
28. Id. at 2462.

might be protected by the First Amendment. The majority opinion held that the alleged purpose and interest served by the Park Service's regulations was the preservation of the parks for all—a seemingly neutral state interest. As Justice Marshall's dissent explored, however, doing so ignored the greater contextual significance of a demonstration over homelessness featuring sleeping in the park. The protest occurred on the first day of winter, with the White House in the background, during a time when the Administration was blamed for insensitivity over homelessness. Is it really so clear that the regulation was content neutral? If a particular symbolic act becomes a popular means of protesting a government action, and the government bans that act in all contexts, the ban is ostensibly content neutral. But there is little likelihood that a communicator would sleep in a cold park to demonstrate *opposition* to homeless people or burn a draft card to *support* a war. Cannot ostensibly neutral regulations be used to stifle popular means of protest?

The final part of the *O'Brien* test mandates that the restriction must be no greater than is necessary to advance or further the government interest. In theory this makes good sense—but in practice, the Court hasn't always been as concerned with this as with, say, determining the existence of an underlying state interest. Even in *O'Brien*, this part of the test is given only cursory treatment. How important to Congress's ability to raise and support armies was continued possession of registration certificates? If O'Brien was drafted, it was his lawful obligation to report. The absence of a certificate would not relieve him from liability if he failed to respond to a draft notice. The American public was highly divided on the desirability of a draft during the Vietnam era, and a volunteer army replaced the draft. To have a capable armed force, was it necessary to stifle a highly visible symbol of protest on such an important issue? Or would punishment of those who failed to report when they were drafted achieve the government's end?

None of the preceding is intended to suggest that the *O'Brien* test is not followed by the Court today; quite to the contrary, it is. The point is that application of the test depends on the given case and symbolic expression. To see this, let us examine how the Court treated a noteworthy symbol and a controversial form of symbolic expression.

### THE CONFLICT BETWEEN FREE EXPRESSION AND PRESERVATION OF A TREASURED NATIONAL SYMBOL

### The Symbolic Importance of the American Flag

Throughout history, flags have been used to convey deeply held feelings. The Colonial-era "Don't Tread on Me" flag, depicting a snake poised to attack, showed American defiance. The flag of the rebellious California Republic bore the image of a grizzly bear,[29] whose reputation for ferocity was legendary.

---

29. James L. Brown, *Dissension in Arcady—the Bear Flag Revolt* (Academy Press, 1978) pp. 5–10.

Today, the Mexican flag is prominently displayed during rallies in support of the rights of Mexican-Americans and undocumented immigrants from Mexico.

The American flag has always held a special place in the hearts of many patriotic citizens. The U.S. national anthem tells the story of the American flag at Fort McHenry in Baltimore: Neither flag nor fort could be destroyed by the British during the War of 1812. Another powerful image is the picture of U.S. Marines raising the flag on Mount Suribachi, Iwo Jima, after many American soldiers had died in the assault on this strategic position in World War II. In 1988, Vice President Bush made Governor Dukakis's veto of a Pledge of Allegiance bill in Massachusetts a significant campaign issue. As President, Mr. Bush pushed for a constitutional amendment to ban flag desecration; this amendment enjoyed widespread support by the American public.

How better, then, to communicate a disdain for the government than to destroy one of its most treasured symbols? Burning the American flag is far more likely to gain attention to a speaker's message than speaking on a streetcorner.

The flag-burning question goes to the heart of government neutrality in the marketplace of ideas. The use of the flag to convey patriotic messages is typical. Flags were flown in support of the wars in Vietnam and the Persian Gulf. During the Iran hostage crisis, a popular poster showed two Iwo Jima Marines mounting the flag in the Ayatolla's behind.[30] Such uses of the flag are never challenged. The question is whether communicative uses of the American flag which are not viewed as patriotic by a majority of Americans are also protected by the First Amendment. The issue has often been difficult for the Court to agree on, and one that the Court has sometimes been content to avoid. The remainder of this section will trace the history of the Court's reasoning in flag desecration cases. As you read the decisions, notice the Court's use of alternative legal doctrines that sidestep the free expression issues. When the Court finally confronts the question head-on in *Texas v. Johnson*, look for what test the Court uses to balance the competing interests of free speech and preservation of a national symbol. Ask yourself if the Court adhered to its precedents in resolving this controversial issue.

### The Supreme Court and the American Flag, 1907–82

The strong feelings of a majority of the American public for their flag were reflected in the fact that every state at one time had a statute prohibiting flag desecration. In addition, Congress enacted a federal flag desecration law.[31] Convictions under several of these statutes were reviewed by the Supreme Court between 1907 and 1982. Although some of these convictions were reversed, none of the statutes were declared unconstitutional, and the extent to which the flag could be used for symbolic communication was never delineated.

---

30. Karal Ann Marling and John Wetenhall, *Iwo Jima* (Cambridge, Mass.: Harvard University Press, 1991), p. 207.
31. Former 18 U.S.C. 700(a) prohibited "knowingly cast[ing] contempt upon any flag of the United States by publicly mutilating, defacing, defiling, burning, or trampling upon it." This law was revised when Congress passed the Flag Protection Act of 1989. See *U.S. v. Eichman*, p. 11–55, *infra*.

In the 1907 case of *Halter v. Nebraska*,[32] the Supreme Court upheld a conviction under a Nebraska flag desecration law that prohibited, among other things, printing or placing a representation of the U.S. flag on merchandise for the purpose of advertising. The defendants in *Halter* were prosecuted because they were selling beer with a representation of the flag on the bottle. Although state laws were not subject to review on freedom of speech grounds until the *Gitlow* decision eighteen years later, the defendants had argued that the law infringed their personal liberty.

The multifaceted reasoning employed by the Court to uphold the conviction in *Halter* is worth reviewing because it is so different from that employed by any modern Supreme Court justice. First was the fact that many of the states had similar statutes, and the Court would pause before concluding that a majority of the states had violated the Constitution. Second, a law would not be held unconstitutional unless it was manifestly so. Finally, the Court discussed the importance of the flag as a symbol of the American republic. The Court did not simply conclude that Nebraska's flag desecration law was permissible. The majority opinion went one step further and suggested that "it may reasonably be affirmed that a *duty* rests upon each state in every legal way to encourage its people to love the Union" (emphasis added).

The Supreme Court first heard a flag-burning case in *Street v. New York*.[33] After civil rights leader James Meredith had been shot by a sniper in Mississippi, Sidney Street took his American flag to the intersection of St. James Place and Lafayette Avenue in Brooklyn. There he set fire to the flag and dropped it to the pavement. About thirty persons were on the corner near the flag. Street testified that he said, "If they let that happen to Meredith we don't need an American flag." He was convicted for violating Section 1725 (16) (d) of the New York law that made it a misdemeanor "publicly [to] mutilate, deface, defile, or defy, trample upon, or cast contempt upon either by words or act [any flag of the United States]."

New York Civil Liberties Union lawyers representing Street asked the Court to find that flag burning was protected symbolic expression, but the case was resolved on a technical issue. The Court noted that the law made it illegal to show contempt for the flag by words or act. After examining the trial record, the Justices could not be certain whether the trial judge found Street guilty based on his speech about the flag, the burning of the flag, or both. Because freedom to express publicly one's opinions about our flag is protected by the First Amendment, and Street may have been found guilty of contemptuous speech about the flag, the conviction was reversed on a 5-4 decision. The Court noted that the proper procedure would have been to indict Street on two separate counts and for the judge to return separate verdicts on each count.

The *Street* majority's decision not to rule on the constitutionality of flag burning may appear to be based on a desire to avoid taking a stand on a controversial issue. Some commentators have made similar allegations about the

32. 205 U.S. 34 (1907).
33. 394 U.S. 576 (1969).

Rehnquist Court's decisions, which chip away at abortion rights rather than reversing *Roe v. Wade*. Justice Harlan's opinion in *Street* explained that "We resist the pulls to decide the constitutional issues involved in this case on a broader basis than the record before us imperatively requires." In other words, because the Court could reverse Street's conviction on a technical issue, there was no need to reverse the conviction on the much more general basis that all flag burning as means of protest is protected expression. This decision is consistent with traditional canons of judicial decision making, which favor avoiding constitutional questions when they are not necessary to the resolution of a case.

An interesting aspect of *Street* is the fact that some of the dissenters were among the Court's more liberal justices. They included justices Warren, Black, and Fortas, who each wrote their own dissent. The Warren Court has been characterized as the most liberal Court in American history, and yet Chief Justice Warren himself noted: "I believe that the States and the Federal Government do have the power to protect the flag from acts of desecration and disgrace." When reading the flag-burning decisions of the Rehnquist Court later in this chapter, it is worth asking if that Court also failed to divide into traditional ideological blocs.

The Chief Justice's dissent also took the Court to task for avoiding the constitutional issue. He accused the majority of searching "microscopically" for the opportunity to decide the case on a peripheral ground when the trial record left no doubt that Street was convicted solely for burning the American flag. Justice Warren noted that the American flag was increasingly becoming an integral part of public protests, and that those who protest and those who enforce the law are entitled to know whether flag burning is constitutional.

*Smith v. Goguen*[34] was another flag misuse case that was not decided on First Amendment grounds. Defendant Goguen wore a four-by-six-inch version of the American flag sewn to the seat of his blue jeans on a public street in Leominster, Massachusetts. Goguen was talking with a group of persons, and unlike Street, did not appear to be engaged in any protest. When a police officer questioned Goguen about his choice of apparel, some of the other persons laughed. Goguen did not take the witness stand in this case, and his motivation for wearing the flag was unknown. He was convicted for violating a Massachusetts law that provided for the punishment of whoever publicly treats contemptuously the flag of the United States.

The Court again explicitly declined to base its decision on First Amendment grounds. Instead, the statute was declared void because it was too vague. The phrase "treats contemptuously" was held too indefinite to adequately warn citizens of forbidden conduct. In addition, the phrase gave so little guidance that the police, court, and jury would be free to react to nothing more than their own preferences for treatment of the flag. The decision was good news for Mr. Goguen, who did not need to return to the Massachusetts House of Corrections. However, the holding left open the question of whether

---

34. 415 U.S. 566 (1974).

a more precise statute could be used to convict other people whose wardrobe included an American flag.

The Supreme Court denied certiorari in a 1982 flag-burning case, *Kime v. United States*.[35] Teresa Kime had set an American flag on fire during a demonstration protesting the prosecution of a leader of her political party. She and Donald Bonwell were convicted for casting contempt on a flag of the United States by publicly burning it,[36] and sentenced to eight months in jail. A federal district court and the Fourth Circuit Court of Appeals both affirmed the conviction. The Supreme Court denied the defendant's petition for certiorari, and therefore did not hear an appeal of the case. No reasons for the Court's decision were given.

Justice Brennan wrote a dissenting opinion maintaining that the Court should have heard the case, because it was highly likely that precedents such as *Spence*, *O'Brien*, and *Barnette* would mandate a reversal of the convictions. Brennan argued that the statute was a content-based censorship of ideas. The only conduct that was punished was that which stated a contemptuous political message about the flag.[37]

Justice Brennan's lone dissent was insufficient to protect the rights of Kime and Bonwell. As you read the next case, however, you will see how the rationale of a solitary justice can come to be embraced by a majority of the Court in later cases.

### TEXAS V. JOHNSON—THE FIRST AMENDMENT QUESTION IS FINALLY ANSWERED

#### The *Texas v. Johnson* Decision

Gregory Johnson participated in a political demonstration called the "Republican War Chest Tour," which coincided with the 1984 Republican national convention in Dallas. The demonstrators marched through the Dallas streets chanting political slogans. During the course of the march, Johnson was handed an American flag, which had been taken from a flagpole outside an office building. In front of Dallas City Hall, Johnson unfurled the flag, doused it with kerosene, and set it on fire. As the flag burned, the demonstrators chanted, "America, the red, white, and blue, we spit on you." Witnesses testified that they had been offended by the burning, but no injuries were inflicted or threatened.

Johnson was convicted for violating the Texas Penal Code, which prohibited the desecration of a venerated object. He was sentenced to one year in prison and fined $2,000. After the case was heard by two Texas appellate courts, the U.S. Supreme Court granted certiorari. As you read the Court's decision, look for

35. 456 U.S. 949 (1982).
36. Id. The federal statute in question prohibited "knowingly cast[ing] contempt upon any flag of the United States by publicly mutilating, defacing, defiling, burning, or trampling on it."
37. Id. at 956 (Brennan, J., dissenting).

the reason why the majority declined to use the test articulated in *O'Brien*, even though flag burning is conduct imbued with elements of communication. The Court's conclusions that the statute could not be justified as a means to prevent breaches of the peace or as a means to promote the flag as a symbol of our nation invokes many of the leading First Amendment cases discussed in this text.[38] Did the Court correctly apply these precedents, or were you more persuaded by the dissent's analysis about the unique nature of the American flag?

### *Texas v. Johnson*, 109 S. Ct. 2533 (1989)

Mr. Justice Brennan delivered the opinion of the Court.

. . . The First Amendment literally forbids the abridgment only of "speech," but we have long recognized that its protection does not end at the spoken or written word. While we have rejected "the view that an apparently limitless variety of conduct can be labeled 'speech' whenever the person engaging in the conduct intends thereby to express an idea" (*U.S. v. O'Brien*), we have acknowledged that conduct may be "sufficiently imbued with elements of communication to fall within the scope of the First and Fourteenth Amendments" (*Spence v. Washington*). . . .

The State of Texas conceded for purposes of its oral argument in this case that Johnson's conduct was expressive conduct. . . . Johnson burned an American flag as part—indeed as the culmination—of a political demonstration that coincided with the convening of the Republican Party and its renomination of Ronald Reagan for President. . . . At his trial, Johnson explained his reasons for burning the flag as follows: "The American Flag was burned as Ronald Reagan was being renominated as President. And a more powerful statement of symbolic speech, whether you agree with it or not, couldn't have been made at that time. . . ."

The government generally has a freer hand in restricting expressive conduct than it has in restricting the written or spoken word. . . . It may not, however, proscribe particular conduct because it has expressive elements. What might be termed the more generalized guarantee of freedom of expression makes the communicative nature of conduct an inadequate basis for singling out that conduct for proscription. A law directed at the communicative nature of conduct must, like a law directed at speech itself, be justified by the substantial showing of need that the First Amendment requires. . . . It is, in short, not simply the verbal or nonverbal nature of the expression, but the governmental interest at stake, that helps to determine whether a restriction on that expression is valid. . . .

In order to decide whether *O'Brien*'s test applies here, therefore, we must decide whether Johnson's conviction is unrelated to the suppression of expression. . . . The State offers two separate interests to justify this conviction: preventing breaches of the peace and preserving the flag as a symbol of nationhood and national unity. We hold that the first interest is not implicated on this record and that the second is related to the suppression of expression.

---

38. See, e.g., *Brandenburg v. Ohio, Terminiello v. Chicago,* and *West Virginia Board of Education v. Barnette, supra.*

Texas claims that its interest in preventing breaches of the peace justifies Johnson's conviction for flag desecration. However, no disturbance of the peace actually occurred or threatened to occur because of Johnson's burning of the flag. . . . To accept Texas' arguments that it need only demonstrate "the potential for breach of the peace," and that every flag burning necessarily possesses that potential, would be to eviscerate our holding in *Brandenburg*. This we decline to do. . . .

It remains to consider whether the State's interest in preserving the flag as a symbol of nationhood and national unity justifies Johnson's conviction. As in *Spence*, "[w]e are confronted with a case of prosecution for the expression of an idea through activity," and "[a]ccordingly, we must examine with particular care the interests advanced by [Texas] to support its prosecution." Johnson was not, we add, prosecuted for the expression of just any idea; he was prosecuted for his expression of dissatisfaction with the policies of this country, expression situated at the core of our First Amendment values. . . .

Texas argues that its interest in preserving the flag as a symbol of nationhood and national unity survives this close analysis. . . . According to Texas, if one physically treats the flag in a way that would tend to cast doubt on either the idea that nationhood and national unity are the flag's referents or that national unity actually exists, the message conveyed thereby is a harmful one and therefore may be prohibited.

If there is a bedrock principle underlying the First Amendment, it is that the government may not prohibit the expression of an idea simply because society finds the idea itself offensive or disagreeable. . . . We have not recognized an exception to this principle even where our flag has been involved. In *Street v. New York*, we held that a State may not criminally punish a person for uttering words critical of the flag. . . .

In holding in *Barnette* that the Constitution did not leave this course open to the government, Justice Jackson described one of our society's defining principles in words deserving of their frequent repetition: "*If there is any fixed star in our constitutional constellation, it is that no official, high or petty, can prescribe what shall be orthodox in politics, nationalism, religion, or other matters of opinion* (emphasis added). . . .

If we were to hold that a State may forbid flag burning wherever it is likely to endanger the flag's symbolic role, but allow it whenever burning a flag promotes that role—as where, for example, a person ceremoniously burns a dirty flag . . . we would be permitting a state to "prescribe what shall be orthodox." . . .

There is, moreover, no indication—either in the text of the Constitution or in our cases interpreting it—that a separate judicial category exists for the American flag alone. Indeed, we would not be surprised to learn that the persons who framed our Constitution and wrote the Amendment that we now construe were not known for their reverence for the Union Jack. The First Amendment does not guarantee that other concepts virtually sacred to our Nation as a whole—such as the principle that discrimination on the basis of race is odious and destructive—will go unquestioned in the marketplace of ideas. . . .

We are fortified in today's conclusion by our conviction that forbidding criminal punishment for conduct such as Johnson's will not endanger the special role played by our flag or the feelings it inspires. . . . Our decision is a reaffirmation of the principles of freedom and inclusiveness that the flag best reflects, and of the conviction that our toleration of criticism such as Johnson's is a sign and source of our strength. . . .

The way to preserve the flag's special role is not to punish those who feel differently about these matters. . . . We can imagine no more appropriate response to burning a flag than waving one's own, no better way to counter a flag burner's message than by saluting the flag that burns, no surer means of preserving the dignity even of the flag that burned than by—as one witness here did—according the remains a respectful burial. We do not consecrate the flag by punishing its desecration, for in doing so we dilute the freedom that this cherished emblem represents.  ◆◆◆

Chief Justice Rehnquist, with whom Justice White and Justice O'Connor join, dissenting.

. . . For more than 200 years, the American flag has occupied a unique position as the symbol of our Nation, a uniqueness that justifies a governmental prohibition against flag burning in the way respondent Johnson did here. At the time of the American Revolution, the flag served to unify the Thirteen Colonies at home, while obtaining recognition of national sovereignty abroad. . . . During the War of 1812 . . . [while] waiting anxiously on [a British warship], [Francis Scott] Key watched the British fleet firing on Fort McHenry. Finally, at daybreak, he saw the fort's American flag still flying; the British attack had failed. Intensely moved, he began to scribble on the back of an envelope the poem that became our national anthem. . . .

In the first and second world wars, thousands of our countrymen died on foreign soil fighting for the American cause. At Iwo Jima in the Second World War, U.S. Marines fought hand to hand against thousands of Japanese. By the time the Marines reached the top of Mount Suribachi, they raised a piece of pipe upright and from one end fluttered a flag. That ascent had cost nearly 6,000 American lives. . . .

The American flag, then, throughout more than 200 years of our history, has come to be the visible symbol embodying our Nation. It does not represent the views of any particular political party, and it does not represent any particular political philosophy. The flag is not simply another "idea" or "point of view" competing for recognition in the marketplace of ideas. Millions and millions of Americans regard it with an almost mystical reverence regardless of what sort of social, political, or philosophical beliefs they may have. . . .

But the Court insists that the Texas statute prohibiting the public burning of the American flag infringes on respondent Johnson's freedom of expression. Such freedom, of course, is not absolute. . . . In *Chaplinsky v. New Hampshire*, a unanimous Court said:

> There are certain well defined and narrowly limited classes of speech,
> the prevention and punishment of which have never been thought to
> raise any Constitutional problem. . . . It has been well observed that

such utterances are no essential part of any exposition of ideas, and are of such slight social value as a step to the truth that any benefit that may be derived from them is clearly outweighed by the social interest in order and morality. . . .

Here, it may equally well be said that the public burning of the American flag by Johnson was no essential part of any exposition of ideas, and at the same time it had a tendency to incite a breach of the peace. Johnson was free to make any verbal denunciation of the flag that he wished; indeed, he was free to burn the flag in private. He could burn other symbols of the Government or effigies of political leaders. . . .

Our prior cases dealing with flag burning have left open the question that the court resolves today. In *Street v. New York* . . . , [the Court] expressly reserved the question whether a defendant could constitutionally be convicted for burning the flag. . . . In another related case, *Smith v. Goguen*, . . . the Court was careful again to point out that "[c]ertainly nothing prevents a legislature from defining with substantial specificity what constitutes forbidden treatment of U.S. flags. . . . "

But the Court today will have none of this. The uniquely deep awe and respect for our flag felt by virtually all of us are bundled off under the rubric of "designated symbols" that the First Amendment prohibits the government from establishing. But the government . . . is simply recognizing as a fact the profound regard for the American flag created by that history when it enacts statutes prohibiting the disrespectful public burning of the flag.

The Court concludes its opinion with a regrettably patronizing civics lecture . . . , [when it states]: "The way to preserve the flag's special role is not to punish those who feel differently about these matters. It is to persuade them that they are wrong." The Court's role as the final expositor of the Constitution is well established, but its role as a platonic guardian admonishing those responsible to public opinion as if they were truant schoolchildren has no similar place in our system of government. The cry of "no taxation without representation" animated those who revolted against the English Crown to found our Nation—the idea that those who submitted to government should have some say as to what kind of laws would be passed. Surely one of the high purposes of a democratic society is to legislate against conduct that is regarded as evil and profoundly offensive to the majority of people—whether it be murder, embezzlement, pollution, or flag burning. . . .

The government may conscript men into the Armed Forces where they must fight and perhaps die for the flag, but the government may not prohibit the public burning of the banner under which they fight. I would uphold the Texas statute as applied in this case. ◆◆◆

## Implications of *Texas v. Johnson*

*Texas v. Johnson* implicated core principles of freedom of speech. The majority insisted on strict government neutrality in the marketplace of ideas, as had Justice Brennan in his dissent in *Kime* seven years earlier, forbidding the government from legislating an "approved" way to use the flag to communicate. The Court's decision protects a core First Amendment interest—the right to protest against the government—and it supports the *Cohen* rationale that the communicator should have the maximum opportunity to select the symbols by which she or he communicates. The Court's remedy for those who find flag burning offensive is a classic marketplace-of-ideas approach—they can respond with *more speech* in support of the flag.

The dissent rather candidly rejected the majority's premises. Chief Justice Rehnquist's opinion suggested that there could be certain "bad ideas" that the government may censor. Because the American flag is uniquely special to a majority of Americans, the offensive message inherent in its burning can be proscribed. Contrary to the rationale of *Cohen*, the dissent argued that this particular means of expression need not be protected. Mr. Johnson and his fellow protesters could easily express their antigovernment views in other ways.

The range of arguments employed by those advocating a more absolutist view of the First Amendment and those supporting restrictions on expression are similar, whether the context is flag burning, obscenity, or hate speech. Those who would restrict speech argue that there are certain "bad ideas" whose illegitimacy is beyond debate. These people simply disagree about which ideas are self-evidently evil. They contend that communitarian values, such as civility and respect for others' values or cultures, can outweigh free speech. They emphasize the availability of less offensive symbols that can express the communicator's ideas equally well.

Those supporting greater protection of speech rely on a different set of arguments. They fear giving the government the power to differentiate between good and bad ideas, and emphasize the importance of allowing the communicator to decide what symbols best express his or her ideas. The answer to "bad" speech, whether it is racist, sexist, or unpatriotic, is to respond with more speech.

### The Flag Protection Act of 1989: Constitutional Antidote to *Texas v. Johnson*?

In the aftermath of *Texas v. Johnson*, there was an outcry against the Supreme Court for permitting the destruction of a revered national symbol. Newspapers from coast to coast carried a syndicated cartoon that showed Supreme Court justices raising a burning flag much as the Marines on Iwo Jima had raised an intact one. Congress responded to this political climate by enacting the Flag Protection Act of 1989, which imposed criminal penalties on anyone who knowingly "mutilates, defaces, physically defiles, burns, maintains upon the floor or ground, or tramples upon" a flag of the United States, but exempted conduct directed toward the disposal of worn or soiled flags.

*U.S. v. Eichman*[39] arose out of two prosecutions for violations of the act. One took place in Washington State, where a flag was set on fire to protest the passage of the Flag Protection Act. The other occurred in Washington, D.C.,

---

39. 496 U.S. 310 (1990).

where defendants had set fire to several U.S. flags while protesting various American policies on the steps of the Capitol Building.

The government argued that the Flag Protection Act was constitutional because, unlike the statute in *Johnson*, this act did not target expressive conduct on the basis of the content of the message. Instead, the act protected the physical integrity of the flag under all circumstances. Any conduct that damages or mistreats a flag is illegal, without regard to the actor's motive, the intended message, or the effect of the conduct on observers.

The Court rejected the government's argument in a 5–4 decision. Justice Brennan's relatively brief majority opinion noted that the act made it permissible to burn a flag to promote its symbolic role (such as a respectful burning of a worn flag), but impermissible to mutilate, deface, defile, or trample on the flag (all words that connote disrespectful treatment). The act did constitute a prescription of what attitudes towards the flag would be orthodox, and was therefore unconstitutional.

The *Eichman* holding reinforced one free speech principle to which the Supreme Court of the 1980s and early 1990s has been loyal. When legislation directly discriminates against private citizens' right to express the viewpoint of their choice on political and social issues, the Court will insist on government neutrality in the marketplace of ideas and uphold freedom of speech.

### SUMMARY

Symbols are the key to the manner in which human beings communicate—and as such, symbolic expression can be protected by the First Amendment, although subject to certain requirements. As defined in the *O'Brien* opinion, for any governmental restriction of symbolic expression to be deemed constitutional, it must be (a) within the constitutional power of government; (b) in furtherance of a significant government interest, that is (c) unrelated to the suppression of expression, and (d) no greater than is necessary to achieve the interest.

Historically, the Court has employed the *O'Brien* test to evaluate restrictions against a wide array of symbolic expression—from nude dancing to flag burning. Although the Court's delineation of this as "expressive conduct" appears to imply that some conduct is not expressive, this is for all purposes a fiction. All conduct is expressive to some degree. The Court in *Spence* sought to further explain this by suggesting that expressive conduct occurred when there was an intent to make a particularized message and the likelihood was great that it would be understood by those exposed to it.

In more recent cases focusing on the expressive use of a national symbol—the American flag—the Court has disapproved of regulations that constrain symbolic speech when the restrictions are not content neutral. This is especially important because such expression involves a form of criticism of our government—the act of criticism being essential to the democratic process in the marketplace of ideas.

CHAPTER 12    *Objectives*

**After reading chapter 12,
you should understand
the following:**

◆ *That speech is sometimes subsidized
by the government, for example through
salaries paid to public employees or grants
given to private citizens.*

◆ *That* **rationalizations** *for denying
freedom of speech for recipients of government funds, such as ensuring that tax dollars are used to pay for speech supported
by the taxpayers, and promoting the efficiency of government services.*

◆ *That there are two competing doctrines sometimes used by the courts to resolve First Amendment rights in subsidized speech cases: the* **right/privilege**
*dichotomy and the* **unconstitutional conditions** *doctrine.*

◆ *How the courts have* **wavered** *between
the right/privilege and unconstitutional
conditions theories in resolving free
speech challenges to subsidized speech
restrictions.*

◆ *How recent Supreme Court decisions
such as* Rust v. Sullivan *and* Waters v.
Churchill *have expanded the government's power to control the speech it
funds.*

◆ *How government control of subsidized
speech* **contradicts** *First Amendment values, such as government neutrality in the
marketplace of ideas, uninhibited debate
on controversial issues, and individual
autonomy of expression.*

# 12 Government-Subsidized Speech

IN DECEMBER 1994, Dr. Joycelin Elders, then U.S. Surgeon General, attended a World AIDS Day conference at the United Nations. There she was asked the following question by Rob Clark of the Society for the Psychological Study of Social Issues: "It seems to me that there still remains a taboo against the discussion about masturbation. . . . [W]hat do you think are the prospects of a more explicit discussion and promotion of masturbation?" Surgeon General Elders responded: "I think you already know that I'm a very strong advocate of a comprehensive health education program . . . starting at a very early age. I feel it should be age appropriate, it should be complete, and we need to teach our children the things they need to know. . . . As per your specific question in regard to masturbation, I think [it] is part of human sexuality and it's a part of something that perhaps should be taught. . . ."[1] Elders' answer was a qualified affirmative response; it was later reported many times over in the press, creating a national controversy. Editorials across the country openly speculated whether the surgeon general was " . . . just popping off in a heedless fashion, almost as if she were looking for trouble."[2] A short time later, a chagrined White House announced her forced resignation, hoping to end the controversy.

Dr. Elders was in effect being punished for her speech. Although her comments were controversial, she was hardly the first person in the medical community to advocate a comprehensive approach to teaching sexuality in schools. In that respect for Dr. Elders, it was less an issue of the outrageousness of the *message* and more a question about the appropriateness of the *messenger*. Citizens have a First Amendment right to express an opinion about teaching schoolchildren about masturbation, but when the citizen also happens to be representing the United States

1. *Washington Post* (December 10, 1994).
2. *Washington Post* (December 11, 1994).

as the surgeon general, the issue becomes more complicated. When a government employee acts in an official capacity, he or she is essentially working for the taxpayers, who are paying her salary. The American public may feel that their money is being used to pay for offensive speech.

Should restrictions on free speech be part of the price that one pays for being a government employee or for accepting government grants? When the government imposes rules telling public officials, employees, or grant recipients what they can and cannot say, is the state practicing a form of censorship? Or is it more accurate to say that the government is merely ensuring that the taxpayers' money is being spent on endeavors that they support?

This chapter will examine these issues, referring to them under the generic heading of *government-subsidized expression*—since in all instances, it is the government that in one form or another is paying the bill when this kind of speech occurs.

## TWO THEORIES RELATING TO FREEDOM OF GOVERNMENT-SUBSIDIZED SPEECH

Two judicial doctrines relate to the free speech rights of government-subsidized speakers. One, the **right/privilege distinction,** theorizes that constraints on subsidized speech pose few First Amendment problems because subsidy recipients are free to decline funding if they would prefer to exercise their First Amendment rights. A competing doctrine is the **unconstitutional conditions** theory, which posits that one should not be compelled to surrender constitutional rights in order to receive funds from the government. As you read the following cases, you will see how the Court has used either philosophy to justify a particular decision without rejecting the competing theory. Before analyzing subsidized speech cases, it is important to understand the theories themselves.

### The Right/Privilege Distinction

The right/privilege distinction argues that we enjoy certain inalienable *rights* as human beings and citizens. These exist independent of and prior to the creation of any state or social contract; they are derived from our existence as humans. *Privileges,* on the other hand, are created by the state and are more analogous to government property than to citizens' entitlements. They can be given freely by the state—and just as easily taken away. The U.S. Supreme Court distinguished between rights and privileges as early as 1839 in *Bank of Augusta v. Earle,*[3] holding that a state could lawfully impose arbitrary and unreasonable conditions for doing business in that state, since it had the right to completely exclude foreign (out-of-state) corporations from doing business there. In this context, entry and the ability to conduct business were *privileges,* not rights, and therefore could be regulated by the state.

3. 38 U.S. 519 (1839).

Generally, when *rights* are infringed by government action, the Court will look carefully at the government's restriction and ensure that the government has an adequate justification for its action. For example, speech that may incite illegal conduct is protected unless the *Brandenburg* test is met; and time, place, or manner restrictions are unconstitutional if the three-pronged test discussed in chapter 10 is not satisfied. If *privileges* are implicated, however, the Court has traditionally employed a weaker standard of review, often deferring to government.

In 1892, Oliver Wendell Holmes penned what might be the definitive statement on the rights/privileges distinction. While serving as a justice on the Supreme Judicial Court of Massachusetts, Holmes decided *McAuliffe v. Mayor etc. of City of New Bedford.*[4] In this case, a police officer, John McAuliffe, had been admonished and fired by the city for talking about political conditions while on duty as a beat cop. As you read this short opinion, observe how the right/privilege distinction is the basis of the decision.

### McAuliffe v. Mayor, Etc., of City of New Bedford
### 29 N.E. 517 (1892)

Holmes, J.

The part of the rule which the petitioner seems certainly to have violated is as follows: "No member of the department shall be allowed to solicit money or any aid, on any pretense, for any political purpose whatever." . . . It is argued by the petitioner that the mayor's finding did not warrant the removal; that the part of the rule violated was invalid, as invading the petitioner's right to express his political opinions. . . .

One answer to this argument . . . is that there is nothing in the [C]onstitution or the statute to prevent the city from attaching obedience to this rule as a condition to the office of policeman, and making it part of the good conduct required. The petitioner may have a constitutional right to talk politics, but he has no constitutional right to be a policeman. There are few employments for hire in which the servant does not agree to suspend his constitutional rights of free speech as well as of idleness by the implied terms of his contract. The servant cannot complain, as he takes the employment on the terms which are offered him. On the same principle the city may impose any reasonable condition upon holding offices within its control. This condition seems to us reasonable, if that be a question open to revision here. . . . ◆◆◆

Do you agree with Holmes's inference that McAuliffe's employment was a privilege and not a right? If you accept Justice Holmes's premises, it is difficult to dispute his conclusion. McAuliffe did not have a right to his job because it was a privilege accorded by the city. As such, he served at the city's pleasure and ac-

4. 29 N.E. 517 (1892).

cording to its rules. McAuliffe's First Amendment rights were not denied; instead, he chose to forego them in return for being employed as a police officer.

Over future decades, numerous courts would use this reasoning to mark their points of departure between permissible government regulation and the denial of constitutional rights. For example, the infamous *Scopes v. State*[5] trial, also known as the Scopes Monkey Trial, concerned the rights of John Thomas Scopes—a public school teacher, and therefore a public employee—to teach evolution. Wrote Chief Justice Green of the Supreme Court of Tennessee:

> . . . The plaintiff in error was a teacher in the public schools of Rhea county. He was an employee of the state of Tennessee or of a municipal agency of the state. He was under contract with the state to work in an institution of the state. He had no right or privilege to serve the state except upon such terms as the state prescribed. His liberty, his privilege, his immunity to teach and proclaim the theory of evolution, elsewhere than in the service of the state, was in no wise touched by this law.
>
> The statute before us is not an exercise of the police power of the state undertaking to regulate the conduct and contracts of individuals in their dealings with each other. On the other hand, it is an act of the state as a corporation, a proprietor, an employer. It is a declaration of a master as to the character of work the master's servant shall, or rather shall not perform. . . .

This kind of reasoning assumes that the state as an employer can engage in behavior that is different, and potentially more questionable, than it can when acting as our government.

There are serious flaws to this thinking, however. The first of these extends from the power left to government when a right/privilege dichotomy is used. If government is accorded the ability to impose restrictions on individuals' expression in return for the "privilege" of employment or the conferring of any other government benefit, the potential for abuse of power is considerable. The principle of government neutrality in the marketplace of ideas is compromised when the speech of all government employees, as well as those receiving grants from the state, can be controlled at will.

Second, and equally problematic, the right/privilege dichotomy incorrectly assumes that no rights are surrendered if they are relinquished in order to accept a privilege. Justice Holmes identified McAuliffe's employment as a privilege and not a right—suggesting he had "no constitutional right to be a policeman." Although it is true that McAuliffe had instituted an action for what amounted to wrongful dismissal, his right to employment as a policeman was never really the issue. Rather, as his complaint clearly stated, McAuliffe alleged that his employment had been wrongfully terminated because his "right to express his political opinions" was violated. The Massachusetts

5. 289 SW 363 (1927).

Supreme Court assumed that his free speech rights were not violated because McAuliffe could simply quit the police force, and then express his political views to his heart's content. Is that choice (to quit one's job) truly a voluntary one? Given high unemployment and the difficulties that accompany changing jobs, many government employees will have little choice but to censor their speech rather than risk losing their jobs. When a court employs a right/privilege analysis, it avoids the challenge of balancing an employee's freedom of speech with any justification the government would have for constraining his or her expression on the job.

Although this theoretical justification for limiting government-subsidized speech has enjoyed a fluctuating history in our jurisprudence, it is precisely because of the above-stated problems that an alternative doctrine developed in review of subsidized speech.

### The Unconstitutional Conditions Doctrine

The doctrine of unconstitutional conditions developed as a rival to the right/privilege distinction. In its base form, this doctrine suggests that government may *not* do indirectly what the Constitution forbids it to do directly. Ordinarily this can occur in situations where a government rule does not directly require the forfeiture of a right (e.g., prohibition of speech), but instead indirectly produces that result by making receipt of a benefit tied to certain rules or restrictions. In many ways, this doctrine was a direct response to the concern over government abuse fostered by a right/privilege distinction. If government qualifies receipt of any of its benefits (such as employment) to the condition that an individual forfeit a constitutional right (such as free expression), the government has created an unconstitutional conditions problem.

A strong statement of this doctrine (and a direct repudiation of Justice Holmes's distinction) was offered by Justice Potter Stewart as the Court considered *Perry v. Sindermann* in 1971.[6] In *Perry,* a college instructor in Texas had argued that he was fired because his employer disagreed with the opinions he expressed. A federal district court granted **summary judgment** for the defendant (the college board of regents), holding that no First Amendment issue was raised by the case. As you read *Perry,* think about whether you feel the Court's approach answers the problems posed by the right/privilege distinction. Are there any risks to society if the reasoning in *Perry* were to replace the right/privilege dichotomy?

### *Perry v. Sindermann,* 408 U.S. 593 (1972)

Mr. Justice Stewart delivered the opinion of the Court.

For at least a quarter-century, this Court has made clear that even though a person has no "right" to a valuable governmental benefit and even though the

---

6. 408 U.S. 593 (1971).

government may deny him the benefit for any number of reasons, there are some reasons upon which the government may not rely. It may not deny a benefit to a person on a basis that infringes his constitutionally protected interests—especially, his interest in freedom of speech. For if the government could deny a benefit to a person because of his constitutionally protected speech or associations, his exercise of those freedoms would in effect be penalized and inhibited. This would allow the government to produce a result which [it] could not command directly. Such interference with constitutional rights is impermissible. . . .

[W]e agree . . . that there is a genuine dispute as to whether the college refused to renew the teaching contract on an impermissible basis—as a reprisal for the exercise of constitutionally protected rights. The respondent has alleged that his nonretention was based on his testimony before legislative committees and his other public statements critical of the Regents' policies. And he has alleged that this public criticism was within the First and Fourteenth Amendments' protection of freedom of speech. Plainly, these allegations present a bona fide constitutional claim. For this Court has held that a teacher's public criticism of his superiors on matters of public concern may be impermissible basis for termination of his employment.

For this reason we hold that the grant of summary judgment against the respondent, without full exploration of this issue, was improper. . . .   ◆◆◆

After reading Justice Stewart's opinion, are you convinced that the unconstitutional conditions approach resolves the problems underlying subsidized speech better than the right/privilege distinction? At one level, it is certainly more accurate from a constitutional perspective to focus the inquiry on the real right in question (e.g., expression instead of employment). Equally so, refocusing the inquiry this way also greatly increases the burden placed on the government when it does condition employment or other benefits on what a person does or does not say.

If the government can *never* condition benefits in this way, then no matter what the justification may be, the government must always lose if an unconstitutional condition is imposed. Yet there may be times when the government should condition employment on the relinquishment of certain rights. A diplomat cannot be free to reveal secret information to an adversary during arms control negotiations, and a firefighter cannot stop to discuss hockey scores while putting out a fire. Kindergarten teachers should not be free to show R-rated movies to their classes. The Supreme Court has recognized that sometimes the government has good reasons for placing constraints on the expression of the people it funds. However, the Court has been inconsistent in the application of the unconstitutional conditions doctrine, sometimes basing a decision on that theory, but then veering back toward Justice Holmes's right/privilege distinction.

The choice of doctrine has varied according to the benefit being conferred, *and* depending upon the status of the recipient of the benefit. Let us see how the Court continues to use strands from both doctrines.

## FREE SPEECH RIGHTS OF PUBLIC EMPLOYEES

Public employees provide a compelling example of individuals who receive government benefits (in this case, employment) and have their speech "subsidized" when expressing themselves on the job. Several cases demonstrate the internal disagreement of the Supreme Court over the previously stated doctrines as applied to public employees. For example, in 1966, the Court decided two cases of note, both of which dealt with the First Amendment rights of public employees.

### Bond v. Floyd: Higher Standard of Loyalty for Legislators?

In *Bond v. Floyd*,[7] the Court reviewed the Georgia state legislature's attempt to bar Julian Bond from taking his legislative seat in the Georgia House of Representatives. Mr. Bond had made statements critical of the American participation in Vietnam. Bond had endorsed a statement expressing "sympathy" and "support" for those "unwilling to respond to a military draft." The same statement had suggested that working in the civil rights movement was "a valid alternative to the draft" and "urge[d] all Americans to seek this alternative." The legislative justification for removing Bond was that the state has a right to insist on loyalty to the Constitution as a condition of office. The Court, in a unanimous opinion by Chief Justice Warren, held that Bond's exclusion violated the First Amendment.

### Bond v. Floyd, 385 U.S. 116 (1966)

Chief Justice Warren delivered the opinion of the Court.

We do not quarrel with the State's contention that the oath provisions of the United States and Georgia Constitutions do not violate the First Amendment. But this requirement does not authorize a majority of state legislators to test the sincerity with which another duly elected legislator can swear to uphold the Constitution. Such a power could be utilized to restrict the right of legislators to dissent from national or state policy or that of a majority of their colleagues under the guise of judging their loyalty to the Constitution.

Certainly there can be no question but that the First Amendment protects expressions in opposition to national foreign policy in Vietnam and to the Selective Service system. . . . The State declines to argue that Bond's statements would violate any law if made by a private citizen, but it does argue that even though such a

7. 385 U.S. 116 (1966).

citizen might be protected by his First Amendment rights, the State may nonetheless apply a stricter standard to its legislators. We do not agree. . . .

Bond's statements were at worst unclear on the question of the means to be adopted to avoid the draft. . . . At the hearing before the Special Committee of the Georgia House, when asked his position on persons who burned their draft cards, Bond replied that he admired the courage of persons who "feel strongly enough about their convictions to take an action like that knowing the consequences that they will face." When pressed as to whether his admiration was based on the violation of federal law, Bond stated:

> I have never suggested or counseled or advocated that any one other
> person burn their draft card. In fact, I have mine in my pocket and will
> produce it if you wish. I do not advocate that people should break
> laws. What I simply try to say was that I admired the courage of some-
> one who could act on his convictions knowing that he faces pretty stiff
> consequences.

Certainly this clarification does not demonstrate any incitement to violation of law. . . .

The State attempts to circumvent the protection the First Amendment would afford to these statements if made by a private citizen by arguing that a State is constitutionally justified in exacting a higher standard of *loyalty* from its legislators than from its citizens. . . . We think the rationale of the *New York Times* case disposes of the claim that Bond's statements fell outside the range of constitutional protection. Just as erroneous statements must be protected to give freedom of expression the breathing space it needs to survive, so statements criticizing public policy and the implementation of it must be similarly protected. . . . The interest of the public in hearing all sides of a public issue is hardly advanced by extending more protection to citizen-critics than to legislators. . . . [T]he disqualification of Bond from membership in the Georgia House because of his statements violated Bond's right of free expression under the First Amendment. . . .   ◆◆◆

In *Bond,* the Court makes it very clear that states and the federal government *can* impose a loyalty oath to the United States Constitution—but here seems to suggest that a loyalty oath cannot be used to gauge the sincerity of the commitment of any legislator. Doing such, the Court clearly implies, would promote an unconstitutional condition.

*Bond* is also noteworthy since it raises the question of whether a public employee can be treated more harshly than a private citizen for controversial speech. Here the Court admits that public employees may be compelled to swear loyalty oaths from which private citizens are exempt—but again says that this difference does not mean that the requirement can be used to punish Bond's antiwar discourse. Why? Because using an oath this way would suppress discussion about public policy—the promotion of which is also part of Bond's job.

### Keyishian v. Board of Regents: Academic Freedom and Unpopular Viewpoints on Campus

In *Keyishian v. Board of Regents*,[8] the Court reviewed New York's statutes calling for a teacher loyalty oath, imposing constraints on "seditious" utterances, and prohibiting involvement with the distribution of written material that advocates forceful overthrow of the government. The appellants, faculty members (and one library employee) at the State University of New York (SUNY), had their continued employment threatened or terminated. All appellants brought action for declaratory and injunctive relief, alleging the state statutes and regulations violated the Constitution. The Supreme Court's opinion in *Keyishian* strongly endorsed freedom of speech in the university environment, and also exemplified an unconstitutional conditions approach to resolving this issue.

### *Keyishian v. Board of Regents*, 385 U.S. 589 (1966)

Mr. Justice Brennan delivered the opinion of the Court.

There can be no doubt of the legitimacy of New York's interest in protecting its education system from subversion. But even though the governmental purpose be legitimate and substantial, that purpose cannot be pursued by means that broadly stifle fundamental personal liberties when the end can be more narrowly achieved. . . .

Our Nation is deeply committed to safeguarding academic freedom, which is of transcendent value to all of us and not merely to the teachers concerned. That freedom is therefore a special concern of the First Amendment, which does not tolerate laws that cast a pall of orthodoxy over the classroom. The vigilant protection of constitutional freedoms is nowhere more vital than in the community of American schools. . . . The classroom is peculiarly the "marketplace of ideas." The Nation's future depends upon leaders trained through wide exposure to that robust exchange of ideas which discovers truth out of a multitude of tongues, [rather] than through any kind of authoritative selection. . . .

[S]tandards of permissible statutory vagueness are strict in the area of free expression. . . . The danger of th[e] chilling effect upon the exercise of vital First Amendment rights must be guarded against by sensitive tools which clearly inform teachers what is being proscribed.

The regulatory maze created by New York is wholly lacking in "terms susceptible of objective measurement." [For example, Section 3021 of New York's Education Law allows dismissal of teachers for treasonable or seditious utterances, without defining these terms]. . . . [M]en of common intelligence must necessarily guess at its meaning and differ as to its application. . . . We therefore hold that Section 3021 of the Education Law . . . [is] unconstitutional.

Appellants have also challenged the constitutionality of the discrete provisions of subdivision 1c of Section 105 and subdivision 2 of the Feinberg Law,

8. 385 U.S. 589 (1966).

which make Communist Party membership, as such, prima facie evidence of disqualification. . . . [C]onstitutional doctrine which has emerged . . . has rejected . . . [the] premise . . . that public employment, including academic employment, may be conditioned upon the surrender of constitutional rights which could not be abridged by direct government action. . . .

[T]he theory that public employment which may be denied altogether may be subjected to any conditions, regardless of how unreasonable, has been uniformly rejected. . . . In *Sherbert v. Verner,* 374 U.S. 398 (1963) . . . we said: "It is too late in the day to doubt that the liberties of religion and expression may be infringed by the denial of or placing of conditions upon a benefit or privilege."

We proceed then to the question of the validity of the provisions of subdivision 1c of Section 105 and subdivision 2 of Section 3022, barring employment to members of listed organizations. . . .

In *Elfbrandt v. Russell,* we said, "those who join an organization but do not share its unlawful purposes and who do not participate in its unlawful activities surely pose no threat, either as citizens or as public employees. . . ." In *Aptheker v. Secretary of State,* we held that Party membership, without knowledge of the Party's unlawful purposes *and* specific intent to further its unlawful aims, could not constitutionally warrant deprivation of the right to travel abroad. . . .

These limitations clearly apply to a provision, like Section 105 [subdivision 1c], which blankets all state employees, regardless of the "sensitivity" of their positions. But even the Feinberg Law provision, applicable primarily to activities of teachers, who have captive audiences of young minds, are subject to these limitations in favor of freedom of expression and association; the stifling effect on the academic mind from curtailing freedom of association in such manner is manifest, and has been documented in recent studies. *Elfbrandt* and *Aptheker* state the governing standard: legislation which sanctions membership unaccompanied by specific intent to further the unlawful goals of the organization or which is not active membership violates constitutional limitations. . . .   ◆◆◆

The *Keyishian* decision has important implications. First, it provides a strong endorsement of academic freedom, explicitly relying on the marketplace of ideas as a metaphor for speech in the university classroom. Second, the *Keyishian* opinion suggests that unconstitutional conditions could not be placed on public employees. When Justice Brennan cited the *Sherbert* opinion for the proposition that it is "too late in the day to doubt" that expression may be suppressed by denying government benefits for those with unpopular views, he was promoting the unconstitutional conditions doctrine. This would seem to suggest that governmental attempts to control the subsidized speech of its employees is subject to the unconstitutional conditions doctrine—which gives greater protection to the speech of public employees. It would *appear* that way based on *Keyishian;* however, in subsequent cases the Court has been inconsistent on this score.

### Public Employee Speech: Governed by the Unconstitutional Conditions Doctrine?

*Statements of Public Concern.*   In 1967, one year after *Bond* and *Keyishian*, Justice Thurgood Marshall delivered the majority opinion in *Pickering v. Board of Education.*[9] Pickering, a public school teacher, had been fired for writing a letter (published in a newspaper) in which he criticized the school board's allocation of funds for education and athletics. Pickering also criticized the board's and the superintendent's methods of informing the public of the real reasons for increasing taxes to support the schools. Some of his statements were correct; others were plainly false. Could his public employment be conditioned upon his willingness to never make such statements?

In reviewing the case, Justice Marshall suggested that the teacher's First Amendment interests as a citizen in making *public comment* (that is, comment on an issue of public concern) had to be balanced against any state interest in promoting the efficiency of its employees' public services.[10] The question became, How would this balance be achieved? Justice Marshall answered by reviewing Pickering's statements and concluding that (1) they were not directed at anyone in particular with whom he had contact as a teacher (thus there was no issue of insubordination or disruption of workplace harmony);[11] (2) even if some of his statements were false, there was no evidence anybody believed them;[12] and (3) his comments did not interfere with his ability to teach in the class or with the operation of the school generally.[13] As such, the Court reversed a lower court opinion that had upheld the dismissal.

*Pickering* was significant because it suggested the need to balance the public employee's interest with that of the state. That balance, however, applied in cases where the employee made statements of "public concern." Of course, the *Pickering* opinion operated on the assumption the teacher's statements were of public concern; but how was one to determine this?

In 1982, the Court addressed this question in *Connick v. Myers,*[14] dealing with the termination of an assistant district attorney. In *Connick*, Sheila Myers had been an assistant district attorney in New Orleans. Harry Connick Sr., the district attorney for the Orleans parish, proposed transferring Myers to a different section of criminal court; Myers protested to her supervisors and wrote a memo in the form of a questionnaire, which she circulated to other assistant DAs. The questionnaire concerned the transfer policy, office morale, the need for a grievance committee, the level of confidence in supervisors, and whether employees felt pressured to work for political campaigns.

9. 391 U.S. 563 (1967).
10. Id. at 568.
11. Id. at 569–70.
12. Id. at 570.
13. Id. at 572–3.
14. 461 U.S. 138 (1982).

A key issue in *Connick* was whether the contents of this questionnaire constituted issues of "public concern," sufficient to trigger the balancing test suggested in *Pickering*. Writing for the Court, Justice White noted:

> *Pickering*, its antecedents, and its progeny lead us to conclude that if Myers' questionnaire cannot be fairly characterized as constituting speech on a matter of public concern, it is unnecessary for us to scrutinize the reasons for her discharge. When employee expression cannot be fairly considered as relating to any matter of political, social, or other concern to the community, government officials should enjoy wide latitude in managing their offices, without intrusive oversight by the judiciary in the name of the First Amendment.[15]   ◆◆◆

Stressing that he was referring to cases where a public employee spoke not as a citizen upon matters of public concern, but "instead upon matters of personal interest,"[16] Justice White then set forth the test for "public concern" as follows:

> Whether an employee's speech addresses a matter of public concern must be determined by the content, form and context of a given statement, as revealed by the whole record.[17]   ◆◆◆

Justice White then applied his *content, form, and context* inquiry to Myers's questionnaire, finding all but one question to be of personal and not public concern. "These questions reflect one employee's dissatisfaction with a transfer and an attempt to turn that displeasure into a cause célèbre."[18] White did feel that one question—dealing with whether Myers's contemporaries ever felt pressured to work in a political campaign—might be of "public concern," but he later said this was of public concern "in only a most limited sense."[19] He added: "[H]er survey, in our view, is most accurately characterized as an employee's grievance concerning internal office policy."[20]

The *Connick* opinion emphasizes the importance of a public employee's speech addressing public concern before it will be protected. Connick indicates that when a statement does not pertain to an issue of public concern, the Court will more likely defer to the government's judgment as to the wisdom of a constraint on speech. The Court's reasoning in the next case, *Waters v. Churchill*,[21] exemplifies this deferential approach.

15. Id. at 146.
16. Id. at 147.
17. Id. at 147–8.
18. Id. at 148.
19. Id. at 154.
20. Id.
21. 114 S.Ct. 1878 (1994).

*Deference to Government Justification for Controlling Employee Speech.* In *Waters,* a public hospital nurse had been fired because she allegedly had made statements critical of management to a co-worker. Writing for the majority, Justice Sandra Day O'Connor (see Figure 12.1) explained why a public employee could receive different treatment than a private citizen.

### Waters v. Churchill, 114 S. Ct. 1878 (1994)

What is it about the government's role as employer that gives it a freer hand in regulating the speech of its employees than it has in regulating the speech of the public at large? . . .

To begin with, even many of the most fundamental maxims of our First Amendment jurisprudence cannot reasonably be applied to speech by government employees. The First Amendment demands a tolerance of "verbal tumult, discord, and even offensive utterance," as "necessary side effects of . . . the process of open debate." . . . But we have never expressed doubt that a government employer may bar its employees from using Mr. Cohen's offensive utterances to members of the public, or to the people with whom they work. "Under the First Amendment there is no such thing as a false idea," . . . the "fitting

*Figure 12.1. Justice Sandra Day O'Connor, nominated to the Court by President Reagan in 1981, was originally thought to be a rock-solid ideological conservative, in step with fellow Arizonan and Stanford Law graduate Chief Rehnquist. After better than a decade of service, however, Justice O'Connor has come to form a moderate center of the Court, often in voting blocs with Justices Kennedy and Souter. She authored the majority opinion in* Waters v. Churchill. *(Richard Strauss, Smithsonian Institution. Collection of the Supreme Court of the United States.)*

remedy for evil counsels is good ones." . . . But when an employee counsels her coworkers to do their job in a way with which the public employer disagrees, her managers may tell her to stop, rather than relying on counter-speech. The First Amendment reflects the "profound national commitment to the principle that debate on public issues should be uninhibited, robust, and wide-open." . . . But though a private person is perfectly free to uninhibitedly and robustly criticize a state governor's legislative program, we have never suggested that the Constitution bars the governor from firing a high-ranking deputy for doing the same thing. . . . Even something as close to the core of the First Amendment as participation in political campaigns may be prohibited to government employees. . . .

[W]e have consistently given greater deference to government predictions of harm used to justify restriction of employee speech than to predictions of harm used to justify restrictions on the speech of the public at large. Few of the examples we have discussed involve tangible, present interference with the agency's operation. The danger in them is mostly speculative. One could make a respectable argument that political activity by government employees is generally not harmful, . . . or that high officials should allow more public dissent by their subordinates, . . . or that even in a government workplace the free market of ideas is superior to a command economy. But we have given substantial weight to government employers' reasonable prediction of disruption, even when the speech involved is on a matter of public concern. . . . Similarly, we have refrained from intervening in government employer decisions that are based on speech that is of entirely private concern. Doubtless some such speech is sometimes nondisruptive; doubtless it is sometimes of value to the speakers and the listeners. But we have declined to question government employers' decisions on such matters. . . .

[T]he extra power the government has in this area comes from the nature of the government's mission as employer. Government agencies are charged by law with doing particular tasks. Agencies hire employees to help do those tasks as effectively and efficiently as possible. When someone who is paid a salary so that she will contribute to an agency's effective operation begins to do or say things that detract from the agency's effective operation, the government employer must have some power to restrain her. The reason the governor may, in the example given above, fire the deputy is not that this dismissal would somehow be narrowly tailored to a compelling government interest. It is that the governor and the governor's staff have a job to do, and the governor justifiably feels that a quieter subordinate would allow them to do this job more effectively.

The key to the First Amendment analysis of government employment decisions, then, is this: The government's interest in achieving its goals as effectively and efficiently as possible is elevated from a relatively subordinate interest when it acts as sovereign to a significant one when it acts as employer. The government cannot restrict the speech of the public at large just in the name of efficiency. But where the government is employing someone for the very purpose of effectively achieving its goals, such restrictions may well be appropriate. ◆◆◆

In the context of public employment, Justice O'Connor's opinion candidly rejects First Amendment principles such as a marketplace of ideas on public issues and the use of more speech as a remedy for "bad" speech. In the majority's viewpoint, a bad tendency is a sufficient basis to limit government employee speech, even if the speech cannot be proven to have harmful consequences.

Justice O'Connor contends that in public employee settings, the government is acting as an employer rather than a sovereign. In other words, when the government tells a teacher or a forest ranger what to say, it is analogous to a McDonald's manager telling his or her subordinates not to suggest that customers' health may profit if they ate elsewhere. Of course, for public employees, the government is a sovereign as well as an employer. If forest rangers at a visitors' center are commanded to defend the sale of national forest land for the clearcutting of timber, or history teachers are required to tell their students that Columbus's arrival in the Americas was an immoral imposition of bankrupt European culture, the government can influence the public debate on controversial issues.

In summary, the following can be said about the free speech rights of government employees. First, if their speech references an issue deemed a private concern, rather than a public one, it can be regulated as a condition of employment. Second, if their speech deals with an issue of public concern, the reviewing court will balance the employee's freedom of speech interest with the government's interest in promoting the efficiency of its employees. As Justice O'Connor described the government-friendly balancing process in *Waters*, it is fair to ask whether the right/privilege philosophy essentially governs public employee speech rights. This same hypothesis will be considered with respect to government grant recipients in the next section.

## FREE SPEECH RIGHTS OF GOVERNMENT GRANT RECIPIENTS

Suppose that instead of public employees we were discussing people who receive funding from the government but are not employed by the government. How would the Supreme Court determine the free speech rights of grant recipients? Would the Court apply a right/privilege framework to resolve this issue, reasoning that the government could limit the speech of grant recipients because such recipients were free to decline the funds? Or would the Court hold that imposing limits on a person's speech as a prerequisite for receiving government funds imposed an unconstitutional condition on grant recipients?

### The *Rust v. Sullivan* Principle

The Supreme Court addressed this in 1991 as it decided *Rust v. Sullivan*.[22] This case dealt with Title X of the Public Service Act, enacted in 1970 for the provision of federal funds to family planning programs.[23] While the record is clear that Congress intended this act to provide comprehensive family planning services and information for indigent and low-income people, it is equally clear it did not intend this as providing funds for performing abortions.[24] The effect of this act was far-reaching, particularly given the worsening gap between rich and poor in this country. Prior to the filing of *Rust*, an estimated 4.5 million women qualified as Title X patients,[25] and of these, an astounding 90 percent had incomes below 150 percent of the poverty level.[26] The recipients of Title X funding are usually low-cost public clinics that may or may not be associated with low-cost abortion clinics, the latter being funded by non-Title X funds.

The original Health and Human Services (HHS) policy interpreted Title X to permit clinics to counsel women about and even encourage abortion, although this was required by rule to be couched in dialogue that was objective and nondirective about a patient's options.[27] This policy was significantly altered in 1988, as HHS decided to issue new regulations aimed at what it considered to be compliance with the original purpose of Title X. The new regulations struck at the nature of the communication between Title X doctors and patients by mandating that clinics could no longer discuss abortions with their clients or make any abortion referrals.[28] In this context, the concept of "family planning as envisioned by the original legislation had now been redefined by HHS as excluding abortion.[29] The new policy required clinics to refer a newly diagnosed pregnant woman to prenatal care, providing her with a list of health care providers who would "promote the welfare of the mother and unborn child."[30] The effect of this policy was also to weight this list of health care providers away from abortion clinics and heavily in favor of clinics encouraging childbirth.

22. 111 S.Ct. 1759 (1991).
23. *Family Planning Services and Population Research Act of 1970,* Pub. L. No. 91-572, 84 Stat. 1504 (codified as amended at 42 *U.S.C.* sections 300-300a-6 [1982]).
24. 42 *U.S.C.* section 300a-6.
25. See Petition for Writ of Certiorari at 3, n.3, *New York v. Sullivan,* 889 F. 2d. 401 (2d Cir. 1989), cert granted, 110 S. Ct. 2559 (1990).
26. Alexandra Shapiro, *Title X, the Abortion Debate, and the First Amendment,* 90 Columbia Law Review 1737, 1738 (1990).
27. See, e.g., *Planned Parenthood Federation of America v. Bowen,* 913 F.2d 1492 (10th Cir. 1990), quoting HHS Program Guidelines for Project Grants and Family Planning Services 13 (1981): pregnant women requesting information about options for dealing with an unintended pregnancy should be given "non-directive counseling . . . and referral upon request" for prenatal care, adoption or abortion.
28. Id. at section 59.8 (a) (1).
29. Id. at section 59.2.
30. Id. at section 59.8 (a) (2).

These changes in Title X unquestionably put the federal government in the position of encouraging childbirth rather than abortion. On the politically charged issue of abortion, it was not surprising that the new regulations were soon challenged. Courts in the first, second, and tenth circuits that heard these challenges were at odds as to how to interpret the changes in Title X, particularly in light of the contention that the new rules imposed unconstitutional conditions on the receipt of a benefit.

Writing for a threadbare 5–4 majority, Chief Justice Rehnquist authored an opinion that resolved the conflict of opinions among the federal appeals courts. As you read this excerpt, decide whether you believe the right/privilege dichotomy or the unconstitutional conditions doctrine is a better approach to the question of grantees' free speech rights. This case should be read from a First Amendment perspective. If one presidential administration can change Title X to preclude abortion counseling, the next administration can reverse this decision and *require* doctors to encourage abortion. Hence the real issue in this case is whether the government, or the health care workers to whom it provides grants, should decide what advice should be given to patients.

### *Rust v. Sullivan,* 114 L.Ed.2d 233 (1991)

Chief Justice Rehnquist (see Figure 12.2) delivered the opinion of the Court.

Petitioners contend that the regulations violate the First Amendment by impermissibly discriminating based on viewpoint because they prohibit "all discussion about abortion as a lawful option—including counseling, referral, and the provision of neutral and accurate information about ending a pregnancy—while compelling the clinic or counselor to provide information that promotes continuing a pregnancy to term." . . . They assert that the regulations violate the "free speech rights of private health care organizations that receive Title X funds, of their staff, and of their patients" by impermissibly imposing "viewpoint-discriminatory conditions on government subsidies." . . .

There is no question but that the statutory prohibition [on counseling, referral, and the provision of information regarding abortion as a method of family planning] is constitutional. . . . The Government can, without violating the Constitution, selectively fund a program to encourage certain activities it believes to be in the public interest, without at the same time funding an alternate program which seeks to deal with the problem in another way. In so doing, the Government has not discriminated on the basis of viewpoint; it has merely chosen to fund one activity to the exclusion of the other. [A] legislature's decision not to subsidize the exercise of a fundamental right does not infringe on the right. . . . A refusal to fund protected activity, without more, cannot be equated with the imposition of a "penalty" on that activity.

. . . This is not a case of the Government "suppressing a dangerous idea," but of a prohibition on a project grantee or its employees from engaging in activities outside of its scope. . . .

*Figure 12.2. William H. Rehnquist, first nominated by President Nixon to the Court in 1971, later succeeded Warren Burger as Chief Justice in 1986, and began tilting the Court to slightly more conservative positions on a range of issues. Chief Justice Rehnquist authored the majority opinion in* **Rust v. Sullivan.** *(Dane Penland. Collection of the Supreme Court of the United States.)*

Petitioners . . . contend that the restrictions on the subsidization of abortion-related speech contained in the regulations are impermissible because they condition the receipt of a benefit, in this case Title X funding, on the relinquishment of a constitutional right, the right to engage in abortion advocacy and counseling. Relying on *Perry,* . . . petitioners argue that "even though the government may deny [a] . . . benefit for any number of reasons, there are some reasons upon which the government may not rely. It may not deny a benefit to a person on a basis that infringes his constitutionally protected interests—especially, his interest in freedom of speech." . . .

[H]ere the government is not denying a benefit to anyone, but is instead simply insisting that public funds be spent for the purposes for which they were authorized. The Secretary's regulations do not force the Title X grantee to give up abortion-related speech; they merely require that the grantee keep such activities separate and distinct from Title X activities. . . .

In contrast, our "unconstitutional conditions" cases involve situations in which the government has placed a condition on the *recipient* of the subsidy rather than on a particular program or service, thus effectively prohibiting the recipient from engaging in the protected conduct outside the scope of the federally funded program. . . .

This is not to suggest that funding by the Government, even when coupled with the freedom of the fund recipients to speak outside the scope of the Government-funded project, is invariably sufficient to justify Government control over the content of expression. For example, this Court has recognized that the existence of a Government "subsidy," in the form of Government-owned property, does not justify the restriction of speech in areas that have "been traditionally open to the public for expressive activity," . . . or have been "expressly dedicated to speech activity. . . ." Similarly, we have recognized that the university is a traditional sphere of free expression so fundamental to the functioning of our society that the Government's ability to control speech within that sphere by means of conditions attached to the expenditure of Government funds is restricted by the vagueness and overbreadth doctrines of the First Amendment. . . . It could be argued by analogy that traditional relationships such as that between doctor and patient should enjoy protection under the First Amendment from Government regulation, even when subsidized by the Government. We need not resolve that question here, however, because the Title X program regulations do not significantly impinge upon the doctor-patient relationship. Nothing in them requires a doctor to represent as his own any opinion that he does not in fact hold. Nor is the doctor-patient relationship established by the Title X program sufficiently all-encompassing so as to justify an expectation on the part of the patient of comprehensive medical advice. The program does not provide post-conception medical care, and therefore a doctor's silence with regard to abortion cannot reasonably be thought to mislead a client into thinking that the doctor does not consider abortion an appropriate option for her. The doctor is always free to make clear that advice regarding abortion is simply beyond the scope of the program. . . .  ◆◆◆

In this opinion, Justice Rehnquist moves back to the right/privilege distinction—and away from the doctrine of unconstitutional conditions. How does he do this? Largely by making use of the *status* of the recipient of the benefit in this case—doctors and their staffs at Title X–funded clinics. When Rehnquist asserts there is no diminution in the First Amendment rights of doctors or staff imposed by the new rules' prohibition of abortion counseling or referral, he grounds this in the claim that doctors or staff, outside of their Title X–funded care, may still engage in abortion-related speech—so long as those activities are kept "separate and distinct from Title X activities." The *Rust* analysis moves the government away from neutrality in the marketplace of ideas. Even though medical workers at Title X clinics are free to participate in pro-choice activities on their own time, the government is allowed to ensure that all patients in the clinics it funds will hear only one side of the abortion issue. The *Rust* principle also gives little weight to the patient's right to receive information. A pregnant woman whose poverty makes a government clinic her only medical option will not receive the same range of advice as a woman who can afford a physician whose abortion counseling is not subject to government control.

After the 1992 elections, Congress changed the rules against abortion counseling, making somewhat irrelevant the factual basis of *Rust*. But the case remains highly significant for subsidized speech as it continues the trend back to the right/privilege distinction. The *Rust* principle has been tested in other contexts.

### The *Rust* Principle in Operation

*Public Funding of the Arts.* Congress had created the National Endowment for the Arts (NEA) in 1965 to "help create and sustain not only a climate encouraging freedom of thought, imagination, and inquiry, but also the material conditions facilitating the release of this creative talent.[31] The NEA was to foster these aims through the awarding of subsidies to needy artists and museums. Applicants were to state the nature of their work, the estimated cost, and information about private sources of funding. Peer panels designated projects with artistic merit, and the National Council on the Arts decided what grants should be awarded. Final discretionary authority, however, rested with the chair of the NEA.

Over time, according to the *Congressional Record,*[32] the NEA has distributed billions of federal dollars to artists and museums—although not always without controversy. In 1988, two artists (Andres Serrano and Robert Mapplethorpe) and their separate projects incurred the wrath of certain members of Congress, who found their work offensive, immoral and sacrilegious.[33] One of Serrano's photographs, entitled "Piss Christ," depicted a crucifix made of plastic, dipped into a jar of the artist's urine. A collection of Mapplethorpe's work, at that time displayed at the Corcoran Gallery, depicted several images of bondage and homoeroticism.

After considerable debate, and amendment of proposed rules for the NEA, Congress passed the so-called decency clause. Under this rule, applicants for NEA grants have to pledge that their art meets "general standards of decency and respect for the diverse beliefs of the American public."[34]

In the case that follows, the "decency clause" was challenged as unconstitutional. This case, which only reached the federal district court level, dealt with many of the issues of subsidized speech we have discussed in earlier cases. As you read this excerpt of *Finley v. NEA*[35] identify how the Court resolves the conflict between the right/privilege distinction and the doctrine of unconstitutional conditions.

31. 20 *U.S.C.* Section 951 (5) (1965).
32. See, e.g., 135 *Cong. Rec.* H3639 (daily ed. July 12, 1989).
33. See, e.g., Parachini, *Endowment Congressmen Feud Over Provocative Art,* Los Angeles Times (June 14, 1989), pp. 6–10.
34. 20 *U.S.C.* 954 (d) (1).
35. 795 F.Supp. 1457 (C.D. Cal. 1992).

*Finley v. National Endowment for the Arts,*
795 F. Supp. 1457 (C.D. Cal. 1992).

Tashima, District Judge.

Plaintiffs are four individual performance artists ("Individual plaintiffs") and the National Association of Artists' Organizations ("NAAO"). Individual plaintiffs allege that defendants the National Endowment for the Arts ("NEA") and John E. Frohnmayer ("Frohnmayer"), NEA Chairperson, violated their constitutional and statutory rights by improperly denying their applications for NEA grants. . . . [P]laintiffs contend that public subsidization of art, like public funding of the press and university activities, demands government neutrality. In effect, plaintiffs ask the court to recognize a protected First Amendment interest in artistic expression funded by the government.

Plaintiffs point out that the Court in *Rust v. Sullivan* cautioned that "funding by the Government, even when coupled with the freedom of the fund recipients to speak outside the scope of the Government-funded project, is [not] invariably sufficient to justify Government control over the content of expression. . . ." The Court cited universities and public fora as two settings in which First Amendment values demand Government neutrality notwithstanding that in both contexts the Government is merely declining to support speech rather than prohibiting it altogether. . . .

Artistic expression, no less than academic speech or journalism, is at the core of a democratic society's cultural and political vitality. Congress recognized as much in establishing the NEA. For example, the Senate Report accompanying the NEA's creating devoted an entire section to "Freedom of Expression." It stated:

> It is the intent of the committee that in the administration of this act there be given the fullest attention to freedom of artistic and humanistic expression. . . . Countless times in history artists and humanists who were vilified by their contemporaries because of their innovations in style or mode of expression have become prophets to a later age.
>
> Therefore, the *committee affirms that the intent of this act should be the encouragement of free inquiry and expression. . . .*

[P]laintiffs analogize funding for the arts to funding of public universities. In both settings, limited public funds are allocated to support expressive activities, and some content-based decisions are unavoidable. Nonetheless, this fact does not permit the Government to impose whatever restrictions it pleases on speech in a public university, nor should it provide such license in the arts funding context. Hiring and promotion decisions based on professional evaluations of academic merit are permissible in a public university setting, but decisions based on vague criteria or intended to suppress unpopular expression are not. . . . Analogously, professional evaluations of artistic merit are permissible, but decisions based on the wholly subjective criterion of "decency" are not.

. . . Thus, the fact that the exercise of professional judgment is inescapable in arts funding does not mean that the Government has free rein to impose whatever content restrictions it chooses, just as the fact that academic judgment is inescapable in the university does not free public universities of First Amendment scrutiny. The right of artists to challenge conventional wisdom and values is a cornerstone of artistic . . . freedom. . . . Therefore, the court holds that Government funding of the arts is subject to the constraints of the First Amendment. . . .

Having concluded that public funding of art is entitled to First Amendment protection, the resolution of plaintiffs' challenge is straightforward. . . .

The decency clause clearly reaches a substantial amount of protected speech. In *Sable Communications of Cal., Inc. v. FCC,* . . . the Supreme Court held that "expression which is indecent but not obscene is protected by the First Amendment." . . . The statute seeks to confine the NEA's funding approval only to what is "decent." Conversely, it seeks to dissuade the NEA from funding what is "indecent." When a statute directed at speech is overbroad, as is the decency clause, it gives rise to the hazard that "a substantial loss or impairment of freedoms of expression will occur." . . .

The decency clause sweeps within its ambit speech and artistic expression which is protected by the First Amendment. The court, therefore, holds that the decency clause, on its face, violates the First Amendment for overbreadth and cannot be given effect.  ◆◆◆

Judge Tashima thus used an analogy between the purpose of academic expression and that of artistic expression to justify the conclusion that government funding of the arts was outside the ambit of the *Rust* principle. Once the *Rust* philosophy was found inapplicable, the decency clause was easily seen as unconstitutionally overbroad.

Judge Tashima's decision is consistent with the rationale that freedom of speech should promote individual autonomy (in this case, the artist's creative spirit). Given the historic role of art as a means of political expression, the district court's exemption of artistic expression from the *Rust* principle enhances government neutrality on political controversies. Another federal court used a different rationale to protect controversial expression from the dictates of *Rust*.

**Federal Grants for AIDS Education.**   The U.S. Centers for Disease Control (CDC) issued guidelines on grant proposals for AIDS education materials. These guidelines included a requirement that these materials should not

> Be offensive to a majority of the intended audience or to a majority of
> adults outside the intended audience unless, in the judgment of the Pro-
> gram Review Panel, the potential offensiveness of such materials is out-

weighed by the potential effectiveness in communicating an important HIV prevention message."[36]

A group of organizations interested in AIDS education challenged the regulation and argued that the grant terms were unconstitutionally vague. In *Gay Men's Health Crisis v. Sullivan*,[37] a New York federal district court agreed that the word *offensive* was vague, and therefore rejected the guidelines on First Amendment grounds. The federal court first set forth a criterion for determining vagueness in subsidized speech cases. Because the consequence of noncompliance with the grant regulations (that is, the penalty if one proposed to develop materials that the CDC deemed offensive) was "merely a reduction of a government subsidy," rather than a criminal or civil penalty, the court adopted a "mixed level of scrutiny" for vagueness. The regulation would be held vague if the grant terms have no "core meaning" that can be "reasonably understood by a person of ordinary intelligence."[38]

Despite the relaxed level of scrutiny, the district court found the regulations to be vague. For example, the grant terms provide no answer to questions such as:

> Can educational material be offensive simply because it mentions homosexuality? Because it depicts an interracial couple? . . . Does offensive apply to all descriptions of sexual behavior, graphic depictions of sexual behavior, or depictions of unusual sexual behavior?[39]

Furthermore, the court pointed out that the grant terms provide no guidance "as to how to balance two subjective, undefined, and seemingly incomparable terms [the effectiveness and offensiveness of education materials] against each other."[40] Hence the terms of the grant regulations were found to be void for vagueness because they had no core meaning. The court feared that self-censorship would result if AIDS education groups had to concentrate on proposals that would likely "pass the 'offensiveness' test with room to spare."[41]

The lesson from cases such as *Finley* and *Gay Men's Health Crisis* is that federal courts are not using the *Rust v. Sullivan* principle to give the government total control of the speech it subsidizes. Judge Tashima held that artistic expression, like academic speech, was of such value to society that it would receive First Amendment protection even if it were government subsidized. In

---

36. 55 *Fed. Reg.* 23414 (June 7, 1990).
37. 792 F. Supp. 278 (S.D.N.Y. 1992).
38. Id. at 293.
39. Id. at 294.
40. Id. at 296.
41. Id. at 303. Concern over the "offensiveness" test led one plaintiff organization to refrain from applying for a CDC grant. The Hetrick Martin Institute, which focuses its attention on gay and lesbian youth, believed that vernacular language and a gay-positive approach were essential in order to reach their target audience. Yet the organization believed there would be no point in attempting to secure funding for such materials.

*Gay Men's Health Crisis,* Judge Kram applied the vagueness doctrine to prevent the government from refusing to fund any "offensive" AIDS education materials. Federal district court opinions do not have the precedential value of Supreme Court decisions, but they have played a valuable role in allowing controversial subsidized expression into the marketplace of ideas.

### SUMMARY

When government subsidizes speech, it often attempts to proscribe what can or cannot be said, sometimes under the guise of an interest in promoting the efficiency of government services. Since the 1800s, control of government-subsidized speech has been justified by reference to the right/privilege dichotomy, suggesting that people receiving government benefits have no *right* to expect funding. Government subsidies are *privileges* that can be taken away or conditioned on the waiver of constitutional rights. More recently, courts have sometimes relied on the doctrine of unconstitutional conditions in subsidized speech cases, suggesting that government may not condition government funding on the surrender of constitutional rights.

When the government controls the speech it funds, the result is power in the marketplace of ideas. The government can use its considerable economic resources to further ideas it supports, and decline to fund ideas it finds objectionable. This effect was exemplified by *Rust v. Sullivan,* as the Court upheld government regulations that prevented health-care workers in government-subsidized clinics from counseling their pregnant patients about abortion. Conversely, it is difficult to defend absolute freedom of government-funded speech. Although a kindergarten teacher has every right to discuss abortion off the job, it *may* not seem unreasonable for the government to ban a discussion of this topic in a classroom full of five-year-olds.

Consequently, it is not surprising that in modern times, courts have wavered between the right/privilege and unconstitutional conditions doctrines in deciding subsidized speech cases. In the 1960s, the courts protected public employee speech on controversial issues such as communism and the war in Vietnam. However, employees received much less protection for speech not deemed a "public concern." Recently, the pendulum has swung further in the direction of government control. *Rust v. Sullivan* affirmed the general rule that governmental limits on speech are constitutional when the speech is government funded. Although this principle does not apply as strongly in contexts such as higher education and the arts, the cliche that "he who pays the piper calls the tune" applies to much subsidized speech. *Waters v. Churchill* made it clear that the courts will ordinarily defer to the government's justification for controlling the speech it funds.

The question of subsidized speech is likely to remain in the forefront of political controversy. As taxpayers become increasingly cynical about their government, and more carefully scrutinize government expenditures, the pressure to bend to majority will when funding expression on controversial topics will be great. If the norm becomes partisan intrusion into the market-place of ideas by the political branches of government, the judicial branch will be constrained by the *Rust v. Sullivan* principle in any effort to require neutrality.

## CHAPTER 13    Objectives

**After reading chapter 13,
you should understand
the following:**

◆ *How twentieth-century communication technologies have been subjected to greater **regulation** than has traditional spoken or printed communication.*

◆ *How the doctrine of **frequency scarcity** has been used to justify content regulation of radio and television broadcasts, with the goal of diversifying the viewpoints expressed in the marketplace of ideas.*

◆ *How the doctrine of radio and television **pervasiveness** has been used to justify regulation of "**indecent**" messages expressed on those media.*

◆ *How new technologies such as **cable television** and **computer networks** are significantly expanding society's options for communicating.*

◆ *The **First Amendment issues** raised by emerging communication technologies, including the questions of whether these media may be subjected to the same constraints as radio and television, and how free expression can be protected in a worldwide marketplace of ideas.*

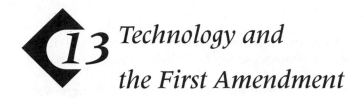

# 13 Technology and the First Amendment

In 1994, THE FEDERAL government attempted to levy 1.2 million dollars in fines against Howard Stern, a popular syndicated radio host sometimes called a "shock jock." Stern and his company—Infinity Broadcasting, which claims a daily audience in excess of 15 million listeners—were accused of violating broadcast codes that limit sexually explicit material on the airwaves.[1] Stern's radio program, which features an entourage/collection of comics, wits, and staff personalities, has been labeled hate-mongering, racist, anti-Semitic, and misogynistic.[2] But one thing this program is *not:* boring.[3]

A different governmental constraint was proposed in response to Stern's fellow talk-show personality Rush Limbaugh. Limbaugh's syndicated radio program is made up primarily of his own monologues, with help from occasional guests and call-ins. He gleefully attacks political liberals and the government programs they defend, such as affirmative action and welfare. Although Limbaugh does not go to the same visceral extremes as Stern,[4] his political opponents take exception to the decidedly partisan rhetoric of the host. His controversial diatribes against feminists (whom he labels "feminazis"), environmentalists ("environmental-whackos"), and Democrats (particularly Bill and Hillary Clinton) have led many to declare him (like Stern) offensive, racist, and crude.[5]

Frustration with the decidedly partisan content of Limbaugh's daily broadcasting material motivated some members of Congress to

1. As a means of punishing Stern the FCC has also considered blocking Infinity's purchase of other radio stations, slowing its expansion in the market. See *U.S. Weighs New Penalties Against Howard Stern,* Reuters World Service (January 1, 1994).
2. See, e.g., Terry Rakolta of Americans for Responsible TV, appearing on *Crossfire* (Transcript #999, Jan. 3, 1994).
3. In preparation for this and other First Amendment projects, at least one of the authors listened to Howard Stern's program for approximately seven months.
4. Compare, for example, Stern's "Adventures of Fart-Man" with Limbaugh's prerecorded songs lampooning Bill or Hillary Clinton.
5. See, e.g., Michael Kinsley, *Crossfire* (Transcript #999, Jan. 3, 1994).

advocate reinstating the **fairness doctrine,** which would have required broadcasters carrying partisan shows to provide airtime to opposing points of view.[6]

The federal government did not reinstate the fairness doctrine (also known as the "Hush Rush" bill). Nevertheless, the government response to Limbaugh's political broadcasts and Stern's indecent material raised another important question: Would either host be targeted for his speech *if he were not broadcasting his particular message?* As we learned in *Cohen v. California,* it is very difficult to regulate profanity unless it constitutes obscenity or fighting words; in chapter 7, we noted that hate speech regulations usually violate the First Amendment. Hence, the *content* of Stern's radio messages would be protected in most communication contexts unless they could be labeled obscene or fighting words. Limbaugh's rhetoric is largely political, serving the core First Amendment value of discussion about public affairs. Partisan rhetoric is a norm in political speech and debate in the United States, and the government could not constitutionally tell a public speaker to devote half of a presentation to opposing views.

What enabled our government to try to regulate Stern and Limbaugh owed less to the *content* of their speech and more to the *technology* that was their medium of expression: radio signals over the public airwaves.

Under current First Amendment law, what role does technology play in determining freedom of expression? Should our channel of communication be relevant in determining our First Amendment rights to express a particular message? In this chapter, we will examine these questions, with an eye toward both existing and developing information technologies.

## GOVERNMENT REGULATION OF TELEPHONE, RADIO, AND TELEVISION COMMUNICATION

Prior to the advent of new information systems such as the Internet, the primary technologies to implicate special government regulation were telephones, radio and television broadcasts, and finally, cable transmission of television.

### Telephone Companies: Common Carriers

Telephone companies have been considered **common carriers,** which means that they allow any person to use their communication technology to transmit messages of that person's design and choosing. By law, common carriers must provide nondiscriminatory service to the public.[7] Common carriers

---

6. This provision passed in the Senate as part of a campaign-finance reform measure. A similar bill was pushed by reps. Edward Markey (D–Mass.) and John Dingel (D–Mich.) in the House.
7. "The fundamental concept of a communications common carrier is that such a carrier makes a public offering to provide, for hire, facilities by wire or radio whereby all members of the public who choose to employ such facilities may communicate or transmit intelligence of their own design and choosing" (*National Association of Regulatory Utility Commissioners v. FCC,* 525 F.2d 630, 641, fn. 58 [D.C. Cir.1976], *cert. denied,* 425 U.S. 992 [1976]).

are generally not held liable for third-party transmissions over their technology (for example, libelous or obscene messages) because they do not have the right to exclude communicators from their services.[8]

Telephone networks are not *scarce,* as any person who can afford the service can use this technology to communicate. Telephone systems generally have been used for *interactive* conversations between two people (or more, with new technology that facilitates conference calls). Recently, telephone networks have also been used in less interactive contexts—for example, the transmission of prerecorded sales solicitations, or the sending of digital signals over a telephone network (as occurs when fax transmissions are sent).

## Radio and Television: Scarcity of Available Frequencies

Radio and television broadcasting has historically used technology that differs greatly from that of the conventional telephone. Radio and television broadcasts are not interactive, involving instead the transmission of signals from sender to receiver. Broadcasting channels are considerably more scarce than those for telephone communication because the technology employs the electromagnetic spectrum, for which there are a finite number of possible frequencies. Because of this limitation, under the Communications Act of 1934, the federal government reserved the right to regulate the licensing of applicants to broadcast along available frequencies. The FCC grants a license only "if public convenience, interest, or necessity will be served thereby."[9]

Radio licenses are usually granted for a term of seven years, while television licenses are granted for five years.[10] Supposedly the FCC has conditioned the awarding of a license upon the applicant's ability and willingness to serve the public interest. But what exactly is operation for the public interest? Originally, this was described as serving " . . . the public, and not for the purpose of furthering the private or selfish interests of individuals or groups of individuals. . . ."[11] This characterization seems almost comical in light of the typical programming of the 1990s. The ability to earn high ratings, which lead to lucrative advertising contracts for station owners, is a major factor in contemporary programming decisions. Today, the FCC tends to characterize public interest as comprising non-entertainment programming responsive to community needs.

## Cable Television: More Options for Broadcasters and the Public

Cable television relies on coaxial cables, rather than the electromagnetic spectrum, to transmit messages. Cable technology is similar to television and

---

8. Phillip H. Miller, *New Technology, Old Problem: Determining the First Amendment Status of Electronic Information Services,* 61 Fordham Law Review 1147, 1195–96 (April 1993).
9. 47 *U.S. Code* section 307(a); see also Section 309(a).
10. Id. at Section 307(c).
11. *Great Lakes Broadcasting Co.,* 3 F.R.C. ANN. REP. 32 (1929), *modified on other grounds* 37 F.2d 993 (D.C. Cir.) *cert. dismissed,* 281 U.S. 706 (1930).

radio broadcasting in that the signals operate in one direction (from sender to multiple receivers). However, cable technology does not suffer from the same scarcity that characterizes the electromagnetic spectrum. Current systems carry approximately seventy-five channels, but technology which can carry over five hundred channels is beginning to be utilized.[12] Cable television thus offers more options for its viewers than does conventional television. Like broadcast television and radio, cable television is regulated by the federal government,[13] which allows local authorities to require cable operators to devote a minimum number of channels to public, educational, and governmental use.

Of these technologies, radio and television broadcasting has provided the most First Amendment controversy. In chief, this has occurred with the development of two legal theories with respect to broadcasting: the aforementioned *scarcity* of broadcast frequencies, and the problem created by *pervasiveness* of the medium. Let us consider these in turn.

## ACCESS, SCARCITY, AND THE FAIRNESS DOCTRINE

### Issues Raised by Frequency Scarcity

If we begin with the premise that the frequencies of the electromagnetic spectrum are a public resource, then their limited or scarce nature may justify government conservancy, in the same way that endangered species or public land are protected. By logical connection, if one further assumes that the value or worth of these frequencies resides in their development for broadcasting purposes, then access to these frequencies can become a critical concern. Who should have this access? Who should be denied?

In a capitalist system, should access be conditioned solely on the ability of the broadcaster to pay the costs of this development and compete in a marketplace? It may be tempting to treat broadcasting licenses like most other goods and services and leave access to be conditioned by one's ability to pay. But so doing may leave us with other problems, for the scarcity of frequencies makes them more powerful in their ability to influence people. Simply put, if viewers have only a *limited* number of radio stations to listen to, or television stations to watch, their outlets for information will also be limited. And, considering that most Americans—even today—admit to getting most of their news from television,[14] it is not much of an inferential leap to claim that those few who hold broadcasting licenses, especially for television, can greatly influence the way many Americans think.

Perhaps the greatest manifestation of this fear was found in the federal government's promulgation of the fairness doctrine. The justification for the regulation was that diverse points of view on public issues might not be aired

---

12. See *The Message in the Medium: The First Amendment on the Information Superhighway,* 107 Harvard Law Review 1062, 1065 (March 1994).
13. See the Cable Communications Act of 1984, 47 *U.S. Code* Sections 534–55 (1988).
14. See Sidney Kraus, *Televised Presidential Debates and Public Policy,* pp. 9–10 (Earlbaum, 1988).

if programming decisions were left to the limited number of communicators who could be licensed to broadcast.

## The *Red Lion* Decision: Scarcity Justifies the Fairness Doctrine

If the government requires broadcasters to present both sides of controversial issues, are the broadcaster's First Amendment rights being denied? Is the fairness doctrine any different from efforts to coerce speech—such as mandating the flag salute—which have been found unconstitutional? The Supreme Court addressed this question in *Red Lion Broadcasting Co. v. FCC*.[15] As you read this decision, see how Justice White applies scarcity theory to justify the fairness doctrine.

### *Red Lion Broadcasting Co. v. FCC*, 395 U.S. 367 (1969)

Mr. Justice White delivered the opinion of the Court.

The Federal Communications Commission has for many years imposed on radio and television broadcasters the requirement that discussion of public issues be presented on broadcast stations, and that each side of those issues must be given fair coverage. This is known as the fairness doctrine. . . .

The Red Lion Broadcasting Company is licensed to operate a Pennsylvania radio station, WGCB. On November 27, 1964, WGCB carried a 15-minute broadcast by the Reverend Billy James Hargis as part of a "Christian Crusade" series. A book by Fred J. Cook entitled *Goldwater—Extremist on the Right* was discussed by Hargis, who said that Cook had been fired by a newspaper for making false charges against city officials; that Cook had then worked for a Communist-affiliated publication, that he had defended Alger Hiss and attacked J. Edgar Hoover and the Central Intelligence Agency; and that he had now written a "book to smear and destroy Barry Goldwater." When Cook heard of the broadcast he concluded that he had been personally attacked and demanded free reply time, which the station refused. After an exchange of letters among Cook, Red Lion, and the FCC, the FCC declared that the Hargis broadcast constituted a personal attack on Cook; that Red Lion had failed to meet its obligation under the fairness doctrine, . . . and that the station must provide reply time whether or not Cook would pay for it. . . .

The broadcasters challenge the fairness doctrine and its specific manifestations in the personal attack and political editorial rules on conventional First Amendment grounds, alleging that the rules abridge their freedom of speech and press. Their contention is that the First Amendment protects their desire to use their allotted frequencies continuously to broadcast whatever they choose, and to exclude whomever they choose from ever using that frequency. . . .

Although broadcasting is clearly a medium affected by a First Amendment interest, differences in the characteristics of new media justify differences in the First Amendment standards applied to them. . . .

15. 395 U.S. 367 (1969).

Where there are substantially more individuals who want to broadcast than there are frequencies to allocate, it is idle to posit an unabridgeable First Amendment right to broadcast comparable to the right of every individual to speak, write, or publish. If 100 persons want broadcast licenses but there are only 10 frequencies to allocate, all of them may have the same "right" to a license; but if there is to be any effective communication by radio, only a few can be licensed and the rest must be barred from the airwaves. . . . No one has a First Amendment right to license or to monopolize a radio frequency; to deny a station license because the public interest requires it is not a denial of free speech.

By the same token, as far as the First Amendment is concerned those who are licensed stand no better than those to whom licenses are refused. A license permits broadcasting, but the licensee has no constitutional right to be the one who holds the license or to monopolize a radio frequency to the exclusion of his fellow citizens. There is nothing in the First Amendment which prevents the Government from requiring a licensee to share his frequency with others and to conduct himself as a proxy or fiduciary with obligations to present those views and voices which are representative of his community and which would otherwise, by necessity, be barred from the airwaves. . . .

*It is the right of the viewers and listeners, not the right of the broadcasters, which is paramount* (emphasis added). It is the purpose of the First Amendment to preserve an uninhibited marketplace of ideas in which truth will ultimately prevail, rather than to countenance monopolization of that market, whether it be by the Government itself or a private licensee. "[S]peech concerning public affairs is more than self-expression; it is the essence of self-government." It is the right of the public to receive suitable access to social, political, esthetic, moral, and other ideas and experiences which is crucial here. That right may not constitutionally be abridged either by Congress or by the FCC. . . .

It is strenuously argued, however, that if political editorials or personal attacks will trigger an obligation in broadcasters to afford the opportunity for expression to speakers who need not pay for time and whose views are unpalatable to the licensees, then broadcasters will be irresistibly forced to self-censorship and and their coverage of controversial public issues will be eliminated or at least rendered wholly ineffective. Such a result would indeed be a serious matter, for should licensees actually eliminate their coverage of controversial issues, the purposes of the doctrine would be stifled.

At this point, however, as the Federal Communications Commission has indicated, that possibility is at best speculative. The communications industry, and in particular the networks, have taken pains to present controversial issues in the past, and even now they do not assert that they intend to abandon their efforts in this regard. . . . [I]f present licensees should suddenly prove timorous, the Commission is not powerless to insist that they give adequate and fair attention to public issues. . . .

In view of the scarcity of broadcast frequencies, the Government's role in allocating those frequencies, and the legitimate claims of those unable without governmental assistance to gain access to those frequencies for expression of their views, we hold the regulations and rulings at issue here are both authorized by statute and constitutional. . . .  ◆◆◆

After reading *Red Lion*, do you agree with Justice White's assumptions about the importance of the fairness doctrine or his dismissal of the broadcasters' First Amendment challenge? While grounding his opinion to uphold the fairness doctrine in a discussion of the scarcity theory, White also clearly implies that the fairness doctrine actually *promotes* speech, rather than restricting it, since allowing for opposing points of view adds to the diversity of viewpoints that enter the marketplace of ideas.

### The Fairness Doctrine Reconsidered

*Criticisms of the Fairness Doctrine.* In the years following *Red Lion*, criticism of the fairness doctrine—and, by implication, the scarcity theory—began to mount. First, the fairness doctrine could be criticized on the basis of its record, which showed spotty subjectivity at best.[16] In part, this was a natural result of FCC procedure, which required the following kind of analysis for a fairness doctrine complaint:

> [A]mong the many factors we are compelled to consider are whether the broadcaster was reasonable in concluding or not concluding that a controversial issue of public importance was represented, whether reasonable opportunities for contrasting viewpoints were given, and whether the program formats utilized and spokespersons chosen for the presentation were reasonable.[17]

Inevitably, where "reasonability" became the standard for determining whether the broadcaster's behavior was appropriate, all hopes of objectivity were dashed. For a broadcaster, what is a "reasonable" conclusion? Or a "reasonable" opportunity? These kinds of standards were inherently subjective.

Second, it was also true that although the fairness doctrine imposed the burden of ensuring a diversity of opinion on broadcasters, the federal government did not impose similar burdens on other media or speakers. Newspapers, magazines, and books had no reciprocal burden of an "opposite point of view."[18]

Third, the doctrine's goal of promoting more speech by requiring diversity of viewpoints proved problematic in practice. Many broadcasters who feared having to produce opposing points of view elected to forgo coverage of

---

16. See Thomas G. Krattenmaker and L. A. Powe, *The Fairness Doctrine Today: A Constitutional Curiosity and an Impossible Dream*, 1985 Duke L. J. 151 (1985).
17. Notice of Inquiry, 49 *Fed. Reg.* 20, 331 (1984).
18. See *Miami Herald v. Tornillo* 418 U.S. 241 (1974). In *Miami Herald*, the Supreme Court declared unconstitutional a Florida statute granting political candidates equal newspaper space to answer criticism and attacks on their records. The Court reasoned: "A newspaper is more than a passive receptacle or conduit for news, comment, and advertising. The choice of material to go into a newspaper, and the decisions made as to limitations on the size and content of the paper, and treatment of public issues and public officials—whether fair or unfair—constitute the exercise of editorial control and judgment. It has yet to be demonstrated how governmental regulation of this crucial process can be exercised consistent with First Amendment guarantees of a free press. . . ." Id. at 258.

the controversial positions.[19] If there was nothing to oppose, there would be no need for opposing viewpoints.

Finally, and perhaps most persuasively, the primary justification for the fairness doctrine—the scarcity theory—became less salient as alternatives to broadcast technology evolved. With the advent of cable television and home-owned satellite dishes, it was no longer realistic to argue that broadcasting options were scarce or limited in any real sense.

*Repeal of the Fairness Doctrine.*    Not surprisingly, the FCC could not ignore the problems associated with the fairness doctrine, and in 1987, repealed it.[20] That same year, Congress passed the Fairness in Broadcasting Act, attempting to reinstate the fairness doctrine. But President Reagan, perhaps being true to his radio and television roots, promptly vetoed it. Some six years later, in response to alleged partisan radio (referenced earlier in this chapter with Rush Limbaugh), some members of Congress tried again. Although this measure failed as well, those who believe there is not a balance of viewpoints in the marketplace of ideas may revive the fairness doctrine or the scarcity theory to support future regulations.

## THE CAPTIVE AUDIENCE: PERVASIVENESS AND THE MEDIUM

A second area of broadcasting regulation with implications for the First Amendment is suggested by the theory of **pervasiveness.** Here, the argument is that certain technologies, such as television and radio broadcasting, are so pervasive that they invade almost every aspect of our lives and cannot be easily ignored or dismissed.

Pervasive communication technologies are seen as particularly troubling when they intrude on a captive audience—one that cannot easily avoid the expression. The Supreme Court historically has been reluctant to deny a regulation that restricts expression, when the rule is directed toward protecting a captive audience that may not desire or appreciate the expression. The Court has shown traditionally favored regulations imposed on expression that targets a recipient in his or her home, since it is there that a viewer's or listener's privacy rights will be greatest.

### *FCC v. Pacifica Foundation:* **Pervasiveness Justifies Limits on "Indecent" Speech**

In *FCC v. Pacifica Foundation,*[21] the Supreme Court observed a connection between the *pervasiveness* of broadcasting and the potentially *captive audience* it reached, with respect to speech that was deemed "indecent" by FCC rules. The argument here assumed that so-called indecent material, when broadcast over

19. See, e.g., *Syracuse Peace Council v. F.C.C.,* 2 F.C.C.R. 5050 (1987), *aff'd,* 867 F.2d 654 (D.C. Cir 1989), *cert. denied,* 493 U.S. 1019 (1990).
20. See *Syracuse Peace Council,* 2 F.C.C.R. 5043.
21. 438 U.S. 726 (1978).

public airwaves, conflicted with the privacy interests of a captive audience, particularly where children might be part of that audience. As such, FCC rules that might proscribe such broadcasts were challenged.

As you read this opinion, see how Justice Stevens uses the pervasiveness theory in evaluating the FCC's rule in question, as well as the proscribed speech. Also note that here the Court is reviewing expression that is indecent but not necessarily obscene; consequently, expression that would ordinarily be protected under the *Miller v. California* test (discussed in chapter 9) may still be subject to regulation when it is broadcast over the airwaves.

The indecent communication at issue in *Pacifica* was a 1973 radio broadcast of a comedy monologue by comedian George Carlin. Presented below is a partial transcript of that monologue, as detailed in the appendix of the Supreme Court's opinion:

> Aruba-du, rube-tu, ruba-tu. I was thinking about the curse words and the swear words . . . that you can't say, that you're not supposed to say all the time. . . . Some guys like to record your words and sell them back to you if they can, *(laughter)* listen in on the telephone, write down what words you say. A guy who used to be in Washington knew that his phone was tapped, used to answer, Fuck Hoover, yes, go ahead. *(laughter)* Okay, I was thinking about the words you couldn't say on the public, ah, airwaves, um, the ones you definitely wouldn't say, ever, [']cause I heard a lady say bitch one night on television, and it was cool like she was talking about . . . the bitch is the first one to notice that in the litter Johnnie . . . And, uh, bastard you can say, and hell and damn, so I have to figure out which ones you couldn't and . . . it came down to seven but the list is open to amendment, and in fact has been changed. . . . The original seven words were: shit, piss, fuck, cunt, cocksucker, motherfucker, and tits. Those are the ones that will curve your spine, grow hair on your hands and *(laughter)* maybe even bring us, God help us, peace without honor *(laughter)*, um, and a bourbon. . . . "

### FCC v. Pacifica Foundation, 438 U.S. 726 (1978)

Mr. Justice Stevens delivered the opinion of the Court.

This case requires that we decide whether the Federal Communications Commission has any power to regulate a radio broadcast that is indecent but not obscene.

A satiric humorist named George Carlin recorded a 12-minute monologue entitled "Filthy Words" before a live audience in a California theater. He began by referring to his thoughts about "the words you couldn't say on the public, ah, airwaves, um, the ones you definitely wouldn't say, ever." He proceeded to list those words and repeat them over and over again in a variety of colloquialisms. The transcript of the recording . . . indicates frequent laughter from the audience.

At about 2 o'clock in the afternoon on Tuesday, October 30, 1973, a New York radio station, owned by respondent Pacifica Foundation, broadcast the "Filthy

Words" monologue. A few weeks later a man, who stated that he had heard the broadcast while driving with his young son, wrote a letter complaining to the Commission. . . .

The complaint was forwarded to the station for comment. In its response, Pacifica explained that the monologue had been played during a program about contemporary society's attitude toward language and that, immediately before its broadcast, listeners had been advised that it included "sensitive language which might be regarded as offensive to some." Pacifica characterized George Carlin as "a significant social satirist" who "like Twain and Sahl before him, examines the language of ordinary people. . . ."

On February 21, 1975, the Commission issued a declaratory order granting the complaint and holding that Pacifica "could have been the subject of administrative sanctions." The Commission did not impose formal sanctions, but it did state that the order would be "associated with the station's license file, and in the event that subsequent complaints are received, the Commission will then decide whether it should utilize any of the available sanctions it has been granted by Congress."

In its memorandum opinion the Commission stated that it intended to "clarify the standards which will be utilized in considering" the growing number of complaints about indecent speech on the airwaves. Advancing several reasons for treating broadcast speech differently from other forms of expression, the Commission found a power to regulate indecent broadcasting in two statutes, which forbids the use of "any obscene, indecent, or profane language by means of radio communications," and which requires the Commission to "encourage the larger and more effective use of radio in the public interest." . . .

[T]he Commission concluded that certain words [in Carlin's monologue] depicted sexual and excretory activities in a patently offensive manner, noted that they "were broadcast at a time when children were undoubtedly in the audience (i.e., in the early afternoon)," and that the prerecorded language, with these offensive words "repeated over and over," was "deliberately broadcast." In summary, the Commission stated: "We therefore hold that the language as broadcast was indecent and prohibited."

The Commission [later] issued another opinion in which it pointed out that it "never intended to place an absolute prohibition on the broadcast of this type of language, but rather sought to channel it to times of day when children most likely would not be exposed to it." . . .

Pacifica argues that inasmuch as the recording is not obscene, the Constitution forbids any abridgment of the right to broadcast it on the radio. . . .

When the issue is narrowed to the facts of this case, the question is whether the First Amendment denies government any power to restrict the public broadcast of indecent language in any circumstances. For if the government has any such power, this was an appropriate occasion for its exercise.

The words of the Carlin monologue are unquestionably "speech" within the meaning of the First Amendment. It is equally clear that the Commission's objections to the broadcast were based in part on its content. The order must therefore fall if, as Pacifica argues, the First Amendment prohibits all governmental regulation that depends on the content of speech. Our past cases demonstrate, however, that no such absolute rule is mandated by the Constitution.

The classic exposition of the proposition that both the content and the context of speech are critical elements of First Amendment analysis is Mr. Justice Holmes' statement for the Court in *Schenck v. United States.*

Other distinctions based on content have been approved in the years since *Schenck.* The government may forbid speech calculated to provoke a fight. . . . It may treat libels against private citizens more severely than libels against public officials. Obscenity may be wholly prohibited. . . .

[T]he fact that society may find speech offensive is not a sufficient reason for suppressing it. Indeed, if it is the speaker's opinion that gives offense, that consequence is a reason for according it constitutional protection. For it is a central tenet of the First Amendment that the government must remain neutral in the marketplace of ideas. If there were any reason to believe that the Commission's characterization of the Carlin monologue as offensive could be traced to its political content—or even to the fact that it satirized contemporary attitudes about four-letter words—First Amendment protection might be required. But that is simply not this case. These words offend for the same reasons that obscenity offends. Their place in the hierarchy of First Amendment values was aptly sketched by Mr. Justice Murphy when he said: "[S]uch utterances are no essential part of any exposition of ideas, and are of such slight social value as a step to truth that any benefit that may be derived from them is clearly outweighed by the social interest in order and morality." . . .

In this case it is undisputed that the content of Pacifica's broadcast was "vulgar," "offensive," and "shocking." Because content of that character is not entitled to absolute constitutional protection under all circumstances, we must consider its context in order to determine whether the Commission's action was constitutionally permissible.

We have long recognized that each medium of expression presents special First Amendment problems. And of all forms of communication, it is broadcasting that has received the most limited First Amendment protection. . . . The reasons for these distinctions [between broadcasting and other modes of communication] are complex but two have relevance to the present case. First, the broadcast media have established a uniquely pervasive presence in the lives of all Americans. Patently offensive, indecent material presented over the airwaves confronts the citizen, not only in public, but also in the privacy of the home, where the individual's right to be left alone plainly outweighs the First Amendment rights of an intruder. Because the broadcast audience is constantly tuning in and out, prior warnings cannot completely protect the listener or viewer from unexpected program content. To say that one may avoid further offense by turning off the radio when he hers indecent language is like saying that the remedy for an assault is to run away after the first blow. One may hang up on an indecent phone call, but that option does not give the caller a constitutional immunity or avoid a harm that has already taken place.

Second, broadcasting is uniquely accessible to children, even those too young to read. Although Cohen's written message might have been incomprehensible to a first grader, Pacifica's broadcast could have enlarged a child's vocabulary in an instant. Other forms of offensive expression may be withheld from the young without restricting the expression at its source. Bookstores and motion picture theaters, for example, may be prohibited from making indecent material available to children. We held in *Ginsberg v. New York,* that the government's interest in the "well-being of its youth" and in supporting "parents' claim to authority in their own household" justified the regulation of otherwise protected expression. The ease with which children may obtain access to broadcast material, coupled with the concerns recognized in *Ginsberg,* amply justify special treatment of indecent broadcasting.

It is appropriate, in conclusion, to emphasize the narrowness of our holding. This case does not involve a two-way radio conversation between a cab driver and a dispatcher, or a telecast of an Elizabethan comedy. We have not decided that an occasional expletive in either setting would justify any sanction or, indeed, that this broadcast would justify a criminal prosecution. The Commission's decision rested entirely on a nuisance rationale under which context is all-important. The concept requires consideration of a host of variables. The time of day was emphasized by the Commission. The content of the program in which the language is used will also affect the composition of the audience, and differences between radio, television, and perhaps closed-circuit transmissions, may also be relevant. As Mr. Justice Sutherland wrote, a "nuisance may be merely a right thing in the wrong place,— like a pig in the parlor instead of the barnyard." We simply hold that when the Commission finds that a pig has entered the parlor, the exercise of its regulatory power does not depend on proof that the pig is obscene. . . .   ◆◆◆

### Implications of the *Pacifica* Decision

Justice Stevens appears to rest his analysis on three premises which, if accurate, lead to his conclusion in upholding the FCC's position. The first revisits a concept we have explored repeatedly throughout this book—categorization. This holds that there are categorical exceptions to the First Amendment, forms of expression that the Constitution will *not* protect. Here Justice Stevens listed most of these exceptions, concluding with obscenity. And while acknowledging that Carlin's words may not have reached obscenity, he said that they were "indecent"—and may fit into a category of words that the First Amendment will not protect *in certain contexts.* Justice Stevens then relied on two other premises to reach the conclusion that broadcasting, at least during daytime hours, was one context in which indecent speech could be limited.

One of these was that broadcasting may receive less First Amendment protection because of its pervasive nature. In Stevens's words, . . . the broadcast media have established a uniquely pervasive presence in the lives of all Americans." This is the theory referenced before, which also suggests that the pervasiveness of broadcasting threatens the privacy interests of its audience in the home by acting as an "intruder."

Second, Justice Stevens assumes that the accessibility of Carlin's monologue to children created an untenable situation. As a captive audience, children were at special risk by the use of this technological medium for this message. A parent or child need only turn on the radio and instantly be exposed to indecent communication without warning (or if the parents are not present, children could listen without their consent). In Stevens's words, " . . . Pacifica's broadcast could have enlarged a child's vocabulary in an instant." Since we already "protect" children from other forms of expression, Stevens suggests, there is little reason not to do the same here.

## Attempted Extensions of the *Pacifica* Rationale

Justice Stevens's use of reasoning in *Pacifica* was specific to indecent speech over the *airwaves*, at a *time* when children were likely to be part of the audience. He was careful to note that the holding might not apply in other contexts. In each case, it would be important to consider "a host of variables," including the time of day, the composition of the audience, and the nature of the communication technology at issue.

Later federal cases have demonstrated what these differences might be. For example, in *Cruz v. Ferre*,[22] the Eleventh Circuit Court of Appeals held that a Miami ordinance prohibiting the distribution of obscene or indecent material on cable television was unconstitutionally overbroad. Indecent cable programming was found less pervasive than broadcast messages for a variety of reasons. Parents could select or reject supplementary cable packages such as HBO (where the indecent programming presumably could be found). Programming guides that warned parents of shows containing nudity, vulgarity, or violence were available, and finally, parents could obtain a lockbox to prevent children from gaining access to objectionable channels.[23]

Likewise, in *Sable Communications, Inc. v. FCC*,[24] the Supreme Court ruled that a restriction of interstate phone-sex telephone services was unconstitutional, although the rule was designed to protect children. A key difference for the Court was the fact that phone-sex services had put into place numerous steps (as the Court referred to them, "affirmative steps"), which required the listener to go to some lengths in order to receive the message.

The time of day during which regulations ban indecent material has also been an important concern when considering their constitutionality. A "safe harbor" was in effect during which indecent material could be broadcast from 10 P.M. through 6 A.M. In *Action for Children's Television v. FCC (ACT I)*,[25] the District of Columbia Circuit Court of Appeals found that an FCC decision to curtail the safe harbor to midnight through 6 A.M. was not based on

22. 755 F.2d 1415 (11th Cir. 1985).
23. Id. at 1420.
24. 492 U.S. 115 (1989).
25. 852 F.2d 1332 (D.C. Cir. 1988).

sufficient evidence. Judge Ruth Bader Ginsburg (who would subsequently be appointed to the Supreme Court by President Clinton) wrote that

> Broadcast material that is indecent but not obscene is protected by the First Amendment; the FCC may regulate such material only with due respect for the high value our Constitution places on freedom and choice in what the people say and hear.[26]   ◆◆◆

The D.C. Circuit Court also rejected a congressional attempt to require the FCC to ban all radio and television broadcasts of indecent material. In *Action for Children's Television v. FCC (ACT II)*,[27] the court rejected the argument that a total ban was justified because significant numbers of children under age eighteen listen to radio and watch television at all hours of the day. Congress could not "preclude access by adults who are interested in seeing or hearing such material" and prevent the FCC from "creating a safe harbor exception to its regulation of indecent broadcasts.[28]

These and other cases suggest that the real issue may not be so much the pervasive presence of the technology in society as much as a question of freedom of choice. Parents are seen as deserving the freedom to control whether their children see and hear indecent broadcasts during the day; however, the freedom of adults to view or listen to indecent broadcasts cannot be denied absolutely.

As any new communication technology gains in popularity, the urge to regulate expression will be ever-present. For example, in chapter 2, you read that British monarchs placed controls on the infant print media to prevent "seditious" expression. Earlier in this chapter, we discussed congressional efforts to limit the caustic diatribes of commentators such as Rush Limbaugh. Popular majorities may also want to impose their values on the American discourse and demand that their representatives limit "harmful" expression on these new technologies. Thus, we are likely to see arguments such as scarcity and pervasiveness used to justify restriction of emerging communication technology. How will the First Amendment impact on efforts to control twenty-first century communication in the next century?

### NEW TECHNOLOGIES, THE FIRST AMENDMENT, AND THE MARKETPLACE OF IDEAS

### New Communication Technologies and the First Amendment

Whenever the government attempts to regulate new communication technologies, First Amendment issues need to be addressed. Will a new technology be constitutionally subjected to the same restrictions as radio and television communication? By what criteria should it be determined whether ex-

26. Id. at 1344.
27. 932 F.2d 1504 (D.C. Cir. 1991), *cert. denied* 112 S. Ct. 1281 (1992).
28. Id. at 1509–10.

pression on new means of communication should be as free as the spoken or printed word, or subjected to heightened regulation?

Some commentators have expressed concern that the federal courts would simply decide which existing technology any new media is most analogous to, and apply the First Amendment rules for that existing technology to the new technology. Such an approach ignores the fact that "a political editorial is still a political editorial whether it is printed in a newspaper, . . . downloaded from a computer network, or faxed over a phone line."[29] Because the courts have often been reluctant to extend full First Amendment protection to new technologies, Harvard Professor Laurence Tribe proposed a constitutional amendment that would apply the guarantees of free speech and free press "without regard to the technological method or medium through which information content is generated, stored, altered, transmitted, or controlled."[30]

The Supreme Court considered the issue of First Amendment rules for one relatively new technology—cable television—in *Turner Broadcasting System, Inc. v. FCC*.[31] This case upheld the constitutionality of a federal law[32] requiring cable operators to carry the signals of a specified number of local commercial television stations and noncommercial educational television stations. (This set of regulations is often called the "must carry" rules, because cable operators are required to carry these stations as part of their programming.)

Justice Kennedy's majority opinion rejected the claim that cable television regulation should be governed by the same First Amendment standard that applies to broadcast television. The Court's reasoning emphasized differences between broadcast and cable technology:

[C]able television does not suffer from the inherent limitations that characterized the broadcast medium. Indeed, given the rapid advances in fiber optics and digital compression technology, soon there may be no practical limitation on the number of speakers who may use the cable medium. Nor is there any danger of physical interference between two cable speakers attempting to share the same channel. In light of these fundamental technological differences between broadcast and cable transmission, application of the more relaxed standard of scrutiny adopted in *Red Lion* and the other broadcast cases is inapt when determining the First Amendment validity of cable regulation.[33]   ◆◆◆

Although the Court held that cable television operators have greater First Amendment rights than do their broadcast counterparts, the must carry regulations were not found unconstitutional. Because the majority believed

---

29. "The Message in the Medium," *supra*, pp. 1062–63.
30. Edward J. Naughton, *Is Cyberspace a Public Forum? Computer Bulletin Boards, Free Speech, and State Action*, 81 Georgetown Law Journal 409, 411 n. 18 (December 1992).
31. 129 L.Ed. 2d 497 (1994).
32. Cable Television Consumer Protection and Competition Act of 1992, 47 *U.S. Code*, Sections 534, 535.
33. 129 L.Ed. 2d at 515.

that the must carry rules were content neutral,[34] the appropriate test for the constitutionality of the regulations was *Ward v. Rock Against Racism*.[35] The question was whether the regulations promote "a substantial government interest that would be achieved less effectively absent the regulation[s]."[36] The case was remanded so that the federal district court that originally heard the case could determine whether the test was met.[37]

The *Turner Broadcasting* decision provided evidence that the Supreme Court would not simply analogize a new technology (cable television) to an older one (broadcast television) and apply the same First Amendment rules. The Court will be called on to make many similar decisions about the free expression rules for new technologies in the future, because technological change is rapidly increasing our communication options.

### The Growth of an Information Superhighway

With the rapidly evolving on-line information services, which connect computers through telephone lines, an individual can now transmit or receive information by means of a computer and a modem device. Common uses of this technology include sending and receiving messages through electronic mail (e-mail), accessing bulletin boards or lists (which serve as forums for discussion), and receiving data from companies providing information services (e.g., LEXIS/NEXIS).

How prevalent is this technology? In 1995 it was reported that 35 percent of all American households have at least one personal computer.[38] More to the point, the recent surge in computer purchases has been for the home market (70 percent of sales, according to a recent estimate),[39] suggesting that what the television was to the last generation, the computer will be to the next.

Computer networks are also gaining popularity. One of the more famous is the Internet, a noncommercial network originally designed to link universities and colleges. Today it also links laboratories and government organizations as well as private individuals. It boasts at least ten million users,[40] among whom the average age is twenty-three and rapidly dropping.[41]

---

34. Id. at 518. Justice O'Connor's dissent, joined by justices Scalia, Ginsburg, and Thomas, disagreed with the conclusion that the must carry rules are content neutral. Justice O'Connor wrote that the justifications for the 1992 Cable Act, such as "preferences for diversity of viewpoints, for localism, for educational programming, and for news and public affairs all make reference to content," even if they do not reflect hostility to particular points of view." Id. at 531.
35. 491 U.S. 781 (1989). This case was discussed in chapter 10.
36. 129 L.Ed. 2d at 530.
37. Id. at 534. Congress asserted that the rules were justified by three government interests: "(1) preserving the benefits of free, over-the-air local broadcast television, (2) promoting the widespread dissemination of information from a multiplicity of sources, and (3) promoting fair competition in the market for television programming." Id. at 530.
38. See Nicholas Negroponte, *homeless@.info.hwy.net*, New York Times, p. 15 (February 11, 1995).
39. Id.
40. See John Markoff, "Building the Electronic Superhighway, *New York Times*, p. 6 (Jan. 23, 1994).
41. See Negroponte, p. 15.

This technology will one day be joined by advanced television technologies capable of offering almost unlimited combinations of television programming (at least 500 channels to start), home shopping, financial and banking services, and entertainment—interactive and with video. When combined, this so-called information superhighway may very well link homes, businesses, government, and schools—as well as nations—all along a fiber optic network.[42] It has been suggested that this technology will fundamentally change the way we think, learn, consume, communicate, and govern our affairs in the next century.

## Challenges to Free Speech on the Information Superhighway

Freedom of speech controversies on the information superhighway have already begun, and they will increase as the use of this network grows. For example, in response to the threat of militia groups, California Senator Dianne Feinstein argued that hate speech and bomb making manuals should be banned from the Internet. Perhaps more significantly, a ban on indecent material was written into a recent Congressional telecommunications bill.[43] The Telecommunications Act of 1996, signed into law by President Clinton, and backed by officials from the House and Senate, demonstrated government's intent to police cyberspace at the Federal level. Included within the Telecommunications Act is language aimed at regulating indecency over the Internet. As noted in the final conference report:

> The conferees intend that the term indecency . . . has the same meaning as established in *FCC v. Pacifica* . . . and *Sable Communications of California Inc. v. FCC*. These cases clearly establish the principle that the federal government has a compelling interest in shielding minors from indecency. . . . The precise contours of the definition of indecency have varied slightly depending on the communications medium to which it has been applied. The essence of the phrase—patently offensive descriptions of sexual and excretory activities—has remained constant, however. . . . There is little doubt that indecency can be applied to computer mediated communications consistent with constitutional strictures, insofar as it has already been applied without rejection in other media contexts, including telephone, cable and broadcast radio.[43a]

As of the time of this writing, the new law had engendered legal action by nearly two dozen groups challenging the Act's constitutionality. Two large cases, *ACLU v. Reno* and *American Library Association v. Reno* were consolidated and heard by a three-judge panel in U.S. District Court in Philadelphia. On June 12, 1996, the 3rd Circuit Court of Appeals found the indecency language

42. "The First Amendment on the Information Superhighway," p. 1067.
43. Rory J. O'Connor, *Cyberspace Hate Speech, Bomb Data Raising Questions*, The Fresno Bee, p. A6 (May 12, 1995).
43a. See PL 104104, The Telecommunications Act of 1996, Conference Report (January 31, 1996) at pp. 188–9.

*Figure 13.1.   University students and users of the internet protest the passage of the Telecommunications Act of 1996, and the threat they feel it poses to free expression in cyberspace. (Joe Tuman.)*

in the Act to be unconstitutional. Justice Dalzell wrote: The Internet may be fairly regarded as a never ending worldwide conversation. The Government may not, through the CDA, interrupt that conversation. As the most participatory form of mass speech yet developed, the Internet deserves the highest protection from governmental intrusion.[43b] Meanwhile, seeking to lead rather than be led by regulations, officials for Prodigy, a privately owned computer network, have begun to use "George Carlin software" to search for objectionable words in subscribers' messages.[44]

Students' expression on the information highway has also been targeted (see Figure 13.1). A high school honor student published an unofficial "Newport High School Home Page" on the Internet, which claimed that classmates "majored in football" and were preoccupied with sex. The home page also offered information about sexually explicit material on the Internet. In response, the high school principal withdrew support for the student as a national merit finalist, and withdrew the school's recommendations from the universities to which the student had applied.[45] A University of Michigan stu-

43b. See civil action no 96–963 (1996).

44. Peter H. Lewis, *No More "Anything Goes": Cyberspace Gets Censors,* The New York Times, p. A1 (June 29, 1994).

45. Melanie J. Mavrides, *ACLU Takes First Internet Censorship Case,* The Fresno Bee, p. A12 (May 28, 1995).

dent was arrested for allegedly writing and transmitting a violent work of fiction, in which the female victim had the same name as a fellow student.[46] The work, which recounted the sexual torture of the woman, was read by a Michigan alum, who alerted university officials; they in turn involved campus police and Federal agents. The FBI charged the young man with transporting threatening material across state lines, a federal offense.

The Supreme Court has yet to rule on freedom of speech on the information highway. The Court will inevitably confront this issue as government regulators and private owners of computer networks attempt to limit expression. Advocates of speech restrictions in cyberspace will argue that heightened regulation is permissible, due to the nature of the technology, much as radio and television have been subjected to greater regulation. How might First Amendment challenges to these restrictions be resolved? The next section of this chapter will analyze this question.

## First Amendment Doctrine and the Information Superhighway

Communication in cyberspace raises many First Amendment issues. One concerns the free expression rights of those who send and receive information through this technology. The rights and responsibilities of entities who *operate* computer networks (such as private enterprises and the government) and sell or give access to communicators must also be considered. Finally, there is the question of freedom of speech on a "worldwide web" of computer networks. When communicators from two nations with very different perspectives on freedom of expression interact in cyberspace, how should free speech rights be determined?

### Freedom of Speech for Communicators on the Information Superhighway

*First Amendment Rights of Network Users.* The pervasiveness rationale that was used in *Pacifica* to justify constraints on radio and television expression does not seem applicable to computer networks. The *Pacifica* majority was concerned that children could inadvertently be exposed to offensive language at the turn of a radio dial. Although there is certainly a risk that computer literate children could encounter indecent discourse while "surfing the net," there are significant differences between radio/television and computer communication. First, a user must take significant and affirmative steps to access a computer network. He or she must purchase the requisite computer technology, subscribe to a computer network, and understand how to access that network (which often requires having a password). A child (or an adult with a child in his or her presence) would need to take several such steps before being exposed to indecent language; the mere act of turning on a computer would be insufficient. Thus, computer networks are more analogous to the

---

46. See Peter Lewis, *An Internet Author of Sexually Violent Fiction Faces Charges*, New York Times, p. 7 (Feb. 11, 1995).

telephone services protected in *Sable Communications*[47] than the radio in *Pacifica.* The logic of the Eleventh Circuit Court of Appeals in *Cruz v. Ferre*[48] provides an additional argument against using the pervasiveness rationale to justify content controls in cyberspace: Parents need not disclose passwords to their children.

Even if the pervasiveness issue is resolved in favor of communicators, expression in cyberspace will still be subject to the rules that generally limit First Amendment rights regardless of the medium. However, the unique nature of computer network communication will help determine whether the free speech rules you have studied in earlier chapters will apply to any particular message in cyberspace. How would issues such as incitement to illegal conduct, defamation, obscenity, and subsidized speech be resolved when the messages are conveyed through cyberspace?

The ease with which ordinary citizens can reach a large and sympathetic audience may increase the probability that incitement to illegal conduct would not be protected by the First Amendment. During World War I, Jacob Abrams circulated his call for draft resistance by dropping leaflets out of an office window, where they floated down to whoever was passing by.[49] A militia group member advocating violence against federal officials could use a computer bulletin board specifically created for those who were sympathetic to the militia movement, and reach the target audience much more effectively than could Mr. Abrams. The result may be an increased likelihood that the third prong of the *Brandenburg*[50] test (illegal conduct must be likely to result before speech can be penalized) could be met.

In defamation or invasion of privacy cases, cyberspace communication raises some interesting questions. Courts will need to address actual malice issues: Would a reporter be justified in deciding that a source of information with whom he or she had only communicated via computer was truthful, or would it constitute "reckless disregard for the truth" to rely on a person known only by a pseudonym on the Internet? Damage awards may increase in some cases because computer networks enable most people to convey a defamatory statement (or disclosure of a private fact) to a larger audience than they could ordinarily reach, thereby increasing the harms caused by a false claim.

Defamation claims will also pose choice of law questions. From state to state, the law varies on several significant issues, such as the standard of fault (e.g., actual malice or negligence) required to sustain a verdict of liability, the rules for determining when a statement is constitutionally protected as opinion, and the availability of punitive damages.[51] Which state law should be ap-

47. See p. 343, *supra.*
48. See p. 343, *supra.*
49. See chapter 4 for a discussion of *Abrams.*
50. See chapter 4.
51. John D. Faucher, *Let the Chips Fall Where They May: Choice of Law in Computer Bulletin Board Defamation Cases,* 26 University of California, Davis Law Review 1045, 1052–53 (Summer 1993).

plied if a defamatory message about a person residing in one state is posted to a computer bulletin board by a person in a second state, and read by persons in many different states? Because existing rules for choice of law are complex, one commentator has argued that the federal courts should develop and apply a federal common law for cases involving defamation on computer bulletin boards.[52]

Obscenity is a category of expression which is unprotected by the Constitution, and the FBI is already investigating online pornography.[53] Presumably a government rule that meets the *Miller*[54] obscenity standard could constitutionally be applied to on-line sexual expression. But two questions are raised. One is how the *Stanley v. Georgia*[55] decision would impact regulation of obscenity in cyberspace. *Stanley* upheld the right to possess obscene materials in the privacy of one's home. If a person is experiencing such materials on a personal computer in his or her own home, the on-line consumer's expectation of privacy is the same as if he or she were reading a book or magazine; hence, the *Stanley* rationale should protect the receiver. However, a Supreme Court that has become more conservative in the past two decades may find a reason to uphold sanctions when cyberspace is the channel of communication.

A second obscenity question relates to the issue of contemporary community standards. Under the *Miller* test, the trier of fact must apply such standards to decide if a work appeals predominantly to the prurient interest. In cyberspace, without boundaries, there are almost limitless combinations of "virtual communities." If a person in Texas transmits an obscene message through electronic mail, which physically passes through Oklahoma as digital data (not pornographic words or images), and is then read on a computer screen in Kansas, where is the community whose standards should be ascertained?

The fact that on-line communication technology may be funded by the government raises a subsidized speech issue. Refer to the two earlier cases involving students' free expression rights on the Internet: If the computers used were property of a public educational institution, school administrators would likely claim that under *Rust v. Sullivan*,[56] they have a right to control expression on those computers. The *Rust* philosophy was evident in *Hazelwood School District v. Kulmeier*,[57] a decision in which the Court upheld a high school principal's censorship of articles on pregnancy and divorce in the student newspaper. In *Hazelwood*, Justice White's majority opinion noted that

> [A] school must also retain the authority to refuse to sponsor student speech that might reasonably be perceived to advocate . . . conduct . . . in-

52. Id. at 1051.
53. Mike Snider, *FBI Probes On-Line Child Pornography*, USA Today, p. D1 (January 23, 1995).
54. See chapter 9.
55. See chapter 9.
56. See chapter 9.
57. 484 U.S. 260 (1987).

consistent with the shared values of a civilized social order, or to . . . associate the school with any position other than neutrality on matters of political controversy.[58]

An elementary or secondary school administrator could probably prevail if he or she wanted to sanction a student for using a school-owned computer to send a controversial message or one that is inconsistent with our nation's "shared values." A cyberspace communicator would have greater rights in a public university, even if the computer were government property. The *Rust* opinion acknowledged that "the university is a traditional sphere of free expression," and that therefore the *Rust* principle "is restricted by the vagueness and overbreadth doctrines of the First Amendment."[59]

Due to this caveat in *Rust,* a public university would need clear rules regarding faculty or student cyberspace communication that would not be permitted, rather than rules that would require ordinary persons to "guess at their meaning."[60] The rule would also need to ban only constitutionally unprotected expression. For example, even if a university could ban a story such as the Michigan student's (described earlier in this chapter) from a computer bulletin board devoted to science, a rule that also excluded a story from an on-line creative writing forum would be overbroad. If the university is funding student participation in a forum devoted to creative writing, the university could not constitutionally ban stories because it objected to their content.[61]

In addition to questions about the user's right to express the content of a particular message, there is also a question of whether a user has a right of *access* to computer networks. Network operators are ordinarily private enterprises who are not bound by the First Amendment's constraints on the *government.* Can the operator of a computer network deny access to those persons or viewpoints the operator finds objectionable?[62]

In 1946, the Supreme Court held that for purposes of the First Amendment the business district in a privately owned company town could be treated as though it were publicly held.[63] It has been argued that computer bulletin boards are fast becoming the "modern day equivalents of the streets, parks, and commons of the eighteenth century town," and that therefore a right of access should be guaranteed.[64] That the Supreme Court would rule in favor of such a right of access is in doubt in light of its holdings in *Lloyd Corpo-*

58. Id. at 272.
59. 114 L.Ed.2d at 260.
60. See chapter 12.
61. The cases in chapter 7 on hate speech stand for the proposition that a university cannot control expression on the grounds that it objects to its content.
62. This issue is discussed in detail in Naughton, supra.
63. *Marsh v. Alabama,* 326 U.S. 501 (1946).
64. Naughton, supra, p. 419. The proposal was developed by Jerry Berman and Marc Rotenberg of the American Civil Liberties Union and the Computer Professionals for Social Responsibility. See *Free Speech in an Electronic Age,* New York Times, p. C13 (January 6, 1991).

*ration v. Tanner*[65] and *Hudgens v. NLRB.*[66] The *Lloyd* and *Hudgens* opinions maintained that there is no First Amendment right of access to a privately owned shopping center, because such an institution is not the equivalent of a municipality.[67]

If the use of technology evolves, and persons increasingly choose to communicate via computer rather than traditional public spaces such as parks and sidewalks, the argument that computer networks are the functional equivalent of these public spaces becomes stronger. Nevertheless, it would be surprising to see the Court granting a right of access to privately owned computer networks. The *Lloyd* opinion distinguished the company town in *Marsh* from a shopping center by noting that the former "involved the assumption by a private enterprise of *all* of the attributes of a state-created municipality" (emphasis added).[68] Operators of a computer network may manage an increasingly large percentage of all public communication in the future, but they will not assume all the attributes of a municipality. Only a very pessimistic futurist would predict a society in which public places such as streets and parks cease to be used for expression because everybody stays at home communicating with others through their impersonal computers.

## First Amendment Rights of On-Line Operators

The First Amendment concerns of on-line network operators do not parallel those of their subscribers. These include questions of the operator's right to ban messages it finds objectionable and the operator's liability for messages that subscribers have sent using its network.

May on-line operators censor the messages of their users? Some businesses that run computer networks have already placed some constraints on their subscribers. Earlier in this chapter we noted how Prodigy had developed "George Carlin" software, which finds messages with objectionable words. Prodigy also banned discussion of an increase in its user fee from its public bulletin boards.[69] America Online shut down forum discussions containing material that may not be suitable for children. This action resulted in the closing of several feminist discussion forums: apparently, AOL was afraid that young girls would see the word *girl* in forum headlines and "go in there looking for information about their Barbies."[70]

Based on the results of cases to date, the courts could easily uphold the First Amendment rights of the network operators, rather than the rights of the users. In *Turner Broadcasting,* the Supreme Court held that restrictions on the programming decisions of cable television operators would receive

65. 407 U.S. 551 (1972).
66. 424 U.S. 507 (1976).
67. 407 U.S. at 568–69, 424 U.S. at 520–21.
68. 407 U.S. at 569.
69. Naughton, supra, p. 410.
70. Lewis, supra, p. A1.

heightened scrutiny.[71] In *Miami Herald,* the Court upheld the right of a newspaper to choose the material it will publish.[72] A lower federal court suggested that in the context of cyberspace, the free expression rights of the network operator would be paramount. In *Cubby, Inc. v. CompuServe, Inc.,*[73] a New York federal district court indicated that a computer service company that operated an electronic news library "may decline to carry a given publication."[74] In *Red Lion,* the Supreme Court did invoke the *scarcity* rationale to legitimize government-imposed radio and television access, so that diverse ideas may be disseminated.[75] Because there will be an almost infinite *physical* capacity for communicating messages on the information superhighway,[76] the frequency scarcity rationale of *Red Lion* would not apply.

If the free expression rights of network operators are given primacy over those of network viewers, the free marketplace of ideas could be compromised, with the probability that the electronic information services industry will be dominated by a few large companies.[77] If these few companies share a similar political ideology, and they wish to control the content of messages on their networks, these companies could keep objectionable ideas off an increasingly significant communication medium. If advertising becomes an important source of revenue for network operators, they may also come under intense pressure to censor messages that network sponsors object to. To avoid this possible constraint on a free marketplace of ideas in cyberspace, some commentators have advocated universal access to the information highway.[78]

In addition to the access issue, there is also a question of whether network operators should be held liable for messages transmitted over their systems. If a message sent over a computer network violates criminal law or commits a tort (such as a defamation or invasion of privacy), should liability be limited to the source of the message, or should the network operator be subject to sanctions as well? The incidence and seriousness of such challenges to network operators are likely to increase in the future. If the government is determined to eradicate a certain type of communication (for example, obscenity), it could limit that communication more efficiently by punishing network operators than by going after individual communicators on the network. In civil cases, the network operator is more likely to have "deep pockets" than an individual user, giving defamation plaintiffs and their lawyers an incentive to sue the operator.

The issue of operator liability was considered in the aforementioned *Cubby* decision, because the plaintiffs had argued that CompuServe should be liable for defamatory statements contained in its electronic library. The state-

71. 129 L.Ed. 2d at 517.
72. 418 U.S. at 258.
73. 776 F. Supp. 135 (S.D.N.Y. 1991).
74. Id. at 140.
75. See 335, supra.
76. *The Message in the Medium,* supra, p. 1088.
77. Miller, supra, p. 1196.
78. See, e.g., Miller, id., and *The Message in the Medium,* supra, p. 1089.

ments allegedly were made on a publication known as *Rumorville USA*, which was not owned or operated by CompuServe. The New York District Court noted that CompuServe had no control over a publication such as *Rumorville*, one of the thousands contained in its database. It would be "no more feasible for CompuServe to examine every publication it carries for potentially defamatory statements than it would be for any other distributor [such as a library or bookstore] to do so." Therefore, CompuServe could not be held liable unless it "knew or had reason to know" of the allegedly defamatory statements.[79]

Of course, since *Cubby* was a federal district court decision, it is possible that other federal courts would reach a different result. The reasoning of the district court in *Cubby* makes sense because it would be unreasonable to expect an operator to screen every message to ensure no criminal or civil wrongs have been committed. The result in *Cubby* also avoids the chilling effect that would result if operators felt safe transmitting only messages that they knew created no risk of legal liability. However, it cannot be said with certainty that the district court's holding will become the law of the land.

Issues of rights and liabilities for network operators and users have implications that extend beyond the borders of the United States. The growth of the information superhighway has enabled a person in one country to communicate with a worldwide audience. International communication between any message source and audience is feasible, as long as all parties have a computer, a modem, and telephone technology to call overseas. The final section of this chapter will consider freedom of expression in this international marketplace of ideas.

### The Information Superhighway: Freedom of Expression Worldwide?

The marketplace of ideas in cyberspace is now global. Twenty-five million people[80] in more than one hundred countries[81] are linked by the Internet. A market research firm projected that by the year 2000, consumers in international markets (particularly Asia-Pacific and European nations) "will spend more than $48 [b]illion on home personal computers, exceeding spending in the United States by nearly 80%."[82]

The freedom of speech environment differs greatly among the many countries linked by the Internet. As one German network user pointed out, "What First Amendment? . . . No such thing here, or in any country besides the U.S.A."[83] The risk of a government searching for objectionable messages and deleting them from the system is very real. There is also a possibility that a user could send an international message that would be illegal to write or

---

79. 776 F. Supp. at 140–41.
80. Lewis, supra, p. D5.
81. *The Message in the Medium*, supra, p. 1066.
82. *Study Says PC Sales Rise Faster Abroad*, New York Times, p. C7 (September 18,1995) (quoting a study by LINK Resources).
83. Lewis, supra, p. D5.

say in the receiver's country. There are no international agreements for re-solving this type of controversy.

The nature of the information superhighway may act as a constraint on censorship in the international marketplace. This is exemplified by the situation in China, where there are now two million personal computers, and users can communicate on the World Wide Web (which translates to "ten thousand dimensional web in heaven and net on Earth" in Chinese).[84] Although the Chinese government censors publishing, broadcasting, and speech, and will likely tap electronic communications as well, leaders may find effective censorship to be too onerous. With the increasing volume of electronic communication, the government will have a more difficult time monitoring the information. Furthermore, because of the importance of the Internet in business and science, China may have no choice but to allow access to the information highway as the nation continues to develop economically.[85] Chinese authorities may take solace from the fact that the global marketplace of ideas is not limited to hostile critiques of Chinese actions.

In a world with so many different perspectives on the value of free expression, how can *our* government (or our First Amendment) hope to regulate or influence expression now taking place on a global basis? If there is to be an international agreement in favor of freedom of speech in cyberspace, the solution may be found in chapter 2 of this text. Although our First Amendment *is* a cornerstone of our individual rights tradition, we can hardly claim that freedom of speech is uniquely an American idea. For centuries many different cultures around the world have struggled with issues of free expression. The American experiment has contributed mightily to the development of this concept, but we are not alone in our efforts to further this liberty.

Thus, it is possible that the solution for protecting expression on the worldwide information superhighway can come about only if we return to a history of free expression rooted in *many* cultures. Only a global, multicultural dialogue and consciousness can provide solutions to questions of expression in cyberspace beyond America's boundaries.

As technology shrinks our world, there is something comforting in that sentiment.

### SUMMARY

In this chapter we examined the influence of technology on communications and its implications for freedom of speech. Technological developments such as the telephone, radio, and television (broadcast and cable) allowed for rapid expansion and dissemination of ideas and communication, although each development also posed its share of problems.

84. Steven Mufson, *The Internet Scales a Great Wall in China*, The Washington Post National Weekly Edition, p. 16 (June 26–July 2, 1995).
85. Id.

Radio and television posed unique dilemmas, since both operated within a limited number of broadcast frequencies and both (especially television) grew to be a dominant communications medium. In many households, television has become the convenient and almost hypnotic babysitter for a new generation of toddlers. Out of such realities grew theories of *scarcity* and *pervasiveness* of communications technology, which our government used to justify regulatory attempts like the fairness doctrine or rules about "indecency." These in effect provided government control over free speech on radio and television. Although the fairness doctrine is now defunct, it is still remembered (and occasionally resurrected) by those in Congress who are seemingly uncomfortable with what they see or hear. Moreover, the concepts of scarcity and pervasiveness have not changed significantly through the years.

However, what has changed—and will continue to change—is the technology of communications. Rapid developments in information technology have led to the creation of computer networks like the Internet, and of current and future advanced television technologies capable of offering a variety of educational, business, and social services. This information superhighway may one day link all homes, businesses, schools, and governments. Although some of this technology is still in development, other parts of it are a reality today.

Such a reality has expanded our concept of the marketplace of ideas metaphor, and in so doing has presented judges, lawyers, and legal scholars with a new set of questions about freedom of speech. The old theories of scarcity and pervasiveness do not so easily apply in this technology context. Categorical exceptions to our First Amendment, such as obscenity or defamation, are more difficult to prosecute. Perhaps most perplexing of all is that this form of technology eradicates geopolitical boundaries as we know them, even bringing into question if or how our country (or any other) can effectively regulate ideas that are expressed and exchanged.

The result of this may very well be a new global consciousness that will address *freedom of speech in the marketplace of ideas,* as we move ahead into the next century and beyond.

# Glossary

**absolutism**   The theory that the First Amendment affords total (absolute) protection of speech rights. To an absolutist, there is no acceptable justification for restricting the expression of any viewpoint.

**actual malice**   A particular state of the communicator's mind at the time of making a false statement. In *New York Times v. Sullivan,* the Supreme Court defined this state of mind to exist when a message source either (1) knows that a statement is false or (2) acts with reckless disregard for whether the statement is false or not.

**ad hoc balancing**   A judicial test for determining the constitutionality of speech restrictions. Under this approach, the court analyzes whether the restriction on expression provides more benefits than harms to society. In making the benefit-harm comparison, freedom of speech is not assigned a uniquely high value relative to other social goals.

**amicus curae**   Friend of the court (Latin). Refers to a person or persons who are not parties to a case, but are invited or permitted to submit information for the court's consideration. For example, the American Civil Liberties Union often submits briefs to the Supreme Court supporting the free speech rights of a party to a case.

**appeal**   A challenge to a judicial decision, in which a higher court is asked to modify the decision of a lower court. Ordinarily, an appeal only involves review of the issues raised and testimony given in the lower court proceedings. Questions of law are more likely to be reversed on appeal than are questions of fact. The factual findings of the jury or trial judge are ordinarily deemed conclusive.

**appellant**   The party to an appeal who argues for reconsideration of the lower court's decision.

**appellate court**   A court that rules on appeals from decisions of a lower court. Appellate courts ordinarily focus on whether the lower court followed the correct rules and procedures in reaching its decision.

**appellee**   The party to an appeal who did not request reconsideration of the lower court's decision. Ordinarily, the appellee argues that the lower court's decision should be upheld.

**as applied**   Refers to a law that is unconstitutional as applied in a particular case, even though the same law might not be found to deprive constitutional rights if applied in a different context. Compare to a law that is unconstitutional **on its face.**

**bad tendency**   Speech is said to have a bad tendency when a communicator intends or hopes that the words will inspire or result in illegal acts, and that his or her speech might have the effect of inspiring such acts. Compare with **clear and present danger.**

**blasphemy**   Expression that is sacrilegious (disrespectful of a deity or belittling of religion). This type of speech includes curses that take a deity's name in vain, and jokes about religious figures and doctrines. Prohibitions on blasphemy have usually been directed at speech that demeans the dominant religion of a society.

**certiorari**    *See* **writ of certiorari.**

**chilling effect**    An effect created by a speech restriction that is written or applied so that persons refrain from expressing ideas that are constitutionally protected, out of fear that their speech will result in legal sanction.

**civil case**    A judicial proceeding in which the complaining party alleges a violation of his or her personal rights, rather than a violation of the criminal laws of society. A defamation lawsuit, or a government employee's lawsuit alleging wrongful termination based on the exercise of protected speech are examples of civil cases.

**clear and present danger**    An effect caused by speech which creates a significant risk of motivating an illegal act. The clear and present danger test requires the government to prove a higher probability that speech will result in a criminal act than does the **bad tendency** test.

**common carrier**    A communication network available on a nondiscriminatory basis to people who are willing to pay for its use.

**common law**    Legal rules established through judicial decisions, rather than by the executive or legislative branch of government. When courts decide cases based on legal principles that have been established in previous judicial opinions, their decisions are based on the common law.

**communitarian**    One who holds that the obligations of citizens to society are equally important as the individual rights guaranteed to citizens. In the freedom of speech context, communitarians argue that we ought to refrain from exercising our freedom of speech if our expression might be dangerous to society or injurious to others.

**concurring opinion**    A judicial opinion that holds in favor of the court's result but is based on reasoning that differs from that of the majority (or plurality) of the justices.

**content neutral**    A law that does not discriminate in its applicability, depending on the nature of the ideas that are expressed, is said to be content neutral. For example, a law forbidding any threats on the President's life would be content neutral, while a law that forbade only threats against Presidents who are Democrats would not be content neutral.

**criminal case**    A legal action based on the violation of a society's criminal laws. Compare with **civil case.**

**defamation**    A false statement (written or oral) that lowers the reputation of another person or subjects him or her to ridicule or shame. *See also* **libel, slander.**

**defendant**    A person who is accused of violating the law (in a criminal case) or is being sued in a civil case (for defamation or invasion of privacy, for example).

**deference**    A judicial decision-making principle maintaining that a decision by the executive or legislative branch of government should be upheld (deferred to) if there is any reasonable basis for that decision. When a court exercises deference, it is unlikely to find an executive or legislative act unconstitutional.

**dicta**    A statement from a judicial opinion that is not part of the reasoning used by the court to decide the issue raised by a case. Dicta does not create precedent for future cases; however, it may provide a persuasive argument to be used in subsequent cases.

**dissenting opinion**    A judicial opinion that disagrees with the result reached by the majority.

**facial challenge**  A claim that a law includes provisions that are unconstitutional. Such a law is sometimes called "void on its face." For example, a law prohibiting political criticism would be void on its face because political criticism is protected by the First Amendment.

**fairness doctrine**  A Federal Communications Commission rule requiring radio and television licensees to provide balanced coverage of all responsible viewpoints on particular issues and providing a right to reply for persons who were the targets of a personal attack on the licensee's station. Repealed in 1987.

**fighting words**  Words that have a direct tendency to cause acts of violence by the person to whom, individually, the remark is addressed. The fighting words doctrine was originally announced in *Chaplinsky v. New Hampshire*, but this definition is based on the Supreme Court's subsequent opinion in *Gooding v. Wilson. See* chapter 6.

**government interest**  A goal or objective the government is attempting to achieve. In freedom of speech cases, the term "government interest" refers to the justifications put forth by the government to support its restrictions on expression.

**hate speech**  Speech that demeans persons, ordinarily based on an immutable characteristic such as ethnicity, gender, or sexual orientation.

**heresy**  A statement of religious doctrine that government or church officials deem to be false.

**indecent**  Vulgar, lewd, or sexually suggestive. Expression can be indecent even if it does not meet the criteria for **obscenity** (see glossary entry).

**intentional infliction of emotional distress**  Language used in tort law to refer to speech and/or actions intended to cause another individual severe emotional suffering. The *New York Times v. Sullivan* requirement of a "false statement of fact" made with "malice" applies to damage actions by public figures bringing suit for intentional infliction of emotional distress. It may also be a remedy in resolving hate speech disputes.

**libel**  Language used in tort law to refer to nonspoken expression that defames (injures the reputation of another). Libelous ideas may be expressed by printing, writing, pictures, signs, or other such symbols.

**majority opinion**  A written decision explaining the reasoning of the majority of justices who decided a particular case.

**marketplace of ideas**  A metaphor used to explain one conception of freedom of speech. Here, as in a real marketplace, ideas or thoughts are freely exchanged, with no external or governmental regulation other than that which the marketplace might impose on itself. In such a system, it is believed that ideas will be exchanged more freely.

**narrowly tailored**  Language used to refer to a requirement for governmental restrictions on speech. When the courts have said that a restriction must be narrowly tailored, they usually have meant that its purpose must be specific and its reach narrow in scope, so as to avoid infringing on more expression than is necessary to achieve a legitimate goal of government.

**obscenity**  For First Amendment purposes, obscenity refers to expression that appeals primarily to sexual impulses. Obscenity does not encompass all vulgar or profane speech. According to the current Supreme Court definition of obscenity (*see Miller v. California*, chapter 9), the average person, applying contemporary community standards, must find that the dominant theme of the material, taken as a whole, appeals to the prurient interest (an "unhealthy" interest in sexual matters), that it is utterly without redeeming social value, and that it is patently offensive.

**on its face**   A legal term referring to the claim that a law, as it is written, imposes a restriction on constitutional rights such as freedom of expression. To suggest that a law is invalid "on its face" (or "facially invalid") is to argue that the plain meaning of the statute denies constitutional rights. For example, a law forbidding criticism of Congress would be void on its face because it is written to prohibit speech protected by the First Amendment.

**original intent**   A term used to refer to what the framers of the Constitution intended when writing a part of that document. This concept is often relied upon by those who do not see the Constitution as a living entity that may evolve over time, but rather as a fixed document that must be interpreted based on the intentions of its creators.

**overbreadth**   A legal term used to describe the reach of a restriction on expression. When a court declares that a statute is overbroad, it means that the challenged restriction reaches speech that is constitutionally protected in addition to that which may be limited. An overbroad law can be analogized to a large fishing net; when the net is used in a manner that is overbroad, it catches not only marine life that may legally be harvested, but also protected (e.g., endangered) species.

**party**   Either side in a legal dispute.

**per curiam**   Latin, meaning "by the court." In practice, it is a phrase used to refer to an opinion by the court for which the author is unspecified. Per curiam opinions do not usually involve a lengthy discussion of the case (*see*, for example, *New York Times v. U.S.* in chapter 5).

**pervasiveness**   Refers to a channel of expression present in a wide variety of public and private places. Ordinarily, a pervasive medium of expression is one that may deliver an offensive message without prior warning. For example, because the audience is constantly tuning a radio station in or out, it may be impossible to warn the audience of objectionable content before the listener (or his or her children) is exposed to it.

**plaintiff**   A party who brings a legal action alleging that he or she is entitled to a remedy because his or her rights have been injured or denied.

**plurality opinion**   An opinion with which a plurality (but not a majority) of justices agree. This type of opinion is written when a court announces a majority decision, but a majority cannot agree on the reasons for that decision. The opinion shared by the greatest number of those in the majority is the plurality opinion.

**politically correct**   The origin of this term has been attributed both to the left and the right; most people would agree that it is used in a pejorative manner to refer to beliefs, ideas, customs, or actions that have gained acceptance with those who think of themselves as more socially progressive. To suggest that something is not "politically correct" is to infer that it would go against those beliefs, ideas, customs, or actions. For example, it would be politically incorrect to use the term "chairman" instead of "chairperson."

**pornography**   Literature, photographs, illustrations, etc. intended to be sexually arousing. Not all pornography falls under the Supreme Court's definition of **obscenity.** Feminist critics of pornography use that term primarily to refer to sexually explicit materials that degrade women.

**precedent** A judgment of a court regarding a point of law, which judgment serves as authority for future courts considering the same issue.

**preferred position** A theory that any restriction that infringes on freedom of speech (or other guarantees of the Bill of Rights) is suspect because the first ten amendments occupy a "preferred position" in the Constitution. Under this theory, a government restriction that appeared to deny a protection of the Bill of Rights would not be presumed constitutional, and the government would need to justify the restriction to the reviewing court.

**prior restraint** A prohibition on expression which is imposed *before* the message is communicated. An example of prior restraint is when the government bans publication of a book or article, as the federal government attempted to do in the Pentagon Papers case (chapter 5).

**privilege** An exemption from a legal obligation or duty that is generally imposed on citizens. For example, the attorney-client privilege exempts an attorney from the obligation to testify that she or he heard a client confess to the commission of a crime.

**procedural** Legal rules are procedural when they refer to the process that will be followed to determine one's rights or obligations in court. For example, the guarantee of a jury trial in all criminal prosecutions for the burning of one's tax return would be a procedural rule. Compare with **substantive.**

**prurient** Relating to an "unhealthy" or "unnatural" interest in sex or sexual matters. See **obscenity.**

**pure speech** The expression of an idea through words or symbols in a manner that requires little physical action beyond transmitting the idea. For example, the wearing of a black armband to protest the Vietnam War, or a yellow ribbon to support U.S. troops overseas, would be deemed very close to pure speech. Restrictions against pure speech are subjected to a more rigorous review by the courts than are restrictions deemed to be directed at conduct.

**reckless** A term used in tort cases to refer to one who is careless, inattentive, or indifferent to the consequences of his or her actions. Recklessness is usually considered an aggravated form of negligence, and is used to imply a more culpable mental state than that caused by inexperience or confusion. In the free speech context, recklessness has been used with the **actual malice** standard in defamation cases, alleging that a statement was made with reckless disregard as to its truth or falsity.

**remand** Literally, to send back. In practice, it means sending a case back to the court from which it came for further adjudication.

**right/privilege distinction doctrine** A legal theory holding that "rights" (which exist independent of and prior to the creation of any state or social contract) are derived from our status as human beings, and distinguishable from "privileges" (created by the state and products of the social contract), which can be given or taken away by the state. This theory was applied in the First Amendment context as courts sought to determine if public employment was a privilege or a right, which would in turn determine when and if the government could restrict public employee speech. The Supreme Court employed this distinction to limit public employee speech in the past.

**scarcity theory** A legal theory said to justify governmental regulation of access to the airwaves, and the content of messages on the airwaves. This theory assumes a limited supply of frequencies, and that the government may act to insure that these limited resources are used in the public interest.

**seditious libel** In English law, this referred to words directed against the Crown or the government, intended to promote the English subjects' dissatisfaction with their leaders or to bring the leaders into hatred or contempt.

**slander** Oral defamation, speech that injures the reputation of another person. Compare with **libel.**

**Star Chamber** A room in England's Palace of Westminster where the King's Council met and meted out whatever punishments were deemed appropriate. The room was said to have stars painted onto the ceiling. Star Chamber proceedings were carried out in secret, and torture was one of the king's prerogatives. Parliament abolished the Star Chamber in 1642.

**substantive** Legal rules are substantive when they refer to the words or actions that may subject a person to civil or criminal liability. For example, a law forbidding the burning of one's tax return or one prohibiting threats to the president's life would be substantive laws. Compare with **procedural.**

**symbolic speech** This term refers to conduct which may be intended to express a message, or perceived as expressing a message. For example, the burning of an American flag is generally considered to be symbolic speech. In truth, all conduct may have meaning to someone, but not all conduct is protected by the First Amendment guarantees of free expression. If there is an important state interest independent of the communicative aspects of such conduct, the conduct may be regulated despite the fact that expression may incidentally be limited,

particularly when the state does not have less restrictive means available to accomplish its ends.

**summary judgment** A legal motion made to the court for judgment to the movant (the side making the motion) without having to go through a full trial. Usually this occurs when questions of law or documentary evidence are uncontroverted, and a trial would be a waste of time.

**time, place, or manner restrictions** A legal term referring to restrictions on expression, particularly where public land and access are involved. A restriction that regulates as to the time, place, or manner in which expression occurs is said to be reasonable if it (a) is content neutral; (b) is narrowly tailored to serve a significant state interest; and (c) leaves open ample alternative channels for communication of information.

**tort** A private or civil wrong or injury. Torts are offenses against a private individual or individuals, whereas violations of the criminal law are offenses against society. Torts that may involve freedom of speech issues include defamation and intentional infliction of emotional distress. In such a case, the plaintiff seeks financial compensation from the defendant as a remedy for the alleged tort.

**unconstitutional conditions doctrine** A rival to the "right/privilege distinction," this doctrine holds that government may not do indirectly (such as conditioning receipt of a government subsidy subject to agreeing not to do something) what it can't do directly (e.g., censor speech). Doing so would create an unconstitutional condition.

**vagueness** A legal term sometimes used in conjunction with **overbreadth.** Vagueness refers to a law that is uncertain, unclear, or susceptible to multiple interpretations by reasonable people. If ordinary persons must guess as to the meaning of a statute, then it is vague. A vague law directed against expression is often found unconstitutional on the grounds that the restriction could deter expression protected by the First Amendment. *See* **chilling effect.**

**writ of certiorari** Literally, a demand by a higher court to a lower court, calling for the record of a case. For example, when the Supreme Court grants certiorari, it has agreed to review the decision of a lower court.

# Table of Cases

# Index